CORPORATE FINANCE

CFA® PROGRAM CURRICULUM
2014 • Level II • Volume 3

WILEY

Please visit our website at
www.WileyGlobalFinance.com.

CONTENTS

Corporate Finance

◙ indicates an optional segment

◙ indicates an optional segment

How to Use the CFA Program Curriculum

Congratulations on passing Level I of the Chartered Financial Analyst (CFA®) Program. This exciting and rewarding program of study reflects your desire to become a serious investment professional. You are embarking on a program noted for its high ethical standards and the breadth of knowledge, skills, and abilities it develops. Your commitment to the CFA Program should be educationally and professionally rewarding.

The credential you seek is respected around the world as a mark of accomplishment and dedication. Each level of the program represents a distinct achievement in professional development. Successful completion of the program is rewarded with membership in a prestigious global community of investment professionals. CFA charterholders are dedicated to life-long learning and maintaining currency with the ever-changing dynamics of a challenging profession. The CFA Program represents the first step towards a career-long commitment to professional education.

The CFA examination measures your mastery of the core skills required to succeed as an investment professional. These core skills are the basis for the Candidate Body of Knowledge (CBOK™). The CBOK consists of four components:

- A broad topic outline that lists the major top-level topic areas (CBOK Topic Outline)
- Topic area weights that indicate the relative exam weightings of the top-level topic areas
- Learning outcome statements (LOS) that advise candidates about the specific knowledge, skills, and abilities they should acquire from readings covering a topic area (LOS are provided in candidate study sessions and at the beginning of each reading)
- The CFA Program curriculum, readings, and end-of-reading questions, which candidates receive upon exam registration

Therefore, the key to your success on the CFA exam is studying and understanding the CBOK™. The following sections provide background on the CBOK, the organization of the curriculum, and tips for developing an effective study program.

CURRICULUM DEVELOPMENT PROCESS

The CFA Program is grounded in the practice of the investment profession. Using the Global Body of Investment Knowledge (GBIK) collaborative website, CFA Institute performs a continuous practice analysis with investment professionals around the world to determine the knowledge, skills, and abilities (competencies) that are relevant to the profession. Regional expert panels and targeted surveys are conducted annually to verify and reinforce the continuous feedback from the GBIK collaborative website. The practice analysis process ultimately defines the CBOK. The CBOK contains the competencies that are generally accepted and applied by investment professionals. These competencies are used in practice in a generalist context and are expected to be demonstrated by a recently qualified CFA charterholder.

A committee consisting of practicing charterholders, in conjunction with CFA Institute staff, designs the CFA Program curriculum in order to deliver the CBOK to candidates. The examinations, also written by practicing charterholders, are designed to allow you to demonstrate your mastery of the CBOK as set forth in the CFA Program curriculum. As you structure your personal study program, you should emphasize mastery of the CBOK and the practical application of that knowledge. For more information on the practice analysis, CBOK, and development of the CFA Program curriculum, please visit www.cfainstitute.org.

ORGANIZATION OF THE CURRICULUM

The Level II CFA Program curriculum is organized into 10 topic areas. Each topic area begins with a brief statement of the material and the depth of knowledge expected.

Each topic area is then divided into one or more study sessions. These study sessions—18 sessions in the Level II curriculum—should form the basic structure of your reading and preparation.

Each study session includes a statement of its structure and objective, and is further divided into specific reading assignments. An outline illustrating the organization of these 18 study sessions can be found at the front of each volume.

The reading assignments are the basis for all examination questions, and are selected or developed specifically to teach the knowledge, skills, and abilities reflected in the CBOK. These readings are drawn from CFA Institute-commissioned content, textbook chapters, professional journal articles, research analyst reports, and cases. Readings include problems and solutions to help you understand and master the topic areas.

Reading-specific Learning Outcome Statements (LOS) are listed at the beginning of each reading. These LOS indicate what you should be able to accomplish after studying the reading. The LOS, the reading, and the end-of-reading questions are dependent on each other, with the reading and questions providing context for understanding the scope of the LOS.

You should use the LOS to guide and focus your study, as each examination question is based on an assigned reading and one or more LOS. The readings provide context for the LOS and enable you to apply a principle or concept in a variety of scenarios. The candidate is responsible for the entirety of all of the required material in a study session, the assigned readings as well as the end-of-reading questions and problems.

We encourage you to review the material on LOS (www.cfainstitute.org/programs/ cfaprogram/courseofstudy/Pages/study_sessions.aspx), including the descriptions of LOS "command words" (www.cfainstitute.org/programs/Documents/cfa_and_cipm_ los_command_words.pdf).

FEATURES OF THE CURRICULUM

OPTIONAL
SEGMENT

Required vs. Optional Segments   You should read all of an assigned reading. In some cases, however, we have reprinted an entire chapter or article and marked certain parts of the reading as "optional." The CFA examination is based only on the required segments, and the optional segments are included only when they might help you to better understand the required segments (by seeing the required material in its full context). When an optional segment begins, you will see text and a dashed vertical bar in the outside margin that will continue until the optional segment ends, accompanied by another icon. *Unless the material is specifically marked as optional, you should assume it is required.* You should rely on the required segments and the reading-specific LOS in preparing for the examination.

Problems/Solutions   *All questions and problems in the readings as well as their solutions (which are provided directly following the problems) are part of the curriculum and are required material for the exam.* When appropriate, we have included problems within and after the readings to demonstrate practical application and reinforce your understanding of the concepts presented. The questions and problems are designed to help you learn these concepts and may serve as a basis for exam questions. Many of these questions are adapted from past CFA examinations.

Margins   The wide margins in each volume provide space for your note-taking.

Six-Volume Structure   For portability of the curriculum, the material is spread over six volumes.

Glossary and Index   For your convenience, we have printed a comprehensive glossary in each volume. Throughout the curriculum, a **bolded** word in a reading denotes a term defined in the glossary. Each volume also contains an index specific to that volume; a combined index can be found on the CFA Institute website with the Level II study sessions.

Source Material   The authorship, publisher, and copyright owners are given for each reading for your reference. We recommend that you use this CFA Institute curriculum rather than the original source materials because the curriculum may include only selected pages from outside readings, updated sections within the readings, and contains problems and solutions tailored to the CFA Program.

LOS Self-Check   We have inserted checkboxes next to each LOS that you can use to track your progress in mastering the concepts in each reading.

DESIGNING YOUR PERSONAL STUDY PROGRAM

Create a Schedule   An orderly, systematic approach to examination preparation is critical. You should dedicate a consistent block of time every week to reading and studying. Complete all reading assignments and the associated problems and solutions in each study session. Review the LOS both before and after you study each reading to ensure that you have mastered the applicable content and can demonstrate the knowledge, skill, or ability described by the LOS and the assigned reading. Use the LOS self-check to track your progress and highlight areas of weakness for later review.

As you prepare for your exam, we will e-mail you important exam updates, testing policies, and study tips. Be sure to read these carefully. Curriculum errata are periodically updated and posted on the study session page at www.cfainstitute.org. You may also sign up for an RSS feed to alert you to the latest errata update.

Successful candidates report an average of over 300 hours preparing for each exam. Your preparation time will vary based on your prior education and experience. For each level of the curriculum, there are 18 study sessions, so a good plan is to devote 15–20 hours per week, for 18 weeks, to studying the material. Use the final four to six weeks before the exam to review what you've learned and practice with sample and mock exams. This recommendation, however, may underestimate the hours needed for appropriate examination preparation depending on your individual circumstances, relevant experience, and academic background. You will undoubtedly adjust your study time to conform to your own strengths and weaknesses, and your educational and professional background.

You will probably spend more time on some study sessions than on others, but on average you should plan on devoting 15-20 hours per study session. You should allow ample time for both in-depth study of all topic areas and additional concentration on those topic areas for which you feel least prepared.

CFA Institute Question Bank   The CFA Institute topic-based question bank is intended to assess your mastery of individual topic areas as you progress through your studies. After each test, you will receive immediate feedback noting the correct responses and indicating the relevant assigned reading so you can identify areas of weakness for further study. The topic tests reflect the question formats and level of difficulty of the actual CFA examinations. For more information on the topic tests, please visit www.cfainstitute.org.

CFA Institute Mock Examinations   In response to candidate requests, CFA Institute has developed mock examinations that mimic the actual CFA examinations not only in question format and level of difficulty, but also in length and topic weight. The three-hour mock exams simulate the morning and afternoon sessions of the actual CFA exam, and are intended to be taken after you complete your study of the full curriculum so you can test your understanding of the curriculum and your readiness for the exam. You will receive feedback at the end of the mock exam, noting the correct responses and indicating the relevant assigned readings so you can assess areas of weakness for further study during your review period. We recommend that you take mock exams during the final stages of your preparation for the actual CFA examination. For more information on the mock examinations, please visit www.cfainstitute.org.

Preparatory Providers   After you enroll in the CFA Program, you may receive numerous solicitations for preparatory courses and review materials. When considering a prep course, make sure the provider is in compliance with the CFA Institute Prep Provider Guidelines Program (www.cfainstitute.org/partners/examprep/Pages/cfa_prep_provider_guidelines.aspx). Just remember, there are no shortcuts to success on the CFA examinations; reading and studying the CFA curriculum is the key to success on the examination. The CFA examinations reference only the CFA Institute assigned curriculum—no preparatory course or review course materials are consulted or referenced.

SUMMARY

Every question on the CFA examination is based on the content contained in the required readings and on one or more LOS. Frequently, an examination question is based on a specific example highlighted within a reading or on a specific end-of-reading question and/or problem and its solution. To make effective use of the CFA Program curriculum, please remember these key points:

1 All pages printed in the curriculum are required reading for the examination except for occasional sections marked as optional. You may read optional pages as background, but you will not be tested on them.

2 All questions, problems, and their solutions - printed at the end of readings - are part of the curriculum and are required study material for the examination.

3 You should make appropriate use of the online sample/mock examinations and other resources available at www.cfainstitute.org.

4   You should schedule and commit sufficient study time to cover the 18 study sessions, review the materials, and take sample/mock examinations.

5   **Note:** Some of the concepts in the study sessions may be superseded by updated rulings and/or pronouncements issued after a reading was published. Candidates are expected to be familiar with the overall analytical framework contained in the assigned readings. Candidates are not responsible for changes that occur after the material was written.

FEEDBACK

At CFA Institute, we are committed to delivering a comprehensive and rigorous curriculum for the development of competent, ethically grounded investment professionals. We rely on candidate and member feedback as we work to incorporate content, design, and packaging improvements. You can be assured that we will continue to listen to your suggestions. Please send any comments or feedback to info@ cfainstitute.org. Ongoing improvements in the curriculum will help you prepare for success on the upcoming examinations, and for a lifetime of learning as a serious investment professional.

Corporate Finance

STUDY SESSIONS

Study Session 8	Corporate Finance
Study Session 9	Corporate Finance: Financing and Control Issues

TOPIC LEVEL LEARNING OUTCOME

The candidate should be able to evaluate capital budget projects, capital structure policy, dividend policy, corporate governance, and mergers and acquisitions.

CORPORATE FINANCE
STUDY SESSION

Corporate Finance

This study session first presents capital budgeting analysis, focusing on the application of concepts in the corporate finance decision-making process. These capital budgeting principles are critical for an analyst inside a company preparing capital budgeting recommendations as well as for an external analyst estimating the value of the company.

The remainder of the study session covers capital structure and dividend policy. The presentation of capital structure starts with the classic Modigliani–Miller irrelevance proposition. This proposition states that a company's value is not affected by capital structure choices. The reading then considers how the optimal capital structure is affected by taxes, agency costs, and the possibility of financial distress. The reading on dividend policy discusses the company's choice between reinvesting or distributing earnings, and the choice between paying cash dividends and repurchasing shares. Analysts are interested in capital structure and dividend policies because of their effect on the risk and return characteristics of corporate equities and bonds.

READING ASSIGNMENTS

Reading 25   Capital Budgeting
Corporate Finance: A Practical Approach, by Michelle R. Clayman, CFA, Martin S. Fridson, CFA, and George H. Troughton, CFA

Reading 26   Capital Structure
by Raj Aggarwal, CFA, Pamela Peterson Drake, CFA, Adam Kobor, CFA, and Gregory Noronha, CFA

(continued)

Reading 27 Dividends and Share Repurchases: Analysis
by Gregory Noronha, CFA, and George H. Troughton, CFA

Capital Budgeting

by John D. Stowe, CFA, and Jacques R. Gagné, CFA

LEARNING OUTCOMES

Mastery	The candidate should be able to:
☐	**a.** calculate the yearly cash flows of expansion and replacement capital projects, and evaluate how the choice of depreciation method affects those cash flows;
☐	**b.** explain the effects of inflation on capital budgeting analysis;
☐	**c.** evaluate capital projects and determine the optimal capital project in situations of 1) mutually exclusive projects with unequal lives, using either the least common multiple of lives approach or the equivalent annual annuity approach, and 2) capital rationing;
☐	**d.** explain how sensitivity analysis, scenario analysis, and Monte Carlo simulation can be used to assess the stand-alone risk of a capital project;
☐	**e.** explain and calculate the discount rate, based on market risk methods, to use in valuing a capital project;
☐	**f.** describe types of real options and evaluate a capital project using real options;
☐	**g.** describe common capital budgeting pitfalls;
☐	**h.** calculate and interpret accounting income and economic income in the context of capital budgeting;
☐	**i.** distinguish among the economic profit, residual income, and claims valuation models for capital budgeting and evaluate a capital project using each.

1   INTRODUCTION

Capital budgeting is the process that companies use for decision making on capital projects—those projects with a life of a year or more. This is a fundamental area of knowledge for financial analysts for many reasons.

- First, capital budgeting is very important for corporations. Capital projects, which make up the long-term asset portion of the balance sheet, can be so large that sound capital budgeting decisions ultimately decide the future of many corporations. Capital decisions cannot be reversed at a low cost, so mistakes are very costly. Indeed, the real capital investments of a company describe a company better than its working capital or capital structures, which are intangible and tend to be similar for many corporations.

- Second, the principles of capital budgeting have been adapted for many other corporate decisions, such as investments in working capital, leasing, mergers and acquisitions, and bond refunding.

- Third, the valuation principles used in capital budgeting are similar to the valuation principles used in security analysis and portfolio management. Many of the methods used by security analysts and portfolio managers are based on capital budgeting methods. Conversely, there have been innovations in security analysis and portfolio management that have also been adapted to capital budgeting.

- Finally, although analysts have a vantage point outside the company, their interest in valuation coincides with the capital budgeting focus of maximizing shareholder value. Because capital budgeting information is not ordinarily available outside the company, the analyst may attempt to estimate the process, within reason, at least for companies that are not too complex. Further, analysts may be able to appraise the quality of the company's capital budgeting process, for example, on the basis of whether the company has an accounting focus or an economic focus.

This reading is organized as follows: Section 2 presents the steps in a typical capital budgeting process. After introducing the basic principles of capital budgeting in Section 3, in Section 4 we discuss the criteria by which a decision to invest in a project may be made. Section 5 presents a crucial element of the capital budgeting process: organizing the cash flow information that is the raw material of the analysis. Section 6 looks further at cash flow analysis. Section 7 demonstrates methods to extend the basic investment criteria to address economic alternatives and risk. Finally, Section 8 compares other income measures and valuation models that analysts use to the basic capital budgeting model.

2   THE CAPITAL BUDGETING PROCESS

The specific capital budgeting procedures that a manager uses depend on the manager's level in the organization, the size and complexity of the project being evaluated, and the size of the organization. The typical steps in the capital budgeting process are as follows:

- Step One, Generating Ideas—Investment ideas can come from anywhere, from the top or the bottom of the organization, from any department or functional area, or from outside the company. Generating good investment ideas to consider is the most important step in the process.

- Step Two, Analyzing Individual Proposals—This step involves gathering the information to forecast cash flows for each project and then evaluating the project's profitability.

- Step Three, Planning the Capital Budget—The company must organize the profitable proposals into a coordinated whole that fits within the company's overall strategies, and it also must consider the projects' timing. Some projects that look good when considered in isolation may be undesirable strategically. Because of financial and real resource issues, scheduling and prioritizing projects is important.

- Step Four, Monitoring and Post-auditing—In a post-audit, actual results are compared to planned or predicted results, and any differences must be explained. For example, how do the revenues, expenses, and cash flows realized from an investment compare to the predictions? Post-auditing capital projects is important for several reasons. First, it helps monitor the forecasts and analysis that underlie the capital budgeting process. Systematic errors, such as overly optimistic forecasts, become apparent. Second, it helps improve business operations. If sales or costs are out of line, it will focus attention on bringing performance closer to expectations if at all possible. Finally, monitoring and post-auditing recent capital investments will produce concrete ideas for future investments. Managers can decide to invest more heavily in profitable areas and scale down or cancel investments in areas that are disappointing.

Planning for capital investments can be very complex, often involving many persons inside and outside of the company. Information about marketing, science, engineering, regulation, taxation, finance, production, and behavioral issues must be systematically gathered and evaluated. The authority to make capital decisions depends on the size and complexity of the project. Lower-level managers may have discretion to make decisions that involve less than a given amount of money, or that do not exceed a given capital budget. Larger and more complex decisions are reserved for top management, and some are so significant that the company's board of directors ultimately has the decision-making authority.

Like everything else, capital budgeting is a cost-benefit exercise. At the margin, the benefits from the improved decision making should exceed the costs of the capital budgeting efforts.

Companies often put capital budgeting projects into some rough categories for analysis. One such classification would be as follows:

1 Replacement projects. These are among the easier capital budgeting decisions. If a piece of equipment breaks down or wears out, whether to replace it may not require careful analysis. If the expenditure is modest and if not investing has significant implications for production, operations, or sales, it would be a waste of resources to overanalyze the decision. Just make the replacement. Other replacement decisions involve replacing existing equipment with newer, more efficient equipment, or perhaps choosing one type of equipment over another. These replacement decisions are often amenable to very detailed analysis, and you might have a lot of confidence in the final decision.

2 Expansion projects. Instead of merely maintaining a company's existing business activities, expansion projects increase the size of the business. These expansion decisions may involve more uncertainties than replacement decisions, and these decisions will be more carefully considered.

3 New products and services. These investments expose the company to even more uncertainties than expansion projects. These decisions are more complex and will involve more people in the decision-making process.

4 Regulatory, safety, and environmental projects. These projects are frequently required by a governmental agency, an insurance company, or some other external party. They may generate no revenue and might not be undertaken by a company maximizing its own private interests. Often, the company will accept the required investment and continue to operate. Occasionally, however, the cost of the regulatory/safety/environmental project is sufficiently high that the company would do better to cease operating altogether or to shut down any part of the business that is related to the project.

5 Other. The projects above are all susceptible to capital budgeting analysis, and they can be accepted or rejected using the net present value (NPV) or some other criterion. Some projects escape such analysis. These are either pet projects of someone in the company (such as the CEO buying a new aircraft) or so risky that they are difficult to analyze by the usual methods (such as some research and development decisions).

3   BASIC PRINCIPLES OF CAPITAL BUDGETING

Capital budgeting has a rich history and sometimes employs some pretty sophisticated procedures. Fortunately, capital budgeting relies on just a few basic principles. Capital budgeting usually uses the following assumptions:

1 Decisions are based on cash flows. The decisions are not based on accounting concepts, such as net income. Furthermore, intangible costs and benefits are often ignored because, if they are real, they should result in cash flows at some other time.

2 Timing of cash flows is crucial. Analysts make an extraordinary effort to detail precisely when cash flows occur.

3 Cash flows are based on opportunity costs. What are the incremental cash flows that occur with an investment compared to what they would have been without the investment?

4 Cash flows are analyzed on an after-tax basis. Taxes must be fully reflected in all capital budgeting decisions.

5 Financing costs are ignored. This may seem unrealistic, but it is not. Most of the time, analysts want to know the after-tax operating cash flows that result from a capital investment. Then, these after-tax cash flows and the investment outlays are discounted at the "required rate of return" to find the net present value (NPV). Financing costs are reflected in the required rate of return. If we included financing costs in the cash flows and in the discount rate, we would be double-counting the financing costs. So even though a project may be financed with some combination of debt and equity, we ignore these costs, focusing on the operating cash flows and capturing the costs of debt (and other capital) in the discount rate.

Capital budgeting cash flows are not accounting net income. Accounting net income is reduced by noncash charges such as accounting depreciation. Furthermore, to reflect the cost of debt financing, interest expenses are also subtracted from accounting net income. (No subtraction is made for the cost of equity financing in arriving at accounting net income.) Accounting net income also differs from economic income, which is the cash inflow plus the change in the market value of the company. Economic income does not subtract the cost of debt financing, and it is based on the changes in the market value of the company, not changes in its book value (accounting depreciation). We will further consider cash flows, accounting income, economic income, and other income measures at the end of this reading.

In assumption 5 above, we referred to the rate used in discounting the cash flows as the "required rate of return." The required rate of return is the discount rate that investors should require given the riskiness of the project. This discount rate is frequently called the "opportunity cost of funds" or the "cost of capital." If the company can invest elsewhere and earn a return of r, or if the company can repay its sources of capital and save a cost of r, then r is the company's opportunity cost of funds. If the company cannot earn more than its opportunity cost of funds on an investment, it should not undertake that investment. Unless an investment earns more than the cost of funds from its suppliers of capital, the investment should not be undertaken. The cost-of-capital concept is discussed more extensively elsewhere. Regardless of what it is called, an economically sound discount rate is essential for making capital budgeting decisions.

Although the principles of capital budgeting are simple, they are easily confused in practice, leading to unfortunate decisions. Some important capital budgeting concepts that managers find very useful are given below.

- A **sunk cost** is one that has already been incurred. You cannot change a sunk cost. Today's decisions, on the other hand, should be based on current and future cash flows and should not be affected by prior, or sunk, costs.

- An **opportunity cost** is what a resource is worth in its next-best use. For example, if a company uses some idle property, what should it record as the investment outlay: the purchase price several years ago, the current market value, or nothing? If you replace an old machine with a new one, what is the opportunity cost? If you invest $10 million, what is the opportunity cost? The answers to these three questions are, respectively: the current market value, the cash flows the old machine would generate, and $10 million (which you could invest elsewhere).

- An **incremental cash flow** is the cash flow that is realized because of a decision: the cash flow *with* a decision minus the cash flow *without* that decision. If opportunity costs are correctly assessed, the incremental cash flows provide a sound basis for capital budgeting.

- An **externality** is the effect of an investment on other things besides the investment itself. Frequently, an investment affects the cash flows of other parts of the company, and these externalities can be positive or negative. If possible, these should be part of the investment decision. Sometimes externalities occur outside of the company. An investment might benefit (or harm) other companies or society at large, and yet the company is not compensated for these benefits (or charged for the costs). **Cannibalization** is one externality. Cannibalization occurs when an investment takes customers and sales away from another part of the company.

- Conventional versus nonconventional cash flows—A **conventional cash flow** pattern is one with an initial outflow followed by a series of inflows. In a **nonconventional cash flow** pattern, the initial outflow is not followed by inflows only, but the cash flows can flip from positive to negative again (or even change signs several times). An investment that involved outlays (negative cash flows) for the first couple of years that were then followed by positive cash flows would be considered to have a conventional pattern. If cash flows change signs once, the pattern is conventional. If cash flows change signs two or more times, the pattern is nonconventional.

Several types of project interactions make the incremental cash flow analysis challenging. The following are some of these interactions:

■ Independent versus mutually exclusive projects. **Independent projects** are projects whose cash flows are independent of each other. **Mutually exclusive projects** compete directly with each other. For example, if Projects A and B are mutually exclusive, you can choose A or B, but you cannot choose both. Sometimes there are several mutually exclusive projects, and you can choose only one from the group.

■ **Project sequencing**. Many projects are sequenced through time, so that investing in a project creates the option to invest in future projects. For example, you might invest in a project today and then in one year invest in a second project if the financial results of the first project or new economic conditions are favorable. If the results of the first project or new economic conditions are not favorable, you do not invest in the second project.

■ Unlimited funds versus capital rationing. An **unlimited funds** environment assumes that the company can raise the funds it wants for all profitable projects simply by paying the required rate of return. **Capital rationing** exists when the company has a fixed amount of funds to invest. If the company has more profitable projects than it has funds for, it must allocate the funds to achieve the maximum shareholder value subject to the funding constraints.

4 INVESTMENT DECISION CRITERIA

Analysts use several important criteria to evaluate capital investments. The two most comprehensive measures of whether a project is profitable or unprofitable are the net present value (NPV) and internal rate of return (IRR). In addition to these, we present four other criteria that are frequently used: the payback period, discounted payback period, average accounting rate of return (AAR), and profitability index (PI). An analyst must fully understand the economic logic behind each of these investment decision criteria as well as its strengths and limitations in practice.

4.1 Net Present Value

For a project with one investment outlay, made initially, the **net present value (NPV)** is the present value of the future after-tax cash flows minus the investment outlay, or

$$\text{NPV} = \sum_{t=1}^{n} \frac{\text{CF}_t}{(1+r)^t} - \text{Outlay} \tag{1}$$

where

CF_t = after-tax cash flow at time t
r = required rate of return for the investment
Outlay = investment cash flow at time zero

To illustrate the net present value criterion, we will take a look at a simple example. Assume that Gerhardt Corporation is considering an investment of €50 million in a capital project that will return after-tax cash flows of €16 million per year for the next four years plus another €20 million in Year 5. The required rate of return is 10 percent.

For the Gerhardt example, the NPV would be

$$NPV = \frac{16}{1.10^1} + \frac{16}{1.10^2} + \frac{16}{1.10^3} + \frac{16}{1.10^4} + \frac{20}{1.10^5} - 50$$

$$NPV = 14.545 + 13.223 + 12.021 + 10.928 + 12.418 - 50$$

$$NPV = 63.136 - 50 = €13.136 \text{ million }[1]$$

The investment has a total value, or present value of future cash flows, of €63.136 million. Since this investment can be acquired at a cost of €50 million, the investing company is giving up €50 million of its wealth in exchange for an investment worth €63.136 million. The investor's wealth increases by a net of €13.136 million.

Because the NPV is the amount by which the investor's wealth increases as a result of the investment, the **decision rule** for the NPV is as follows:

Invest if $\quad\quad$ NPV > 0

Do not invest if $\quad\quad$ NPV < 0

Positive NPV investments are wealth-increasing, while negative NPV investments are wealth-decreasing.

Many investments have cash flow patterns in which outflows may occur not only at time zero, but also at future dates. It is useful to consider the NPV to be the present value of all cash flows:

$$NPV = CF_0 + \frac{CF_1}{(1+r)^1} + \frac{CF_2}{(1+r)^2} + \ldots + \frac{CF_n}{(1+r)^n}, \text{ or}$$

$$NPV = \sum_{t=0}^{n} \frac{CF_t}{(1+r)^t}$$

(2)

In Equation 2, the investment outlay, CF_0, is simply a negative cash flow. Future cash flows can also be negative.

4.2 Internal Rate of Return

The internal rate of return (IRR) is one of the most frequently used concepts in capital budgeting and in security analysis. The IRR definition is one that all analysts know by heart. For a project with one investment outlay, made initially, the IRR is the discount rate that makes the present value of the future after-tax cash flows equal that investment outlay. Written out in equation form, the IRR solves this equation:

$$\sum_{t=1}^{n} \frac{CF_t}{(1+IRR)^t} = \text{Outlay}$$

where IRR is the internal rate of return. The left-hand side of this equation is the present value of the project's future cash flows, which, discounted at the IRR, equals the investment outlay. This equation will also be seen rearranged as

$$\sum_{t=1}^{n} \frac{CF_t}{(1+IRR)^t} - \text{Outlay} = 0$$

(3)

---

1 Occasionally, you will notice some rounding errors in our examples. In this case, the present values of the cash flows, as rounded, add up to 63.135. Without rounding, they add up to 63.13627, or 63.136. We will usually report the more accurate result, the one that you would get from your calculator or computer without rounding intermediate results.

In this form, Equation 3 looks like the NPV equation, Equation 1, except that the discount rate is the IRR instead of r (the required rate of return). Discounted at the IRR, the NPV is equal to zero.

In the Gerhardt Corporation example, we want to find a discount rate that makes the total present value of all cash flows, the NPV, equal zero. In equation form, the IRR is the discount rate that solves this equation:

$$-50 + \frac{16}{(1 + \text{IRR})^1} + \frac{16}{(1 + \text{IRR})^2} + \frac{16}{(1 + \text{IRR})^3}$$

$$+ \frac{16}{(1 + \text{IRR})^4} + \frac{20}{(1 + \text{IRR})^5} = 0$$

Algebraically, this equation would be very difficult to solve. We normally resort to trial and error, systematically choosing various discount rates until we find one, the IRR, that satisfies the equation. We previously discounted these cash flows at 10 percent and found the NPV to be €13.136 million. Since the NPV is positive, the IRR is probably greater than 10 percent. If we use 20 percent as the discount rate, the NPV is − €0.543 million, so 20 percent is a little high. One might try several other discount rates until the NPV is equal to zero; this approach is illustrated in Table 1:

Table 1	Trial and Error Process for Finding IRR
Discount Rate (%)	**NPV**
10	13.136
20	−0.543
19	0.598
19.5	0.022
19.51	0.011
19.52	0.000

The IRR is 19.52 percent. Financial calculators and spreadsheet software have routines that calculate the IRR for us, so we do not have to go through this trial and error procedure ourselves. The IRR, computed more precisely, is 19.5197 percent.

The decision rule for the IRR is to invest if the IRR exceeds the required rate of return for a project:

| Invest if | IRR > r |
| Do not invest if | IRR < r |

In the Gerhardt example, since the IRR of 19.52 percent exceeds the project's required rate of return of 10 percent, Gerhardt should invest.

Many investments have cash flow patterns in which the outlays occur at time zero and at future dates. Thus, it is common to define the IRR as the discount rate that makes the present values of all cash flows sum to zero:

$$\sum_{t=0}^{n} \frac{\text{CF}_t}{(1 + \text{IRR})^t} = 0 \tag{4}$$

Equation 4 is a more general version of Equation 3.

4.3 Payback Period

The payback period is the number of years required to recover the original investment in a project. The payback is based on cash flows. For example, if you invest $10 million in a project, how long will it be until you recover the full original investment? Table 2 below illustrates the calculation of the payback period by following an investment's cash flows and cumulative cash flows.

Table 2	Payback Period Example					
Year	**0**	**1**	**2**	**3**	**4**	**5**
Cash flow	−10,000	2,500	2,500	3,000	3,000	3,000
Cumulative cash flow	−10,000	−7,500	−5,000	−2,000	1,000	4,000

In the first year, the company recovers 2,500 of the original investment, with 7,500 still unrecovered. You can see that the company recoups its original investment between Year 3 and Year 4. After three years, 2,000 is still unrecovered. Since the Year 4 cash flow is 3,000, it would take two-thirds of the Year 4 cash flow to bring the cumulative cash flow to zero. So, the payback period is three years plus two-thirds of the Year 4 cash flow, or 3.67 years.

The drawbacks of the payback period are transparent. Since the cash flows are not discounted at the project's required rate of return, the payback period ignores the time value of money and the risk of the project. Additionally, the payback period ignores cash flows after the payback period is reached. In the table above, for example, the Year 5 cash flow is completely ignored in the payback computation!

Example 1 below is designed to illustrate some of the implications of these drawbacks of the payback period.

EXAMPLE 1

Drawbacks of the Payback Period

The cash flows, payback periods, and NPVs for Projects A through F are given in Table 3. For all of the projects, the required rate of return is 10 percent.

Table 3	Examples of Drawbacks of the Payback Period					
	Cash Flows					
Year	**Project A**	**Project B**	**Project C**	**Project D**	**Project E**	**Project F**
0	−1,000	−1,000	−1,000	−1,000	−1,000	−1,000
1	1,000	100	400	500	400	500
2		200	300	500	400	500
3		300	200	500	400	10,000
4		400	100		400	
5		500	500		400	

(continued)

| Table 3 | (Continued) | | | | | |

	Cash Flows					
Year	**Project A**	**Project B**	**Project C**	**Project D**	**Project E**	**Project F**
Payback period	1.0	4.0	4.0	2.0	2.5	2.0
NPV	−90.91	65.26	140.60	243.43	516.31	7,380.92

Comment on why the payback period provides misleading information about the following:

1   Project A
2   Project B versus Project C
3   Project D versus Project E
4   Project D versus Project F

Solution 1:

Project A does indeed pay itself back in one year. However, this result is misleading because the investment is unprofitable, with a negative NPV.

Solution 2:

Although Projects B and C have the same payback period and the same cash flow after the payback period, the payback period does not detect the fact that Project C's cash flows within the payback period occur earlier and result in a higher NPV.

Solution 3:

Projects D and E illustrate a common situation. The project with the shorter payback period is the less profitable project. Project E has a longer payback and higher NPV.

Solution 4:

Projects D and F illustrate an important flaw of the payback period—that the payback period ignores cash flows after the payback period is reached. In this case, Project F has a much larger cash flow in Year 3, but the payback period does not recognize its value.

The payback period has many drawbacks—it is a measure of payback and not a measure of profitability. By itself, the payback period would be a dangerous criterion for evaluating capital projects. Its simplicity, however, is an advantage. The payback period is very easy to calculate and to explain. The payback period may also be used as an indicator of project liquidity. A project with a two-year payback may be more liquid than another project with a longer payback.

Because it is not economically sound, the payback period has no decision rule like that of the NPV or IRR. If the payback period is being used (perhaps as a measure of liquidity), analysts should also use an NPV or IRR to ensure that their decisions also reflect the profitability of the projects being considered.

4.4 Discounted Payback Period

The discounted payback period is the number of years it takes for the cumulative discounted cash flows from a project to equal the original investment. The discounted payback period partially addresses the weaknesses of the payback period. Table 4 gives an example of calculating the payback period and discounted payback period. The example assumes a discount rate of 10 percent.

Table 4	Payback Period and Discounted Payback Period					
Year	**0**	**1**	**2**	**3**	**4**	**5**
Cash flow (CF)	−5,000	1,500.00	1,500.00	1,500.00	1,500.00	1,500.00
Cumulative CF	−5,000	−3,500.00	−2,000.00	−500.00	1,000.00	2,500.00
Discounted CF	−5,000	1,363.64	1,239.67	1,126.97	1,024.52	931.38
Cumulative discounted CF	−5,000	−3,636.36	−2,396.69	−1,269.72	−245.20	686.18

The payback period is three years plus 500/1500 = 1/3 of the fourth year's cash flow, or 3.33 years. The discounted payback period is between four and five years. The discounted payback period is four years plus 245.20/931.38 = 0.26 of the fifth year's discounted cash flow, or 4.26 years.

The discounted payback period relies on discounted cash flows, much as the NPV criterion does. If a project has a negative NPV, it will usually not have a discounted payback period since it never recovers the initial investment.

The discounted payback does account for the time value of money and risk within the discounted payback period, but it ignores cash flows after the discounted payback period is reached. This drawback has two consequences. First, the discounted payback period is not a good measure of profitability (like the NPV or IRR) because it ignores these cash flows. Second, another idiosyncrasy of the discounted payback period comes from the possibility of negative cash flows after the discounted payback period is reached. It is possible for a project to have a negative NPV but to have a positive cumulative discounted cash flow in the middle of its life and, thus, a reasonable discounted payback period. The NPV and IRR, which consider all of a project's cash flows, do not suffer from this problem.

4.5 Average Accounting Rate of Return

The average accounting rate of return (AAR) can be defined as

$$\text{AAR} = \frac{\text{Average net income}}{\text{Average book value}}$$

To understand this measure of return, we will use a numerical example.

Assume a company invests $200,000 in a project that is depreciated straight-line over a five-year life to a zero salvage value. Sales revenues and cash operating expenses for each year are as shown in Table 5. The table also shows the annual income taxes (at a 40 percent tax rate) and the net income.

Table 5	Net Income for Calculating an Average Accounting Rate of Return				
	Year 1	**Year 2**	**Year 3**	**Year 4**	**Year 5**
Sales	$100,000	$150,000	$240,000	$130,000	$80,000
Cash expenses	50,000	70,000	120,000	60,000	50,000
Depreciation	40,000	40,000	40,000	40,000	40,000
Earnings before taxes	10,000	40,000	80,000	30,000	−10,000
Taxes (at 40 percent)	4,000	16,000	32,000	12,000	−4,000[a]
Net income	6,000	24,000	48,000	18,000	−6,000

[a]Negative taxes occur in Year 5 because the earnings before taxes of −$10,000 can be deducted against earnings on other projects, thus reducing the tax bill by $4,000.

For the five-year period, the average net income is $18,000. The initial book value is $200,000, declining by $40,000 per year until the final book value is $0. The average book value for this asset is ($200,000 −$0) / 2 = $100,000. The average accounting rate of return is

$$\text{AAR} = \frac{\text{Average net income}}{\text{Average book value}} = \frac{18,000}{100,000} = 18\%$$

The advantages of the AAR are that it is easy to understand and easy to calculate. The AAR has some important disadvantages, however. Unlike the other capital budgeting criteria discussed here, the AAR is based on accounting numbers and not based on cash flows. This is an important conceptual and practical limitation. The AAR also does not account for the time value of money, and there is no conceptually sound cutoff for the AAR that distinguishes between profitable and unprofitable investments. The AAR is frequently calculated in different ways, so the analyst should verify the formula behind any AAR numbers that are supplied by someone else. Analysts should know the AAR and its potential limitations in practice, but they should rely on more economically sound methods like the NPV and IRR.

4.6 Profitability Index

The profitability index (PI) is the present value of a project's future cash flows divided by the initial investment. It can be expressed as

$$\text{PI} = \frac{\text{PV of future cash flows}}{\text{Initial investment}} = 1 + \frac{\text{NPV}}{\text{Initial investment}} \tag{5}$$

You can see that the PI is closely related to the NPV. The PI is the *ratio* of the PV of future cash flows to the initial investment, while an NPV is the *difference* between the PV of future cash flows and the initial investment. Whenever the NPV is positive, the PI will be greater than 1.0, and conversely, whenever the NPV is negative, the PI will be less than 1.0. The investment decision rule for the PI is as follows:

Invest if   PI > 1.0
Do not invest if   PI < 1.0

Because the PV of future cash flows equals the initial investment plus the NPV, the PI can also be expressed as 1.0 plus the ratio of the NPV to the initial investment, as shown in Equation 5 above. Example 2 illustrates the PI calculation.

EXAMPLE 2

Example of a PI Calculation

The Gerhardt Corporation investment (discussed earlier) had an outlay of €50 million, a present value of future cash flows of €63.136 million, and an NPV of €13.136 million. The profitability index is

$$PI = \frac{\text{PV of future cash flows}}{\text{Initial investment}} = \frac{63.136}{50.000} = 1.26$$

The PI can also be calculated as

$$PI = 1 + \frac{\text{NPV}}{\text{Initial investment}} = 1 + \frac{13.136}{50.000} = 1.26$$

Because the PI > 1.0, this is a profitable investment.

The PI indicates the value you are receiving in exchange for one unit of currency invested. Although the PI is used less frequently than the NPV and IRR, it is sometimes used as a guide in capital rationing, which we will discuss later. The PI is usually called the profitability index in corporations, but it is commonly referred to as a "benefit-cost ratio" in governmental and not-for-profit organizations.

4.7 NPV Profile

The NPV profile shows a project's NPV graphed as a function of various discount rates. Typically, the NPV is graphed vertically (on the y-axis) and the discount rates are graphed horizontally (on the x-axis). The NPV profile for the Gerhardt capital budgeting project is shown in Example 3.

EXAMPLE 3

NPV Profile

For the Gerhardt example, we have already calculated several NPVs for different discount rates. At 10 percent the NPV is €13.136 million; at 20 percent the NPV is −€0.543 million; and at 19.52 percent (the IRR), the NPV is zero. What is the NPV if the discount rate is 0 percent? The NPV discounted at 0 percent is €34 million, which is simply the sum of all of the undiscounted cash flows. Table 6 and Figure 1 show the NPV profile for the Gerhardt example for discount rates between 0 percent and 30 percent.

Table 6	Gerhardt NPV Profile
Discount Rate (%)	**NPV (in € Millions)**
0	34.000
5.00	22.406
10.00	13.136
15.00	5.623
19.52	0.000
20.00	−0.543

(continued)

Table 6	(Continued)
Discount Rate (%)	**NPV (in € Millions)**
25.00	−5.661
30.00	−9.954

Figure 1	Gerhardt NPV Profile

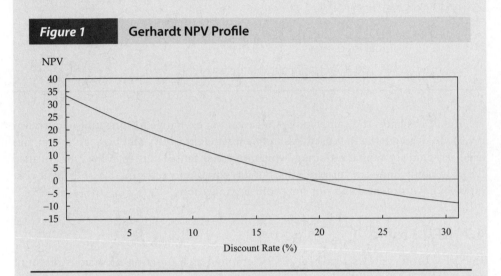

Three interesting points on this NPV profile are where the profile goes through the vertical axis (the NPV when the discount rate is zero), where the profile goes through the horizontal axis (where the discount rate is the IRR), and the NPV for the required rate of return (NPV is €13.136 million when the discount rate is the 10 percent required rate of return).

The NPV profile in Figure 1 is very well-behaved. The NPV declines at a decreasing rate as the discount rate increases. The profile is convex from the origin (convex from below). You will shortly see some examples in which the NPV profile is more complicated.

4.8 Ranking Conflicts between NPV and IRR

For a single conventional project, the NPV and IRR will agree on whether to invest or to not invest. For independent, conventional projects, no conflict exists between the decision rules for the NPV and IRR. However, in the case of two mutually exclusive projects, the two criteria will sometimes disagree. For example, Project A might have a larger NPV than Project B, but Project B has a higher IRR than Project A. In this case, should you invest in Project A or in Project B?

Differing cash flow patterns can cause two projects to rank differently with the NPV and IRR. For example, suppose Project A has shorter-term payoffs than Project B. This situation is presented in Example 4.

EXAMPLE 4

Ranking Conflict Due to Differing Cash Flow Patterns

Projects A and B have similar outlays but different patterns of future cash flows. Project A realizes most of its cash payoffs earlier than Project B. The cash flows as well as the NPV and IRR for the two projects are shown in Table 7. For both projects, the required rate of return is 10 percent.

Table 7	Cash Flows, NPV, and IRR for Two Projects with Different Cash Flow Patterns						
	Cash Flows						
Year	**0**	**1**	**2**	**3**	**4**	**NPV**	**IRR (%)**
Project A	−200	80	80	80	80	53.59	21.86
Project B	−200	0	0	0	400	73.21	18.92

If the two projects were not mutually exclusive, you would invest in both because they are both profitable. However, you can choose either A (which has the higher IRR) or B (which has the higher NPV).

Table 8 and Figure 2 show the NPVs for Project A and Project B for various discount rates between 0 percent and 30 percent.

Table 8	NPV Profiles for Two Projects with Different Cash Flow Patterns	
Discount Rate (%)	**NPV for Project A**	**NPV for Project B**
0	120.00	200.00
5.00	83.68	129.08
10.00	53.59	73.21
15.00	28.40	28.70
15.09	27.98	27.98
18.92	11.41	0.00
20.00	7.10	−7.10
21.86	0.00	−18.62
25.00	−11.07	−36.16
30.00	−26.70	−59.95

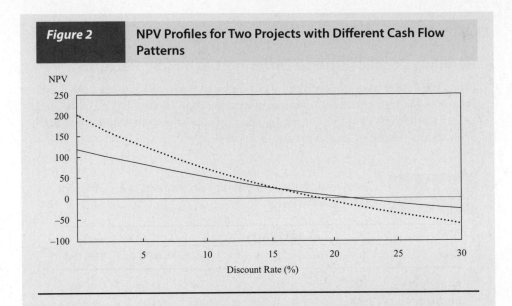

Figure 2	NPV Profiles for Two Projects with Different Cash Flow Patterns

Note that Project B has the higher NPV for discount rates between 0 percent and 15.09 percent. Project A has the higher NPV for discount rates exceeding 15.09 percent. The crossover point of 15.09 percent in Figure 2 corresponds to the discount rate at which both projects have the same NPV (of 27.98). Project B has the higher NPV below the crossover point, and Project A has the higher NPV above it.

Whenever the NPV and IRR rank two mutually exclusive projects differently, as they do in the example above, you should choose the project based on the NPV. Project B, with the higher NPV, is the better project because of the reinvestment assumption. Mathematically, whenever you discount a cash flow at a particular discount rate, you are implicitly assuming that you can reinvest a cash flow at that same discount rate.[2] In the NPV calculation, you use a discount rate of 10 percent for both projects. In the IRR calculation, you use a discount rate equal to the IRR of 21.86 percent for Project A and 18.92 percent for Project B.

Can you reinvest the cash inflows from the projects at 10 percent, or 21.86 percent, or 18.92 percent? When you assume the required rate of return is 10 percent, you are assuming an opportunity cost of 10 percent—you are assuming that you can either find other projects that pay a 10 percent return or pay back your sources of capital that cost you 10 percent. The fact that you earned 21.86 percent in Project A or 18.92 percent in Project B does not mean that you can reinvest future cash flows at those rates. (In fact, if you can reinvest future cash flows at 21.86 percent or 18.92 percent, these should have been used as your required rate of return instead of 10 percent.) Because the NPV criterion uses the most realistic discount rate—the opportunity cost of funds—the NPV criterion should be used for evaluating mutually exclusive projects.

---

2 For example, assume that you are receiving $100 in one year discounted at 10 percent. The present value is $100/1.10 = $90.91. Instead of receiving the $100 in one year, invest it for one additional year at 10 percent, and it grows to $110. What is the present value of $110 received in two years discounted at 10 percent? It is the same $90.91. Because both future cash flows are worth the same, you are implicitly assuming that reinvesting the earlier cash flow at the discount rate of 10 percent has no effect on its value.

Another circumstance that frequently causes mutually exclusive projects to be ranked differently by NPV and IRR criteria is project scale—the sizes of the projects. Would you rather have a small project with a higher rate of return or a large project with a lower rate of return? Sometimes, the larger, low rate of return project has the better NPV. This case is developed in Example 5.

EXAMPLE 5

Ranking Conflicts Due to Differing Project Scale

Project A has a much smaller outlay than Project B, although they have similar future cash flow patterns. The cash flows as well as the NPVs and IRRs for the two projects are shown in Table 9. For both projects, the required rate of return is 10 percent.

Table 9	Cash Flows, NPV, and IRR for Two Projects of Differing Scale						

	Cash Flows						
Year	**0**	**1**	**2**	**3**	**4**	**NPV**	**IRR (%)**
Project A	−100	50	50	50	50	58.49	34.90
Project B	−400	170	170	170	170	138.88	25.21

If they were not mutually exclusive, you would invest in both projects because they are both profitable. However, you can choose either Project A (which has the higher IRR) or Project B (which has the higher NPV).

Table 10 and Figure 3 show the NPVs for Project A and Project B for various discount rates between 0 percent and 30 percent.

Table 10	NPV Profiles for Two Projects of Differing Scale	

Discount Rate (%)	**NPV for Project A**	**NPV for Project B**
0	100.00	280.00
5.00	77.30	202.81
10.00	58.49	138.88
15.00	42.75	85.35
20.00	29.44	40.08
21.86	25.00	25.00
25.00	18.08	1.47
25.21	17.65	0.00
30.00	8.31	−31.74
34.90	0.00	−60.00
35.00	−0.15	−60.52

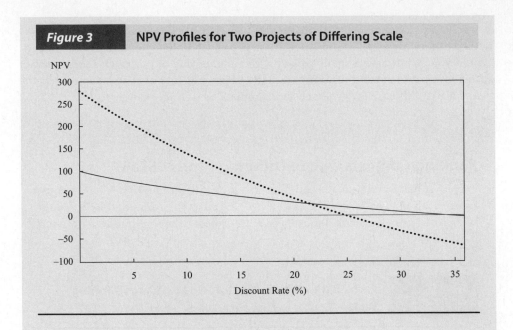

Figure 3   NPV Profiles for Two Projects of Differing Scale

Note that Project B has the higher NPV for discount rates between 0 percent and 21.86 percent. Project A has the higher NPV for discount rates exceeding 21.86 percent. The crossover point of 21.86 percent in Figure 3 corresponds to the discount rate at which both projects have the same NPV (of 25.00). Below the crossover point, Project B has the higher NPV, and above it, Project A has the higher NPV. When cash flows are discounted at the 10 percent required rate of return, the choice is clear—Project B, the larger project, which has the superior NPV.

The good news is that the NPV and IRR criteria will usually indicate the same investment decision for a given project. They will usually both recommend acceptance or rejection of the project. When the choice is between two mutually exclusive projects and the NPV and IRR rank the two projects differently, the NPV criterion is strongly preferred. There are good reasons for this preference. The NPV shows the amount of gain, or wealth increase, as a currency amount. The reinvestment assumption of the NPV is the more economically realistic. The IRR does give you a rate of return, but the IRR could be for a small investment or for only a short period of time. As a practical matter, once a corporation has the data to calculate the NPV, it is fairly trivial to go ahead and calculate the IRR and other capital budgeting criteria. However, the most appropriate and theoretically sound criterion is the NPV.

4.9 The Multiple IRR Problem and the No IRR Problem

A problem that can arise with the IRR criterion is the "multiple IRR problem." We can illustrate this problem with the following nonconventional cash flow pattern:[3]

Time	0	1	2
Cash Flow	−1,000	5,000	−6,000

The IRR for these cash flows satisfies this equation:

---

3 This example is adapted from Hirschleifer (1958).

$$-1{,}000 + \frac{5{,}000}{\left(1 + IRR\right)^{1}} + \frac{-6{,}000}{\left(1 + IRR\right)^{2}} = 0$$

It turns out that there are two values of IRR that satisfy the equation: IRR = 1 = 100% and IRR = 2 = 200%. To further understand this problem, consider the NPV profile for this investment, which is shown in Table 11 and Figure 4.

Table 11	NPV Profile for a Multiple IRR Example
Discount Rate (%)	**NPV**
0	−2,000.00
25	−840.00
50	−333.33
75	−102.04
100	0.00
125	37.04
140	41.67
150	40.00
175	24.79
200	0.00
225	−29.59
250	−61.22
300	−125.00
350	−185.19
400	−240.00
500	−333.33
1,000	−595.04
2,000	−775.51
3,000	−844.95
4,000	−881.62
10,000	−951.08
1,000,000	−999.50

Figure 4	NPV Profile for a Multiple IRR Example

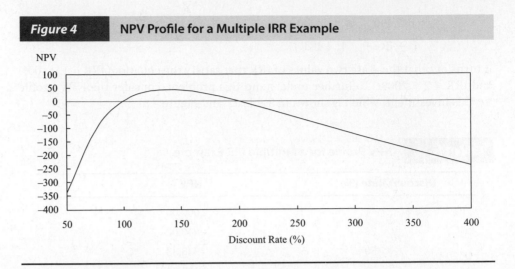

As you can see in the NPV profile, the NPV is equal to zero at IRR = 100% and IRR = 200%. The NPV is negative for discount rates below 100 percent, positive between 100 percent and 200 percent, and then negative above 200 percent. The NPV reaches its highest value when the discount rate is 140 percent.

It is also possible to have an investment project with no IRR. The "no-IRR problem" occurs with this cash flow pattern:[4]

Time	0	1	2
Cash Flow	100	−300	250

The IRR for these cash flows satisfies this equation:

$$100 + \frac{-300}{(1 + \text{IRR})^1} + \frac{250}{(1 + \text{IRR})^2} = 0$$

For these cash flows, no discount rate exists that results in a zero NPV. Does that mean this project is a bad investment? In this case, the project is actually a good investment. As Table 12 and Figure 5 show, the NPV is positive for all discount rates. The lowest NPV, of 10, occurs for a discount rate of 66.67 percent, and the NPV is always greater than zero. Consequently, no IRR exists.

Table 12	NPV Profile for a Project with No IRR

Discount Rate (%)	NPV
0	50.00
25	20.00
50	11.11
66.67	10.00
75	10.20
100	12.50
125	16.05
150	20.00

---

4 This example is also adapted from Hirschleifer.

Table 12	(Continued)
Discount Rate (%)	**NPV**
175	23.97
200	27.78
225	31.36
250	34.69
275	37.78
300	40.63
325	43.25
350	45.68
375	47.92
400	50.00

Figure 5	NPV Profile for a Project with No IRR

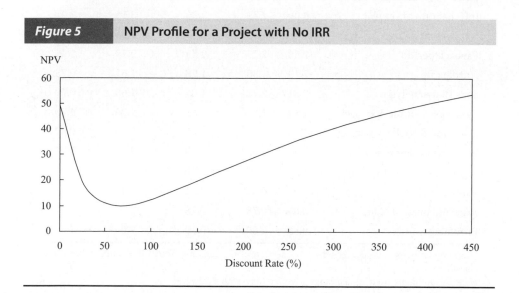

For conventional projects that have outlays followed by inflows—negative cash flows followed by positive cash flows—the multiple IRR problem cannot occur. However, for nonconventional projects, as in the example above, the multiple IRR problem can occur. The IRR equation is essentially an nth degree polynomial. An nth degree polynomial can have up to n solutions, although it will have no more real solutions than the number of cash flow sign changes. For example, a project with two sign changes could have zero, one, or two IRRs. Having two sign changes does not mean that you *will* have multiple IRRs; it just means that you *might*. Fortunately, most capital budgeting projects have only one IRR. Analysts should always be aware of the unusual cash flow patterns that can generate the multiple IRR problem.

4.10 Popularity and Usage of the Capital Budgeting Methods

Analysts need to know the basic logic of the various capital budgeting criteria as well as the practicalities involved in using them in real corporations. Before delving into the many issues involved in applying these models, we would like to present some feedback on their popularity.

The usefulness of any analytical tool always depends on the specific application. Corporations generally find these capital budgeting criteria useful. Two recent surveys by Graham and Harvey (2001) and Brounen, De Jong, and Koedijk (2004) report on the frequency of their use by U.S. and European corporations. Table 13 gives the mean responses of executives in five countries to the question "How frequently does your company use the following techniques when deciding which projects or acquisitions to pursue?"

Table 13	Mean Responses about Frequency of Use of Capital Budgeting Techniques				
	U.S.	**U.K.**	**Netherlands**	**Germany**	**France**
Internal rate of return[a]	3.09	2.31	2.36	2.15	2.27
Net present value[a]	3.08	2.32	2.76	2.26	1.86
Payback period[a]	2.53	2.77	2.53	2.29	2.46
Hurdle rate	2.13	1.35	1.98	1.61	0.73
Sensitivity analysis	2.31	2.21	1.84	1.65	0.79
Earnings multiple approach	1.89	1.81	1.61	1.25	1.70
Discounted payback period[a]	1.56	1.49	1.25	1.59	0.87
Real options approach	1.47	1.65	1.49	2.24	2.20
Accounting rate of return[a]	1.34	1.79	1.40	1.63	1.11
Value at risk	0.95	0.85	0.51	1.45	1.68
Adjusted present value	0.85	0.78	0.78	0.71	1.11
Profitability index[a]	0.85	1.00	0.78	1.04	1.64

[a]These techniques were described in this section of the reading. You will encounter the others elsewhere.
Note: Respondents used a scale ranging from 0 (never) to 4 (always).

Although financial textbooks preach the superiority of the NPV and IRR techniques, it is clear that several other methods are heavily used.[5] In the four European countries, the payback period is used as often as, or even slightly more often than, the NPV and IRR. In these two studies, larger companies tended to prefer the NPV and IRR over the payback period. The fact that the U.S. companies were larger, on average, partially explains the greater U.S. preference for the NPV and IRR. Other factors influence the choice of capital budgeting techniques. Private corporations used the payback period more frequently than did public corporations. Companies managed by an MBA had a stronger preference for the discounted cash flow techniques. Of course, any survey research also has some limitations. In this case, the persons in these large corporations responding to the surveys may not have been aware of all of the applications of these techniques.

---

5 Analysts often refer to the NPV and IRR as "discounted cash flow techniques" because they accurately account for the timing of all cash flows when they are discounted.

These capital budgeting techniques are essential tools for corporate managers. Capital budgeting is also relevant to external analysts. Because a corporation's investing decisions ultimately determine the value of its financial obligations, the corporation's investing processes are vital. The NPV criterion is the criterion most directly related to stock prices. If a corporation invests in positive NPV projects, these should add to the wealth of its shareholders. Example 6 illustrates this scenario.

EXAMPLE 6

NPVs and Stock Prices

Freitag Corporation is investing €600 million in distribution facilities. The present value of the future after-tax cash flows is estimated to be €850 million. Freitag has 200 million outstanding shares with a current market price of €32.00 per share. This investment is new information, and it is independent of other expectations about the company. What should be the effect of the project on the value of the company and the stock price?

Solution:

The NPV of the project is €850 million − €600 million = €250 million. The total market value of the company prior to the investment is €32.00 × 200 million shares = €6,400 million. The value of the company should increase by €250 million to €6,650 million. The price per share should increase by the NPV per share, or €250 million/200 million shares = €1.25 per share. The share price should increase from €32.00 to €33.25.

The effect of a capital budgeting project's positive or negative NPV on share price is more complicated than Example 6 above, in which the value of the stock increased by the project's NPV. The value of a company is the value of its existing investments plus the net present values of all of its future investments. If an analyst learns of an investment, the impact of that investment on the stock price will depend on whether the investment's profitability is more or less than expected. For example, an analyst could learn of a positive NPV project, but if the project's profitability is less than expectations, this stock might drop in price on the news. Alternatively, news of a particular capital project might be considered as a signal about other capital projects underway or in the future. A project that by itself might add, say, €0.25 to the value of the stock might signal the existence of other profitable projects. News of this project might increase the stock price by far more than €0.25.

The integrity of a corporation's capital budgeting processes is important to analysts. Management's capital budgeting processes can demonstrate two things about the quality of management: the degree to which management embraces the goal of shareholder wealth maximization, and its effectiveness in pursuing that goal. Both of these factors are important to shareholders.

END OPTIONAL SEGMENT

CASH FLOW PROJECTIONS　　　　　　　　　**5**

In Section 4, we presented the basic capital budgeting models that managers use to accept or reject capital budgeting proposals. In that section, we assumed the cash flows were given, and we used them as inputs to the analysis. In Section 5, we detail how these cash flows are found for an "expansion" project. An expansion project is an independent investment that does not affect the cash flows for the rest of the company.

In Section 6, we will deal with a "replacement" project, in which the cash flow analysis is more complicated. A replacement project must deal with the differences between the cash flows that occur with the new investment and the cash flows that would have occurred for the investment being replaced.

5.1 Table Format with Cash Flows Collected by Year

The cash flows for a conventional expansion project can be grouped into 1) the investment outlays, 2) after-tax operating cash flows over the project's life, and 3) terminal year after-tax non-operating cash flows. Table 14 gives an example of the cash flows for a capital project where all of the cash flows are collected by year.

Table 14	Capital Budgeting Cash Flows Example (Cash Flows Collected by Year)					
Year	**0**	**1**	**2**	**3**	**4**	**5**
Investment outlays:						
Fixed capital	−200,000					
Net working capital	−30,000					
Total	−230,000					
Annual after-tax operating cash flows:						
Sales		220,000	220,000	220,000	220,000	220,000
Cash operating expenses		90,000	90,000	90,000	90,000	90,000
Depreciation		35,000	35,000	35,000	35,000	35,000
Operating income before taxes		95,000	95,000	95,000	95,000	95,000
Taxes on operating income		38,000	38,000	38,000	38,000	38,000
Operating income after taxes		57,000	57,000	57,000	57,000	57,000
Add back: Depreciation		35,000	35,000	35,000	35,000	35,000
After-tax operating cash flow		92,000	92,000	92,000	92,000	92,000
Terminal year after-tax non-operating cash flows:						
After-tax salvage value						40,000
Return of net working capital						30,000
Total						70,000
Total after-tax cash flow	−230,000	92,000	92,000	92,000	92,000	162,000
Net present value at 10 percent required rate of return	162,217					
Internal rate of return	32.70%					

The investment outlays include a $200,000 outlay for fixed capital items. This outlay includes $25,000 for nondepreciable land, plus $175,000 for equipment that will be depreciated straight-line to zero over five years. The investment in net working capital is the net investment in short-term assets required for the investment. This is the investment in receivables and inventory needed, less the short-term payables generated by the project. In this case, the project required $50,000 of current assets but generated $20,000 in current liabilities, resulting in a total investment in net working capital of $30,000. The total investment outlay at time zero is $230,000.

Each year, sales will be $220,000 and cash operating expenses will be $90,000. Annual depreciation for the $175,000 depreciable equipment is $35,000 (one-fifth of the cost). The result is an operating income before taxes of $95,000. Income taxes at a 40 percent rate are $0.40 \times \$95,000 = \$38,000$. This leaves operating income after taxes of $57,000. Adding back the depreciation charge of $35,000 gives the annual after-tax operating cash flow of $92,000.[6]

At the end of Year 5, the company will sell off the fixed capital assets. In this case, the fixed capital assets (including the land) are sold for $50,000, which represents a gain of $25,000 over the remaining book value of $25,000. The gain of $25,000 is taxed at 40 percent, resulting in a tax of $10,000. This leaves $40,000 for the fixed capital assets after taxes. Additionally, the net working capital investment of $30,000 is recovered, as the short-term assets (such as inventory and receivables) and short-term liabilities (such as payables) are no longer needed for the project. Total terminal year non-operating cash flows are then $70,000.

The investment project has a required rate of return of 10 percent. Discounting the future cash flows at 10 percent and subtracting the investment outlay gives an NPV of $162,217. The internal rate of return is 32.70 percent. Because the investment has a positive NPV, this project should be accepted. The IRR investment decision criterion would also recommend accepting the project because the IRR is greater than the required rate of return.

5.2 Table Format with Cash Flows Collected by Type

In the layout in Table 14, we essentially collected the cash flows in the columns, by *year*, and then found the NPV by summing the present values of the annual cash flows (at the bottom of each column). There is another way of organizing the same information. We could also find the NPV by finding the present values of the cash flows in Table 14 by rows, which are the *types* of cash flows. This approach is shown in Table 15:

Table 15	Capital Budgeting Cash Flows Example (Cash Flows Collected by Type)			
Time	Type of Cash Flow	Before-Tax Cash Flow	After-Tax Cash Flow	PV at 10%
0	Fixed capital	−200,000	−200,000	−200,000
0	Net working capital	−30,000	−30,000	−30,000
1–5	Sales minus cash expenses	220,000 −90,000 = 130,000	130,000(1 − 0.40) = 78,000	295,681
1–5	Depreciation tax savings	None	0.40(35,000) = 14,000	53,071
5	After-tax salvage value	50,000	50,000 −0.40(50,000 − 25,000) = 40,000	24,837
5	Return of net working capital	30,000	30,000	18,628
			NPV=	162,217

---

6 Examining the operating cash flows in Table 14, we have a $220,000 inflow from sales, a $90,000 outflow for cash operating expenses, and a $38,000 outflow for taxes. This is an after-tax cash flow of $92,000.

As Table 15 shows, the outlays in fixed capital and in net working capital at time zero total $230,000. For Years 1 through 5, the company realizes an after-tax cash flow for sales minus cash expenses of $78,000, which has a present value of $295,681. The depreciation charge results in a tax savings of $14,000 per year, which has a present value of $53,071. The present values of the after-tax salvage and of the return of net working capital are also shown in the table. The present value of all cash flows is an NPV of $162,217. Obviously, collecting the after-tax cash flows by year, as in Table 14, or by type, as in Table 15, results in the same NPV.

5.3 Equation Format for Organizing Cash Flows

The capital budgeting cash flows in the example project above were laid out in one of two alternative tabular formats. Analysts may wish to take even another approach. Instead of producing a table, you can also look at the cash flows using equations such as the following:

1   Initial outlay: For a new investment:

$$\text{Outlay} = \text{FCInv} + \text{NWCInv}$$

where

$\quad$ FCInv = investment in new fixed capital
$\quad$ NWCInv = investment in net working capital

This equation can be generalized for a replacement project (covered in Section 6.2), in which existing fixed capital is sold and provides some of the funding for the new fixed capital purchased. The outlay is then

$$\text{Outlay} = \text{FCInv} + \text{NWCInv} - \text{Sal}_0 + T(\text{Sal}_0 - B_0) \tag{6}$$

where

$\quad$ Sal_0 = cash proceeds (salvage value) from sale of old fixed capital
$\quad$ T = tax rate
$\quad$ B_0 = book value of old fixed capital

2   Annual after-tax operating cash flow:

$$CF = (S - C - D)(1 - T) + D, \text{ or} \tag{7}$$

$$CF = (S - C)(1 - T) + TD \tag{8}$$

where

$\quad$ S = sales
$\quad$ C = cash operating expenses
$\quad$ D = depreciation charge

3   Terminal year after-tax non-operating cash flow:

$$\text{TNOCF} = \text{Sal}_T + \text{NWCInv} - T(\text{Sal}_T - B_T) \tag{9}$$

where

$\quad$ Sal_T = cash proceeds (salvage value) from sale of fixed capital on **termination date**
$\quad$ B_T = book value of fixed capital on termination date

The outlay in the example is found with Equation 6:

Outlay $= 200,000 + 30,000 - 0 + 0 = \$230,000$

For a replacement project, the old fixed capital would be sold for cash (Sal_0) and then there would be taxes paid on the gain (if $Sal_0 - B_0$ were positive) or a tax saving (if $Sal_0 - B_0$ were negative). In this example, Sal_0 and $T(Sal_0 - B_0)$ are zero because no existing fixed capital is sold at time zero.

Using Equation 7, we find that the annual after-tax operating cash flow is

$$CF = (S - C - D)(1 - T) + D$$
$$= (220,000 - 90,000 - 35,000)(1 - 0.40) + 35,000 = 95,000$$
$$\times (0.60) + 35,000$$
$$= 57,000 + 35,000 = \$92,000$$

Equation 7 is the project's net income plus depreciation. An identical cash flow results if we use Equation 8:

$$CF = (S - C)(1 - T) + TD$$
$$= (220,000 - 90,000)(1 - 0.40) + 0.40(35,000)$$
$$= 130,000(0.60) + 0.40(35,000) = 78,000 + 14,000 = \$92,000$$

Equation 8 is the after-tax sales and cash expenses plus the depreciation tax savings. The analyst can use either equation.

Equation 9 provides the terminal year non-operating cash flow:

$$TNOCF = Sal_T + NWCInv - T(Sal_T - B_T)$$
$$= 50,000 + 30,000 - 0.40(50,000 - 25,000)$$
$$= 50,000 + 30,000 - 10,000 = \$70,000$$

The old fixed capital (including land) is sold for $50,000, but $10,000 of taxes must be paid on the gain. Including the $30,000 return of net working capital gives a terminal year non-operating cash flow of $70,000.

The NPV of the project is the present value of the cash flows—an outlay of $230,000 at time zero, an annuity of $92,000 for five years, plus a single payment of $70,000 in five years:

$$NPV = -230,000 + \sum_{t=1}^{5} \frac{92,000}{(1.10)^t} + \frac{70,000}{(1.10)^5}$$
$$= -230,000 + 348,752 + 43,465 = \$162,217$$

We obtain an identical NPV of $162,217 whether we use a tabular format collecting cash flows by year, a tabular format collecting cash flows by type, or an equation format using Equations 6 through 9. The analyst usually has some flexibility in choosing how to solve a problem. Furthermore, the analysis that an analyst receives from someone else could be in varying formats. The analyst must interpret this information correctly regardless of format. An analyst may need to present information in alternative formats, depending on what the client or user of the information wishes to see. All that is important is that the cash flows are complete (with no cash flows omitted and none double-counted), that their timing is recognized, and that the discounting is done correctly.

6 MORE ON CASH FLOW PROJECTIONS

Cash flow analysis can become fairly complicated. Section 6 extends the analysis of the previous section to include more details on depreciation methods, replacement projects (as opposed to simple expansion projects), the use of spreadsheets, and the effects of inflation.

6.1 Straight-Line and Accelerated Depreciation Methods

Before going on to more complicated investment decisions, we should mention the variety of depreciation methods that are in use. The example in Section 5.1 assumed straight-line depreciation down to a zero salvage value. Most accounting texts give a good description of the straight-line method, the sum-of-years digits method, the double-declining balance method (and the 150 percent declining balance method), and the units-of-production and service hours method.[7]

Many countries specify the depreciation methods that are acceptable for tax purposes in their jurisdictions. For example, in the U.S., corporations use the MACRS (modified accelerated cost recovery system) for tax purposes. Under MACRS, real property (real estate) is usually depreciated straight-line over a 27.5- or 39-year life, and other capital assets are usually grouped into MACRS asset classes and subject to a special depreciation schedule in each class. These MACRS classes and the depreciation rates for each class are shown in Table 16.

Table 16	Depreciation Rates under U.S. MACRS					
	Recovery Period Class					
Year	**3-Year**	**5-Year**	**7-Year**	**10-Year**	**15-Year**	**20-Year**
1	33.33%	20.00%	14.29%	10.00%	5.00%	3.75%
2	44.45	32.00	24.49	18.00	9.50	7.22
3	14.81	19.20	17.49	14.40	8.55	6.68
4	7.41	11.52	12.49	11.52	7.70	6.18
5		11.52	8.93	9.22	6.93	5.71
6		5.76	8.93	7.37	6.23	5.28
7			8.93	6.55	5.90	4.89
8			4.45	6.55	5.90	4.52
9				6.55	5.90	4.46
10				6.55	5.90	4.46
11				3.29	5.90	4.46
12					5.90	4.46
13					5.90	4.46
14					5.90	4.46
15					5.90	4.46
16					2.99	4.46
17						4.46

---

7 White, Sondhi, and Fried (2003) is a good example. Consult their Chapter 8, "Analysis of Long-Lived Assets: Part II—Analysis of Depreciation and Impairment," for review and examples.

			Recovery Period Class			
Year	**3-Year**	**5-Year**	**7-Year**	**10-Year**	**15-Year**	**20-Year**
18						4.46
19						4.46
20						4.46
21						2.25

For the first four MACRS classes (3-year, 5-year, 7-year, and 10-year), the depreciation is double-declining-balance with a switch to straight-line when optimal and with a half-year convention. For the last two classes (15-year and 20-year), the depreciation is 150 percent-declining-balance with a switch to straight-line when optimal and with a half-year convention. Take 5-year property in Table 16 as an example. With double-declining-balance, the depreciation each year is $2/5 = 40\%$ of the beginning-of-year book value. However, with a half-year convention, the asset is assumed to be in service for only six months during the first year, and only one-half of the depreciation is allowed the first year. After the first year, the depreciation rate is 40 percent of the beginning balance until Year 4, when straight-line depreciation would be at least as large, so we switch to straight-line. In Year 6, we have one-half of a year of the straight-line depreciation remaining because we assumed the asset was placed in service half-way through the first year.

Accelerated depreciation generally improves the NPV of a capital project compared to straight-line depreciation. For an example of this effect, we will assume the same capital project as in Table 14, except that the depreciation is MACRS 3-year property. When using straight-line, the depreciation was 20 percent per year ($35,000). The depreciation percentages for MACRS 3-year property are given in Table 16. The first-year depreciation is $0.3333 \times 175,000 = \$58,327.50$, second year depreciation is $0.4445 \times 175,000 = \$77,787.50$, third year depreciation is $0.1481 \times 175,000 = \$25,917.50$, fourth year depreciation is $0.0741 \times 175,000 = \$12,967.50$, and fifth year depreciation is zero. The impact on the NPV and IRR of the project is shown in Table 17.

Table 17	Capital Budgeting Example with MACRS					
Year	**0**	**1**	**2**	**3**	**4**	**5**
Investment outlays:						
Fixed capital	−200,000					
Net working capital	−30,000					
Total	−230,000					
Annual after-tax operating cash flows:						
Sales		220,000	220,000	220,000	220,000	220,000
Cash operating expenses		90,000	90,000	90,000	90,000	90,000
Depreciation		58,328	77,788	25,918	12,968	0
Operating income before taxes		71,673	52,213	104,083	117,033	130,000
Taxes on operating income (40%)		28,669	20,885	41,633	46,813	52,000
Operating income after taxes		43,004	31,328	62,450	70,220	78,000

(continued)

Table 17	(Continued)					
Year	0	1	2	3	4	5
Add back: Depreciation		58,328	77,788	25,918	12,968	0
After-tax operating cash flow		101,331	109,115	88,367	83,187	78,000
Terminal year after-tax non-operating cash flows:						
After-tax salvage value						40,000
Return of net working capital						30,000
Total						70,000
Total after-tax cash flows	−230,000	101,331	109,115	88,367	83,187	148,000
Net present value at 10% required rate of return	$167,403					
Internal rate of return		34.74%				

As the table shows, the depreciation charges still sum to $175,000 (except for $2 of rounding), but they are larger in Years 1 and 2 and smaller in Years 3, 4, and 5. Although this method reduces operating income after taxes in Years 1 and 2 (and increases it in Years 3, 4, and 5), it reduces tax outflows in Years 1 and 2 and increases them later. Consequently, the after-tax operating cash flows (which were $92,000 per year) increase in early years and decrease in later years. This increases the NPV from $162,217 to $167,403, a difference of $5,186. The IRR also increases from 32.70 percent to 34.74 percent.[8]

The impact of accelerated depreciation can be seen without going through the complete analysis in Table 17. We previously showed in Table 15 that the present value of the depreciation tax savings (which was an annuity of 0.40 × $35,000 = $14,000 a year for five years) was $53,071. The present value of the tax savings from accelerated depreciation is shown in Table 18.

Table 18	Present Value of Tax Savings from Accelerated Depreciation		
Year	Depreciation ($)	Tax Savings	PV at 10% ($)
1	58,327.50	0.40 × $58,327.5 = $23,331	21,210
2	77,787.50	0.40 × $77,787.5 = $31,115	25,715
3	25,917.50	0.40 × $25,917.5 = $10,367	7,789
4	12,967.50	0.40 × $12,967.5 = $5,187	3,543
5	0	0.40 × $0 = $0	0
Total present value			58,257

---

[8] This example assumes that the investment occurs on the first day of the tax year. If the outlay occurs later in the tax year, the depreciation tax savings for the tax years are unchanged, which means that the cash savings occur sooner, increasing their present values. The result is a higher NPV and IRR.

By using the accelerated depreciation schedule, we increase the present value of the tax savings from $53,071 (from Table 15) to $58,257, an increase of $5,186. The tax deferral associated with the accelerated depreciation (compared to straight-line) adds $5,186 to the NPV of the project.

There are a myriad of tax and depreciation schedules that apply to investment projects around the world. These tax and depreciation schedules are also subject to change from year to year. To accurately assess the profitability of a particular capital project, it is vital to identify and apply the schedules that are relevant to the capital budgeting decision at hand.

6.2 Cash Flows for a Replacement Project

In Section 5.1, we evaluated the cash flows for an expansion project, basing our after-tax cash flows on the outlays, annual operating cash flows after tax, and salvage value for the project by itself. In many cases, however, investing in a project will be more complicated. Investing could affect many of the company's cash flows. In principle, the cash flows relevant to an investing decision are the incremental cash flows: the cash flows the company realizes *with* the investment compared to the cash flows the company would realize *without* the investment. For example, suppose we are investing in a new project with an outlay of $100,000 and we sell off existing assets that the project replaces for $30,000. The incremental outlay is $70,000.

A very common investment decision is a replacement decision, in which you replace old equipment with new equipment. This decision requires very careful analysis of the cash flows. The skills required to detail the replacement decision cash flows are also useful for other decisions in which an investment affects other cash flows in the company. We use the term "replacement" loosely, primarily to indicate that the cash flow analysis is more complicated than it was for the simpler expansion decision.

Assume we are considering the replacement of old equipment with new equipment that has more capacity and is less costly to operate. The characteristics of the old and new equipment are given below:

Old Equipment		New Equipment	
Current book value	$400,000		
Current market value	$600,000	Acquisition cost	$1,000,000
Remaining life	10 years	Life	10 years
Annual sales	$300,000	Annual sales	$450,000
Cash operating expenses	$120,000	Cash operating expenses	$150,000
Annual depreciation	$40,000	Annual depreciation	$100,000
Accounting salvage value	$0	Accounting salvage value	$0
Expected salvage value	$100,000	Expected salvage value	$200,000

If the new equipment replaces the old equipment, an additional investment of $80,000 in net working capital will be required. The tax rate is 30 percent, and the required rate of return is 8 percent.

The cash flows can be found by carefully constructing tables like Table 14 or by using Equations 6 through 9. The initial outlay is the investment in the new equipment plus the additional investment in net working capital less the after-tax proceeds from selling the old equipment:

$$\text{Outlay} = \text{FCInv} + \text{NWCInv} - \text{Sal}_0 + T(\text{Sal}_0 - B_0)$$

$$\text{Outlay} = 1{,}000{,}000 + 80{,}000 - 600{,}000$$

$$+ 0.3(600{,}000 - 400{,}000) = \$540{,}000$$

In this case, the outlay of $540,000 is $1,080,000 for new equipment and net working capital minus the after-tax proceeds of $540,000 the company receives from selling the old equipment. The incremental operating cash flows are

$$\begin{aligned}
\text{CF} &= (S - C - D)(1 - T) + D \\
&= \big[(450{,}000 - 300{,}000) - (150{,}000 - 120{,}000) \\
&\quad - (100{,}000 - 40{,}000)\big](1 - 0.30) + (100{,}000 - 40{,}000) \\
&= (150{,}000 - 30{,}000 - 60{,}000)(1 - 0.30) + 60{,}000 = \$102{,}000
\end{aligned}$$

The incremental sales are $150,000, incremental cash operating expenses are $30,000, and incremental depreciation is $60,000. The incremental after-tax operating cash flow is $102,000 per year.

At the project termination, the new equipment is expected to be sold for $200,000, which constitutes an incremental cash flow of $100,000 over the $100,000 expected salvage price of the old equipment. Since the accounting salvage values for both the new and old equipment were zero, this gain is taxable at 30 percent. The company also recaptures its investment in net working capital. The terminal year after-tax non-operating cash flow is

$$\begin{aligned}
\text{TNOCF} &= \text{Sal}_T + \text{NWCInv} - T(\text{Sal}_T - B_T) \\
&= (200{,}000 - 100{,}000) + 80{,}000 - 0.30 \\
&\quad \big[(200{,}000 - 100{,}000) - (0 - 0)\big] \\
&= \$150{,}000
\end{aligned}$$

Once the cash flows are identified, the NPV and IRR are readily found. The NPV, found by discounting the cash flows at the 8 percent required rate of return, is

$$\text{NPV} = -540{,}000 + \sum_{t=1}^{10} \frac{102{,}000}{1.08^t} + \frac{150{,}000}{1.08^{10}} = \$213{,}907$$

The IRR, found with a financial calculator, is 15.40 percent. Because the NPV is positive, this equipment replacement decision is attractive. The fact that the IRR exceeds the 8 percent required rate of return leads to the same conclusion.

The key to estimating the incremental cash flows for the replacement is to compare the cash flows that occur with the new investment to the cash flows that would have occurred without the new investment. The analyst is comparing the cash flows with a particular course of action to the cash flows with an alternative course of action.

6.3 Spreadsheet Modeling

Although the examples in this reading can be readily solved with a financial calculator, capital budgeting is usually done with the assistance of personal computers and spreadsheets such as Microsoft Excel®. Spreadsheets are heavily used for several reasons. Spreadsheets provide a very effective way of building even complex models. Built-in spreadsheet functions (such as those for finding rates of return) are easy to use. The model's assumptions can be changed and solved easily. Models can be shared with other analysts, and they also help in presenting the results of the analysis. The example below shows how a spreadsheet can be used to solve a capital budgeting problem.

EXAMPLE 7

Capital Budgeting with a Spreadsheet

Lawton Enterprises is evaluating a project with the following characteristics:

- Fixed capital investment is $2,000,000.

- The project has an expected six-year life.

- The initial investment in net working capital is $200,000. At the end of each year, net working capital must be increased so that the cumulative investment in net working capital is one-sixth of the next year's projected sales.

- The fixed capital is depreciated 30 percent in Year 1, 35 percent in Year 2, 20 percent in Year 3, 10 percent in Year 4, 5 percent in Year 5, and 0 percent in Year 6.

- Sales are $1,200,000 in Year 1. They grow at a 25 percent annual rate for the next two years, and then grow at a 10 percent annual rate for the last three years.

- Fixed cash operating expenses are $150,000 for Years 1–3 and $130,000 for Years 4–6.

- Variable cash operating expenses are 40 percent of sales in Year 1, 39 percent of sales in Year 2, and 38 percent in Years 3–6.

- Lawton's marginal tax rate is 30 percent.

- Lawton will sell its fixed capital investments for $150,000 when the project terminates and recapture its cumulative investment in net working capital. Income taxes will be paid on any gains.

- The project's required rate of return is 12 percent.

- If taxable income on the project is negative in any year, the loss will offset gains elsewhere in the corporation, resulting in a tax savings.

1 Determine whether this is a profitable investment using the NPV and IRR.

2 If the tax rate increases to 40 percent and the required rate of return increases to 14 percent, is the project still profitable?

Solution to 1:

Table 19	Cash Flows for Lawton Investment (Rounded to Nearest $1,000)						
Year	**0**	**1**	**2**	**3**	**4**	**5**	**6**
Fixed capital investment	−2,000						
NWC investments	−200	−50	−63	−31	−34	−38	
Sales		1,200	1,500	1,875	2,063	2,269	2,496
Fixed cash expenses		150	150	150	130	130	130
Variable cash expenses		480	585	713	784	862	948
Depreciation		600	700	400	200	100	0
Operating income before taxes		−30	65	613	949	1,177	1,417
Taxes on operating income		−9	20	184	285	353	425
Operating income after taxes		−21	45	429	664	824	992
Add back: Depreciation		600	700	400	200	100	0
After-tax operating cash flow		579	745	829	864	924	992
Salvage value							150

(continued)

Year	0	1	2	3	4	5	6
Table 19 (Continued)							
Taxes on salvage value							−45
Return of NWC							416
Total after-tax cash flows	−2,200	529	682	798	830	886	1,513
NPV (at r = 12 percent)	1,181						
IRR		26.60%					

Because the NPV of $1,181,000 is positive, the project is profitable for Lawton to undertake. The IRR investment decision rule also indicates that the project is profitable because the IRR of 26.60 percent exceeds the 12 percent required rate of return.

Solution to 2:

The tax rate and required return can be changed in the spreadsheet model. When these changes are made, the NPV becomes $736,000 and the IRR becomes 24.02 percent. (The revised spreadsheet is not printed here.) Although profitability is lower, the higher tax rate and required rate of return do not change the investment decision.

6.4 Effects of Inflation on Capital Budgeting Analysis

Inflation affects capital budgeting analysis in several ways. The first decision the analyst must make is whether to do the analysis in "nominal" terms or in "real" terms. Nominal cash flows include the effects of inflation, while real cash flows are adjusted downward to remove the effects of inflation. It is perfectly acceptable to do the analysis in either nominal or real terms, and sound decisions can be made either way. However, inflation creates some issues regardless of the approach.

The cash flows and discount rate used should both be nominal or both be real. In other words, nominal cash flows should be discounted at a nominal discount rate, and real cash flows should be discounted at a real rate. The real rate, just like real cash flows, has had the effect of inflation taken out. In general, the relationship between real and nominal rates is

$$(1 + \text{Nominal rate}) = (1 + \text{Real rate})(1 + \text{Inflation rate})$$

Inflation reduces the value of depreciation tax savings (unless the tax system adjusts depreciation for inflation). The effect of expected inflation is captured in the discounted cash flow analysis. If inflation is higher than expected, the profitability of the investment is correspondingly lower than expected. Inflation essentially shifts wealth from the taxpayer to the government. Higher-than-expected inflation increases the corporation's real taxes because it reduces the value of the depreciation tax shelter. Conversely, lower-than-expected inflation reduces real taxes (the depreciation tax shelters are more valuable than expected).

Inflation also reduces the value of fixed payments to bondholders. When bonds are originally issued, bondholders pay a price for the bonds reflecting their inflationary expectations. If inflation is higher than expected, the real payments to bondholders are lower than expected. Higher-than-expected inflation shifts wealth from bondholders to the issuing corporations. Conversely, if inflation is lower than expected, the real interest expenses of the corporation increase, shifting wealth from the issuing corporation to its bondholders.

Finally, inflation does not affect all revenues and costs uniformly. The company's after-tax cash flows will be better or worse than expected depending on how particular sales outputs or cost inputs are affected. Furthermore, contracting with customers, suppliers, employees, and sources of capital can be complicated as inflation rises.

The capital budgeting model accommodates the effects of inflation, although inflation complicates the capital budgeting process (and the operations of a business, in general).

PROJECT ANALYSIS AND EVALUATION

7

Assessing the opportunity costs and analyzing the risks of capital investments becomes more complex and sophisticated as you examine real cases. The first project interaction we examine in this section is that of comparing mutually exclusive projects with unequal lives. We will briefly describe other project interactions, but will not examine them in detail. We also examine the process of capital budgeting under capital rationing.

Up to this point, we have largely ignored the issue of accounting for risk. We will introduce risk analysis in two ways. The first is accounting for risk on a stand-alone basis. The second is accounting for risk on a systematic basis.

7.1 Mutually Exclusive Projects with Unequal Lives

We have previously looked at mutually exclusive projects and decided that the best project is the one with the greatest NPV. However, if the mutually exclusive projects have differing lives and the projects will be replaced (or replicated) repeatedly when they wear out, the analysis is more complicated. The analysis of a one-shot (one time only) investment differs from that of an investment chain (in which the asset is replaced regularly in the future).

For example, assume we have two projects with unequal lives of two and three years, with the following after-tax cash flows:

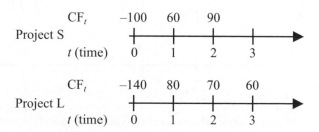

Both projects have a 10 percent required rate of return. The NPV of Project S is $28.93 and the NPV of Project L is $35.66. Given that the two projects are mutually exclusive, Project L, with the greater NPV, should be chosen.

However, let us now assume that these are not one-shot investments, but investments in assets that the company will need to replace when they wear out. Project S would be replaced every two years and Project L every three years. This situation is often referred to as a replacement chain. In this type of problem, you should examine the entire chain and not just the first link in the chain. If the projects are part of a replacement chain, examining the cash flows for only the initial investment for Projects S and L is improper because Project L provides cash flows during Year 3, when Project S provides none.

There are two logically equivalent ways of comparing mutually exclusive projects in a replacement chain. They are the "least common multiple of lives" approach and the "equivalent annual annuity" approach.

7.1.1 Least Common Multiple of Lives Approach

For the least common multiple of lives approach, the analyst extends the time horizon of analysis so that the lives of both projects will divide exactly into the horizon. For Projects S and L, the least common multiple of 2 and 3 is 6: The two-year project would be replicated three times over the six-year horizon and the three-year project would be replicated two times over the six-year horizon.[9] The cash flows for replicating Projects S and L over a six-year horizon are shown below.

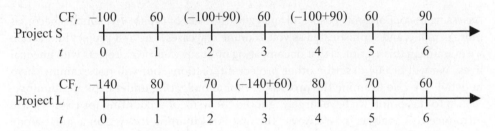

Discounting the cash flows for the six-year horizon results in an NPV for Project S of $72.59 and an NPV for Project L of $62.45. Apparently, investing in Project S and replicating the investment over time has a greater NPV than choosing Project L and replicating it. This decision is the reverse of the one we made when looking solely at the NPVs of the initial investments!

Because the NPV of a single investment represents the present values of its cash flows, you can also visualize the NPV of a replacement chain as the present value of the NPVs of each investment (or link) in the chain. For Projects S and L, the NPVs of each investment are shown on the timelines below:

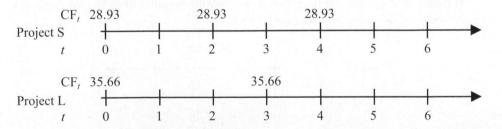

Investing in Project S is equivalent to receiving values of $28.93 at times 0, 2, and 4, while investing in Project L is equivalent to receiving values of $35.66 at times 0 and 3. The present values of these cash flow patterns are $72.59 for Project S and $62.45 for Project L. Discounting the NPVs of each investment in the chain is equivalent to discounting all of the individual cash flows in the chain.

---

9 The least common multiple of lives is not necessarily the product of the two lives, as in the case of Projects S and L. For example, if two projects have lives of 8 and 10 years, the least common multiple of lives is 40 years, not 80. Both 8 and 10 are exactly divisible into 40.

7.1.2 *Equivalent Annual Annuity Approach*

The other method for properly evaluating a replacement chain is called the equivalent annual annuity (EAA) approach. The name for this approach is very descriptive. For an investment project with an outlay and variable cash flows in the future, the project NPV summarizes the equivalent value at time zero. For this same project, the EAA is the annuity payment (series of equal annual payments over the project's life) that is equivalent in value to the NPV.

Analysts can use a simple two-step procedure to find the EAA. The first step is to find the present value of all of the cash flows for an investment—the investment's NPV. The second step is to calculate an annuity payment that has a value equivalent to the NPV. For Project S above, we already calculated the NPV of the project over its two-year life to be $28.93. The second step is to find an annuity payment for the two-year life that is equivalent. For a two-year life and a 10 percent discount rate, a payment of $16.66 is the equivalent annuity.

The EAA for Project L is found by annuitizing its $35.66 NPV over three years, so the EAA for Project L is $14.34.

The decision rule for the EAA approach is to choose the investment chain that has the highest EAA, which in this case is Project S.

Given these two approaches to comparing replacement chains, which one should the analyst use? As a practical matter, the two approaches are logically equivalent and will result in the same decision.[10] Consequently, the analyst can choose one approach over the other based on personal preference. Or, if the audience for the analyst's work prefers to see the analysis using one approach, the analyst can simply produce the analysis in that format.

7.2 Capital Rationing

Capital rationing is the case in which the company's capital budget has a size constraint. For example, the capital budget is a fixed money amount. A fixed capital budget can place the company in several interesting situations. To illustrate these, we will assume that the company has a fixed $1,000 capital budget and has the opportunity to invest in four projects. The projects are of variable profitability.

In the first situation, the budget is adequate to invest in all profitable projects. Consider the four projects in Table 20.

Table 20	First Capital Rationing Example			
	Investment Outlay	**NPV**	**PI**	**IRR (%)**
Project 1	600	220	1.37	15
Project 2	200	70	1.35	16
Project 3	200	−60	0.70	10
Project 4	400	−100	0.75	8

In this case, the company has two positive-NPV projects, Projects 1 and 2, which involve a total outlay of $800. Their total NPV is $290. The company should choose these projects, and it will have $200 in its capital budget left over. These excess funds can be used elsewhere in the company (moved to someone else's budget, used to pay dividends or repurchase shares, or used to pay down debt). If a manager is afraid to return the excess funds and chooses to invest in Project 3, the manager will consume the whole capital budget but reduce the total NPV to $230, essentially destroying $60 of wealth for the company.

A second case exists in which the company has more profitable projects than it can choose, but it is able to invest in the most profitable ones available. Continuing with the $1,000 capital budget, this second case is illustrated in Table 21.

Table 21	Second Capital Rationing Example			
	Investment Outlay	**NPV**	**PI**	**IRR (%)**
Project 5	600	300	1.50	16
Project 6	200	80	1.40	18
Project 7	200	60	1.30	12
Project 8	200	40	1.20	14

When the analyst has a fixed budget, the PI is especially useful because it shows the profitability of each investment per currency unit invested. If we rank these projects by their PIs, Projects 5, 6, and 7 are the best projects and we are able to select them. This selection results in a total NPV of $440. The IRRs, shown in the last column, are not a reliable guide to choosing projects under capital rationing because a high-IRR project may have a low NPV. Wealth maximization is best guided by the NPV criterion.

A third case exists in which the company has more profitable projects than it can choose, but it is not able to invest in the most profitable ones available. Assume the company cannot invest in fractional projects: It must take all or none of each project it chooses. Continuing with the $1,000 capital budget, this case is illustrated in Table 22.

Table 22	Third Capital Rationing Example			
	Investment Outlay	**NPV**	**PI**	**IRR (%)**
Project 9	600	300	1.50	15
Project 10	600	270	1.45	16
Project 11	200	80	1.40	12
Project 12	400	100	1.25	11

In this example, an unlimited budget of $1,800 would generate a total NPV of $750. However, when the budget constraint is imposed, the highest NPV results from choosing Projects 9 and 12. The company is forced to choose its best project and its fourth-best project, as indicated by their relative PIs. Any other combination of projects either violates the budget or has a lower total NPV.

Capital rationing has the potential to misallocate resources. Capital markets are supposed to allocate funds to their highest and best uses, with the opportunity cost of funds (used as the discount rate for NPVs or the hurdle rate for IRRs) guiding this allocation process. Capital rationing violates market efficiency if society's resources are not allocated where they will generate the best returns. Companies that use capital rationing may be doing either "hard" or "soft" capital rationing. Under hard capital rationing, the budget is fixed and the managers cannot go beyond it. Under soft capital rationing, managers may be allowed to over-spend their budgets if they argue effectively that the additional funds will be deployed profitably.

In the case of hard rationing, choosing the optimal projects that fit within the budget and maximize the NPV of the company can be computationally intensive. Sometimes, managers use estimates and trial and error to find the optimal set of projects. The PI can be used as a guide in this trial and error process. Other times, the number of possibilities is so daunting that mathematical programming algorithms are used.

7.3 Risk Analysis of Capital Investments—Stand-Alone Methods

So far, we have evaluated projects by calculating a single NPV to decide whether a project is profitable. We took a single value, or point estimate, of each input into the model and combined the values to calculate the NPV.

Risk is usually measured as a dispersion of outcomes. In the case of stand-alone risk, we typically measure the riskiness of a project by the dispersion of its NPVs or the dispersion of its IRRs. Sensitivity analysis, scenario analysis, and simulation analysis are very popular stand-alone risk analysis methods. These risk measures depend on the variation of the project's cash flows.

To illustrate the stand-alone risk tools, we will use the following "base case" capital project:

Unit price	$5.00
Annual unit sales	40,000
Variable cost per unit	$1.50
Investment in fixed capital	$300,000
Investment in working capital	$50,000
Project life	6 years
Depreciation (straight-line)	$50,000
Expected salvage value	$60,000
Tax rate	40 percent
Required rate of return	12 percent

The outlay, from Equation 6, is $300,000 plus $50,000, or $350,000. The annual after-tax operating cash flow, from Equation 7, is

$$CF = (S - C - D)(1 - T) + D$$

$$= \left[(5 \times 40{,}000)) - (1.50 \times 40{,}000) - (50{,}000)\right](1 - 0.40) + 50{,}000$$

$$= \$104{,}000$$

The terminal year after-tax non-operating cash flow, from Equation 9, is

$$TNOCF = Sal_6 + NWCInv - T(Sal_6 - B_6)$$

$$= 60{,}000 + 50{,}000 - 0.40(60{,}000 - 0) = \$86{,}000$$

The project NPV is

$$NPV = -350,000 + \sum_{t=1}^{6} \frac{104,000}{1.12^t} + \frac{86,000}{1.12^6} = -350,000 + 471,157 = \$121,157$$

7.3.1 Sensitivity Analysis

Sensitivity analysis calculates the effect on the NPV of changes in one input variable at a time. The base case above has several input variables. If we wish to do a sensitivity analysis of several of them, we must specify the changes in each that we wish to evaluate. Suppose we want to consider the following:

	Base Value	Low Value	High Value
Unit price	$5.00	$4.50	$5.50
Annual unit sales	40,000	35,000	45,000
Variable cost per unit	$1.50	$1.40	$1.60
Expected salvage value	$60,000	$30,000	$80,000
Tax rate	40%	38%	42%
Required rate of return	12%	10%	14%

We have changed each of six input variables. Table 23 shows the NPV calculated for the base case. Then the NPV is recalculated by changing one variable from its base case value to its high or low value.

| Table 23 | Sensitivity of Project NPV to Changes in a Variable |

	Project NPV			
Variable	**Base Case ($)**	**With Low Estimate ($)**	**With High Estimate ($)**	**Range of Estimates ($)**
Unit price	121,157	71,820	170,494	98,674
Annual unit sales	121,157	77,987	164,326	86,339
Cost per unit	121,157	131,024	111,289	19,735
Salvage value	121,157	112,037	127,236	15,199
Tax rate	121,157	129,165	113,148	16,017
Required return	121,157	151,492	93,602	57,890

As Table 23 shows, the project's NPV is most sensitive to changes in the unit price variable. The project's NPV is least sensitive to changes in the salvage value. Roughly speaking, the project's NPV is most sensitive to changes in unit price and in unit sales. It is least affected by changes in cost per unit, salvage value, and the tax rate. Changes in the required rate of return also have a substantial effect, but not as much as changes in price or unit sales.

In a sensitivity analysis, the manager can choose which variables to change and by how much. Many companies have access to software that can be instructed to change a particular variable by a certain amount—for example, to increase or decrease unit price, unit sales, and cost per unit by 10 percent. The software then produces the changes in NPV for each of these changes. Sensitivity analysis can be used to establish which variables are most influential on the success or failure of a project.

7.3.2 Scenario Analysis

Sensitivity analysis calculates the effect on the NPV of changes in one variable at a time. In contrast, scenario analysis creates scenarios that consist of changes in several of the input variables and calculates the NPV for each scenario. Although corporations could do a large number of scenarios, in practice they usually do only three. They can be labeled variously, but we will present an example with "pessimistic," "most likely," and "optimistic" scenarios. Continuing with the basic example from the section above, the values of the input variables for the three scenarios are given in the table below.

Table 24	Input Variables and NPV for Scenario Analysis		
	Scenario		
Variable	**Pessimistic**	**Most Likely**	**Optimistic**
Unit price	$4.50	$5.00	$5.50
Annual unit sales	35,000	40,000	45,000
Variable cost per unit	$1.60	$1.50	$1.40
Investment in fixed capital	$320,000	$300,000	$280,000
Investment in working capital	$50,000	$50,000	$50,000
Project life	6 years	6 years	6 years
Depreciation (straight-line)	$53,333	$50,000	$46,667
Salvage value	$40,000	$60,000	$80,000
Tax rate	40%	40%	40%
Required rate of return	13%	12%	11%
NPV	−$5,725	$121,157	$269,685
IRR	12.49%	22.60%	34.24%

The most likely scenario is the same as the base case we used above for sensitivity analysis, and the NPV for the most likely scenario is $121,157. To form the pessimistic and optimistic scenarios, managers change several of the assumptions for each scenario. For the pessimistic scenario, several of the input variables are changed to reflect higher costs, lower revenues, and a higher required rate of return. As the table shows, the result is a negative NPV for the pessimistic scenario and an IRR that is less than the pessimistic scenario's 13 percent required rate of return. For the optimistic scenario, the more favorable revenues, costs, and required rate of return result in very good NPV and IRR.

For this example, the scenario analysis reveals the possibility of an unprofitable investment, with a negative NPV and with an IRR less than the cost of capital. The range for the NPV is fairly large compared to the size of the initial investment, which indicates that the investment is fairly risky. This example included three scenarios for which management wants to know the profitability of the investment for each set of assumptions. Other scenarios can be investigated if management chooses to do so.

7.3.3 Simulation (Monte Carlo) Analysis

Simulation analysis is a procedure for estimating a probability distribution of outcomes, such as for the NPV or IRR for a capital investment project. Instead of assuming a single value (a point estimate) for the input variables in a capital budgeting spreadsheet, the analyst can assume several variables to be stochastic, following their own probability distributions. By simulating the results hundreds or thousands of times, the analyst can build a good estimate of the distributions for the NPV or IRR. Because of the volume of computations, analysts and corporate managers rely heavily on their personal computers and specialized simulation software such as @RISK.[11] Example 8 presents a simple simulation analysis.

EXAMPLE 8

Capital Budgeting Simulation

Gouhua Zhang has made the following assumptions for a capital budgeting project:

▪ Fixed capital investment is 20,000; no investment in net working capital is required.

▪ The project has an expected five-year life.

▪ The fixed capital is depreciated straight-line to zero over a five-year life. The salvage value is normally distributed with an expected value of 2,000 and a standard deviation of 500.

▪ Unit sales in Year 1 are normally distributed with a mean of 2,000 and a standard deviation of 200.

▪ Unit sales growth after Year 1 is normally distributed with a mean of 6 percent and standard deviation of 4 percent. Assume the same sales growth rate for Years 2–5.

▪ The sales price is 5.00 per unit, normally distributed with a standard deviation of 0.25 per unit. The same price holds for all five years.

▪ Cash operating expenses as a percentage of total revenue are normally distributed with a mean and standard deviation of 30 percent and 3 percent, respectively.

▪ The discount rate is 12 percent and the tax rate is 40 percent.

1 What are the NPV and IRR using the expected values of all input variables?

2 Perform a simulation analysis and provide probability distributions for the NPV and IRR.

Solution to 1:

Table 25	Expected Cash Flows for Simulation Example					
Time	0	1	2	3	4	5
Fixed capital	−20,000					
After-tax salvage value						1,200
Price		5.00	5.00	5.00	5.00	5.00
Output		2,000	2,120	2,247	2,382	2,525
Revenue		10,000	10,600	11,236	11,910	12,625
Cash operating expenses		3,000	3,180	3,371	3,573	3,787
Depreciation		4,000	4,000	4,000	4,000	4,000
Operating income before taxes		3,000	3,420	3,865	4,337	4,837
Taxes on operating income		1,200	1,368	1,546	1,735	1,935
Operating income after taxes		1,800	2,052	2,319	2,602	2,902
Depreciation		4,000	4,000	4,000	4,000	4,000
Total after-tax cash flow	−20,000	5,800	6,052	6,319	6,602	8,102

---

11 @RISK is a popular and powerful risk analysis tool sold by Palisade Corporation. @RISK is an add-in for Microsoft Excel that allows simulation techniques to be incorporated into spreadsheet models.

Table 25	(Continued)						
Time		**0**	**1**	**2**	**3**	**4**	**5**
NPV (at r = 12 percent)		3,294					
IRR		18.11%					

Based on the point estimates for each variable (the mean values for each), which are shown in Table 25 above, Zhang should find the NPV to be 3,294 and the IRR to be 18.11 percent.

Solution to 2:

Zhang performs a simulation using @RISK with 10,000 iterations. For each iteration, values for the five stochastic variables (price, output, output growth rate, cash expense percentage, and salvage value) are selected from their assumed distributions and the NPV and IRR are calculated. After the 10,000 iterations, the resulting information about the probability distributions for the NPV and IRR is shown in Figure 6 and Table 26.

Figure 6A	Distribution for NPV

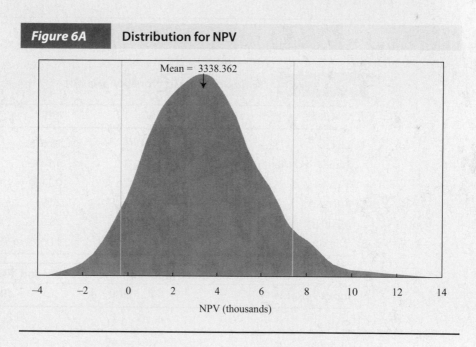

Figure 6B	Distribution for IRR

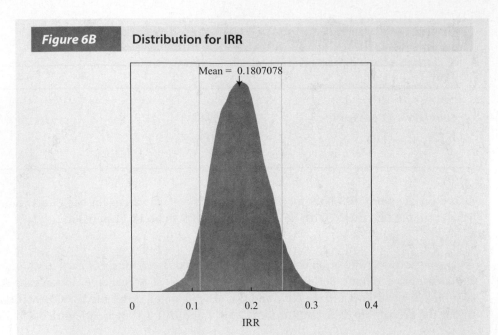

Table 26	Summary Statistics for NPV and IRR

Statistic	NPV	IRR
Mean	3,338	18.07%
Standard deviation	2,364	4.18%
Skewness	0.2909	0.1130
Kurtosis	3.146	2.996
Median	3,236	18.01%
90% confidence interval	−379 to 7,413	11.38% to 25.13%

Correlations between Input Variables and NPV and IRR		
Input Variable	NPV	IRR
Output	0.71	0.72
Output growth rate	0.49	0.47
Price	0.34	0.34
Cash expense proportion	−0.28	−0.29
Salvage value	0.06	0.05

As the figure shows, the distributions for the NPV and IRR are somewhat normal looking. The means and standard deviations for each are given in Table 26. Both distributions have a slight positive skewness, which means the distributions are skewed to the right. The two kurtosis values are fairly close to 3.0, which means that the distributions are not peaked or fat-tailed compared to the standard normal distribution. The median is the value at which 50 percent of the 10,000 outcomes fall on either side. The 90 percent confidence intervals show that 90 percent of the observations fall between −379 and 7,413 for the

NPV and between 11.38 percent and 25.13 percent for the IRR. Although not shown in the table, 7.04 percent of the observations had a negative NPV and an IRR less than the 12 percent discount rate.

The means of the NPV and IRR from the simulation (in Table 26) are fairly close to their values calculated using point estimates for all of the input variables (in Table 25). This is not always the case, but it is here. The additional information from a simulation is the dispersions of the NPV and IRR. Given his assumptions and model, the simulation results show Zhang the distributions of NPV and IRR outcomes that should be expected. Managers and analysts often prefer to know these total distributions rather than just their mean values.

The correlations in Table 26 can be interpreted as sensitivity measures. Changes in the "output" variable have the highest correlation with NPV and IRR outcomes. The salvage value has the lowest (absolute value) correlation.

This capital budgeting simulation example was not very complex, with only five stochastic variables. The example's five input variables were assumed to be normally distributed—in reality, many other distributions can be employed. Finally, the randomly chosen values for each variable were assumed to be independent. They can be selected jointly instead of independently. Simulation techniques have proved to be a boon for addressing capital budgeting problems.

Sensitivity analysis, scenario analysis, and simulation analysis are well-developed stand-alone risk analysis methods. These risk measures depend on the variation of the project's cash flows. Market risk measures, presented in the next section, depend not only on the variation of a project's cash flows, but also on how those cash flows covary with (or correlate with) market returns.

7.4 Risk Analysis of Capital Investments—Market Risk Methods

When using market risk methods, the discount rate to be used in evaluating a capital project is the rate of return required on the project by a diversified investor. The discount rate should thus be a risk-adjusted discount rate, which includes a premium to compensate investors for risk.[12] This risk premium should reflect factors that are priced or valued in the marketplace. The two equilibrium models for estimating this risk premium are the capital asset pricing model (CAPM) and arbitrage pricing theory (APT). We will discuss the CAPM as a way of finding risk-adjusted discount rates, although you should be aware that other methods can be used.

In the CAPM, total risk can be broken into two components: systematic risk and unsystematic risk. Systematic risk is the portion of risk that is related to the market and that cannot be diversified away. Unsystematic risk is non-market risk, risk that is idiosyncratic and that can be diversified away. Diversified investors can demand a risk premium for taking systematic risk, but not unsystematic risk.[13] Hence, the

---

12 Our approach to capital budgeting is to discount expected cash flows at a risk-adjusted cost of capital. An alternative approach, which is also conceptually sound, is the "certainty-equivalent method." In this method, certainty-equivalent cash flows (expected cash flows that are reduced to certainty equivalents) are valued by discounting them at a risk-free discount rate. The use of risk-adjusted discount rates is more intuitive and much more popular.

13 The capital asset pricing model uses this intuition to show how risky assets should be priced relative to the market. While the CAPM assigns a single market risk premium for each security, the APT develops a set of risk premia. The CAPM and APT are developed in detail elsewhere in the CFA curriculum.

stand-alone risk measures—total risk measured by the dispersion of the NPV or the IRR—are inappropriate when the corporation is diversified, or, as is more likely, when the corporation's investors are themselves diversified.

In the capital asset pricing model, a project's or asset's "beta," or β, is generally used as a measure of systematic risk. The security market line (SML) expresses the asset's required rate of return as a function of β:

$$r_i = R_F + \beta_i \left[E(R_M) - R_F \right] \tag{10}$$

where

r_i = required return for project or asset i

R_F = risk-free rate of return

β_i = beta of project or asset i

$[E(R_M) - R_F]$ = market risk premium, the difference between the expected market return and the risk-free rate of return

The project's required rate of return is equal to the risk-free rate plus a risk premium, where the risk premium is the product of the project beta and the market risk premium.

Here, the required rate of return (sometimes called a hurdle rate) is specific to the risk of the project. There is no one hurdle rate appropriate for all projects.

The security market line (SML) is graphed in Figure 7. This line indicates the required rate of return for a project, given its beta. The required rate of return can be used in two ways:

▪ The SML is used to find the required rate of return. The required rate of return is then used to find the NPV. Positive NPV projects are accepted and negative NPV projects are rejected.

▪ The SML is used to find the required rate of return. The project's IRR is compared to the required rate of return. If the IRR is greater than the required return, the project is accepted (this point would plot above the SML in Figure 7). If the IRR is less than the required rate of return (below the SML), the project is rejected.

Figure 7   **SML for Capital Budgeting Projects**

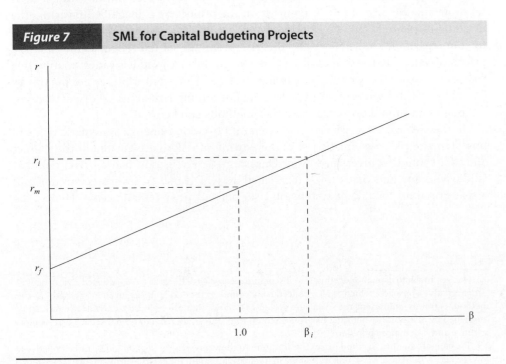

Example 9 illustrates how the capital asset pricing model and the security market line are used as part of the capital budgeting process.

Using the SML to Find the Project Required Rate of Return

Premont Systems is evaluating a capital project with the following characteristics:

- The initial outlay is €150,000.
- Annual after-tax operating cash flows are €28,000.
- After-tax salvage value at project termination is €20,000.
- Project life is 10 years.
- The project beta is 1.20.
- The risk-free rate is 4.2 percent and the expected market return is 9.4 percent.

1 Compute the project NPV. Should the project be accepted?

2 Compute the project IRR. Should the project be accepted?

Solution to 1:

The project's required rate of return is

$$r_i = R_F + \beta_i[E(R_M) - R_F] = 4.2\% + 1.20(9.4\% - 4.2\%)$$
$$= 4.2\% + 6.24\% = 10.44\%$$

The cash flows discounted at 10.44 percent give an NPV of

$$NPV = -150,000 + \sum_{t=1}^{10} \frac{28,000}{1.1044^t} + \frac{20,000}{1.1044^{10}} = €26,252$$

The project should be accepted because it has a positive NPV.

Solution to 2:

The IRR, found with a financial calculator, is 14.24 percent. The required rate of return, established with the SML as in the solution to Question 1 above, is 10.44 percent. Since the IRR exceeds the required rate of return, the project should be accepted. For a beta of 1.20, the IRR of 14.24 percent would plot above the SML.

Using project betas to establish required rates of return for capital projects is especially important when a project's risk differs from that of the company. The cost of capital for a company is estimated for the company as a whole—it is based on the average riskiness of the company's assets as well as its financial structure. The required rates of return of debt and equity are used to estimate the weighted (overall) average cost of capital (WACC) for the company. When a project under consideration is more risky or less risky than the company, the WACC should not be used as the project's required rate of return.

For example, assume that the risk-free rate of return is 3 percent, the market return is 8 percent, and the company beta is 0.9. Assume also that the company is considering three projects: Project A with a 0.5 beta, Project B with a 0.9 beta, and Project C with a 1.1 beta. The required rates of return for the company and for each project are as follows:

Company $3\% + 0.9(8\% - 3\%) = 7.5\%$

Project A $3\% + 0.5(8\% - 3\%) = 5.5\%$

Project B $3\% + 0.9(8\% - 3\%) = 7.5\%$

Project C $3\% + 1.1(8\% - 3\%) = 8.5\%$

If management uses the company WACC as the required return for all projects, this rate is too high for Project A, making it less likely that Project A would be accepted. Project B has the same risk as the company, so it would be evaluated fairly. Using the WACC for Project C makes the error of using a discount rate that is too low, which would make it more likely that this high-risk project would be accepted. Whenever possible, it is desirable to use project-specific required rates of return instead of the company's overall required rate of return.

Market returns are readily available for publicly traded companies. The stock betas of these companies can then be calculated, and this calculation assists in estimating the companies' betas and WACC. Unfortunately, however, the returns for specific capital projects are not directly observable, and we have to use proxies for their betas. Frequently, we can employ the pure-play method, in which the analyst identifies other publicly traded stocks in the same business as the project being considered. The betas for the stocks of these companies are used to estimate a project beta. In the pure-play method, these proxy companies need to be relatively focused in the same line of business as the project. When the pure-play method is not possible, other methods, such as estimating accounting betas or cross-sectional regression analysis, are used.

7.5 Real Options

Real options are capital budgeting options that allow managers to make decisions in the future that alter the value of capital budgeting investment decisions made today. Instead of making all capital budgeting decisions now, at time zero, managers can wait and make additional decisions at future dates when these future decisions are contingent upon future economic events or information. These sequential decisions, in which future decisions depend on the decisions made today as well as on future economic events, are very realistic capital budgeting applications.

Real options are like financial options—they just deal with real assets instead of financial assets. A simple financial option could be a call option on a share of stock. Suppose the stock is selling for $50, the exercise (strike) price is $50, and the option expires in one year. If the stock goes up to $60, you exercise the option and have a gain of $10 in one year. If the stock goes down to $40, you do not exercise, and you have no gain. However, no gain is better than the $10 loss you would have had if you had purchased the stock at the beginning of the year. Real options, like financial options, entail the right to make a decision, but not the obligation. The corporation should exercise a real option only if it is value-enhancing.

Just as financial options are contingent on an underlying asset, real options are contingent on future events. The flexibility that real options give to managers can greatly enhance the NPV of the company's capital investments. The following are several types of these real options:

Timing Options   Instead of investing now, the company can delay investing. Delaying an investment and basing the decision on hopefully improved information that you might have in, say, a year could help improve the NPV of the projects selected.

Sizing Options   If after investing, the company can abandon the project when the financial results are disappointing, it has an **abandonment option**. At some future date, if the cash flow from abandoning a project exceeds the present value of the cash flows from continuing the project, managers should exercise the abandonment option. Conversely, if the company can make additional investments when future financial results are strong, the company has a **growth option** or an expansion option.

Flexibility Options   Once an investment is made, other operational flexibilities may be available besides abandonment or expansion. For example, suppose demand exceeds capacity. Management may be able to exercise a **price-setting option**. By increasing prices, the company could benefit from the excess demand, which it cannot do by increasing production. There are also **production-flexibility** options. Even though it is expensive, the company can profit from working overtime or from adding additional shifts. The company can also work with customers and suppliers for their mutual benefit whenever a demand–supply mismatch occurs. This type of option also includes the possibility of using different inputs or producing different outputs.

Fundamental Options   In cases like those above, there are options embedded in a project that can raise its value. In other cases, the whole investment is essentially an option. The payoffs from the investment are contingent on an underlying asset, just like most financial options. For example, the value of an oil well or refinery investment is contingent upon the price of oil. The value of a gold mine is contingent upon the price of gold. If oil prices are low, you may not drill a well. If oil prices are high, you go ahead and drill. Many R&D (research and development) projects also look like options.

There are several approaches to evaluating capital budgeting projects with real options. One of the difficulties with real options is that the analysis can be very complicated. Although some of the problems are simple and can be readily solved, many of them are so complex that they are expensive to evaluate or you may not have much confidence in the analysis. Four common sense approaches to real options analysis are presented below.

1   Use DCF analysis without considering options. If the NPV is positive without considering real options, and the project has real options that would simply add more value, it is unnecessary to evaluate the options. Just go ahead and make the investment.

2   Consider the Project NPV = NPV(based on DCF alone) – Cost of options + Value of options. Go ahead and calculate the NPV based on expected cash flows. Then simply add the value associated with real options. For example, if a project has a negative NPV based on DCF alone of $50 million, will the options add at least that much to its value?

3   Use decision trees. Although they are not as conceptually sound as option pricing models, decision trees can capture the essence of many sequential decision making problems.

4   Use option pricing models. Except for simple options, the technical requirements for solving these models may require you to hire special consultants or "quants." Some large companies have their own specialists.

The analyst is confronted with 1) a variety of real options that investment projects may possess and 2) a decision about how to reasonably value these options. Example 10 deals with production flexibility; in this case, an additional investment outlay gives the company an option to use alternative fuel sources.

EXAMPLE 10

Production-Flexibility Option

Sackley AquaFarms estimated the NPV of the expected cash flows from a new processing plant to be – $0.40 million. Sackley is evaluating an incremental investment of $0.30 million that would give management the flexibility to switch between coal, natural gas, and oil as an energy source. The original plant relied only on coal. The option to switch to cheaper sources of energy when they are available has an estimated value of $1.20 million. What is the value of the new processing plant including this real option to use alternative energy sources?

Solution:

The NPV, including the real option, should be

$$\text{Project NPV} = \text{NPV}(\text{based on DCF alone}) - \text{Cost of options}$$
$$+ \text{Value of options}$$
$$\text{Project NPV} = -0.40 \text{ million} - 0.30 \text{ million} + 1.20 \text{ million}$$
$$= \$0.50 \text{ million}$$

Without the flexibility offered by the real option, the plant is unprofitable. The real option to adapt to cheaper energy sources adds enough to the value of this investment to give it a positive NPV.

Two of the most valuable options are to abandon or expand a project at some point after the original investment. Example 11 illustrates the abandonment option.

EXAMPLE 11

Abandonment Option

Nyberg Systems is considering a capital project with the following characteristics:

- The initial outlay is €200,000.
- Project life is four years.
- Annual after-tax operating cash flows have a 50 percent probability of being €40,000 for the four years and a 50 percent probability of being €80,000.
- Salvage value at project termination is zero.
- The required rate of return is 10 percent.
- In one year, after realizing the first-year cash flow, the company has the option to abandon the project and receive the salvage value of €150,000.

1 Compute the project NPV assuming no abandonment.
2 What is the optimal abandonment strategy? Compute the project NPV using that strategy.

Solution to 1:

The expected annual after-tax operating cash flow is 0.50(40,000) + 0.50(80,000) = €60,000. The cash flows discounted at 10 percent give an NPV of

$$\text{NPV} = -200,000 + \sum_{t=1}^{4} \frac{60,000}{1.10^t} = -€9,808$$

The project should be rejected because it has a negative NPV.

Solution to 2:

The optimal abandonment strategy would be to abandon the project in one year if the subsequent cash flows are worth less than the abandonment value. If at the end of the first year the low cash flow occurs, you can abandon for €150,000 and give up €40,000 for the following three years. The €40,000 annual cash flow, discounted for three years at 10 percent, has a present value of only €99,474, so you should abandon. Three years of the higher €80,000 cash flow has a present value of €198,948, so you should not abandon. After the first year, abandon if the low cash flow occurs, and do not abandon if the high cash flow occurs.

If the high cash flow occurs and you do not abandon, the NPV is

$$NPV = -200,000 + \sum_{t=1}^{4} \frac{80,000}{1.10^t} = €53,589$$

If you abandon when the low cash flow occurs, you receive the first year cash flow and the abandonment value and then no further cash flows. In that case, the NPV is

$$NPV = -200,000 + \frac{40,000 + 150,000}{1.10} = -€27,273$$

The expected NPV is then

$$NPV = 0.50(53,589) + 0.50(-27,273) = €13,158$$

Optimal abandonment raises the NPV by 13,158 − (− €9,808) = €22,966.

A fundamental real option could be a gold mine or an oil well. Example 12 looks at the possibility of purchasing the rights to a gold mining property.

EXAMPLE 12

Erichmann Gold Mine

The Erichmann family has offered a five-year option on one of its small gold mining properties for $10 million. The current price of gold is $400 per ounce. The mine holds an estimated 500,000 ounces that could be mined at an average cost of $450 per ounce. The maximum production rate is 200,000 ounces per year. How would you assess the Erichmann family's offer?

Solution:

A binomial option model can be built for the underlying price of gold. These binomial models are very common in assessing the value of financial options such as puts and calls on stocks, callable bonds, or mortgages with prepayment options. Whenever the price path for gold is above $450 per ounce, it might be attractive to commence mining. Of course, you would cease mining whenever the price is lower. With additional information about the volatility of gold prices and the risk-free interest rate, an expert could build this binomial model and value the real option. Comparing the value of this real option to its $10 million cost would enable you to make an investment decision.

A critical assumption of many applications of traditional capital budgeting tools is that the investment decision is made now, with no flexibility considered in future decisions. A more reasonable approach is to assume that the corporation is making sequential decisions, some now and some in the future. A combination of optimal current and future decisions is what will maximize company value. Real options analysis tries to incorporate rational future decisions into the assessment of current investment decision making. This future flexibility, exercised intelligently, enhances the value of capital investments. Some real options can be valued with readily available option pricing models, such as the binomial model or the Black–Scholes–Merton option pricing model.[14] Unfortunately, many real options are very complex and hard to value, which poses a challenge as the analyst tries to lay out the economic contingencies of an investment and assess their values. A real option, with the future flexibility it provides, can be an important piece of the value of many projects.

7.6 Common Capital Budgeting Pitfalls

Although the principles of capital budgeting may be easy to learn, applying the principles to real world investment opportunities can be challenging. Some of the common mistakes that managers make are listed in Table 27.

Table 27	Common Capital Budgeting Pitfalls

Not incorporating economic responses into the investment analysis

Misusing capital budgeting templates

Pet projects

Basing investment decisions on EPS, net income, or return on equity

Using IRR to make investment decisions

Bad accounting for cash flows

Overhead costs

Not using the appropriate risk-adjusted discount rate

Spending all of the investment budget just because it is available

Failure to consider investment alternatives

Handling sunk costs and opportunity costs incorrectly

Economic Responses   Economic responses to an investment often affect its profitability, and these responses have to be correctly anticipated. For example, in response to a successful investment, competitors can enter and reduce the investment's profitability. Similarly, vendors, suppliers, and employees may want to gain from a profitable enterprise. Companies that make highly profitable investments often find that a competitive marketplace eventually causes profitability to revert to normal levels.

Template Errors   Because hundreds or even thousands of projects need to be analyzed over time, corporations have standardized capital budgeting templates for managers to use in evaluating projects. This situation creates risks in that the template model may not match the project, or employees may input inappropriate information.

Pet Projects   **Pet projects** are projects that influential managers want the corporation to invest in. Ideally, pet projects will receive the normal scrutiny that other investments receive and will be selected on the strength of their own merits. Often, unfortunately,

---

14 Chapter 4 of Chance (2003) gives an excellent overview of option pricing models.

pet projects are selected without undergoing normal capital budgeting analysis. Or the pet project receives the analysis, but overly optimistic projections are used to inflate the project's profitability.

EPS, Net Income, or ROE   Managers sometimes have incentives to boost EPS, net income, or ROE. Many investments, even those with strong NPVs, do not boost these accounting numbers in the short run and may even reduce them. Paying attention to short-run accounting numbers can result in choosing projects that are not in the long-run economic interests of the business.

Basing Decisions on the IRR   The NPV criterion is economically sound. The IRR criterion is also sound for independent projects (with conventional cash flow patterns). If projects are mutually exclusive or competitive with each other, investing in projects based on the IRR will tend to result in choosing smaller, short-term projects with high IRRs at the expense of larger, longer-term, high NPV projects. Basing decisions on paybacks or accounting rates of return is even more dangerous. These measures can be economically unsound.

Bad Accounting for Cash Flows   In analyzing a complicated project, it is easy to omit relevant cash flows, double count cash flows, and mishandle taxes.

Overhead Costs   In large companies, the cost of a project must include the overhead it generates for such things as management time, information technology support, financial systems, and other support. Although these items are hard to estimate, over- or underestimating these overhead costs can lead to poor investment decisions.

Discount Rate Errors   The required rate of return for a project should be based on its risk. If a project is being financed with debt (or with equity), you should still use the project's required rate of return and not the cost of debt (or the **cost of equity**). Similarly, a high-risk project should not be discounted at the company's overall cost of capital, but at the project's required rate of return. Discount rate errors have a huge impact on the computed NPVs of long-lived projects.

Overspending and Underspending the Capital Budget   Politically, many managers will spend all of their budget and argue that their budget is too small. In a well-run company, managers will return excess funds whenever their profitable projects cost less than their budget, and managers will make a sound case for extra funds if their budget is too small.

Failure to Consider Investment Alternatives   Generating good investment ideas is the most basic step in the capital budgeting process, and many good alternatives are never even considered.

Sunk Costs and Opportunity Costs   Ignoring sunk costs is difficult for managers to do. Furthermore, not identifying the economic alternatives (real and financial) that are the opportunity costs is probably the biggest failure in much analysis. Only costs that change with the decision are relevant.

8   OTHER INCOME MEASURES AND VALUATION MODELS

Capital budgeting was one of the first widespread applications of discounted cash flow analysis. In the basic capital budgeting model, the analyst values an investment by discounting future after-tax cash flows at the rate of return required by investors. Subtracting the initial investment results in the project's NPV. The future cash flows consist of after-tax operating cash flows plus returns of investment (such as salvage value and sale of working capital).

Analysts will employ and encounter other concepts of income and other valuation approaches besides this basic capital budgeting model. Because some of these other approaches are economically sound and widely employed, we will briefly describe some of them here. By considering these approaches, you can see the distinguishing features of each approach and that they should result in consistent valuations (if they are used correctly).

To facilitate the comparison of income measures and valuation models, we will employ as an example a simple company (the Granite Corporation) that invests in one project. The company goes out of business when that project expires. After evaluating that project with the NPV and IRR capital budgeting models, we will examine that same project using the following alternative methods:

- economic income and accounting income;
- economic profit valuation;
- residual income valuation; and
- claims valuation.

Our purpose is to show how the various income measures and valuation methods are related to each other.

8.1 The Basic Capital Budgeting Model

The basic capital budgeting model (presented earlier) identifies the after-tax operating cash flows from an investment as well as non-operating cash flows (such as the initial investment or future recovery of invested capital or net working capital). Then, these cash flows are discounted at the required rate of return for the asset to establish the NPV.

The base-case capital budgeting project is the following. The company is going to invest $150,000 and generate sales for the next five years as shown in Table 28. Variable cash operating expenses will be 50 percent of sales each year, and fixed cash operating expenses are $20,000. Depreciation is straight-line to zero, $30,000 per year with a zero book value at the end of five years. The income tax rate is 40 percent. Salvage value is $10,000, which is taxable at 40 percent, leaving an after-tax salvage value of $6,000 at the end of five years. The required rate of return is 10 percent.

Table 28	Basic Capital Budgeting Example for Granite Corporation					
Year	**0**	**1**	**2**	**3**	**4**	**5**
Fixed capital investment	−150,000					
Sales		150,000	200,000	250,000	200,000	150,000
Variable cash expenses		75,000	100,000	125,000	100,000	75,000

Table 28	(Continued)					
Year	**0**	**1**	**2**	**3**	**4**	**5**
Fixed cash expenses		20,000	20,000	20,000	20,000	20,000
Depreciation		30,000	30,000	30,000	30,000	30,000
Operating income before taxes		25,000	50,000	75,000	50,000	25,000
Taxes at 40 percent		10,000	20,000	30,000	20,000	10,000
Operating income after taxes		15,000	30,000	45,000	30,000	15,000
After-tax operating cash flow		45,000	60,000	75,000	60,000	45,000
Salvage value						10,000
Taxes on salvage value						4,000
After-tax salvage value						6,000
Total after-tax cash flow	−150,000	45,000	60,000	75,000	60,000	51,000
NPV (at r = 10 percent)	69,492					
IRR	26.27%					

The present value of the after-tax cash flows for Years 1-5 is $219,492. Subtracting the investment of $150,000 results in the NPV of $69,492. The IRR for the investment is 26.27 percent.

8.2 Economic and Accounting Income

Economic income and accounting income differ from the after-tax operating cash flows used in the basic capital budgeting model.

Economic income is the profit realized from an investment. For a given year, economic income is the investment's after-tax cash flow plus the change in the market value:

Economic income = Cash flow + Change in market value

Economic income = Cash flow + (Ending market value   **(11)**

       − Beginning market value)

Or

Economic income = Cash flow − (Beginning market value

       −Ending market value)

Economic income = Cash flow − Economic depreciation[15]

For the Granite Corporation, the cash flows are already calculated in Table 28. The beginning market value at time zero is the present value of the future after-tax cash flows at the 10 percent required rate of return, or $219,492. The market value at any future date is the present value of subsequent cash flows discounted back to that date. For the Granite Corporation, the cash flows, changes in market value, and economic incomes are shown in Table 29.

---

[15] These equations are conceptually identical because economic depreciation is the negative of the change in market value. For example, assume the cash flow is 10, the beginning market value is 30, and the ending market value is 25. Cash flow + Change in market value = Cash flow + (Ending market value − Beginning market value) = 10 + (25 − 30) = 5. Or, Cash flow − Economic depreciation = Cash flow − (Beginning market value − Ending market value) = 10 − (30 − 25) = 5.

Table 29	Economic Income for Granite Corporation				
Year	**1**	**2**	**3**	**4**	**5**
Beginning market value	219,492	196,441	156,086	96,694	46,364
Ending market value	196,441	156,086	96,694	46,364	0
Change in market value	−23,051	−40,356	−59,391	−50,331	−46,364
After-tax cash flow	45,000	60,000	75,000	60,000	51,000
Economic income	21,949	19,644	15,609	9,669	4,636
Economic rate of return	10%	10%	10%	10%	10%

In Year 1, the beginning value is $219,492 and the ending value is $196,441, so the change in value is −$23,051. The economic income is the cash flow plus the change in value, or $45,000 + (−$23,051) = $21,949. The economic income for Years 2–5 is found similarly. The economic rate of return is the year's economic income divided by its beginning market value. Notice that the economic rate of return is precisely 10 percent each year, which was the required rate of return on the project.

Accounting income for this company will differ from the economic income for two reasons. First, the accounting depreciation is based on the original cost of the investment (not the market value of the investment). Consequently, the accounting depreciation schedule does not follow the declines in the market value of an asset. Besides being based on accounting depreciation instead of economic depreciation, accounting net income is the after-tax income remaining after paying interest expenses on the company's debt obligations. In contrast, interest expenses are ignored when computing the economic income for an asset or the after-tax operating cash flows in the basic capital budgeting model. As explained in Section 3, the effects of financing costs are captured in the discount rate, not in the cash flows. In the capital budgeting model, if we included interest expenses in the cash flows, we would be double counting them.

To illustrate these differences, we will assume that the company borrows an amount equal to one-half of the value of the company, which is 50 percent of $219,492, or $109,746, and that it pays 8 1/3 percent interest each year on the beginning balance. With a 40 percent tax rate, the after-tax interest cost is 8 1/3% (1 − 0.40) = 5.0%. Because the Granite Corporation has a five-year life, it does not need to borrow or retain earnings for the future, and all cash flows will be distributed to bondholders and stockholders. Granite will maintain a 50 percent debt/value ratio on the company's debt, so bondholders will receive 8 1/3 percent interest on their beginning bond balance and the debt will also be amortized (paid down) whenever the value of the company goes down. Furthermore, after all operating costs, interest expenses, and taxes are paid, stockholders will receive all remaining cash flows each year as a cash dividend or share repurchase.[16]

The financial statements for the Granite Corporation are shown in Table 30.

---

16 The assumptions may be unrealistic, but this is a very simple corporation.

Table 30	Condensed Financial Statements for Granite Corporation					
Year	0	1	2	3	4	5
Balance sheets:						
Assets	150,000	120,000	90,000	60,000	30,000	0
Liabilities	109,746	98,221	78,043	48,347	23,182	0
Net worth	40,254	21,779	11,957	11,653	6,818	0
Income statements:						
Sales		150,000	200,000	250,000	200,000	150,000
Variable cash expenses		75,000	100,000	125,000	100,000	75,000
Fixed cash expenses		20,000	20,000	20,000	20,000	20,000
Depreciation		30,000	30,000	30,000	30,000	30,000
EBIT		25,000	50,000	75,000	50,000	25,000
Interest expense		9,146	8,185	6,504	4,029	1,932
EBT		15,854	41,815	68,496	45,971	23,068
Taxes at 40 percent		6,342	16,726	27,399	18,388	9,227
Net income before salvage		9,513	25,089	41,098	27,583	13,841
After-tax salvage value						6,000
Net income		9,513	25,089	41,098	27,583	19,841
Statements of cash flows:						
Operating cash flows:						
Net income		9,513	25,089	41,098	27,583	19,841
Depreciation		30,000	30,000	30,000	30,000	30,000
Total		39,513	55,089	71,098	57,583	49,841
Financing cash flows:						
Debt repayment		−11,525	−20,178	−29,696	−25,165	−23,182
Dividends/repurchases		−27,987	−34,911	−41,402	−32,417	−26,659
Total		−39,513	−55,089	−71,098	−57,583	−49,841
Investing cash flows		0	0	0	0	0
Total cash flows		0	0	0	0	0

The income statement for financial reporting purposes differs from that used in the capital budgeting model because the interest on debt obligations is now taken out as an expense before arriving at net income. The book value of the company's assets is based on the original accounting cost minus accumulated accounting depreciation. Note that the liabilities and net worth are also declining in the balance sheet. The liabilities decline each year, reflecting the amounts that were paid annually to reduce the principal of the loan. Notice, also, that the net worth is declining. Normally, the net worth of a company increases because beginning equity is increased by net retentions—the excess of net income over dividends paid. In this case, the company is shrinking and going out of business in five years, so the distributions to shareholders (which can be either cash dividends or share repurchases) exceed net income and net worth declines. The amounts that are paid each year to reduce debt and for dividends/ share repurchases are shown in the financing section of the statement of cash flows.

Accounting measures of performance also can differ from economic measures of performance. Table 31 repeats the economic income and accounting income from Tables 29 and 30. The table also shows the economic rate of return each year and two popular accounting measures of performance: the return on equity (ROE = Net income divided by Beginning equity) and return on assets (ROA = EBIT divided by Beginning assets).

Table 31	Economic Income, Accounting Income, and Rates of Return for Granite Corporation				
Year	1	2	3	4	5
Economic income	21,949	19,644	15,609	9,669	4,636
Accounting income	9,513	25,089	41,098	27,583	19,841
Economic rate of return	10.00%	10.00%	10.00%	10.00%	10.00%
Return on equity (ROE)	23.63%	115.20%	343.71%	236.70%	291.00%
Return on assets (ROA)	16.67%	41.67%	83.33%	83.33%	83.33%

As Table 31 illustrates, economic and accounting incomes differ substantially. Over the five years, economic income is much less than accounting income, and the patterns certainly differ. In addition, the accounting rates of return, the ROE and ROA, for this admittedly unusual company are quite different from the economic rate of return.

8.3 Economic Profit, Residual Income, and Claims Valuation

Although the capital budgeting model is widely employed, analysts have used other procedures to divide up the cash flows from a company or project and then value them using discounted cash flow methods. We present three of these alternative models here: the economic profit model, the residual income model, and the claims valuation model. Used correctly, they are all consistent with the basic capital budgeting model and with each other.

8.3.1 Economic Profit

The first alternative method for measuring income and valuing assets is based on economic profit (EP).[17] Economic profit has been used in asset valuation as well as in performance measurement and management compensation. Its calculation is loosely as follows:

$$EP = NOPAT - \$WACC \qquad (12)$$

where

$$EP = \text{economic profit}$$
$$NOPAT = \text{net operating profit after tax} = EBIT\,(1-\text{Tax rate})$$
$$EBIT = \text{operating income before taxes, or earnings before interest and taxes}$$
$$\$WACC = \text{dollar cost of capital} = WACC \times \text{Capital}$$
$$WACC = \text{weighted average (or overall) cost of capital}$$
$$\text{Capital} = \text{investment}$$

---

17 Economic Value Added or EVA®, trademarked by the consulting firm Stern Stewart & Company, is a well-known commercial application of the economic profit approach. See Stewart (1991) and Peterson and Peterson (1996) for complete discussion.

EP is a periodic measure of profit above and beyond the dollar cost of the capital invested in the project. The dollar cost of capital is the dollar return that the company must make on the project in order to pay the debt holders and the equity holders their respective required rates of return.[18]

For the Granite Corporation, for the first year, we have the following:

$$\text{NOPAT} = \text{EBIT}(1 - \text{Tax rate}) = 25,000(1 - 0.40) = \$15,000$$

$$\$\text{WACC} = \text{WACC} \times \text{Capital} = 10\% \times 150,000 = \$15,000$$

$$\text{EP} = \text{NOPAT} - \$\text{WACC} = 15,000 - 15,000 = \$0$$

Table 32 shows the EP for all five years for the Granite Corporation.

Table 32	EP for Granite Corporation				
Year	**1**	**2**	**3**	**4**	**5**[b]
Capital[a]	150,000	120,000	90,000	60,000	30,000
NOPAT	15,000	30,000	45,000	30,000	21,000
$WACC	15,000	12,000	9,000	6,000	3,000
EP	0	18,000	36,000	24,000	18,000

[a]Depreciation is $30,000 per year.
[b]The $6,000 after-tax gain from salvage is included in NOPAT in Year 5.

EP is readily applied to valuation of an asset or a security. The NPV found by discounted cash flow analysis in the basic capital budgeting model will be equal to the present value of future EP discounted at the weighted average cost of capital.

$$\text{NPV} = \sum_{t=1}^{\infty} \frac{\text{EP}_t}{(1 + \text{WACC})^t} \tag{13}$$

This NPV is also called the market value added (MVA).[19] So we have

$$\text{NPV} = \text{MVA} = \sum_{t=1}^{\infty} \frac{\text{EP}_t}{(1 + \text{WACC})^t} \tag{14}$$

Discounting the five years of EP for the Granite Corporation at the 10 percent WACC gives an NPV (and MVA) of $69,492. The total value of the company (of the asset) is the original investment of $150,000 plus the NPV of $69,492, or $219,492. The valuation using EP is the same as that found with the basic capital budgeting model.

8.3.2 Residual Income

Another method for estimating income and valuing an asset is the residual income method.[20] This method focuses on the returns to equity, where

Residual income = Net income − Equity charge,

or

---

[18] You have already studied the relationship between the required rate of return on the project or WACC (here 10 percent), the rate of return required by debtholders (here 8 1/3 percent), and the rate of return required by equityholders (here 15 percent).

[19] Peterson and Peterson define MVA as the market value of the company minus the capital invested, which is an NPV.

[20] See Chapter 5 in Stowe, Robinson, Pinto, and McLeavey (2002) and Edwards and Bell (1961) for treatments of residual income analysis.

$$RI_t = NI_t - r_e B_{t-1} \tag{15}$$

where

$\qquad RI_t$ = residual income during period t

$\qquad NI_t$ = net income during period t

$\qquad r_e B_{t-1}$ = equity charge for period t, which is the required rate of return on equity, r_e, times the beginning-of-period book value of equity, B_{t-1}

For the first year for the Granite Corporation, the net income is \$9,513. The beginning book value of equity is \$40,254 (from the balance sheet in Table 30), and the required rate of return on equity is 15 percent. Consequently, the residual income for Year 1 is:

$$RI_t = NI_t - r_e B_{t-1} = 9,513 - 0.15(40,254) = 9,513 - 6,038 = \$3,475$$

The residual income for all five years for Granite is shown in Table 33.

Table 33	Residual Income for Granite Corporation				
Year	**1**	**2**	**3**	**4**	**5[a]**
NI_t	9,513	25,089	41,098	27,583	19,841
$r_e B_{t-1}$	6,038	3,267	1,794	1,748	1,023
RI_t	3,475	21,822	39,304	25,835	18,818

[a]The \$6,000 after-tax gain from salvage is included in NI in Year 5.

Residual income, like EP, can also be applied to valuation of an asset or security. The NPV of an investment is the present value of future residual income discounted at the required rate of return on equity.

$$NPV = \sum_{t=1}^{\infty} \frac{RI_t}{(1 + r_e)^t} \tag{16}$$

Discounting the residual income for the Granite Corporation at the 15 percent required rate of return on equity gives an NPV of \$69,492. The total value of the company (of the asset) is the present value of the residual income, the original equity investment, plus the original debt investment:

PV of residual income	\$69,492
Equity investment	40,254
Debt investment	109,746
Total value	\$219,492

The value of the company is the original book value of its debt and equity plus the present value of the residual income (which is the project's NPV). Again, this is the same value we found with the basic capital budgeting model and with the EP model.

8.3.3 Claims Valuation

To value a company, the EP valuation approach essentially adds the present value of EP to the original investment. The residual income approach adds the present value of residual income to the original debt and equity investments in the company. Since the EP approach is from the perspective of all suppliers of capital, EP is discounted at the overall WACC. The residual income approach takes the perspective of equity investors, so residual income is discounted at the cost of equity.

The third and final alternative valuation approach that we present is to divide the operating cash flows between securityholder classes (in this example, debt and equity), and then value the debt and equity cash flows separately.

Balance Sheet

Assets	Liabilities
	Equity

The basic capital budgeting approach is to value the asset, which is on the left-hand side of the balance sheet above. The claims valuation approach values the liabilities and equity, the claims against the assets, which are on the right-hand side of the balance sheet. The value of the claims should equal the value of the assets.

For the Granite Corporation, the cash flows to debtholders are the interest payments and principal payments. These are valued by discounting them at the cost of debt, which is 8 1/3 percent. The cash flows to stockholders are the dividends and share repurchases, which are valued by discounting them at the 15 percent cost of equity. Table 34 lists the future cash flows for debt and equity.

Table 34	Payments to Bondholders and Stockholders of Granite Corporation				
Year	**1**	**2**	**3**	**4**	**5**
Interest payments	9,146	8,185	6,504	4,029	1,932
Principal payments	11,525	20,178	29,696	25,165	23,182
Total debt payments	20,671	28,363	36,199	29,194	25,114
Equity distributions	27,987	34,911	41,402	32,417	26,659

The present value of the total debt payments, discounted at the cost of debt, is $109,746. The value of the equity distributions, discounted at the cost of equity, is $109,746. The total value of the company is the combined value of debt and equity, which is $219,492.

In our example, the basic capital budgeting model, the economic profit model, the residual income model, and the claims valuation model all result in the same valuation of the company. In the real world, analysts must deal with many accounting complications. Some of these complications may include pension liability adjustments, valuations of marketable securities held, exchange rate gains and losses, and adjustments for leases, inventories, goodwill, deferred taxes, etc. In theory, all of the valuation models are equivalent. In practice, even with due diligence and care, analysts may prefer one approach over others and disagree about valuations.

There are other approaches to valuation that analysts use and run across. Two common ones are the free cash flow to the firm and **free cash flow to equity** approaches.[21] The free cash flow to the firm approach is fundamentally the same as the basic capital budgeting approach. The free cash flow to equity approach is related to the claims valuation approach. In corporate finance, corporate managers usually

---

21 The free cash flow to the firm and free cash flow to equity approaches are developed in Chapter 3 of Stowe, Robinson, Pinto, and McLeavey (2002).

value an asset by valuing its total after-tax cash flows. Security analysts typically value equity by valuing the cash flows to stockholders. Real estate investors often evaluate real estate investments by valuing the cash flows to the equity investor after payments to creditors, which is like the claims valuation approach.

SUMMARY

Capital budgeting is the process that companies use for decision making on capital projects—those projects with a life of a year or more. This reading developed the principles behind the basic capital budgeting model, the cash flows that go into the model, and several extensions of the basic model.

OPTIONAL
SEGMENT

- Capital budgeting undergirds the most critical investments for many corporations—their investments in long-term assets. The principles of capital budgeting have been applied to other corporate investing and financing decisions and to security analysis and portfolio management.

- The typical steps in the capital budgeting process are: 1) generating ideas, 2) analyzing individual proposals, 3) planning the capital budget, and 4) monitoring and post-auditing.

- Projects susceptible to capital budgeting process can be categorized as: 1) replacement, 2) expansion, 3) new products and services, and 4) regulatory, safety and environmental.

- Capital budgeting decisions are based on incremental after-tax cash flows discounted at the opportunity cost of funds. Financing costs are ignored because both the cost of debt and the cost of other capital are captured in the discount rate.

- The net present value (NPV) is the present value of all after-tax cash flows, or

$$\text{NPV} = \sum_{t=0}^{n} \frac{\text{CF}_t}{(1+r)^t}$$

where the investment outlays are negative cash flows included in the CF_ts and where r is the required rate of return for the investment.

- The IRR is the discount rate that makes the present value of all future cash flows sum to zero. This equation can be solved for the IRR:

$$\sum_{t=0}^{n} \frac{\text{CF}_t}{(1+\text{IRR})^t} = 0$$

- The payback period is the number of years required to recover the original investment in a project. The payback is based on cash flows.

- The discounted payback period is the number of years it takes for the cumulative discounted cash flows from a project to equal the original investment.

- The average accounting rate of return (AAR) can be defined as follows:

$$\text{AAR} = \frac{\text{Average net income}}{\text{Average book value}}$$

- The profitability index (PI) is the present value of a project's future cash flows divided by the initial investment:

$$PI = \frac{\text{PV of future cash flows}}{\text{Initial investment}} = 1 + \frac{\text{NPV}}{\text{Initial investment}}$$

- The capital budgeting decision rules are to invest if the NPV > 0, if the IRR > r, or if the PI > 1.0. There are no decision rules for the payback period, discounted payback period, and AAR because they are not always sound measures.

- The NPV profile is a graph that shows a project's NPV graphed as a function of various discount rates.

- For mutually exclusive projects that are ranked differently by the NPV and IRR, it is economically sound to choose the project with the higher NPV.

- The "multiple IRR problem" and the "no IRR problem" can arise for a project with nonconventional cash flows—cash flows that change signs more than once during the project's life.

- The fact that projects with positive NPVs theoretically increase the value of the company and the value of its stock could explain the popularity of NPV as an evaluation method.

END OPTIONAL SEGMENT

- Analysts often organize the cash flows for capital budgeting in tables, summing all of the cash flows occurring at each point in time. These totals are then used to find an NPV or IRR. Alternatively, tables collecting cash flows by type can be used. Equations for the capital budgeting cash flows are as follows:

  Initial outlay:

  $$\text{Outlay} = \text{FCInv} + \text{NWCInv} - \text{Sal}_0 + T(\text{Sal}_0 - B_0)$$

  Annual after-tax operating cash flow:

  $$CF = (S - C - D)(1 - T) + D, \text{ or}$$

  $$CF = (S - C)(1 - T) + TD$$

  Terminal year after-tax non-operating cash flow:

  $$\text{TNOCF} = \text{Sal}_T + \text{NWCInv} - T(\text{Sal}_T - B_T)$$

- Depreciation schedules affect taxable income, taxes paid, and after-tax cash flows, and therefore capital budgeting valuations.

- Spreadsheets are heavily used for capital budgeting valuation.

- When inflation exists, the analyst should perform capital budgeting analysis in "nominal" terms if cash flows are nominal and in "real" terms if cash flows are real.

- Inflation reduces the value of depreciation tax savings (unless the tax system adjusts depreciation for inflation). Inflation reduces the value of fixed payments to bondholders. Inflation usually does not affect all revenues and costs uniformly. Contracting with customers, suppliers, employees, and sources of capital can be complicated as inflation rises.

- Two ways of comparing mutually exclusive projects in a replacement chain are the "least common multiple of lives" approach and the "equivalent annual annuity" approach.

- For the least common multiple of lives approach, the analyst extends the time horizon of analysis so that the lives of both projects will divide exactly into the horizon. The projects are replicated over this horizon, and the NPV for the total cash flows over the least common multiple of lives is used to evaluate the investments.

- The equivalent annual annuity is the annuity payment (series of equal annual payments over the project's life) that is equivalent in value to the project's actual cash flows. Analysts find the present value of all of the cash flows for an investment (the NPV) and then calculate an annuity payment that has a value equivalent to the NPV.

- With capital rationing, the company's capital budget has a size constraint. Under "hard" capital rationing, the budget is fixed. In the case of hard rationing, managers use trial and error and sometimes mathematical programming to find the optimal set of projects. In that situation, it is best to use the NPV or PI valuation methods.

- Sensitivity analysis calculates the effect on the NPV of changes in one input variable at a time.

- Scenario analysis creates scenarios that consist of changes in several of the input variables and calculates the NPV for each scenario.

- Simulation (Monte Carlo) analysis is used to estimate probability distributions for the NPV or IRR of a capital project. Simulations randomly select values for stochastic input variables and then repeatedly calculate the project NPV and IRR to find their distributions.

- Risk-adjusted discount rates based on market risk measures should be used as the required rate of return for projects when the investors are diversified. The capital asset pricing model (CAPM) and arbitrage pricing theory (APT) are common approaches for finding market-based risk-adjusted rates.

- In the CAPM, a project's or asset's beta, or β, is used as a measure of systematic risk. The security market line (SML) estimates the asset's required rate of return as $r_i = R_F + \beta_i [E(R_M) - R_F]$.

- Project-specific betas should be used instead of company betas whenever the risk of the project differs from that of the company.

- Real options can be classified as 1) timing options; 2) sizing options, which can be abandonment options or growth (expansion) options; 3) flexibility options, which can be price-setting options or production-flexibility options; and 4) fundamental options. Simple options can be evaluated with decision trees; for more complex options, the analyst should use option pricing models.

- Economic income is the investment's after-tax cash flow plus the change in the market value. Accounting income is revenues minus expenses. Accounting depreciation, based on the original cost of the investment, is the decrease in the book (accounting) value, while economic depreciation is the decrease in the market value of the investment. Accounting net income is net of the after-tax interest expenses on the company's debt obligations. In computing economic income, financing costs are ignored.

- Economic profit is

$$EP = NOPAT - \$WACC$$

where NOPAT = Net operating profit after tax = EBIT(1 − Tax rate) and $WACC = Dollar cost of capital = WACC × Capital. When applied to the valuation of an asset or security, the NPV of an investment (and its market value added) is the present value of future EP discounted at the weighted average cost of capital.

$$NPV = MVA = \sum_{t=1}^{\infty} \frac{EP_t}{(1 + WACC)^t}$$

The total value of the company (of the asset) is the original investment plus the NPV.

- Residual income = Net income − Equity charge, or $RI_t = NI_t − r_e B_{t-1}$ where RI_t = Residual income during period t, NI_t = Net income during period t, r_e = Cost of equity, and B_{t-1} = Beginning-of-period book value of equity. The NPV of an investment is the present value of future residual income discounted at the required rate of return on equity:

$$NPV = \sum_{t=1}^{\infty} \frac{RI_t}{\left(1 + r_e\right)^t}$$

The total value of the company (of the asset) is the NPV plus the original equity investment plus the original debt investment.

- The claims valuation approach values an asset by valuing the claims against the asset. For example, an asset financed with debt and equity has a value equal to the value of the debt plus the value of the equity.

PRACTICE PROBLEMS

1 FITCO is considering the purchase of new equipment. The equipment costs $350,000, and an additional $110,000 is needed to install it. The equipment will be depreciated straight-line to zero over a five-year life. The equipment will generate additional annual revenues of $265,000, and it will have annual cash operating expenses of $83,000. The equipment will be sold for $85,000 after five years. An inventory investment of $73,000 is required during the life of the investment. FITCO is in the 40 percent tax bracket and its cost of capital is 10 percent. What is the project NPV?

   A $52,122.

   B $64,090.

   C $97,449.

2 After estimating a project's NPV, the analyst is advised that the fixed capital outlay will be revised upward by $100,000. The fixed capital outlay is depreciated straight-line over an eight-year life. The tax rate is 40 percent and the required rate of return is 10 percent. No changes in cash operating revenues, cash operating expenses, or salvage value are expected. What is the effect on the project NPV?

   A $100,000 decrease.

   B $73,325 decrease.

   C $59,988 decrease.

3 When assembling the cash flows to calculate an NPV or IRR, the project's after-tax interest expenses should be subtracted from the cash flows for:

   A the IRR calculation, but not the NPV calculation.

   B both the NPV calculation and the IRR calculation.

   C neither the NPV calculation nor the IRR calculation.

4 Standard Corporation is investing $400,000 of fixed capital in a project that will be depreciated straight-line to zero over its ten-year life. Annual sales are expected to be $240,000, and annual cash operating expenses are expected to be $110,000. An investment of $40,000 in net working capital is required over the project's life. The corporate income tax rate is 30 percent. What is the after-tax operating cash flow expected in year one?

   A $63,000.

   B $92,000.

   C $103,000.

5 Five years ago, Frater Zahn's Company invested £38 million—£30 million in fixed capital and another £8 million in working capital—in a bakery. Today, Frater Zahn's is selling the fixed assets for £21 million and liquidating the investment in working capital. The book value of the fixed assets is £15 million and the marginal tax rate is 40 percent. The fifth year's after-tax non-operating cash flow to Frater Zahn's is *closest* to:

   A £20.6 million.

   B £23.0 million.

   C £26.6 million.

The following information relates to Questions 6–8

McConachie Company is considering the purchase of a new 400-ton stamping press. The press costs $360,000, and an additional $40,000 is needed to install it. The press will be depreciated straight-line to zero over a five-year life. The press will generate no additional revenues, but it will reduce cash operating expenses by $140,000 annually. The press will be sold for $120,000 after five years. An inventory investment of $60,000 is required during the life of the investment. McConachie is in the 40 percent tax bracket.

6   What is the McConachie net investment outlay?

   A $400,000.

   B $420,000.

   C $460,000.

7   McConachie's incremental annual after-tax operating cash flow is *closest* to:

   A $116,000.

   B $124,000.

   C $140,000.

8   What is the terminal year after-tax non-operating cash flow at the end of year five?

   — return of working cap + gain on sale

   A $108,000.

   B $132,000.

   C $180,000.

The following information relates to Questions 9–14

Linda Pyle is head of analyst recruiting for PPA Securities. She has been very frustrated by the number of job applicants who, in spite of their stellar pedigrees, seem to have little understanding of basic financial concepts. Pyle has written a set of conceptual questions and simple problems for the human resources department to use to screen for the better candidates in the applicant pool. A few of her corporate finance questions and problems are given below.

Concept 1   "A company invests in depreciable assets, financed partly by issuing fixed-rate bonds. If inflation is lower than expected, the value of the real tax savings from depreciation and the value of the real after-tax interest expense are both reduced."

Concept 2   "Sensitivity analysis and scenario analysis are useful tools for estimating the impact on a project's NPV of changing the value of one capital budgeting input variable at a time."

Concept 3   "When comparing two mutually exclusive projects with unequal lives, the IRR is a good approach for choosing the better project because it does not require equal lives."

Concept 4   "Project-specific betas should be used instead of company betas whenever the risk of the project differs from that of the company."

Problem   "Fontenot Company is investing €100 in a project that is being
                 depreciated straight-line to zero over a two-year life with no sal-
                 vage value. The project will generate earnings before interest and
                 taxes of €50 each year for two years. Fontenot's weighted average
                 cost of capital and required rate of return for the project are both
                 12 percent, and its tax rate is 30 percent."

9 For Concept 1, the statement is correct regarding the effects on:

    A the real tax savings from depreciation, but incorrect regarding the real after-tax interest expense.

    B both the real tax savings from depreciation and the real after-tax interest expense.

    C neither the real tax savings from depreciation nor the real after-tax interest expense.

10 For Concept 2, the statement is correct regarding:

    A sensitivity analysis, but not correct regarding scenario analysis.

    B scenario analysis, but not correct regarding sensitivity analysis.

    C both sensitivity analysis and scenario analysis.

11 Are the statements identified as Concept 3 and Concept 4 correct?

    A No for Concepts 3 and 4.

    B No for Concept 3, but yes for Concept 4.

    C Yes for Concept 3, but no for Concept 4.

12 The after-tax operating cash flows in euros for the Fontenot Company are:

    A 50 in both years.

    B 70 in both years.

    C 85 in both years.

13 The economic income in euros for the Fontenot Company is:

    A 17.24 in Year 1 and 9.11 in Year 2.

    B 17.76 in Year 1 and 24.89 in Year 2.

    C 24.89 in Year 1 and 17.76 in Year 2.

14 The market value added (MVA) in euros for the Fontenot Company is *closest* to:

    A 38.87.

    B 39.92.

    C 43.65.

The following information relates to Questions 15–20

The capital budgeting committee for Laroche Industries is meeting. Laroche is a North American conglomerate that has several divisions. One of these divisions, Laroche Livery, operates a large fleet of vans. Laroche's management is evaluating whether it is optimal to operate new vans for two, three, or four years before replacing them. The managers have estimated the investment outlay, annual after-tax operating expenses, and after-tax salvage cash flows for each of the service lives. Because revenues and some operating costs are unaffected by the choice of service life, they were ignored in the analysis. Laroche Livery's opportunity cost of funds is 10 percent. The following table gives the cash flows in thousands of Canadian dollars (C$).

Service Life	Investment	Year 1	Year 2	Year 3	Year 4	Salvage
2 years	−40,000	−12,000	−15,000			20,000
3 years	−40,000	−12,000	−15,000	−20,000		17,000
4 years	−40,000	−12,000	−15,000	−20,000	−25,000	12,000

Schoeman Products, another division of Laroche, has evaluated several investment projects and now must choose the subset of them that fits within its C$40 million capital budget. The outlays and NPVs for the six projects are given below. Schoeman cannot buy fractional projects, and must buy all or none of a project. The currency amounts are in millions of Canadian dollars.

Project	Outlay	PV of Future Cash Flows	NPV
1	31	44	13
2	15	21	6
3	12	16.5	4.5
4	10	13	3
5	8	11	3
6	6	8	2

Schoeman wants to determine which subset of the six projects is optimal.

A final proposal comes from the division Society Services, which has an investment opportunity with a real option to invest further if conditions warrant. The crucial details are as follows:

- The original project:
  - An outlay of C$190 million at time zero.
  - Cash flows of C$40 million per year for Years 1–10 if demand is "high."
  - Cash flows of C$20 million per year for Years 1–10 if demand is "low."
- Additional cash flows with the optional expansion project:
  - An outlay of C$190 million at time one.
  - Cash flows of C$40 million per year for Years 2–10 if demand is "high."
  - Cash flows of C$20 million per year for Years 2–10 if demand is "low."
- Whether demand is "high" or "low" in Years 1–10 will be revealed during the first year. The probability of "high" demand is 0.50, and the probability of "low" demand is 0.50.
- The option to make the expansion investment depends on making the initial investment. If the initial investment is not made, the option to expand does not exist.
- The required rate of return is 10 percent.

Society Services wants to evaluate its investment alternatives.

The internal auditor for Laroche Industries has made several suggestions for improving capital budgeting processes at the company. The internal auditor's suggestions are as follows:

Suggestion 1   "In order to put all capital budgeting proposals on an equal footing, the projects should all use the risk-free rate for the required rate of return."

Suggestion 2   "Because you cannot exercise both of them, you should not permit a given project to have both an abandonment option and an expansion/growth option."

Suggestion 3   "When rationing capital, it is better to choose the portfolio of investments that maximizes the company NPV than the portfolio that maximizes the company IRR."

Suggestion 4   "Project betas should be used for establishing the required rate of return whenever the project's beta is different from the company's beta."

15 What is the optimal service life for Laroche Livery's fleet of vans?

   A   Two years.

   B   Three years.

   C   Four years.

16 The optimal subset of the six projects that Schoeman is considering consists of Projects:

   A   1 and 5.

   B   2, 3, and 4.

   C   2, 4, 5, and 6.

17 What is the NPV (C$ millions) of the original project for Society Services without considering the expansion option?

   A   −6.11.

   B   −5.66.

   C   2.33.

18 What is the NPV (C$ millions) of the optimal set of investment decisions for Society Services including the expansion option?

   A   6.34.

   B   12.68.

   C   31.03.

19 Should the capital budgeting committee accept the internal auditor's first and second suggestions, respectively?

   A   No for Suggestions 1 and 2.

   B   No for Suggestion 1 and Yes for Suggestion 2.

   C   Yes for Suggestion 1 and No for Suggestion 2.

20 Should the capital budgeting committee accept the internal auditor's third and fourth suggestions, respectively?

   A   No for Suggestions 3 and 4.

   B   Yes for Suggestions 3 and 4.

   C   No for Suggestion 3 and Yes for Suggestion 4.

The following information relates to Questions 21–26

Maximilian Böhm is reviewing several capital budgeting proposals from subsidiaries of his company. Although his reviews deal with several details that may seem like minutiae, the company places a premium on the care it exercises in making its investment decisions.

The first proposal is a project for Richie Express, which is investing $500,000, all in fixed capital, in a project that will have operating income after taxes of $20,000 and depreciation of $40,000 each year for the next three years. Richie Express will sell the asset in three years, paying 30 percent taxes on any excess of the selling price over book value. The proposal indicates that a $647,500 terminal selling price will enable the company to earn a 15 percent internal rate of return on the investment. Böhm doubts that this terminal value estimate is correct.

Another proposal concerns Gasup Company, which does natural gas exploration. A new investment has been identified by the Gasup finance department with the following projected cash flows:

- Investment outlays are $6 million immediately and $1 million at the end of the first year.

- After-tax operating cash flows are $0.5 million at the end of the first year and $4 million at the end of each of the second, third, fourth, and fifth years. In addition, an after-tax outflow occurs at the end of the five-year project that has not been included in the operating cash flows: $5 million required for environmental cleanup.

- The required rate of return on natural gas exploration is 18 percent.

The Gasup analyst is unsure about the calculation of the NPV and the IRR because the outlay is staged over two years.

Finally, Dominion Company is evaluating two mutually exclusive projects: The Pinto grinder involves an outlay of $100,000, annual after-tax operating cash flows of $45,000, an after-tax salvage value of $25,000, and a three-year life. The Bolten grinder has an outlay of $125,000, annual after-tax operating cash flows of $47,000, an after-tax salvage value of $20,000, and a four-year life. The required rate of return is 10 percent. The net present value (NPV) and equivalent annual annuity (EAA) of the Pinto grinder are $30,691 and $12,341, respectively. Whichever grinder is chosen, it will have to be replaced at the end of its service life. The analyst is unsure about which grinder should be chosen.

Böhm and his colleague Beth Goldberg have an extended conversation about capital budgeting issues, including several comments listed below. Goldberg makes two comments about real options:

Comment 1   "The abandonment option is valuable, but it should be exercised only when the abandonment value is above the amount of the original investment."

Comment 2   "If the cost of a real option is less than its value, this will increase the NPV of the investment project in which the real option is embedded."

Böhm also makes several comments about specific projects under consideration:

Comment A   The land and building were purchased five years ago for $10 million. This is the amount that should now be included in the fixed capital investment."

Comment B   "We can improve the project's NPV by using the after-tax cost of debt as the discount rate. If we finance the project with 100 percent debt, this discount rate would be appropriate."

Comment C   "It is generally safer to use the NPV than the IRR in making capital budgeting decisions. However, when evaluating mutually exclusive projects, if the projects have conventional cash flow patterns and have the same investment outlays, it is acceptable to use either the NPV or IRR."

Comment D   "You should not base a capital budgeting decision on its immediate impact on earnings per share (EPS)."

21 What terminal selling price is required for a 15 percent internal rate of return on the Richie project?

   A $588,028.

   B $593,771.

   C $625,839.

22 The NPV and IRR, respectively, of the Gasup Company investment are *closest* to:

   A $509,600 and 21.4%.

   B $509,600 and 31.3%.

   C $946,700 and 31.3%.

23 Of the two grinders that the Dominion Company is evaluating, Böhm should recommend the:

   A   Bolten grinder because its NPV is higher than the Pinto grinder NPV.

   B   Bolten grinder because its EAA is higher than the Pinto grinder EAA.

   C   Pinto grinder because its EAA is higher than the Bolten grinder EAA.

24 Are Goldberg's comments about real options correct?

   A   No for Comment 1 and Comment 2.

   B   No for Comment 1 and Yes for Comment 2.

   C   Yes for Comment 1 and No for Comment 2.

25 Is Böhm most likely correct regarding Comment A about the $10 million investment and Comment B about using the after-tax cost of debt?

   A   No for both comments.

   B   Yes for both comments.

   C   No for Comment A and Yes for Comment B.

26 Is Böhm most likely correct regarding Comment C that it is acceptable to use either NPV or IRR and Comment D about the immediate impact on EPS?

   A   No for both comments.

   B   Yes for both comments.

   C   No for Comment C and Yes for Comment D.

The following information relates to Questions 27–32

Barbara Simpson is a sell-side analyst with Smith Riccardi Securities. Simpson covers the pharmaceutical industry. One of the companies she follows, Bayonne Pharma, is evaluating a regional distribution center. The financial predictions for the project are as follows:

- Fixed capital outlay is €1.50 billion.
- Investment in net working capital is €0.40 billion.
- Straight-line depreciation is over a six-year period with zero salvage value.
- Project life is 12 years.
- Additional annual revenues are €0.10 billion.
- Annual cash operating expenses are reduced by €0.25 billion.
- The capital equipment is sold for €0.50 billion in 12 years.
- Tax rate is 40 percent.
- Required rate of return is 12 percent.

Simpson is evaluating this investment to see whether it has the potential to affect Bayonne Pharma's stock price. Simpson estimates the NPV of the project to be €0.41 billion, which should increase the value of the company.

Simpson is evaluating the effects of other changes to her capital budgeting assumptions. She wants to know the effect of a switch from straight-line to accelerated depreciation on the company's operating income and the project's NPV. She also believes that the initial outlay might be much smaller than initially assumed. Specifically, she thinks the outlay for fixed capital might be €0.24 billion lower, with no change in salvage value.

When reviewing her work, Simpson's supervisor provides the following comments. "I note that you are relying heavily on the NPV approach to valuing the investment decision. I don't think you should use an IRR because of the multiple IRR problem that is likely to arise with the Bayonne Pharma project. However, the equivalent annual annuity would be a more appropriate measure to use for the project than the NPV. I suggest that you compute an EAA."

27 Simpson should estimate the after-tax operating cash flow for Years 1–6 and 7–12, respectively, to be *closest* to:

  A €0.31 billion and €0.21 billion.

  B €0.31 billion and €0.25 billion.

  C €0.35 billion and €0.25 billion.

28 Simpson should estimate the initial outlay and the terminal year non-operating cash flow, respectively, to be *closest* to:

  A €1.50 billion and €0.70 billion.

  B €1.90 billion and €0.70 billion.

  C €1.90 billion and €0.90 billion.

29 Is Simpson's estimate of the NPV of the project correct?

  A Yes.

  B No. The NPV is −€0.01 billion.

  C No. The NPV is €0.34 billion.

30 A switch from straight-line to accelerated depreciation would:

  A increase the NPV and decrease the first year operating income after taxes.

    B increase the first year operating income after taxes and decrease the NPV.

    C increase both the NPV and first year operating income after taxes.

31 If the outlay is lower by the amount that Simpson suggests, the project NPV should increase by an amount *closest* to:

    A €0.09 billion.

    B €0.14 billion.

    C €0.17 billion.

32 How would you evaluate the comments by Simpson's supervisor about not using the IRR and about using the EAA? The supervisor is:

    A incorrect about both.

    B correct about IRR and incorrect about EAA.

    C incorrect about IRR and correct about EAA.

The following information relates to Questions 33–38

Mun Hoe Yip is valuing Pure Corporation. Pure is a simple corporation that is going out of business in five years, distributing its income to creditors and bondholders as planned in the financial statements below. Pure has a 19 percent cost of equity, 8 1/3 percent before-tax cost of debt, 12 percent weighted average cost of capital, and 40 percent tax rate, and it maintains a 50 percent debt/value ratio.

    Yip is valuing the company using the basic capital budgeting method as well as other methods, such as EP, residual income, and claims valuation. Yip's research assistant, Linda Robinson, makes three observations about the analysis.

Observation 1	"The present value of the company's economic income should be equal to the present value of the cash flows in the basic capital budgeting approach."
Observation 2	"The economic income each year is equal to the cash flow minus the economic depreciation."
Observation 3	"The market value added is the present value of the company's economic profit (EP), which equals the net worth of 77,973."

Year	0	1	2	3	4	5
Balance Sheets:						
Assets	200,000	160,000	120,000	80,000	40,000	0
Liabilities	122,027	107,671	88,591	64,222	33,929	0
Net worth	77,973	52,329	31,409	15,778	6,071	0
Income Statements:						
Sales		180,000	200,000	220,000	240,000	200,000
Variable cash expenses		90,000	100,000	110,000	120,000	100,000
Fixed cash expenses		20,000	20,000	20,000	20,000	20,000
Depreciation		40,000	40,000	40,000	40,000	40,000
EBIT		30,000	40,000	50,000	60,000	40,000
Interest expense		10,169	8,973	7,383	5,352	2,827

Year	0	1	2	3	4	5
EBT		19,831	31,027	42,617	54,648	37,173
Taxes at 40 percent		7,932	12,411	17,047	21,859	14,869
Net income before salvage		11,899	18,616	25,570	32,789	22,304
After-tax salvage value						12,000
Net income		11,899	18,616	25,570	32,789	34,304
Statements of Cash Flows:						
Operating cash flows:						
Net income		11,899	18,616	25,570	32,789	34,304
Depreciation		40,000	40,000	40,000	40,000	40,000
Total		51,899	58,616	65,570	72,789	74,304
Financing cash flows:						
Debt repayment		14,357	19,080	24,369	30,293	33,929
Dividends/repurchases		37,542	39,536	41,201	42,496	40,375
Total		−51,899	−58,616	−65,570	−72,789	−74,304
Investing cash flows:		0	0	0	0	0
Total cash flows:		0	0	0	0	0

33 Economic income during year one is *closest* to:

  A 23,186.

  B 29,287.

  C 46,101.

34 What is EP during Year 1?

  A −12,101.

  B −6,000.

  C 6,000.

35 What is residual income during Year 1?

  A −2,916.

  B 2,542.

  C 8,653.

36 What is the value of equity at time zero?

  A 44,055.

  B 77,973.

  C 122,027.

37 Are Robinson's first two observations, respectively, correct?

  A Yes for both observations.

  B No for the first and Yes for the second.

  C Yes for the first and No for the second.

38 Which of the following would be Yip's *most appropriate* response to Robinson's third observation?

  A The market value added is not equal to the present value of EP, although the market value of equity is equal to 122,027.

   B The market value added is equal to the present value of EP, which in this case is 44,055.

   C The market value added is not equal to the present value of EP, and market value added is equal to 44,055.

The following information relates to Questions 39–44

Carlos Velasquez, CFA, is a financial analyst with Embelesado, S.A., a Spanish manufacturer of sailboats and sailing equipment. Velasquez is evaluating a proposal for Embelesado to build sailboats for a foreign competitor that lacks production capacity and sells in a different market. The sailboat project is perceived to have the same risk as Embelesado's other projects.

The proposal covers a limited time horizon—three years—after which the competitor expects to be situated in a new, larger production facility. The limited time horizon appeals to Embelesado, which currently has excess capacity but expects to begin its own product expansion in slightly more than three years.

Velasquez has collected much of the information necessary to evaluate this proposal in Exhibits 1 and 2.

Exhibit 1	Selected Data for Sailboat Proposal (Currency Amounts in € Millions)
Initial fixed capital outlay	60
Annual contracted revenues	60
Annual operating costs	25
Initial working capital outlay (recovered at end of the project)	10
Annual depreciation expense (both book and tax accounting)	20
Economic life of facility (years)	3
Salvage (book) value of facility at end of project	0
Expected market value of facility at end of project	5

Exhibit 2	Selected Data for Embelesado, S.A.
Book value of long-term debt/total assets	28.6%
Book value of equity/total assets	71.4%
Market value of long-term debt/market value of company	23.1%
Market value of equity/market value of company	76.9%
Coupon rate on existing long-term debt	8.5%
Interest rate on new long-term debt	8.0%
Cost of equity	13.0%

Exhibit 2	(Continued)	

Marginal tax rate	35.0%
Maximum acceptable payback period	2 years

Velasquez recognizes that Embelesado is currently financed at its target capital structure and expects that the capital structure will be maintained if the sailboat project is undertaken. Embelesado's managers disagree, however, about the method that should be used to evaluate capital budgeting proposals.

One of Embelesado's vice presidents asks Velasquez the following questions:

Question 1   Will projects that meet a corporation's payback criterion for acceptance necessarily have a positive net present value (NPV)?

Question 2   For mutually exclusive projects, will the NPV and internal rate of return (IRR) methods necessarily agree on project ranking?

Question 3   For the sailboat project, what will be the effects of using accelerated depreciation (for both book and tax accounting) instead of straight-line depreciation on a) the NPV and b) the total net cash flow in the terminal year?

Question 4   Assuming a 13 percent discount rate, what will be the increase in the sailboat project's NPV if the expected market value of the facility at end of project is €15 million rather than €5 million?

39 The weighted average cost of capital for Embelesado is *closest* to:

A   10.78%.

B   11.20%.

C   11.85%.

40 The total net cash flow (in € millions) for the sailboat project in its terminal year is *closest* to:

A   33.00.

B   39.75.

C   43.00.

41 The IRR for the sailboat project is *closest* to:

A   18.5%.

B   19.7%.

C   20.3%.

42 The best responses that Velasquez can make to Question 1 and Question 2 are:

	Question 1	Question 2
A	No	No
B	No	Yes
C	Yes	No

43 In response to Question 3, what are the *most likely* effects on the NPV and the total net cash flow in the terminal year, respectively?

	NPV	Total Net Cash Flow in Terminal Year
A	Increase	Increase
B	Increase	Decrease
C	Decrease	Increase

44 In response to Question 4, the increase in the sailboat project's NPV(in € millions) is *closest* to:

A 4.50.

B 6.50.

C 6.76.

The following information relates to Questions 45–50

María Hernández is a sell-side analyst covering the electronics industry in Spain. One of the companies she follows, SG Electronics, S.A., has recently announced plans to begin producing and selling a new series of video cameras. Hernández estimates that this project will increase the value of the company and, consequently, she plans on changing her research opinion on the company from a "hold" to a "buy." Her initial financial predictions for the project are:

- Fixed capital equipment outlay is €2,750,000.
- At the beginning of the project, a required increase in current assets of €200,000 and a required increase in current liabilities of €125,000.
- Straight-line depreciation to zero over a five-year life.
- Project life of five years.
- Incremental annual unit sales of 3,000 at a unit price of €600.
- Annual fixed cash expenses of €125,000; variable cash expenses of €125 per unit.
- The capital equipment is expected to be sold for €450,000 at the end of Year 5. At the end of the project, the net working capital investment will be recovered.
- Tax rate of 40 percent.
- Based on the capital asset pricing model, the required rate of return is 12 percent.

Hernández estimates the expected net present value (NPV) of the project to be €975,538 and the internal rate of return (IRR) to be 24.6 percent. She also performs a sensitivity analysis by changing the input variable assumptions used in her initial analysis.

When reviewing Hernández's work, her supervisor, Arturo Costa, notes that she did not include changes in the depreciation method, initial fixed capital outlay, or inflation assumptions in her sensitivity analysis. As a result, Costa asks the following questions:

Question 1   "What would be the effect on the project's NPV if the initial fixed capital equipment outlay increased from €2,750,000 to €3,000,000, everything else held constant?"

Question 2   "How would a higher than expected inflation rate affect the value of the real tax savings from depreciation and the value of the real after-tax interest expense, everything else held constant?"

Question 3   "You are using a required rate of return of 12 percent when the company's weighted average cost of capital (WACC) is 10 percent. Why are you using a required rate of return for the project greater than the company's WACC?"

Before ending the meeting, Costa tells Hernández: "Last year the company produced a prototype at a cost of €500,000. Now management is having doubts about the market appeal of the product in its current design, and so they are considering delaying the start of the project for a year, until the prototype can be shown to industry experts."

45 Using Hernández's initial financial predictions, the estimated annual after-tax operating cash flow is *closest* to:

A   €780,000.

B   €1,000,000.

C   €1,075,000.

46 Using Hernández's initial financial predictions, the estimated terminal year after-tax non-operating cash flow is *closest* to:

A   €195,000.

B   €270,000.

C   €345,000.

47 Hernández's best response to Costa's first question is that the project's NPV would decrease by an amount *closest* to:

A   €142,000.

B   €178,000.

C   €250,000.

48 Hernández's *best* response to Costa's second question is that:

A   real tax savings from depreciation and real interest expense would be lower.

B   real tax savings from depreciation would be higher and real interest expense would be lower.

C   real tax savings from depreciation would be lower and real interest expense would be higher.

49 Hernández's *best* response to Costa's third question is: "Because:

A   the project will plot above the security market line."

B   the project's beta is greater than the company's beta."

C   the project's IRR is greater than the required rate of return."

50 Should Costa's end-of-meeting comments result in changes to Hernández's capital budgeting analysis?

A   No.

B   Yes, but only to incorporate the possible delay.

C   Yes, to incorporate both the possible delay and the cost of producing the prototype.

SOLUTIONS

1 C is correct.

Outlay = FCInv + NWCInv − Sal_0 + $T(\text{Sal}_0 − B_0)$

Outlay = (350,000 + 110,000) + 73,000 − 0 + 0 = $533,000

The installed cost is $350,000 + $110,000 = $460,000, so the annual depreciation is $460,000/5 = $92,000. The annual after-tax operating cash flow for Years 1–5 is

$$CF = (S − C − D)(1 − T) + D = (265,000 − 83,000 − 92,000)$$
$$(1 − 0.40) + 92,000$$
$$CF = \$146,000$$

The terminal year after-tax non-operating cash flow in Year 5 is

$$TNOCF = \text{Sal}_5 + \text{NWCInv} − T(\text{Sal}_5 − B_5) = 85,000 + 73,000$$
$$−0.40(85,000 − 0)$$
$$TNOCF = \$124,000$$

The NPV is

$$NPV = −533,000 + \sum_{t=1}^{5} \frac{146,000}{1.10^t} + \frac{124,000}{1.10^5} = \$97,449$$

2 B is correct. The additional annual depreciation is $100,000/8 = $12,500. The depreciation tax savings is 0.40 ($12,500) = $5,000. The change in project NPV is

$$−100,000 + \sum_{t=1}^{8} \frac{5,000}{(1.10)^t} = −100,000 + 26,675 = −\$73,325$$

3 C is correct. Financing costs are not subtracted from the cash flows for either the NPV or the IRR. The effects of financing costs are captured in the discount rate used.

4 C is correct. The annual depreciation charge is $400,000/10 = $40,000. The after-tax operating cash flow in Year 1 should be

$$CF = (S − C − D)(1 − T) + D$$
$$= (240,000 − 110,000 − 40,000)(1 − 0.30) + 40,000$$
$$= 63,000 + 40,000 = \$103,000$$

5 C is correct. The terminal year after-tax non-operating cash flow is

$$TNOCF = \text{Sal}_5 + \text{NWCInv} − T(\text{Sal}_5 − B_5)$$
$$= 21 + 8 − 0.40(21 − 15) = £26.6 \text{ million}$$

6 C is correct. The investment outlay is

$$\text{Outlay} = \text{FCInv} + \text{NWCInv} − \text{Sal}_0 + T(\text{Sal}_0 − B_0)$$
$$= (360,000 + 40,000) + 60,000 − 0 + 0 = \$460,000$$

7 A is correct. Depreciation will be $400,000/5 = $80,000 per year. The annual after-tax operating cash flow is

$$CF = (S - C - D)(1 - T) + D$$
$$= \left[0 - (-140,000) - 80,000\right](1 - 0.40) + 80,000 = \$116,000$$

8 B is correct. The terminal year non-operating cash flow is

$$TNOCF = Sal_5 + NWCInv - T(Sal_5 - B_5)$$
$$= 120,000 + 60,000 - 0.40(120,000 - 0) = \$132,000$$

9 C is correct. The value of the depreciation tax savings is increased, and the value of the real after-tax interest expense is also increased. Due to the lower inflation, the value has increased (essentially discounting at a lower rate).

10 A is correct. The statement is correct for sensitivity analysis, but not for scenario analysis (in which several input variables are changed for each scenario).

11 B is correct. Either the least-common multiple of lives or the equivalent annual annuity approach should be used (both use the NPV, not the IRR). Concept 4 is correct as given.

12 C is correct. The problem gives EBIT not EBITDA.

$$CF = (S - C - D)(1 - T) + D = 50(1 - 0.3) + 50 = €85 \text{ each year}$$

13 A is correct. Economic income is the cash flow plus the change in value, or economic income is the cash flow minus the economic depreciation (we will use the second expression):

$$V_0 = \frac{85}{1.12} + \frac{85}{1.12^2} = 143.65 \quad V_1 = \frac{85}{1.12} = 75.89 \quad V_2 = 0$$

$$\text{Economic income(Year 1)} = CF_1 - (V_0 - V_1)$$
$$= 85 - (143.65 - 75.89)$$
$$= 85 - 67.76 = €17.24$$
$$\text{Economic income(Year 2)} = CF_2 - (V_1 - V_2)$$
$$= 85 - (75.89 - 0)$$
$$= 85 - 75.89 = €9.11$$

14 C is correct.

$$EP = NOPAT - \$WACC = EBIT(1 - T) - WACC \times Capital$$
$$EP(\text{Year 1}) = 50(1 - 0.30) - 0.12(100) = 35 - 12 = €23$$
$$EP(\text{Year 2}) = 50(1 - 0.30) - 0.12(50) = 35 - 6 = €29$$
$$MVA = \frac{EP(\text{Year 1})}{1 + WACC} + \frac{EP(\text{Year 2})}{(1 + WACC)^2} = \frac{23}{1.12} + \frac{29}{1.12^2} = €43.65$$

(An alternative way to get MVA is simply to find the NPV of the investment project.)

15 B is correct. The way to solve the problem is to calculate the equivalent annual annuity and choose the service life with the lowest annual cost. For a two-year service life, the NPV is

$$NPV = -40,000 + \frac{-12,000}{1.10^1} + \frac{-15,000}{1.10^2} + \frac{20,000}{1.10^2} = -46,776.86$$

The EAA (PV = −46,776.86, $N = 2$, and $i = 10\%$) is −26,952.38.

For a three-year service life, the NPV is

$$NPV = -40,000 + \frac{-12,000}{1.10^1} + \frac{-15,000}{1.10^2} + \frac{-20,000}{1.10^3} + \frac{17,000}{1.10^3}$$
$$= -65,559.73$$

The EAA (PV = –65,559.73, N = 3, and i = 10%) is –26,362.54.

For a four-year service life, the NPV is

$$NPV = -40,000 + \frac{-12,000}{1.10^1} + \frac{-15,000}{1.10^2} + \frac{-20,000}{1.10^3} + \frac{-25,000}{1.10^4}$$
$$+\frac{12,000}{1.10^4} = -87,211.26$$

The EAA (PV = –87,211.26, N = 4, and i = 10%) is –27,512.61.

The three-year service life has the lowest annual cost. Laroche should replace the vans every three years.

16 A is correct. To help the selection process, use the profitability index for each project, which shows the total present value per dollar invested.

Project	Outlay	PV of Future Cash Flows	NPV	PI	PI Rank
1	31	44	13	1.419	1
2	15	21	6	1.400	2
3	12	16.5	4.5	1.375	(tie) 3
4	10	13	3	1.300	6
5	8	11	3	1.375	(tie) 3
6	6	8	2	1.333	5

Try to incorporate the high PI projects into the budget using trial and error. These trials include the following:

Set of Projects	Total Outlay	Total NPV
1 and 5	39	16
2, 3, and 4	37	13.5
2, 3, and 5	35	13.5
2, 4, 5, and 6	39	14

Among the sets of projects suggested, the optimal set is the one with the highest NPV, provided its total outlay does not exceed C$40 million. The set consisting of Projects 1 and 5 produces the highest NPV.

17 B is correct.

If demand is "high," the NPV is

$$NPV = -190 + \sum_{t=1}^{10} \frac{40}{1.10^t} = C\$55.783 \text{ million}$$

If demand is "low," the NPV is

$$NPV = -190 + \sum_{t=1}^{10} \frac{20}{1.10^t} = -C\$67.109 \text{ million}$$

The expected NPV is $0.50(55.783) + 0.50(-67.109) = -C\$5.663$ million.

18 B is correct. Assume we are at time = 1. The NPV of the expansion (at time 1) if demand is "high" is

$$NPV = -190 + \sum_{t=1}^{9} \frac{40}{1.10^t} = C\$40.361 \text{ million}$$

The NPV of the expansion (at time 1) if demand is "low" is

$$NPV = -190 + \sum_{t=1}^{9} \frac{20}{1.10^t} = -C\$74.820 \text{ million}$$

The optimal decision is to expand if demand is "high" and not expand if "low."

Because the expansion option is exercised only when its value is positive, which happens 50 percent of the time, the expected value of the expansion project, at time zero, is

$$NPV = \frac{1}{1.10} 0.50(40.361) = C\$18.346 \text{ million}$$

The total NPV of the initial project and the expansion project is

$$NPV = -C\$5.663 \text{ million} + C\$18.346 \text{ million} = C\$12.683 \text{ million}$$

The optional expansion project, handled optimally, adds sufficient value to make this a positive NPV project.

19 A is correct. Both suggestions are bad. In valuing projects, expected cash flows should be discounted at required rates of return that reflect their risk, not at a risk-free rate that ignores risk. Even though both options cannot be simultaneously exercised, they can both add value. If demand is high, you can exercise the growth option, and if demand is low, you can exercise the abandonment option.

20 B is correct. Both suggestions are good. Choosing projects with high IRRs might cause the company to concentrate on short-term projects that reduce the NPV of the company. Whenever the project risk differs from the company risk, a project-specific required rate of return should be used.

21 C is correct. The after-tax operating cash flow for each of the next three years is $\$20,000 + \$40,000 = \$60,000$. The book value in three years will be $\$380,000$ (the original cost less three years' depreciation). So the terminal year after-tax non-operating cash flow will be $Sal_3 - 0.30(Sal_3 - \$380,000)$, where Sal_3 is the selling price. For a 15 percent return, the PV of future cash flows must equal the investment:

$$500,000 = \frac{60,000}{1.15} + \frac{60,000}{1.15^2} + \frac{60,000}{1.15^3} + \frac{Sal_3 - 0.30(Sal_3 - 380,000)}{1.15^3}$$

There are several paths to follow to solve for Sal_3.

$$363,006.5 = \frac{Sal_3 - 0.30(Sal_3 - 380,000)}{1.15^3}$$

$$Sal_3 - 0.30(Sal_3 - 380,000) = 552,087.5$$

$$0.70 \, Sal_3 = 438,087.5$$

$$Sal_3 = \$625,839$$

22 A is correct. The cash flows (in $ million) for the 5-year gas project are as
follows:

Time	Outlays	After-Tax Operating Cash Flows	Total After-Tax Cash Flows
0	6.0	0.0	−6.0
1	1.0	0.5	−0.5
2	0.0	4.0	4.0
3	0.0	4.0	4.0
4	0.0	4.0	4.0
5	5.0	4.0	−1.0

Given the required rate of return of 18 percent, the NPV can be calculated with
Equation 2 or with a financial calculator:

$$NPV = -6.0 + \frac{-0.5}{1.18} + \frac{4.0}{1.18^2} + \frac{4.0}{1.18^3} + \frac{4.0}{1.18^4} + \frac{-1.0}{1.18^5}$$

$$NPV = \$509,579$$

Similarly, the IRR can be calculated from Equation 3:

$$-6.0 + \frac{-0.5}{1+r} + \frac{4.0}{(1+r)^2} + \frac{4.0}{(1+r)^3} + \frac{4.0}{(1+r)^4} + \frac{-1.0}{(1+r)^5} = 0$$

Solving for r with a financial calculator or spreadsheet software will yield
21.4 percent for the internal rate of return. Note that in spite of the fact that
we are dealing with a nonconventional cash flow pattern, the IRR has a unique
solution. The NPV profile declines as the required rate of return increases, and
the NPV value crosses the x-axis (required rate of return) only one time, at
21.4 percent.

23 C is correct. Because the mutually exclusive projects have unequal lives, the
EAA should be used instead of the NPV. The NPV and EAA for the Pinto
grinder are correct. For the Bolten grinder, the NPV is

$$NPV = -125,000 + \sum_{t=1}^{4} \frac{47,000}{1.10^t} + \frac{20,000}{1.10^4} = 37,644$$

To find the Bolten EAA, take the NPV for Bolten and annualize it for four years
($N = 4$, PV = 37,644, and $i = 10\%$). The Bolten EAA is $11,876. Consequently,
the Pinto grinder has the better EAA of $12,341.

24 B is correct. Goldberg's first comment is wrong. A project should be abandoned
in the future only when its abandonment value is more than the discounted
value of the remaining cash flows. Goldberg's second comment is correct.

25 A is correct. The $10 million original cost is a sunk cost and not relevant. The
correct investment is today's opportunity cost, the market value today. The
correct discount rate is the project required rate of return.

26 C is correct. Even if they are the same size, a short-term project with a high IRR
can have a lower NPV than a longer-term project. The immediate impact on
EPS does not capture the full effect of the cash flows over the project's entire
life.

27 A is correct. The annual depreciation charge for Years 1–6 is $1.5/6 = 0.25$.
Annual after-tax operating cash flows for Years 1–6 are:

$$CF = (S - C - D)(1 - T) + D$$
$$CF = [0.10 - (-0.25) - 0.25](1 - 0.40) + 0.25$$
$$CF = 0.06 + 0.25 = €0.31 \text{ billion}$$

Annual after-tax operating cash flows for Years 7–12 are:

$$CF = (S - C - D)(1 - T) + D$$
$$CF = [0.10 - (-0.25) - 0](1 - 0.40) + 0$$
$$CF = €0.21 \text{ billion}$$

28 B is correct.

Outlay at time zero is:

$$\text{Outlay} = FCInv + NWCInv - Sal_0 + T(Sal_0 - B_0)$$
$$\text{Outlay} = 1.50 + 0.40 - 0 + 0 = €1.90 \text{ billion}$$

Terminal year after-tax non-operating cash flow is

$$TNOCF = Sal_{12} + NWCInv - T(Sal_{12} - B_{12})$$
$$TNOCF = 0.50 + 0.40 - 0.40(0.50 - 0) = €0.70 \text{ billion}$$

29 B is correct. The cash flows, computed in the first two questions, are as follows:

Time 0	−€1.90 billion
Time 1–6	€0.31 billion
Time 7–12	€0.21 billion
Time 12	€0.70 billion

The NPV is

$$NPV = -1.90 + \sum_{t=1}^{6} \frac{0.31}{1.12^t} + \sum_{t=7}^{12} \frac{0.21}{1.12^t} + \frac{0.70}{1.12^{12}}$$
$$NPV = -1.90 + 1.2745 + 0.4374 + 0.1797 = -€0.0084 \text{ billion}$$
$$\approx -€0.01 \text{ billion}$$

30 A is correct. Accelerated depreciation shifts depreciation expense toward the earlier years so that first-year operating income after taxes will be lower. However, because depreciation is a noncash expense, it must be added back to operating income after taxes in order to obtain after-tax operating cash flow. This process shifts cash flows from later years to earlier years, increasing the NPV.

31 C is correct. The outlay is lower by €0.24, which will decrease the annual depreciation by €0.04 for the first six years. The annual additional taxes from the loss of the depreciation tax shelter are €0.04(0.40) = €0.016. The after-tax cash flows are higher by €0.24 at time zero (because of the smaller investment) and lower by €0.016 for the first six years. The NPV increases by

$$NPV = +0.24 - \sum_{t=1}^{6} \frac{0.016}{1.12^t} = 0.24 - 0.0658 = 0.1742 = €0.17 \text{ billion}$$

32 A is correct. Both of the supervisor's comments are incorrect. Because the Bayonne Pharma project is a conventional project (an outflow followed by inflows), the multiple IRR problem cannot occur. The EAA is preferred over the NPV when dealing with mutually exclusive projects with differing lives, a scenario which is not relevant for this decision. The Bayonne Pharma project is free-standing, so the NPV approach is appropriate.

33 B is correct.

Economic income = Cash flow − Economic depreciation

Economic income$(\text{Year 1}) = CF_1 - (V_0 - V_1)$

After-tax operating cash flow $(CF) = (S - C - D)(1 - T) + D +$ After-tax

salvage $= EBIT(1 - T) + D +$ After-tax salvage

Year	1	2	3	4	5
EBIT	30,000	40,000	50,000	60,000	40,000
EBIT(1 − 0.40)	18,000	24,000	30,000	36,000	24,000
D	40,000	40,000	40,000	40,000	40,000
After-tax salvage					12,000
CF	58,000	64,000	70,000	76,000	76,000

$CF_1 = 58,000$

$$V_0 = \frac{58,000}{1.12} + \frac{64,000}{1.12^2} + \frac{70,000}{1.12^3} + \frac{76,000}{1.12^4} + \frac{76,000}{1.12^5} = 244,054.55$$

$$V_1 = \frac{64,000}{1.12} + \frac{70,000}{1.12^2} + \frac{76,000}{1.12^3} + \frac{76,000}{1.12^4} = 215,341.10$$

Economic income (Year 1) = 58,000 − (244,054.55 − 215,341.10)

Economic income (Year 1) = 58,000 − 28,713.45 = 29,286.55

34 B is correct.

EP = NOPAT − $WACC

NOPAT $= EBIT(1 - \text{Tax rate}) = 30,000(1 - 0.40) = 18,000$

$WACC $= WACC \times \text{Capital} = 0.12(200,000) = 24,000$

EP $= 18,000 - 24,000 = -6,000$

35 A is correct.

$RI_t = NI_t - r_e B_{t-1}$

$RI_1 = 11,899 - 0.19(77,973) = 11,899 - 14,815 = -2,916$

36 C is correct. The value of equity is the PV of cash distributions to equity:

$$PV = \frac{37,542}{1.19} + \frac{39,536}{1.19^2} + \frac{41,201}{1.19^3} + \frac{42,496}{1.19^4} + \frac{40,375}{1.19^5} = 122,027$$

37 B is correct. Robinson's first statement is wrong. The value of an asset is the present value of its future cash flows. Economic income each year is the cash flow minus economic depreciation, EI = CF − ED. For this company, which is declining in value each year, the economic depreciation is positive and EI is less than CF each year. Consequently, the present value of economic income (EI) will be less than the present value of future cash flows (CF). Robinson's second statement is correct.

38 B is correct. Market value added is equal to the present value of EP. Its value, however, is not equal to the book value of equity. The calculation of MVA is shown below:

Year	1	2	3	4	5*
EBIT	30,000	40,000	50,000	60,000	60,000
NOPAT = EBIT(1 − 0.40)	18,000	24,000	30,000	36,000	36,000
Capital (beginning)	200,000	160,000	120,000	80,000	40,000
$WACC = 0.12 × Capital	24,000	19,200	14,400	9,600	4,800
EP = NOPAT − $WACC	−6,000	4,800	15,600	26,400	31,200

*The fifth year figures include the effects of salvage. Before-tax salvage of 20,000 (= 12,000/(1 − 0.40)) is added to EBIT. The after-tax salvage of 12,000 is included in NOPAT.

$$\text{MVA} = \frac{-6,000}{1.12} + \frac{4,800}{1.12^2} + \frac{15,600}{1.12^3} + \frac{26,400}{1.12^4} + \frac{31,200}{1.12^5} = 44,054.55$$

39 B is correct. The weighted average cost of capital for Embelesado is calculated as:

$$\text{WACC} = \left(\text{Market weight of debt} \times \text{After-tax cost of debt}\right)$$
$$+\left(\text{Market weight of equity} \times \text{Cost of equity}\right)$$
$$\text{WACC} = w_d k_d\left(1 - T\right) + w_{cs} k_{cs} = 0.231(8.0\%)(1 - 0.35) + 0.769(13.0\%)$$
$$= 1.201\% + 9.997\%$$
$$\text{WACC} = 11.198\% = 11.20\%$$

40 C is correct. The terminal year cash flow is:

Revenues	€60.00
Less operating costs	25.00
Less depreciation expenses	20.00
= Taxable Income	15.00
Less taxes @ 35%	(5.25)
= Net Income	9.75
Plus depreciation expenses	20.00
= After-tax operating CF	29.75
+ Recover WC	10.00
+ Ending market value	5.00
Less taxes on sale proceeds @ 35%	(1.75)*
= Terminal Year CF	€43.00

*The tax on the sale proceeds is 35% times the gain of €5.00 = €1.75

41 C is correct. This is the IRR for a project with the following cash flows: (€70,000) in Year 0, €29,750 at Years 1 and 2, and €43,000 at Year 3.

	Years 1 & 2	Year 3
Revenues	€60,000	€60,000
Less operating costs	25,000	25,000
Less depreciation expense	20,000	20,000
= Taxable income	15,000	15,000
Less taxes @ 35%	5,250	5,250
= Net income	9,750	9,750
Plus depreciation expense	20,000	20,000
= After-tax operating CF	€29,750	29,750
+ Recover WC		10,000
+ Salvage value		5,000
– Less taxes on sal. value @ 35%		1,750
= Terminal year CF		€43,000

The IRR of 20.29% is readily found with a financial calculator:

$$70,000 = \frac{29,750}{(1 + IRR)^1} + \frac{29,750}{(1 + IRR)^2} + \frac{43,000}{(1 + IRR)^3}$$

You can also "reverse-engineer" the answer using the choices given in the question.

42 A is correct. Projects with shorter paybacks do not necessarily have a positive NPV. For mutually exclusive projects, the NPV and IRR criteria will not necessarily provide the same project ranking.

43 B is correct. Additional depreciation in earlier time periods will shield Embelesado from additional taxes, thus increasing the net cash flows in earlier years of the project and increasing the project's NPV. However, this also means that there will be less depreciation expense in the terminal year of the project, thus shielding less income and increasing taxes. Terminal-year net cash flow will likely decrease.

44 A is correct. The entire €10 million will be subject to taxes, resulting in an additional €6.5 million after taxes. As indicated below, when discounted at 13 percent for three years, this has a present value of €4.5048 (rounded to €4.50 million):

$$PV = \frac{10.0(1 - 0.35)}{(1.13)^3} = \frac{6.50}{(1.13)^3} = 4.50$$

45 B is correct. Using equation CF = (S – C) × (1 – T) + TD, the numbers are:

$$\text{Sales} = \text{P} \times \text{Q} = €600 \times 3{,}000 = €1{,}800{,}000$$

$$\text{Costs} = \text{Variable cost} \times \text{Q} + \text{Fixed costs} = (125 \times 3{,}000) + €125{,}000$$

$$= 500{,}000$$

$$\text{Depreciation expense} = €2{,}750{,}000 \div 5 = €550{,}000$$

$$\text{CF} = (1{,}800{,}000 - 500{,}000) \times (1 - 0.40) + (550{,}000 \times 0.40)$$

$$= 780{,}000 + 220{,}000 = €1{,}000{,}000$$

46 C is correct. The terminal year non-operating cash flow includes the after-tax salvage value and the recovery of net working capital = €450,000 × (1 −0.40) + €75,000 = €345,000.

> (Note: Terminal year recovery of net working capital investment = Decrease in current assets − Decrease in current liabilities = €200,000 −€125,000 = €75,000.)

47 B is correct. Calculations: The outlay is higher by €250,000, which will increase annual depreciation by €50,000 over the 5-year period. The annual additional tax savings from the higher depreciation expense is: 50,000 × (0.40) = 20,000. Therefore NPV should decrease by:

$$\text{NPV} = -250{,}000 + \sum_{t=1}^{5} \frac{20{,}000}{1.12^t} = -250{,}000 + 72{,}095.524 = -177{,}904$$

48 A is correct. Higher than expected inflation increases the corporation's real taxes because it reduces the value of the depreciation tax shelter; it also decreases the real interest expense because payments to bondholders in real terms are lower than expected.

49 B is correct. When a project is more or less risky than the company, project beta and not WACC should be used to establish the required rate of return for the capital project. In this case, the required rate of return is greater than the WACC, which means the project beta (risk) is greater than the company's beta.

50 B is correct. Timing options (e.g., delay investing) should be included in the NPV analysis, but sunk costs should not.

READING

26

Capital Structure

by Raj Aggarwal, CFA, Pamela Peterson Drake, CFA, Adam Kobor, CFA, and Gregory Noronha, CFA

LEARNING OUTCOMES

Mastery	The candidate should be able to:
☐	a. explain the Modigliani–Miller propositions regarding capital structure, including the effects of leverage, taxes, financial distress, agency costs, and asymmetric information on a company's cost of equity, cost of capital, and optimal capital structure;
☐	b. describe the target capital structure and explain why a company's actual capital structure may fluctuate around its target;
☐	c. describe the role of debt ratings in capital structure policy;
☐	d. explain factors an analyst should consider in evaluating the effect of capital structure policy on valuation;
☐	e. describe international differences in the use of financial leverage, factors that explain these differences, and implications of these differences for investment analysis.

INTRODUCTION

1

The most important decision a company makes in its pursuit of maximizing its value is typically the decision concerning what products to manufacture and/or what services to offer. The decision on how to finance investments (e.g., in factories and equipment), the so-called capital structure decision, is often seen as less important, even secondary. As we will see in this reading, the importance of the capital structure decision depends on the assumptions one makes about capital markets and the agents operating in it.

Under the most restrictive set of assumptions, the capital structure decision—the choice between how much debt and how much equity a company uses in financing its investments—is irrelevant. That is, any level of debt is as good as any other, and the capital structure decision is not only secondary, it is irrelevant. However, as some of the underlying assumptions are relaxed, the choice of how much debt to have in the capital structure becomes meaningful. Under a particular set of assumptions, it is even possible to have an optimal level of debt in the capital structure; that is, a level of debt at which company value is maximized.

The reading is organized as follows: In Section 2 we introduce the capital structure decision and discuss the assumptions and theories that lead to alternative capital structures. In Section 3 we present important practical issues for the analyst, such as the role of debt ratings in the capital structure decision and international differences in capital structure policies. The final section summarizes the reading.

2   THE CAPITAL STRUCTURE DECISION

A company's **capital structure** is the mix of debt and equity the company uses to finance its business. The goal of a company's capital structure decision is to determine the financial leverage or capital structure that maximizes the value of the company by minimizing the weighted average cost of capital. The **weighted average cost of capital** (WACC) is given by the weighted average of the marginal costs of financing for each type of financing used. For a company with both debt and equity in its capital structure for which interest expense is tax deductible at a rate t, the WACC, which we will denote r_{wacc} is

$$r_{wacc} = \left(\frac{D}{V}\right)r_d(1-t) + \left(\frac{E}{V}\right)r_e \qquad\qquad \textbf{(1)}$$

where r_d is the before-tax marginal cost of debt, r_e is the marginal cost of equity, and t is the marginal tax rate.[1] Variables D and E denote the market value of the shareholders' outstanding debt and equity, respectively, and the value of the company is given by $V = D + E$. You will notice that the debt and equity costs of capital and the tax rate are all understood to be "marginal" rates. The overall cost of capital is therefore a marginal cost also: what it costs the company to raise additional capital using the specified mixture of debt and equity. Further, this is the current cost: what it would cost the company today. What it cost in the past is not relevant. Therefore, the cost of equity, the cost of debt, and the tax rate that we use throughout the remainder of this reading are marginal: the cost or tax rate for additional capital.

In the following section, we first consider the theoretical relationship between leverage and a company's value. We then examine the practical relationship between leverage and company value in equal depth.

2.1 Proposition I without Taxes: Capital Structure Irrelevance

In a now-classic paper, Nobel Prize–winning economists Franco Modigliani and Merton Miller argued the important theory that, given certain assumptions, a company's choice of capital structure does not affect its value.[2] The assumptions relate to expectations and markets:

1   Investors agree on the expected cash flows from a given investment. This means that all investors have the same expectations with respect to the cash flows from an investment in bonds or stocks. In other words, expectations are homogeneous.

---

1 For simplicity, this discussion ignores preferred stock.
2 Modigliani and Miller (1958).

2   Bonds and shares of stock are traded in **perfect capital markets**. This means that there are no transactions costs, no taxes, no bankruptcy costs, and everyone has the same information. In a perfect capital market, any two investments with identical cash flow streams and risk must trade for the same price.

3   Investors can borrow and lend at the risk-free rate.

4   There are no agency costs. This means that managers always act to maximize shareholder wealth.

5   The financing decision and the investment decision are independent of each other. This means that operating income is unaffected by changes in the capital structure.

Many of these assumptions are unrealistic, and we will examine the consequences of relaxing some of them later in this section. The important point is that Modigliani and Miller provided a basis for thinking about capital structure and the starting point for analysis. Consider the capital of a company to be a pie: Each slice represents how much of total capital is provided by a specific type of capital, e.g., by common equity. One can split it in any number of ways, but the size of the pie remains the same. Saying that the pie remains the same size is equivalent to saying that the present value of cash flows to the company remains the same. This can only happen if the future cash flow stream is expected to remain the same and the risk of that cash flow stream, as reflected by the cost of capital, remains the same. Modigliani and Miller prove that under these conditions, and given their assumptions, changing the capital structure (i.e., how the pie is sliced) does not affect value. In other words, in a perfect capital market with risk-free borrowing and lending and with investment and financing decisions independent of each other, investors can create the capital structure which they individually prefer for the company by borrowing and lending on their own accounts. The capital structure chosen by management does not matter because it can be adjusted to the desired capital structure by investors at no cost.

Suppose that a company has a capital structure consisting of 50 percent debt and 50 percent equity and that an investor would prefer that the company's capital structure be 70 percent debt and 30 percent equity. The investor uses borrowed money to finance his or her share purchases so that effectively ownership of company assets reflects the preferred 70 percent debt financing. To the extent this changing capital structure has no effect on the company's expected operating cash flows, the capital structure decision has no impact on company value. Modigliani and Miller use the concept of arbitrage to demonstrate their point: If the value of an unlevered company—that is, a company without any debt—is not equal to that of a levered company, investors could make an arbitrage profit. The arbitrage operation (selling the overvalued asset and using the proceeds to buy the undervalued asset) would quickly force the values to be equivalent.

The importance of the Modigliani and Miller theory is that it demonstrates that managers cannot create value simply by changing the company's capital structure. Consider why this might be true. The operating earnings of a business are available to the providers of its capital. In an all-equity company (that is, a company with no debt), all of the operating earnings are available to the equityholders and the value of the company is the present value of these operating earnings. If, on the other hand, a company is partially financed by debt, these operating earnings are split between the providers of capital: the equityholders and the debtholders. Under market equilibrium, the sum of the values of debt and equity in such a case should equal the value of the all-equity company. In other words, the value of a company is determined solely by its cash flows, not by the relative reliance on debt and equity capital.

This principle does not change the fact of the relative risks of leverage to debtholders versus equityholders. Adding leverage does increase the risk faced by the equityholders. In such a case, equityholders seek compensation for this extra risk by requiring a higher return. Indeed, in equilibrium, the increase in equity returns is exactly offset by increases in the risk and the associated increase in the required rate of return on equity, so that there is no change in the value of the company.[3]

Modigliani and Miller (MM) first illustrated the capital structure irrelevance proposition under the condition of no taxes:

> *MM Proposition I:*
>
> The market value of a company is not affected by the capital structure of the company.

In other words, the value of the company levered (V_L) is equal to the value unlevered (V_U), or $V_L = V_U$. A crucial implication of MM Proposition I is that the weighted average cost of capital for a company in the no-tax case is unaffected by its capital structure.

To understand this proposition, we can think about two companies with the same expected, perpetual cash flows and uncertainty and, hence, the same discount rate applied to value these cash flows. Even if the companies have different capital structures, these two companies must have the same present value using discounted cash flow models. If capital structure changes were to have any effect on a company's value, there would exist an arbitrage opportunity to make riskless profits.

In a perfect market, investors can substitute their own leverage for a company's leverage by borrowing or lending appropriate amounts in addition to holding shares of the company. Because this process is costless for investors (we assume perfect markets), a company's financial leverage should have no impact on its value. Therefore, a company's capital structure is irrelevant in perfect markets (which assume no taxes).

2.2 Proposition II without Taxes: Higher Financial Leverage Raises the Cost of Equity

Modigliani and Miller's second proposition focuses on the cost of capital of the company:

> *MM Proposition II:*
>
> The cost of equity is a linear function of the company's debt/equity ratio.

Assuming that financial distress has no costs and that debtholders have prior claim to assets and income relative to equityholders, the cost of debt is less than the cost of equity. According to this proposition, as the company increases its use of debt financing, the cost of equity rises. We know from MM Proposition I that the value of the company is unchanged and the weighted average cost of capital remains constant if the company changes its capital structure. What Proposition II then means is that the cost of equity increases in such a manner as to exactly offset the increased use of cheaper debt in order to maintain a constant WACC.

The risk of the equity depends on two factors: the risk of the company's operations (business risk) and the degree of financial leverage (financial risk). Business risk determines the cost of capital, whereas the capital structure determines financial risk.

The weighted average cost of capital, or r_{wacc}, *ignoring taxes*, is

$$r_{wacc} = \left(\frac{D}{V}\right)r_d + \left(\frac{E}{V}\right)r_e \tag{2}$$

---

[3] As a final point, in the absence of taxes, MM's capital structure irrelevance result holds whether debt is assumed to be risk-free (as MM assumed in their 1958 article) or risky, so long as there are no bankruptcy costs.

where

r_{wacc} = the weighted average cost of capital of the company

r_d = the before-tax marginal cost of debt capital, and is equal to the after-tax marginal cost of debt because there are no taxes by assumption

r_e = the marginal cost of equity capital

D = the market value of debt

E = the market value of equity

V = the value of the company, which is equal to $D + E$

Let us define r_0 as the cost of capital for a company financed only by equity (an "all-equity company"). Then, by MM Proposition I, $r_{wacc} = r_0$, so

$$r_{wacc} = \left(\frac{D}{V}\right)r_d + \left(\frac{E}{V}\right)r_e = r_0 \qquad (3)$$

Recalling that $D + E = V$ and using this to substitute for V, we can rearrange Equation 3 to solve for the cost of equity:

$$r_e = r_0 + (r_0 - r_d)\frac{D}{E} \qquad (4)$$

☆ r_0 = cost of equity for firm 100% equity-financed

Equation 4 is the precise expression for the cost of equity in MM Proposition II. As shown in Equation 4, the cost of equity is a linear function of the debt/equity ratio (D/E) with the intercept equal to r_0 and the slope coefficient equal to the positive quantity ($r_0 - r_d$). We know that ($r_0 - r_d$) is positive because the cost of equity must be an increasing function of the debt/equity ratio for WACC to be unchanged as the use of debt in financing is increased, as required by Proposition I. Thus, as the debt/equity ratio increases, the cost of equity capital also increases. See Exhibit 1 later in this section.

Consider the example of the Leverkin Company, which currently has an all-equity capital structure. Leverkin has an expected operating income of $5,000 and a cost of equity, which is also its WACC, of 10 percent. Adopting a common practice, we represent operating income by earnings before interest and taxes, EBIT. For simplicity, we will assume that the EBIT and other cash flows are perpetual. Let us suppose that Leverkin is planning to issue $15,000 in debt at a cost of 5 percent in order to buy back $15,000 worth of its equity.

Because there are no taxes and the EBIT is a perpetuity, we can compute the value of the all-equity Leverkin as the present value of its expected cash flows:

$$V = \frac{\text{EBIT}}{r_{wacc}} = \frac{\$5,000}{0.10} = \$50,000$$

Under MM Proposition I, because $V_L = V_U$, the value of Leverkin remains the same whether it is all-equity financed or has $15,000 of debt. When it issues the debt, Leverkin pays an interest charge of 5% on this debt. That is, Leverkin's interest payment is 0.05($15,000) = $750.

By MM Proposition II, the cost of Leverkin's equity when it has $15,000 debt and $50,000 − $15,000 = $35,000 equity is

$$r_e = 0.10 + (0.10 - 0.05)\frac{\$15,000}{\$35,000} \approx 0.12143 = 12.143\%$$

The value of Leverkin with $15,000 debt in its capital structure must equal the sum of the present value of cash flows to debtholders and equityholders. With $15,000 debt, Leverkin makes an interest payment of $750 to debtholders, leaving $5,000 − $750 = $4,250 for equityholders.

$$V = D + E = \frac{\$750}{0.05} + \frac{\$4,250}{0.12143} = \$15,000 + \$34,999.59 \approx \$50,000$$

It is straightforward to demonstrate that Leverkin's value remains at $50,000 at any level of debt.[4] We can also confirm, using Equation 3, that Leverkin's WACC with the new capital structure remains at 10% as required by Proposition I:

$$r_{wacc} = \left(\frac{\$15,000}{\$50,000}\right)0.05 + \left(\frac{\$35,000}{\$50,000}\right)0.12143 = 0.10 = 10\%$$

Just as we can express the beta of any investment portfolio as a market-value weighted average of the betas of the investments in that portfolio, we can express the systematic risk of each of the sources of a company's capital in a similar manner.[5] In other words, we can represent the systematic risk of the assets of the entire company as a weighted average of the systematic risk of the company's debt and equity:

$$\beta_a = \left(\frac{D}{V}\right)\beta_d + \left(\frac{E}{V}\right)\beta_e \qquad (5)$$

where β_a is the asset's systematic risk, or **asset beta**, β_d is the beta of debt, and β_e is the equity beta. The asset beta represents the amount of the assets' risk that is non-diversifiable (cannot be eliminated by holding those assets as part of a large, well-diversified portfolio).

According to Modigliani and Miller, the company's cost of capital does not depend on its capital structure but rather is determined by the business risk of the company. On the other hand, as the level of debt rises, the risk of the company defaulting on its debt increases. These costs are borne by the equityholders. So as the proportionate use of debt rises, the equity's beta, β_e, also rises. By reordering the formula of β_a to solve for β_e, we get

$$\beta_e = \beta_a + \left(\beta_a - \beta_d\right)\left(\frac{D}{E}\right) \qquad (6)$$

In the next section, we look at the decision to use debt financing given the taxes and market imperfections found in the real world.

2.3 Taxes, the Cost of Capital, and the Value of the Company

Taxes are the first practical consideration in modifying the results of the MM propositions. In the discussion below we will present MM Propositions I and II with taxes.

Because interest paid is deductible from income for tax purposes in most countries, the use of debt provides a tax shield that translates into savings that enhance the value of a company. Indeed, ignoring other practical realities of costs of financial distress and bankruptcy, the value of the company increases with increasing levels of debt. In effect, by making the interest costs deductible for income taxes, the government subsidizes companies' use of debt. The actual cost of debt is reduced by the level of the company's tax benefit:

After-tax cost of debt = Before-tax cost of debt × (1 – Marginal tax rate)

---

4 Note that this statement is true even with 100 percent debt financing because in that case, the debtholders are effectively the company's owners (equityholders).
5 Hamada (1972).

Modigliani and Miller show that, in the presence of corporate taxes,[6] the value of the company with debt is greater than that of the all-equity company by an amount equal to the tax rate multiplied by the value of the debt. That is, MM Proposition I with corporate taxes is:

$$V_L = V_U + tD \qquad\qquad (7)$$

where t is the marginal tax rate. The term tD is often referred to as the debt tax shield.

By introducing corporate tax, we adjust the weighted average cost of capital formula to reflect the impact of the tax benefit:

$$r_{wacc} = \left(\frac{D}{V}\right)r_d(1-t) + \left(\frac{E}{V}\right)r_e \qquad\qquad (8)$$

Because by Proposition I with taxes the value of a company with debt is greater than that of the same company without debt, *for the same level of operating income*, it must follow that the WACC for the company with debt *must be lower* than that for the all-equity company. If we continue to define r_0 as the cost of capital for an all-equity company, MM show that the cost of equity for the same company with debt is:

$$r_e = r_0 + (r_0 - r_d)(1-t)\frac{D}{E} \qquad\qquad (9) \quad \text{☆ Know this!}$$

This is MM Proposition II when there are corporate taxes.[7] Notice that the difference between Equation 9 and MM Proposition II in the no-tax case (Equation 4) is the presence of the term $(1-t)$. When t is not zero, the term $(1-t)$ is less than 1 and serves to lower the cost of leveraged equity when compared to the no-tax case.[8] That is, the cost of equity becomes greater as the company increases the amount of debt in its capital structure, but the cost of equity does not rise as fast as it does in the no-tax case. Equivalently, the slope coefficient is $(r_0 - r_d)(1-t)$, which is smaller than the slope coefficient $(r_0 - r_d)$ in the case of no taxes. As a consequence, the WACC for the leveraged company falls as debt increases, and overall company value increases. Therefore, if taxes are considered but financial distress and bankruptcy costs are not, debt financing is highly advantageous, and in the extreme, a company's optimal capital structure is all debt.

Let us return to the example of the Leverkin Company, which is currently all-equity, has an EBIT of $5,000, and a WACC, which is also its cost of equity, of 10%. As before, Leverkin is planning to issue $15,000 of debt in order to buy back an equivalent amount of equity. Now, however, Leverkin pays corporate taxes at a rate of 25%.

Because Leverkin must pay taxes, the after-tax cash flow available to its shareholders is earnings before taxes, EBT, times $(1-t)$, or $EBT(1-t)$. $EBT(1-t)$ is the same here as $EBIT(1-t)$ because $I = 0$. If we continue to assume perpetual cash flows, the value of the all-equity, or unlevered, Leverkin is:

$$V_U = \frac{EBT(1-t)}{WACC} = \frac{\$5,000(1-0.25)}{0.10} = \$37,500$$

☆ value of unleveraged firm
EBT = EBIT if no debt

Note that the value of Leverkin when there are corporate taxes is less than its value in the no-tax case. This is simply because a new claimant on Leverkin's cash flows, the government through its ability to impose taxes, has entered the picture.

Let us now see what happens to Leverkin's value when it issues $15,000 in debt and buys back stock. According to MM Proposition I, when there are corporate taxes, i.e., Equation 7,

---

6 We continue to assume that there are no personal taxes.

7 The derivation of Equation 9 can be found in more advanced texts. See, for example, Copeland, Weston, and Shastri (2005).

8 *Leveraged* and *levered* as used in discussion of capital structure are synonyms. Both terms are commonly used.

$$V_L = V_U + tD = \$37,500 + 0.25(\$15,000) = \$41,250$$

Because the value of the debt is \$15,000, the value of the equity (after the buy-back) must be (\$41,250 − \$15,000) = 26,250. According to MM Proposition II with corporate taxes (Equation 9), the cost of the levered equity is:

$$r_e = 0.10 + (0.10 - 0.05)(1 - 0.25)\frac{\$15,000}{\$26,250} = 0.12143 = 12.143\%$$

Because the value of the company must equal the present value of cash flows to debt and to equity,

$$V_L = D + E = \frac{r_d D}{r_d} + \frac{(EBIT - r_d D)(1 - t)}{r_e}$$

$$= \frac{\$750}{0.05} + \frac{(\$5,000 - \$750)(1 - 0.25)}{0.12143} \approx \$41,250$$

This is the value of the company as given by MM Proposition I. As a further check, using Equation 8, the WACC for the levered Leverkin is:

$$r_{wacc} = \frac{\$15,000}{\$41,250}(0.05)(1 - 0.25) + \frac{\$26,250}{\$41,250}(0.12143)$$

$$= 0.09091 = 9.091\%$$

As expected, this is lower than the unlevered WACC of 10%. Because after taxes are paid, whatever is left of the cash flows can be claimed by debtholders and equityholders, we must also have:

$$V_L = \frac{EBIT(1 - t)}{WACC} = \frac{\$5,000(1 - 0.25)}{0.09091} \approx \$41,250$$

We can see the effect of taxes on the cost of capital in Exhibit 1. Here, we see that if there are no taxes, as shown in Panel B, the cost of capital is constant at $r_{wacc} = r_0$. If, on the other hand, interest is tax deductible, the cost of capital declines for ever-increasing use of debt financing, as shown in Panel C.

Exhibit 1　　**Modigliani and Miller Propositions**

Panel A. Value of the Company and Cost of Capital for Propositions without and with Taxes

	Without Taxes	With Taxes
Proposition I	$V_L = V_U$	$V_L = V_U + tD$
Proposition II	$r_e = r_0 + (r_0 - r_d)\frac{D}{E}$	$r_e = r_0 + (r_0 - r_d)(1 - t)\frac{D}{E}$

Panel B. Costs of Capital if There Are No Taxes

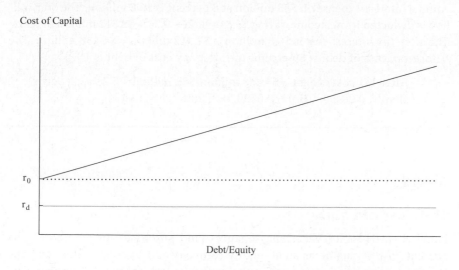

Panel C. Costs of Capital if There Are Taxes

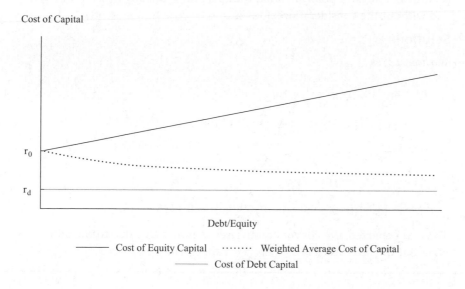

——— Cost of Equity Capital   ⋯⋯⋯ Weighted Average Cost of Capital
————— Cost of Debt Capital

EXAMPLE 1

The After-Tax Cost of Debt

Payment People, a provider of temporary accounting workers, is considering an $85 million acquisition. The company could raise capital by selling either debt or equity. If the company finances the acquisition with debt at 8 percent interest, what is the after-tax cost of issuing debt if the company's marginal tax rate is 34 percent?

Solution:

Annual interest expense on $85 million at 8 percent is $6.8 million. The $6.8 million is deducted from income, saving $6.8 million × 0.34 = $2.312 million in taxes. The after-tax interest cost is $6.8 million − $2.312 million = $4.488 million. The before-tax cost of debt is 8 percent; the after-tax cost of debt is

> After-tax cost of debt = $4.488 million/$85 million = 5.28%, or, equivalently, 0.08(1 − 0.34) = 0.0528, or 5.28%

EXAMPLE 2

The Cost of Equity

Hotel chain Hostales Vacaciones finances land purchases for new hotels. Its current cost of capital, as an all-equity company, is 13 percent. The company is opening ten new hotels and is considering issuing debt at 9 percent for its financing needs. If it issues debt, its debt-to-equity ratio would be 0.5. The corporate tax rate is 32 percent. What would be the company's cost of equity with and without the consideration of taxes?

Solution:

Without taxes

$$r_e = r_0 + (r_0 - r_d)\left(\frac{D}{E}\right)$$

$$r_e = 0.13 + \left[(0.13 - 0.09)(0.5)\right] = 0.15, \text{ or } 15\%$$

With taxes

$$r_e = r_0 + (r_0 - r_d)(1 - t)\frac{D}{E}$$

$$r_e = 0.13 + \left[(0.13 - 0.09)(1 - 0.32)(0.5)\right] = 0.1436, \text{ or } 14.36\%$$

Thus, as expected, the cost of equity rises in both cases due to the addition of debt, but the increase is less when taxes are considered.

Miller (1977) introduced another aspect into the analysis of the tax benefits from the use of debt financing. He argued that if investors face different tax rates on dividend and interest income for their personal taxes, this situation may reduce the advantage of debt financing somewhat. If investors face a higher personal rate of tax on income from debt investments relative to stock investments, they will demand a higher return on debt—driving up the cost of debt to the company.[9] Thus, in the Miller model, whether or not financing with debt adds value to the company depends on the corporate tax rate, the personal tax rate on interest income, and the personal tax rate on dividend income. It is therefore possible in the Miller model, depending on the levels of the various tax rates, for debt to add value, lower value, or to have no effect on value.

---

9 It can be argued that there is a higher personal tax on debt income because debt instruments typically provide investors with taxable interest periodically, whereas taxable income from stock investments could, conceivably, be lower because the tax consequences of investing in non-dividend-paying stocks are deferred until the stock is sold.

In practice, however, the value of a levered company is affected by more than the tax issues surrounding the use of debt. The analysis gets more complicated once we introduce factors such as the cost of financial distress, agency costs, and asymmetric information. We address these additional factors next.

2.4 Costs of Financial Distress

The downside of operating and financial leverage is that earnings are magnified downward during economic slowdowns. Lower or negative earnings put companies under stress, and this **financial distress** adds costs—both explicit and implicit—to a company. Even before taking the drastic step of filing for bankruptcy, companies under stress may lose customers, creditors, suppliers, and valuable employees to more secure competitors.

EXAMPLE 3

Costs of Financial Distress

Enron is an extreme example of the loss of value due to financial distress. Up until its demise in 2001, Enron was a large player in the natural gas industry. Events leading up to the eventual bankruptcy protection filing caused investors to flee the common stock as creditors refused new lending. Enron went from a favored to a disdained company in record time.

According to a company presentation made ten days after its 2 December 2001 bankruptcy filing, the company's common stock price plunged from $80 per share to $1 per share prior to the bankruptcy announcement, losing $25 billion in market value.[10] This loss in value was due to a number of factors, including:

- investors' and creditors' lost confidence;
- financial market reaction from a lack of access to capital markets;
- current maturities greatly exceeding operating cash flow because of the inability to refinance debt;
- nervous trade creditors;
- Dynegy pulling out of the merger on 28 November 2001; and
- the bond ratings downgrade on 28 November 2001.

Cash bankruptcy expenses listed in the bankruptcy filing documents totaled $17.3 million, though the bankruptcy costs including accountants', advisors', and lawyers' fees were over $500 million by November of 2003.[11]

The expected cost of financial distress is composed of two key ingredients: 1) the costs of financial distress and bankruptcy, in the event they happen, and 2) the probability that financial distress and bankruptcy happen. We can classify the costs of financial distress into direct and indirect costs. Direct costs of financial distress include the actual cash expenses associated with the bankruptcy process, such as legal and administrative fees. Indirect costs of financial distress include forgone investment opportunities, impaired ability to conduct business, and agency costs associated with the debt during periods in which the company is near or in bankruptcy.

---

10 Enron Corporation Organizational Meeting, 12 December 2001.
11 *Houston Business Journal*, 19 November 2003.

Companies whose assets have a ready secondary market have lower costs associated with financial distress. Companies with relatively marketable tangible assets, such as airlines, shipping companies, and steel manufacturers, incur lower costs from financial distress because such assets are usually more readily marketable. On the other hand, companies with few tangible assets, such as high-tech growth companies, pharmaceutical companies, information technology companies, and others in the service industry, have less to liquidate and therefore have a higher cost associated with financial distress.

The probability of bankruptcy increases as the degree of leverage increases. The probability of bankruptcy for a given company depends on how the fixed costs of debt service interact with the instability of the business environment and the reserves available to the company to delay bankruptcy. In other words, the probability of bankruptcy depends, in part, on the company's business risk. Other factors that affect the likelihood of bankruptcy include the company's corporate governance structure and the management of the company.

2.5 Agency Costs

Agency costs are the costs associated with the fact that all public companies and the larger private companies are managed by non-owners. Agency costs are the incremental costs arising from conflicts of interest when an agent makes decisions for a principal. In the context of a corporation, agency costs arise from conflicts of interest between managers, shareholders, and bondholders. In the following, "perquisite consumption" refers to items that executives may legally authorize for themselves that have a cost to shareholders, such as subsidized dining, a corporate jet fleet, chauffeured limousines, and so forth.

The smaller the stake that managers have in the company, the less is their share in bearing the cost of excessive perquisite consumption or not giving their best efforts in running the company. The costs arising from this conflict of interest have been called the **agency costs of equity**. Given that outside shareholders are aware of this conflict, they will take actions to minimize the loss, such as requiring audited financial statements. The net agency costs of equity therefore have three components:[12]

1 **Monitoring costs**. These are the costs borne by owners to monitor the management of the company and include the expenses of the annual report, board of director expenses, and the cost of the annual meeting.

2 **Bonding costs**. These are the costs borne by management to assure owners that they are working in the owners' best interest. These include the implicit cost of noncompete employment contracts and the explicit cost of insurance to guarantee performance.

3 **Residual loss**. This consists of the costs that are incurred even when there is sufficient monitoring and bonding, because monitoring and bonding mechanisms are not perfect.

The better a company is governed, the lower the agency costs. Good governance practices translate into higher shareholder value, reflecting the fact that managers' interests are better aligned with those of shareholders. Additionally, agency theory predicts that a reduction in net agency costs of equity results from an increase in the use of debt versus equity. That is, there are equity-agency cost savings associated with the use of debt. Similarly, the more financially leveraged a company is, the less freedom managers have to either take on more debt or unwisely spend cash. This is

---

12 Jensen and Meckling (1976) provide this breakdown of agency costs.

the foundation of Michael Jensen's **free cash flow hypothesis**.[13] According to Jensen's hypothesis, higher debt levels discipline managers by forcing them to manage the company efficiently so the company can make its interest and principal payments and by reducing the company's free cash flow and thus management's opportunities to misuse cash.[14]

2.6 Costs of Asymmetric Information

Asymmetric information (an unequal distribution of information) arises from the fact that managers have more information about a company's performance and prospects (including future investment opportunities) than do outsiders such as owners and creditors. Whereas all companies have a certain level of asymmetric information, companies with comparatively high asymmetry in information are those with complex products like high-tech companies, companies with little transparency in financial accounting information, or companies with lower levels of institutional ownership. Providers of both debt and equity capital demand higher returns from companies with higher asymmetry in information because they have a greater likelihood of agency costs.

Some degree of asymmetric information always exists because investors never know as much as managers and other insiders. Consequently, investors often closely watch manager behavior for insight into insider opinions on the company's future prospects. Being aware of this scrutiny, managers take into account how their actions might be interpreted by outsiders. The signaling model of capital structure suggests there may be a hierarchy ("pecking order") to the selection of methods for financing new investments.

The **pecking order theory**, developed by Myers and Majluf (1984), suggests that managers choose methods of financing according to a hierarchy that gives first preference to methods with the least potential information content (internally generated funds) and lowest preference to the form with the greatest potential information content (public equity offerings).[15] In brief, managers prefer internal financing; and if internal financing is insufficient, managers next prefer debt, and finally equity. Another implication of the work of Myers and Majluf is that financial managers tend to issue equity when they believe the stock is overvalued but are reluctant to issue equity if they believe the stock is undervalued. Thus, additional issuance of stock is often interpreted by investors as a negative signal.

We can read the signals that managers provide in their choice of financing method. For example, commitments to fixed payments, such as dividends and debt service payments, may be interpreted as the company's management having confidence in the company's future prospects of making payments. Such signals are considered too costly for poorly performing companies to afford. Alternatively, the signal of raising money at the top of the pecking order and issuing equity at the bottom of the pecking order holds other clues. If, for instance, the company's cost of capital increases after an equity issuance, we may interpret this effect as an indication that management needed capital beyond what comes cheaply; in other words, this is a negative signal regarding the company's future prospects.

---

13 Jensen (1986).

14 Harvey, Lins, and Roper (2004) observe that this discipline is especially important in emerging markets, in which there is a tendency to overinvest.

15 In general, public equity offerings are very closely scrutinized because investors are typically skeptical that existing owners would share ownership of a company with a great future with other investors.

2.7 The Optimal Capital Structure According to the Static Trade-Off Theory

When companies make decisions about financial leverage, they must weigh the value-enhancing effects of leverage from the tax deductibility of interest against the value-reducing impact of the costs of financial distress or bankruptcy, agency costs of debt, and asymmetric information. Putting together all the pieces of the theory of Modigliani and Miller, along with the taxes, costs of financial distress, debt agency costs, and asymmetric information, we see that as financial leverage is increased, there comes a point beyond which further increases in value from value-enhancing effects are offset completely by value-reducing effects. This point is known as the **optimal capital structure**. In other words, the optimal capital structure is that capital structure at which the value of the company is maximized.

Considering only the tax shield provided by debt and the costs of financial distress, the expression for the value of a leveraged company becomes

$$V_L = V_U + tD - PV(\text{Costs of financial distress})$$ **(10)**

Equation 10 represents the **static trade-off theory of capital structure**. It results in an optimal capital structure such that debt constitutes less than 100 percent of a company's capital structure. We diagram this optimum in Exhibit 2.

Exhibit 2	Trade-off Theory with Taxes and Cost of Financial Distress

Panel A. Value of the Company and the Debt/Equity Ratio

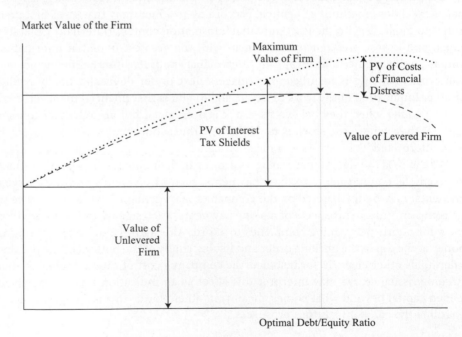

Exhibit 2	(Continued)

Panel B. Cost of Capital and the Debt/Equity Ratio

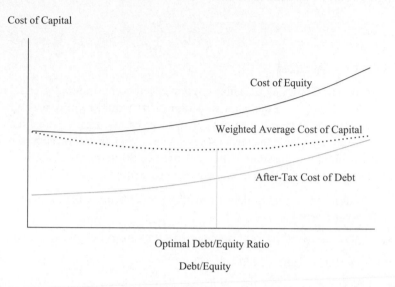

The static trade-off theory of capital structure is based on balancing the expected costs from financial distress against the tax benefits of debt service payments, as shown in Panel A of Exhibit 2. Unlike the Modigliani and Miller proposition of no optimal capital structure, or a structure with almost all debt when the tax shield is considered, static trade-off theory puts forth an optimal capital structure with an optimal proportion of debt. Optimal debt usage is found at the point where any additional debt would cause the costs of financial distress to increase by a greater amount than the benefit of the additional tax shield.

We cannot say precisely at which level of debt financing a company reaches its optimal capital structure. The optimal capital structure depends on the company's business risk, combined with its tax situation, corporate governance, and financial accounting information transparency, among other factors. However, what we can say, based on this theory, is that a company should consider a number of factors, including its business risk and the possible costs of financial distress, in determining its capital structure.

A company's management uses these tools to decide the level of debt appropriate for the company. The tax benefit from the deductibility of the interest expense on debt must be balanced against the risk associated with the use of debt. The extent of financial leverage used should thus depend on owners' and management's appetites for risk, as well as the stability of the company's business environment. Indeed, as we show in Panel B of Exhibit 2, as the proportion of debt in a business rises, the costs of both debt and equity are likely to rise to offset the higher risks associated with higher levels of debt. These cost increases reduce or even negate the cost savings due to the greater use of debt, the cheaper source of financing. The result is a U-shaped weighted average cost of capital curve.

When the company recognizes its most appropriate or best capital structure, it may adopt this as its **target capital structure**. Because management may exploit short-term opportunities in one or another financing source and because market-value fluctuations continuously affect the company's capital structure, a company's capital structure at any point in time may differ from the target. In addition, it may be impractical (due to market conditions making it inadvisable to raise capital) and expensive (because of flotation costs) for a company to continuously maintain its target structure. Nevertheless, so long as the assumptions of the analysis and the target are unchanged, analysts and management should focus on the target capital structure.

EXAMPLE 4

Financial Leverage and the Cost of Capital

The (hypothetical) Singapore-based Chuang Ho Company provides copper-wired components for cellular telephone manufacturers globally. Chuang Ho is going to establish a subsidiary that would require assets of SGD 3 billion, and wants to select a capital structure that would minimize its cost of capital for the subsidiary. Alex Ahn, the company's CFO, wants to evaluate a target leverage structure and uses a scenario approach to evaluate the cost of capital for the present 0 percent debt and possible 50 percent debt or 80 percent debt. Chuang Ho's marginal tax rate is 35 percent. Ahn has gathered the following information regarding costs of capital:

- The marginal cost of equity rises with increased levels of debt from 13.5 percent (no debt) to 18 percent (50 percent debt), to 28 percent (80 percent debt).

- The marginal cost of borrowing is 12 percent on 50 percent debt, and 18 percent on 80 percent debt.

Which capital structure is expected to have the lowest cost of capital?

Solution:

First, calculate the cost of capital under the three scenarios:

Exhibit 3	Chuang Ho Subsidiary		
	Leverage		
	No Debt	**50% Debt**	**80% Debt**
Assets	$3,000,000,000	$3,000,000,000	$3,000,000,000
Debt	$0	$1,500,000,000	$2,400,000,000
Equity	$3,000,000,000	$1,500,000,000	$600,000,000
Debt/Equity ratio	0	1	4
Proportion of debt	0%	50%	80%
Proportion of equity	100%	50%	20%
Before-tax cost of debt	—	12%	18%
Cost of equity	13.5%	18%	28%
After-tax cost of debt = $r_d(1-t)$	—	7.8%	11.7%
Weighted average cost of capital	13.5%	12.9%	14.96%

Of the three capital structures that we are evaluating, the cost of capital is lowest for 50 percent debt.

PRACTICAL ISSUES IN CAPITAL STRUCTURE POLICY

Although capital structure theories should serve to inform an analyst's decision-making process in valuing a company, there are several practical aspects of capital structure to consider. These include the evaluation of company credit-worthiness by independent agencies, an understanding of the industry to which the company belongs, and an analysis of the legal, institutional, and macroeconomic environment in which the company operates. We consider these factors next.

3.1 Debt Ratings

Debt ratings are an important consideration in the practical management of leverage. As leverage rises, rating agencies tend to lower the ratings of the company's debt to reflect the higher credit risk resulting from the increasing leverage. Lower ratings signify higher risk to both equity and debt capital providers, who therefore demand higher returns.

Most large companies pay one or more rating services to rate their bonds. Debt issues are rated for credit-worthiness by credit rating agencies. Among credit rating agencies with status as "Nationally Recognized Statistical Rating Organizations" from the U.S. Securities and Exchange Commission (SEC), the three largest are Moody's, Standard & Poor's, and Fitch. Rating agencies perform a financial analysis of the company's ability to pay the promised cash flows, as well as an analysis of the bond's indenture, the set of complex legal documents associated with the issuance of debt instruments.

Exhibit 4	Bond Ratings by Moody's, Standard & Poor's, and Fitch		
	Moody's	**Standard & Poor's**	**Fitch**
Highest quality	Aaa	AAA	AAA
High quality	Aa	AA	AA
Upper medium grade	A	A	A
Medium grade	Baa	BBB	BBB
Speculative	Ba	BB	BB
Highly speculative	B	B	B
Substantial risk	Caa	CCC	CCC
Extremely speculative	Ca		
Possibly in default	C		
Default		D	DDD-D

Rows 1–4 are bracketed as **Investment grade**; rows 5–10 are bracketed as **Speculative grade**.

These agencies evaluate a wealth of information about the issuer and the bond, including the bond's characteristics and indenture, and provide investors with an assessment of the company's ability to pay the interest and principal on the bond as promised. We provide the bond rating classifications in Exhibit 4. Although there is significant agreement in ratings among the three major services, some disagreements do occur. For example, Standard & Poor's lowered the credit rating of General Motors to speculative grade in early May of 2005, but Moody's did not do so until late August of 2005.

In practice, most managers consider the company's debt rating in their policies regarding capital structure. Managers must be mindful of their company's bond ratings because the cost of capital is tied closely to bond ratings. Consider the difference in the yields on Aaa and Baa rated corporate bonds, as shown in Exhibit 5. Typically, a difference of 100 basis points exists between the yields of Aaa and Baa bonds, though this spread widens in economic recessions.[16] The cost of debt increases significantly when a bond's rating drops from investment grade to speculative grade. For example, when the rating of General Motors' unsecured 7.2 percent bond maturing in 2011 was changed by Moody's from Baa to Ba, the bond's price fell by over 7.5 percent and its yield rose from 7.541 percent to 9.364 percent.

Exhibit 5	Yields on Aaa and Baa Rated Corporate Bonds, 1984–2005

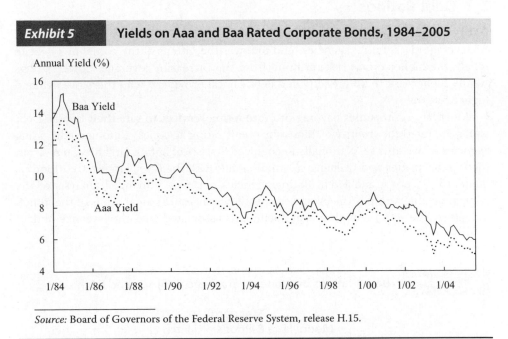

Source: Board of Governors of the Federal Reserve System, release H.15.

3.2 Evaluating Capital Structure Policy

In evaluating a company's capital structure, the financial analyst must look at the capital structure of the company over time, the capital structure of competitors that have similar business risk, and company-specific factors, such as the quality of corporate governance, that may affect agency costs, among other factors.[17] The financial analyst is not privy to the company's target capital structure but rather can evaluate the company's ability to handle its financial obligations and the potential role of costs of financial distress in determining how much financial leverage a company can handle.

Several practical considerations are important in this regard, such as the industry in which a company operates, the volatility of the company's cash flows, and its need for financial flexibility. Regulatory aspects can also play a role. For example, companies in the utility industry have relatively stable cash flows because they have a natural monopoly. Such companies usually also have a low degree of information asymmetry. As a result, utility companies tend to have much more debt than companies in other

---

16 The Board of Governors of the Federal Reserve System H.15 series of Aaa and Baa corporate yields shows an average spread of 119 basis points between Aaa and Baa rated bonds, on average, from 1919 to mid-2005. The largest spread occurred in 1932, with 565 bps, and the lowest spread occurred in 1966, with a 32 bp difference.

17 Good corporate governance should lower the net agency costs of equity.

industries. Similarly, the guarantee afforded by deposit insurance in the United States, for example, allows banks in the U.S. to have debt levels in excess of 80 percent of assets. In contrast, companies in the technology or pharmaceutical industries tend to have little or no debt for the following reasons: 1) they have few tangible assets (their assets are chiefly human capital, patents, ideas, etc.), 2) there is a high degree of information asymmetry (such companies spend a lot on research and development and are very secretive about their products), and 3) they have a great need for financial flexibility (they need to respond quickly to competitive and other changes in their operating environment).

A common goal of capital structure decisions is to finance at the lowest cost of capital. Analysts can use a scenario approach to assess this point for a particular company, starting with the current cost of capital for a company and considering various changes to answer the following questions:

1   What happens to the cost of capital as the debt ratio is changed?

2   At what debt ratio is the cost of capital minimized and company value maximized?

3   To what extent are stock price and company value affected when market conditions make it difficult or impossible for a company to maintain its optimal capital structure?

3.3 Leverage in an International Setting

Modigliani and Miller told us that under several conditions the market value of a company is independent of its capital structure. However, we know that a company's capital structure is indeed relevant in the real world because of the effects of taxation, the costs of financial distress, and agency costs. The static trade-off theory suggests that the optimal level of leverage should be the level at which the value of the company is maximized; this is the level of debt financing at which any additional debt increases the costs of financial distress by an amount greater than the benefit from interest deductibility.

A company's capital structure largely depends on company-specific factors such as the probability of bankruptcy, profitability, quality and structure of assets, and growth opportunities. Beyond these factors, the company's industry affiliation, as well as the characteristics of the country where the company operates, can also account for differences in capital structure.

The general business environment differs from one country to another, and researchers show that country-specific factors have explanatory power similar to or even greater than that of the company's industry affiliation in determining a company's capital structure.[18] Comparing financial leverage indicators of a U.S.-based energy company and a Japanese energy company is not meaningful if we do not take country-specific differences into account. Tradition, tax policy, and regulation may largely explain the different degrees of leverage in the two countries.

In examining the capital structure and debt maturity structure of corporations in an international context, researchers generally find that differences in the capital structures exist between developed and emerging markets, as well as across the developed countries. Moreover, the debt maturity structure—another important capital structure decision—also tends to vary across the international setting. Therefore, when analysts focus on the capital structure of companies in an international setting,

---

18 See, for example, Fan, Titman, and Twite (2004).

they must consider both the relative use of debt and the maturity structure of debt. In fact, short-term and long-term debt ratios follow very different patterns in an international comparison:

- Taking total debt into account, companies in France, Italy, and Japan tend to be more highly levered than companies in the United States and the United Kingdom.

- Focusing on the use of long-term debt, on the other hand, a different picture emerges: North American companies tend to use more long-term debt than do Japanese companies.

- Companies in developed markets typically use more long-term debt and tend to have higher long-term debt to total debt ratios compared to their emerging market peers.

Beyond the pure comparison of the capital structures, it is equally or even more important to identify and understand the country-specific factors that explain the cross-country differences.[19] Three major types of factors may be used to explain most capital structure differences in an international comparison:

1 *Institutional and legal environment*: These factors represent the legal and regulatory environment in which companies operate, as well as the requirements related to financial reporting. These institutional factors—including taxation, accounting standards, and even the presence or lack of corruption—may affect a company's optimal capital structure.

2 *Financial markets and banking sector*: These factors include characteristics of the banking sector, as well as the size and activity of the financial markets. Financial institutions are crucial for companies' access to financing.

3 *Macroeconomic environment*: These factors capture the general economic and business environment, addressing the influence of economic growth and inflation on the capital structure.

3.3.1 *Institutional and Legal Environment*

Taxation, financial legislation, the content of laws (e.g., bankruptcy law), and the quality of enforcement all differ from one country to another. These differences may influence the capital structures of companies and explain many of the differences that we observe across countries.

The apparent conflict of interest between a company's management and outside investors has already been addressed as the agency problem. This problem is, in fact, one of the key determinants of a company's ability to obtain capital; hence, agency costs are one of the major factors determining the capital structure. This conflict may be mitigated by carefully prepared contracts. The quality of investors' legal protections depends on both the content and the enforcement of the contracts and laws. As a result, we expect to see higher financial leverage in those countries that have weaker legal systems. Further, in countries with weaker legal systems, we expect a greater use of short-term debt financing versus long-term debt financing. Researchers find that companies operating in countries with an efficient legal system tend to use more long-term debt than short-term debt and exhibit lower leverage than comparable companies in countries with weaker legal systems.

---

19 We should note that conclusions drawn in different studies are not always consistent with each other. The results of empirical studies, in fact, may depend on several factors, such as the set of countries and companies taken into the data sample, the analyzed historical period, the hypotheses that the researchers intended to test, and even the definition of leverage that they considered.

Some researchers assume that legal systems based on common law offer external capital providers (both equity and debt providers) better protection compared to the legal systems of civil-law countries. Common law originated in England and is also followed in other countries, such as the United States, Canada, Australia, New Zealand, Singapore, India, and Malaysia. Civil law, on the other hand, has origins going back to ancient Rome; the countries of continental Europe and most of the rest of the world have legal systems based on this tradition. Researchers find mixed and limited evidence that companies operating in common-law countries tend to have longer debt maturity structures compared to their peers in civil-law countries, and use less debt and more equity in their capital structure.

Similar to the rationale described in the case of legal system efficiency, a high level of information asymmetry between insiders and outsiders encourages a greater use of debt relative to equity, as well as a greater reliance on short-term debt than on long-term debt in the capital structure. This is likely due to the fact that enforcing the debt contract is easier than enforcing the less clearly contracted shareholders' rights. Auditors and financial analysts can help reduce information asymmetries and increase the level of transparency.[20] Researchers confirm that the presence of auditors and analysts is associated with lower financial leverage. The importance of auditors is usually strongest in emerging markets, whereas the presence of analysts is more important in developed markets.

As we discussed earlier, taxes affect the capital structure decision by lowering the cost of debt financing to the issuer in those jurisdictions in which interest expense is tax deductible. In the absence of debt agency costs and bankruptcy costs, the benefit from the tax deductibility of interest encourages companies to use debt financing instead of equity financing. However, if dividend income is taxed at lower rates than interest income, some of the advantage of debt versus equity financing may be reduced from the corporate perspective because the price at which equity can be sold should reflect that advantage. Taxes are an important factor in a company's capital structure decision.

Researchers find mixed results on the effect of the corporate tax rate on capital structures, but they find that personal tax rates do matter. Because the tax treatment of dividends differs across countries, researchers can examine the importance of different tax treatments of dividend income.[21] They find that companies in countries that have lower tax rates on dividend income also have less debt in their capital structures.

3.3.2 *Financial Markets and the Banking Sector*

The size, activity, and liquidity of capital markets are crucial for corporations' access to capital. Several researchers have analyzed the impact of capital markets' characteristics on companies' capital structures. Some find that liquid and active capital markets affect companies' debt maturity structure. Specifically, they find that companies in countries that have liquid and active capital markets tend to use more long-term (as opposed to short-term) debt with longer maturity (30-year maturity is preferred to 15-year maturity). Researchers attribute this finding to the heightened external monitoring of companies by market participants in active markets.[22]

The banking sector is one of the primary sources of funds for the corporate sector in many countries, and its role is especially significant in countries that do not have a corporate bond market. The importance of the banking sector relative to the capital markets can vary from one country to another, however. Countries with a common-law tradition, where the shareholders' rights are stronger, tend to be more market-based, whereas civil-law countries tend to be more bank-based. Because the relationship

---

20 Fan et al. (2003).
21 Fan et al. (2003).
22 See Demirguc-Kunt and Maksimovic (1998).

between a bank and a company is stronger and closer than between a company and a bondholder, banks can handle information asymmetries more efficiently. This effect may partly explain why civil-law countries are more bank-oriented.

However, researchers' findings are mixed regarding the effect of the banking system. Some researchers claim that banks have no effect on companies' financial leverage and that the difference between the bank-oriented and market-oriented countries is more reflected by the relative importance of public financing (i.e., stock and bonds) and private financing (i.e., bank loans).[23] On the other hand, some researchers find that companies in bank-based countries exhibit higher financial leverage compared to those that operate in market-based countries.[24]

The presence of institutional investors may also affect the companies' capital structure choice. Some institutional investors may have preferred debt maturities ("preferred habitats"), and this preference may affect companies' debt maturity structure. Insurance companies and pension plans, for example, may prefer investing in long-term debt securities in order to match the interest rate risk of their long-term liabilities. Researchers find limited results regarding the influence of preferred habitats; companies in countries that have more institutional investors in their markets tend to have more long-term debt and somewhat lower debt-to-equity ratios.[25]

3.3.3 *Macroeconomic Environment*

Inflation is a widely recognized macroeconomic indicator. High inflation has a negative impact on both the level of debt financing and the use of long-maturity debt.[26] Companies in higher-inflation countries usually exhibit lower levels of financial leverage, rely more on equity financing, and have a shorter debt maturity structure compared to their peers in lower-inflation countries.

Researchers have also found that the growth in gross domestic product is associated with longer debt maturity in developed markets. In addition, researchers focusing on developing countries find that companies in countries with high growth rely more on equity financing.[27]

3.3.4 *Conclusions*

Financial analysts must consider country-specific factors when analyzing and comparing companies that operate in different countries. We have summarized these factors in Exhibit 6.

Exhibit 6	Country-Specific Factors and Their Assumed Impacts on the Companies' Capital Structure		
Country-Specific Factor	**If a Country**	**. . . Then D/E Ratio Is Potentially**	**. . . And Debt Maturity Is Potentially**
Institutional framework			
Legal system efficiency	Is more efficient	Lower	Longer
Legal system origin	Has common law as opposed to civil law	Lower	Longer
Information intermediaries	Has auditors and analysts	Lower	Longer
Taxation	Has taxes that favor equity	Lower	

---

23 Rajan (1995).

24 See, for example, Claessens, Djankov, and Nevova (2001).

25 See Fan et al. and Domowitz, Glen, and Madhavan (2000).

26 Demirguc-Kunt and Maksimovic (1999), Domowitz et al., and Fan et al.

27 See Domowitz et al.

Exhibit 6	(Continued)		

Country-Specific Factor	If a Country	. . . Then D/E Ratio Is Potentially	. . . And Debt Maturity Is Potentially
Banking system, financial markets			
Equity and bond markets	Has active bond and stock markets		Longer
Bank-based or market-based country	Has a bank-based financial system	Higher	
Investors	Has large institutional investors	Lower	Longer
Macroeconomic environment			
Inflation	Has high inflation	Lower	Shorter
Growth	Has high GDP growth	Lower	Longer

These factors include the differences in the business and legal environments in other countries, taxes, and macroeconomic factors, among others. Companies' optimal capital structures may differ simply as a consequence of these many country-specific differences. In addition to presenting challenges for international financial and credit analysis, these international differences in debt ratios present some challenges in developing debt policies for the foreign subsidiaries of multinational companies. Theory provides little guidance, and corporate practices in this area seem to vary widely.

SUMMARY

In this reading, we have reviewed theories of capital structure and considered practical aspects that an analyst should examine when making investment decisions.

- The goal of the capital structure decision is to determine the financial leverage that maximizes the value of the company (or minimizes the weighted average cost of capital).

- In the Modigliani and Miller theory developed without taxes, capital structure is irrelevant and has no effect on company value.

- The deductibility of interest lowers the cost of debt and the cost of capital for the company as a whole. Adding the tax shield provided by debt to the Modigliani and Miller framework suggests that the optimal capital structure is all debt.

- In the Modigliani and Miller propositions with and without taxes, increasing a company's relative use of debt in the capital structure increases the risk for equity providers and, hence, the cost of equity capital.

- When there are bankruptcy costs, a high debt ratio increases the risk of bankruptcy.

- Using more debt in a company's capital structure reduces the net agency costs of equity.

- The costs of asymmetric information increase as more equity is used versus debt, suggesting the pecking order theory of leverage, in which new equity issuance is the least preferred method of raising capital.

- According to the static trade-off theory of capital structure, in choosing a capital structure, a company balances the value of the tax benefit from deductibility of interest with the present value of the costs of financial distress. At the optimal target capital structure, the incremental tax shield benefit is exactly offset by the incremental costs of financial distress.

- A company may identify its target capital structure, but its capital structure at any point in time may not be equal to its target for many reasons, including that management may exploit tactical opportunities in financing sources, market-value fluctuations in its securities, or just be unable to maintain the capital structure due to market conditions.

- Many companies have goals for maintaining a certain credit rating, and these goals are influenced by the relative costs of debt financing among the different rating classes.

- In evaluating a company's capital structure, the financial analyst must look at the capital structure of the company over time, the capital structure of competitors that have similar business risk, and company-specific factors, such as the quality of corporate governance, that may affect agency costs, among other factors.

- Good corporate governance and accounting transparency should lower the net agency costs of equity.

- When comparing capital structures of companies in different countries, an analyst must consider a variety of characteristics that might differ and affect both the typical capital structure and the debt maturity structure. The major characteristics fall into three categories: institutional and legal environment, financial markets and banking sector, and macroeconomic environment.

REFERENCES

Claessens, Stijn, Simeon Djankov, and Titiana Nenova. 2001. "Corporate Risk around the World." *Financial Crises in Emerging Markets*. Edited by Reuven Glick, Ramon Moreno, and Mark Speigel. New York: Cambridge University Press.

Copeland, Thomas E.J. Fred Weston, and Kuldeep Shastri. 2005. *Financial Theory and Corporate Policy*, 4th edition. Boston: Pearson/Addison Wesley.

Demirguc-Kunt, Asli, and Voljislav Maksimovic. 1998. "Law, Finance, and Company Growth." *Journal of Finance*, vol. 53, no. 6: 2107–2137.

Domowitz, Ian, Jack Glen, and Ananth Madhavan. 2000. "International Evidence on Aggregate Corporate Financing Decisions." Working paper, Pennsylvania State University.

Fan, J. P. H., Sheridan Titman, and Garry J. Twite. 2004. "An International Comparison of Capital Structure and Debt Maturity Choices." European Finance Association 2003 Annual Conference. Paper No. 769.

Hamada, Robert. 1972. "The Effect of the Firm's Capital Structure on the Systematic Risk of Common Stocks." *Journal of Finance*, vol. 27, no. 2: 435–452.

Harvey, Campbell R., Karl V. Lins, and Andrew H. Roper. 2004. "The Effect of Capital Structure When Expected Agency Costs Are Extreme." *Journal of Financial Economics*, vol. 74, no. 1: 3–30.

Jensen, Michael C. 1986. "Agency Costs of Free Cash Flow, Corporate Finance, and Takeovers." *American Economic Review*, vol. 76, no. 2: 323–329.

Jensen, Michael C., and William H. Meckling. 1976. "Theory of the Company: Managerial Behavior, Agency Costs, and Ownership Structure." *Journal of Financial Economics*, vol. 3, no. 4: 305–360.

Miller, Merton H. 1977. "Debt and Taxes." *Journal of Finance*, vol. 32, no. 2: 261–275.

Modigliani, Franco, and Merton H. Miller. 1958. "The Cost of Capital, Corporation Finance, and the Theory of Investment." *American Economic Review*, vol. 48, no. 3: 261–297.

Myers, Stewart, and Nicholas S. Majluf. 1984. "Corporate Financing and Investment Decisions When Firms Have Information That Investors Do Not Have." *Journal of Financial Economics*, vol. 13: 187–221.

Rajan, Raghuram G., and Luigi Zingales. 1995. "What Do We Know about Capital Structure? Some Evidence from International Data." *Journal of Finance*, vol. 50, no. 5: 1421–1460.

PRACTICE PROBLEMS

1 If investors have homogeneous expectations, the market is efficient, and there are no taxes, no transactions costs, and no bankruptcy costs, the Modigliani and Miller Proposition I states that:

   A bankruptcy risk rises with more leverage.

   B managers cannot change the value of the company by using more or less debt.

   C managers cannot increase the value of the company by employing tax saving strategies.

2 According to Modigliani and Miller's Proposition II without taxes:

   A the capital structure decision has no effect on the cost of equity.

   B investment and the capital structure decisions are interdependent.

   C the cost of equity increases as the use of debt in the capital structure increases.

3 Suppose the weighted average cost of capital of the Gadget Company is 10 percent. If Gadget has a capital structure of 50 percent debt and 50 percent equity, a before-tax cost of debt of 5 percent, and a marginal tax rate of 20 percent, then its cost of equity capital is *closest* to:

   A 12 percent.

   B 14 percent.

   C 16 percent.

4 The current weighted average cost of capital (WACC) for Van der Welde is 10 percent. The company announced a debt offering that raises the WACC to 13 percent. The *most likely* conclusion is that for Van der Welde:

   A the company's prospects are improving.

   B equity financing is cheaper than debt financing.

   C the company's debt/equity ratio has moved beyond the optimal range.

5 All else equal, the use of long-maturity debt is expected to be *greater* in those markets in which:

   A inflation is low.

   B capital markets are passive and illiquid.

   C the legal system's protection of bondholders' interests is weak.

6 According to the pecking order theory:

   A new debt is preferable to new equity.

   B new debt is preferable to internally generated funds.

   C new equity is always preferable to other sources of capital.

7 According to the static trade-off theory:

   A debt should be used only as a last resort.

   B companies have an optimal level of debt.

   C the capital structure decision is irrelevant.

The following information relates to Questions 8–13

Barbara Andrade is an equity analyst who covers the entertainment industry for Greengable Capital Partners, a major global asset manager. Greengable owns a significant position with a large unrealized capital gain in Mosely Broadcast Group (MBG). On a recent conference call, MBG's management states that they plan to increase the proportion of debt in the company's capital structure. Andrade is concerned that any changes in MBG's capital structure will negatively affect the value of Greengable's investment.

To evaluate the potential impact of such a capital structure change on Greengable's investment, she gathers the information about MBG given in Exhibit 1.

Exhibit 1	Current Selected Financial Information for MBG
Yield to maturity on debt (cost before tax)	8.00%
Market value of debt	$100 million
Number of shares of common stock	10 million
Market price per share of common stock	$30
Cost of capital if all equity-financed	10.3%
Marginal tax rate	35%

Andrade expects that an increase in MBG's financial leverage will increase its costs of debt and equity. Based on an examination of similar companies in MBG's industry, Andrade estimates MBG's cost of debt and cost of equity at various debt-to-total capital ratios, as shown in Exhibit 2.

Exhibit 2	Estimates of MBG's before Tax Costs of Debt and Equity	
Debt-to-Total Capital Ratio (%)	**Cost of Debt (%)**	**Cost of Equity (%)**
20	7.7	12.5
30	8.4	13.0
40	9.3	14.0
50	10.4	16.0

8 MBG is *best described* as currently: ☆ cap. structure based on market value
   A 25% debt-financed and 75% equity-financed.
   B 33% debt-financed and 66% equity-financed.
   C 75% debt-financed and 25% equity-financed.

9 Based on Exhibits 1 and 2, the current after-tax cost of debt for MBG is *closest* to:
   A 2.80%.
   B 5.20%.

C 7.65%.

10 Based on Exhibits 1 and 2, MBG's current cost of equity capital is *closest* to:

  A 10.30%.

  B 10.80%.

  C 12.75%.

11 Based on Exhibits 1 and 2, what debt-to-total capital ratio would minimize MBG's weighted average cost of capital?

  A 20%.

  B 30%.

  C 40%.

12 Holding operating earnings constant, an increase in the marginal tax rate to 40 percent would:

  A result in a lower cost of debt capital.

  B result in a higher cost of debt capital.

  C not affect the company's cost of capital.

13 According to the pecking order theory, MBG's announced capital structure change:

  A is optimal because debt is cheaper than equity on an after-tax basis.

  B may be optimal if new debt is issued after new equity is made complete use of as a source of capital.

  C may be optimal if new debt is issued after internally generated funds are made complete use of as a source of capital.

The following information relates to Questions 14–19[1]

Lindsay White, CFA, is an analyst with a firm in London, England. She is responsible for covering five companies in the Consumer Staples industry. White believes the domestic and global economies will grow slightly below average over the next two years, but she is also concerned about the possibility of a mild recession taking hold. She has been asked to review the companies that she covers, and she has collected information about them, presented in Exhibit 1. White has estimated that earnings before interest and taxes (EBIT) will remain constant for all five companies for the foreseeable future. Currency is in terms of the British pound (£). The marginal corporate tax rate is 30% for all five companies.

Exhibit 1	Selected Company Financial Data				
	Aquarius	**Bema**	**Garth**	**Holte**	**Vega**
EBIT (£)	600,000	600,000	400,000	400,000	400,000
Debt-to-equity ratio (market value)	0.60	0.00	0.00	0.71	0.62

Exhibit 1	(Continued)				
	Aquarius	**Bema**	**Garth**	**Holte**	**Vega**
Debt (market value) (£)	2,000,000	0	0	2,000,000	2,000,000
S&P debt rating	A+	n.a.	n.a.	A–	A
Weighted average cost of capital	—	10%	10%	—	—

Based on conversations with management of the five companies, as well as on her own independent research and analysis, White notes the following:

Aquarius:

- has lower bonding costs than does Bema.
- has a higher percentage of tangible assets to total assets than does Bema.
- has a higher degree of operating leverage than does Bema.

Garth:

- invests significantly less in research and development than does Holte.
- has a more highly developed corporate governance system than does Holte.
- has more business risk than does Holte.

In addition, White has reached various conclusions regarding announcements by Bema, Garth, and Vega:

Announcement	Bema has announced that it will issue debt and use the proceeds to repurchase shares. As a result of this debt-financed share repurchase program, Bema indicates that its debt/equity ratio will increase to 0.6 and its before-tax cost of debt will be 6%.
Conclusion	As a result of the announced program, Bema's total market value should decrease relative to Aquarius's.
Announcement	Garth has announced that it plans to abandon the prior policy of all-equity financing by the issuance of £1 million in debt in order to buy back an equivalent amount of equity. Garth's before-tax cost of debt is 6%.
Conclusion	This change in capital structure is reasonable, but Garth should take care subsequently to maintain a lower D/E ratio than Holte.
Announcement	Vega has announced that it intends to raise capital next year, but is unsure of the appropriate method of raising capital.
Conclusion	White has concluded that Vega should apply the pecking order theory to determine the appropriate method of raising capital.

14 Based on the Modigliani and Miller (MM) propositions with corporate taxes, Aquarius's WACC is *closest* to:

A 3.38%.

    B 7.87%.

    C 11.25%.

15 Based on MM propositions with corporate taxes, what is Bema's weighted average cost of capital after the completion of its announced debt-financed share repurchase program?

    A 6.52%.

    B 7.83%.

    C 8.88%.

16 Based on Exhibit 1 and White's notes, which of the following is *least* consistent with White's conclusion regarding Bema's announcement?

    A Bema's bonding costs will be higher than Aquarius's.

    B Bema will have a lower degree of operating leverage than does Aquarius.

    C Bema will have a lower percentage of tangible assets to total assets than does Aquarius.

17 Based on the MM propositions with corporate taxes, Garth's cost of equity after the debt issuance is *closest* to:

    A 10.00%.

    B 10.85%.

    C 11.33%.

18 Based on Exhibit 1 and White's notes, which of the following is *most* consistent with White's conclusion regarding Garth's announcement?

    A Garth has more business risk than does Holte.

    B Garth invests significantly less in research and development than does Holte.

    C Garth has a more highly developed corporate governance system than does Holte.

19 Based on White's conclusion regarding determining the appropriate method of raising capital, Vega should raise capital in the following order:

    A debt, internal financing, equity.

    B equity, debt, internal financing.

    C internal financing, debt, equity.

SOLUTIONS

1   B is correct. Proposition I, or the capital structure irrelevance theorem, states that the level of debt versus equity in the capital structure has no effect on company value in perfect markets.

2   C is correct. The cost of equity rises with the use of debt in the capital structure, e.g., with increasing financial leverage.

3   C is correct. Using Equation 1 from the reading:

$$0.10 = (0.50)(0.05)(1 - 0.20) + (0.50)r_e$$
$$r_e = 0.16 \text{ or } 16 \text{ percent.}$$

4   C is correct. If the company's WACC increases as a result of taking on additional debt, the company has moved beyond the optimal capital range. The costs of financial distress may outweigh any tax benefits to the use of debt.

5   A is correct. The use of long-maturity debt is expected to be inversely related to the level of inflation.

6   A is correct. According to the pecking order theory, internally generated funds are preferable to both new equity and new debt. If internal financing is insufficient, managers next prefer new debt, and finally new equity.

7   B is correct. The static trade-off theory indicates that there is a trade-off between the tax shield from interest on debt and the costs of financial distress, leading to an optimal amount of debt in a company's capital structure.

8   A is correct. The market value of equity is ($30)(10,000,000) = $300,000,000. With the market value of debt equal to $100,000,000, the market value of the company is $100,000,000 + $300,000,000 = $400,000,000. Therefore, the company is $100,000,000/$400,000,000 = 0.25 or 25% debt-financed.

9   B is correct.

$$r_d(1 - t) = 0.08(1 - 0.35) = 0.052 = 5.20\%$$

10   B is correct.

$$r_e = r_0 + (r_0 - r_d)(1 - t)\frac{D}{E}$$

$$= 0.103 + (0.103 - 0.08)(1 - 0.35)\left(\frac{\$100\,\text{million}}{\$300\,\text{million}}\right)$$

$$= 0.108 = 10.80\%$$

11   B is correct. Let $V = D + E$:

$$r_{wacc} = \left(\frac{D}{V}\right)r_d(1 - t) + \left(\frac{E}{V}\right)r_e$$

$$\text{At } D/V = 20\%, r_a = (0.2)(0.077)(1 - 0.35) + (0.8)(0.125) = 0.1100$$
$$= 11.00\%$$

At $D/V = 30\%, r_a = (0.3)(0.084)(1 - 0.35) + (0.7)(0.130) = 0.1074$
$= 10.74\%$

$$\text{At } D/V = 40\%, r_a = (0.4)(0.093)(1 - 0.35) + (0.6)(0.140) = 0.1082$$
$$= 10.82\%$$

$$\text{At } D/V = 50\%, r_a = (0.5)(0.104)(1 - 0.35) + (0.5)(0.160) = 0.1138$$
$$= 11.38\%$$

12 A is correct. The after-tax cost of debt decreases as the marginal tax rate increases.

13 C is correct. If internally generated funds have already been fully used, the use of new debt may be optimal, according to the pecking order theory of capital structure.

14 B is correct. $V_L = \dfrac{\text{EBIT}(1 - t)}{r_{wacc}}$

Because $D/E = 0.60$ and $D = £2m$, then $E = £2m/(0.60) = £3,333,333$

So, Value of company $(V_L) = D + E = £2,000,000 + £3,333,333 = £5,333,333$

Because $V_L = \dfrac{\text{EBIT}(1 - t)}{r_{wacc}} = \dfrac{(600,000)(1 - 0.30)}{r_{wacc}} = 5,333,333$

So, $r_{wacc} = \dfrac{(600,000)(1 - 0.30)}{5,333,333} = 0.0787 = 7.87\%$

15 C is correct. $r_e = r_0 + (r_0 - r_d)(1 - t)\left(\dfrac{D}{E}\right)$, and $r_{wacc} = \left(\dfrac{D}{V}\right)r_d(1 - t) + \left(\dfrac{E}{V}\right)r_e$

$$r_e = r_0 + (r_0 - r_d)(1 - t)\left(\dfrac{D}{E}\right) = 10 + (10 - 6)(1 - 0.30)(0.60)$$
$$= 10 + 1.68 = 11.68\%$$

Therefore,

$$r_{wacc} = \left(\dfrac{D}{V}\right)r_d(1 - t) + \left(\dfrac{E}{V}\right)r_e = \left(\dfrac{0.6}{1.6}\right)(6)(1 - 0.30) + \left(\dfrac{1.0}{1.6}\right)(11.68)$$
$$= 1.58 + 7.30 = 8.88\%$$

16 B is correct. If Bema's degree of operating leverage declines relative to that of Aquarius, Bema's business risk will also decline relative to Aquarius. All else being equal, this decline would be expected to *increase* Bema's market value relative to Aquarius; e.g., by decreasing Bema's cost of equity.

17 C is correct.

$$r_e = r_0 + (r_0 - r_d)(1 - t)\left(\dfrac{D}{E}\right)$$

$$V_U = \dfrac{\text{EBIT}(1 - t)}{r_0} = \dfrac{400,000(1 - 0.30)}{0.10} = 2,800,000$$

$$V_L = V_U + tD = (2.8\,\text{million}) + (0.30)(1\,\text{million}) = 3.10\,\text{million}$$

$$E = V_L - D = (3.10\,\text{million}) - (1\,\text{million}) = 2.10\,\text{million}$$

$$r_e = r_0 + (r_0 - r_d)(1 - t)\left(\dfrac{D}{E}\right) = 10 + (10 - 6)(1 - 0.30)\left(\dfrac{1}{2.10}\right)$$

$$= 10 + 1.33 = 11.33\%$$

18 A is correct. The statement implies that Garth possesses a lower ability to assume debt than does Holte, all else being equal.

19 C is correct. According to the pecking order theory, managers prefer internal financing. If internal financing is not sufficient, managers next prefer debt, and finally equity.

27

Dividends and Share Repurchases: Analysis

by Gregory Noronha, CFA, and George H. Troughton, CFA

LEARNING OUTCOMES

Mastery	The candidate should be able to:
☐	**a.** compare theories of dividend policy, and explain implications of each for share value given a description of a corporate dividend action;
☐	**b.** describe types of information (signals) that dividend initiations, increases, decreases, and omissions may convey;
☐	**c.** explain how clientele effects and agency issues may affect a company's payout policy;
☐	**d.** explain factors that affect dividend policy;
☐	**e.** calculate and interpret the effective tax rate on a given currency unit of corporate earnings under double taxation, dividend imputation, and split-rate tax systems;
☐	**f.** compare stable dividend, constant dividend payout ratio, and residual dividend payout policies, and calculate the dividend under each policy;
☐	**g.** explain the choice between paying cash dividends and repurchasing shares;
☐	**h.** describe broad trends in corporate dividend policies;
☐	**i.** calculate and interpret dividend coverage ratios based on 1) net income and 2) free cash flow;
☐	**j.** identify characteristics of companies that may not be able to sustain their cash dividend.

CFA Institute gratefully acknowledges the contributions of Catherine E. Clark, CFA, as co-author of a prior version of this reading.

1   INTRODUCTION

One of the longest running debates in corporate finance concerns the impact, if any, on common shareholders' wealth of a company's **payout policy** (i.e., the principles by which a company distributes cash to common shareholders by means of cash dividends and/or share repurchases).[1] Payout decisions, along with financing (capital structure) decisions, generally involve the board of directors and most senior level of management and are closely watched by investors and analysts. This reading introduces the theory and practice of dividend policy with reference to world markets.

This reading is organized as follows. In Section 2, we present theories of the effects of dividend policy on company value. In Section 3, we discuss factors that affect dividend policy. In Section 4, we cover the types of dividend policies, the dividend-share repurchase decision, and global trends in payout policy. Section 5 covers analysis of dividend safety, and we conclude the reading with a summary.

2   DIVIDEND POLICY AND COMPANY VALUE: THEORY

Over the last forty years, financial theorists have debated the extent to which dividend policy should and does matter to a company's shareholders. One group of theorists believes that dividend policy is irrelevant to shareholders. This group typically holds that only the decisions of the company that are directly related to investment in working and fixed capital affect shareholders' wealth. A second group holds that dividend policy does matter to investors, for one or more reasons, and that a company can affect shareholders' wealth through its dividend policy. Typically, dividend relevance is attributed to either a presumption that investors value a unit of dividends more highly than an equal amount of uncertain capital gains, or to one or more market imperfections. Such imperfections include taxes (in which a given amount of dividends is taxed differently than an equal amount of capital gains), asymmetric information (specifically, that corporate insiders are better informed about their company's prospects than outside investors), and agency costs (in particular, that management has a tendency to squander extra cash). We examine these positions and the assumptions that underlie them in the following subsections.

2.1 Dividend Policy Does Not Matter

In a 1961 paper, Miller and Modigliani ("MM") argued that in a world without taxes, transaction costs, and equal ("symmetric") information among all investors—that is, under **perfect capital market** assumptions—a company's dividend policy should have no impact on its cost of capital or on shareholder wealth.[2] Their argument begins by assuming a company has a given capital budget (e.g., it accepts all projects with a positive net present value [NPV]), and that its current capital structure and debt ratio are optimal. Another way of stating this argument is that the dividend decision is independent of a company's investment and financing decisions. For example, suppose that a company decided to pay out all of its earnings as dividends. To finance capital projects, it could issue additional common shares in the amount of its capital budget (such financing would keep its capital structure unchanged). The value of the newly

---

1 The term *payout policy*, or sometimes *distribution policy*, is more general than *dividend policy* because it reflects the fact that companies can return cash to shareholders by means of share repurchases and cash dividends.
2 See Miller and Modigliani (1961).

issued shares would exactly offset the value of the dividend. Thus, if a company paid out a dividend that represented 5 percent of equity, its share price would be expected to drop by 5 percent. If a common stock in Australia is priced at A$20 before an A$1 a share dividend, the implied new price would be A$19. The shareholder has assets worth A$20 if the dividend is not paid or assets worth A$20 if the stock drops to A$19 and an A$1 dividend is paid.

Note that under the MM assumptions, there is no meaningful distinction between dividends and share repurchases (repurchases of outstanding common shares by the issuing company)—they are both ways for a company to return cash to shareholders. If a company had few investment opportunities such that its current cash flow was more than that needed for positive NPV projects, it could distribute the excess cash flow via a dividend or a share repurchase. Shareholders selling shares would receive A$20 a share, and shareholders not selling would hold shares whose value continued to be A$20. To see this, suppose the company being discussed has 10,000 shares outstanding, a current free cash flow of A$10,000, and the present value of its future cash flows is A$190,000. Thus, the share price is (A$10,000 + A$190,000)/10,000 = A$20. Now if the company uses the free cash flow to repurchase shares, in lieu of paying a dividend of A$1, it will repurchase 500 shares (A$10,000/A$20 = 500). The 9,500 shares left outstanding have a claim on the A$190,000 future cash flow, which results in a share price of A$20.

An intuitive understanding of MM dividend irrelevance also follows from the concept of a "homemade dividend."[3] In a world with no taxes or transactions costs, if shareholders wanted or needed income, they could construct their own dividend policy by selling sufficient shares to create their desired cash flow stream. Using the example above, assume the company did not pay the A$1 dividend and the stock remained at A$20. A holder of 1,000 shares who desired A$1,000 in cash could sell 50 shares at A$20 reducing his or her holdings to 950 shares. Note that by reducing share holdings, second period dividend income is reduced: higher dividend income in one period is at the expense of exactly offsetting lower dividend income in subsequent periods. The irrelevance argument does not state that dividends per se are irrelevant to share value but that dividend *policy* is irrelevant because by taking the earning power of assets as a given and assuming perfect capital markets, policy alternatives merely involve tradeoffs of different dividend streams of equal present value.

In the real world, there are market imperfections that create some problems for MM's dividend policy irrelevance propositions. First, both companies and individuals incur transactions costs. A company issuing new shares incurs **flotation costs** (i.e., costs in selling shares to the public that include underwriters' fees, legal costs, registration expenses, and possible negative price effects) often estimated to be as much as 4 percent to 10 percent of the capital raised, depending on the size of the company and the size of the issue.[4] Shareholders selling shares to create a "homemade" dividend would incur transaction costs and, in some countries, capital gains taxes (of course, cash dividends incur taxes in most countries). Furthermore, selling shares

---

3 MM use a similar idea in their irrelevance proposition for capital structure—that of "homemade leverage." If a shareholder can undo anything a company does at no cost, then it follows that whatever the company does in terms of capital structure or dividend decisions should not have an impact on shareholder value because the shareholder can always alter the outcome to suit his or her own needs. Thus under the MM assumptions, only investment decisions, which determine the amount of future cash flows from operations, have an effect on company value.

4 Because net income is calculated after payment of interest, net income is considered a flow to equity or internally generated equity. New share issuance—externally generated equity—is thus the closest financing substitute to internally generated equity. Dividends also may be financed with debt (if bond covenants permit), which is subject to flotation costs.

on a periodic basis to create an income stream of dividends can be problematic over time if share prices are volatile. If share prices decline, shareholders have to sell more shares to create the same dividend stream.

2.2 Dividend Policy Matters: The Bird in the Hand Argument

Financial theorists, such as Myron Gordon (1963), John Lintner (1962), and Benjamin Graham (1934), have argued that, even under perfect capital markets assumptions, investors prefer a dollar of dividends to a dollar of potential capital gains from reinvesting earnings because they view dividends as less risky. Graham's viewpoint is that " . . . the typical dollar of reinvestment has less economic value to the shareholder than a dollar paid in dividends."[5] The Gordon, Lintner, and Graham arguments are similar and have sometimes been called the "bird in the hand" argument, a reference to the proverb "a bird in the hand is worth two in the bush." By assuming that a given amount of dividends is less risky than the same amount of capital gains, the argument is that a company that pays dividends will have a lower cost of equity capital than an otherwise similar company that does not pay dividends; the lower cost of equity should result in a higher share price. MM contend that this argument is incorrect because, under their assumptions, paying or increasing the dividend today does not affect the risk of future cash flows. Such actions only lower the ex-dividend price of the share (the **ex-dividend price** is the share price when the share first trades without the right to receive an upcoming dividend).

2.3 Dividend Policy Matters: The Tax Argument

In some countries, dividend income has traditionally been taxed at higher rates than capital gains. For instance in the 1970s, tax rates on dividend income in the United States were as high as 70 percent, whereas the long-term capital gains rate was 35 percent. Even as recently as 2002, U.S. tax rates were as high as 39.1 percent on dividends and 20 percent on long-term capital gains. (From 2003 to 2010, dividends and long-term capital gains were taxed at 15 percent in the United States.)

An argument could be made that in a country that taxes dividends at higher rates than capital gains, taxable investors should prefer companies that pay low dividends and reinvest earnings in profitable growth opportunities. Presumably, any growth in earnings in excess of the opportunity cost of funds would translate into a higher share price. If, for any reason, a company lacked growth opportunities sufficient to consume its annual retained earnings, it could distribute such funds through shares repurchases (again, the assumption is that capital gains are taxed more lightly than dividends). Taken to its extreme, this argument would advocate a *zero* payout ratio. Real world market considerations may complicate the picture; for example, in some jurisdictions governmental regulation may preclude companies from never distributing excess earnings as dividends or deem share repurchases to be dividends if the repurchases appear to be ongoing in lieu of dividend payments.

2.4 Other Theoretical Issues

In the following section we present other important issues that arise in theory of dividend policy.

---

5 Graham, Dodd, Cottle, and Tatham (1962), p. 486.

2.4.1 *Clientele Effect*

Another factor that may affect a company's dividend policy is a clientele effect. In this context, a **clientele effect** is the existence of groups of investors (clienteles) attracted by (and drawn to invest in) companies with specific dividend policies.

For example, some retired investors may have a preference for higher current income and prefer to hold stocks with relatively high dividend payouts and yields. Alternatively, other investor groups, such as younger workers with a long time horizon, might favor owning shares of companies that reinvest a high proportion of their earnings for long-term capital growth and thus prefer stocks that pay little or no dividends.

When the investor's marginal tax rate on capital gains (i.e., the tax on the next euro of capital gains) is lower than the marginal tax rate on dividends (i.e., the tax on the next euro of dividends), the investor may be influenced by tax considerations to have a preference for returns in the form of capital gains. All else being equal, however, tax-exempt investors would be expected to be indifferent about returns in the forms of capital gains or dividends from a tax perspective. Taxable investors might be similarly indifferent regarding investments held in tax-exempt accounts.

Many investors indicate a preference for dividends. Some institutional investors, including certain mutual funds, banks, and insurance companies, will only invest in companies that pay a dividend. Some investors require a specific minimum dividend yield or require that the dividend yield be in the top quartile (or half) of the relevant stock universe. Some mutual funds and exchange-traded funds specifically seek high-dividend yield. Various high-yield equity indices exist in response to this demand (e.g., the Dow Jones Select Dividend Index family or the MSCI High Dividend Yield Indices). Trusts and foundations may be under a restriction that only income (i.e., interest and dividends) may be distributed to beneficiaries. Some individual investors use a discipline of "only spend the dividends, not the principal" to preserve their capital.[6] Furthermore, in some jurisdictions, there are *legal* or *approved lists of equity investments* for institutions, such as insurance companies, or trusts for individuals. Such lists typically mandate that permissible investments consist only of companies that pay dividends. Often, such restrictive lists are intended to discourage investment in high-risk stocks. All of these considerations suggest that a clientele effect does exist and that equity market participants can be sorted by those who prefer to receive returns in the form of dividends and those who prefer capital gains returns.

Even if a clientele effect exists, however, it would not follow that dividend policy affects equity values; only that investors care about dividends and gravitate toward owning companies with the dividend policies they prefer. In particular, if the dividend market is in equilibrium in the sense that the demands of all clienteles for various dividend policies are satisfied by sufficient numbers of companies, a company cannot affect its own share value by changing its dividend policy. The change would only result in a switch in clientele. Thus, dividend clienteles may tend to promote stability of dividend policy and do not contradict dividend policy irrelevance.

Investors seeking yield will often be found to consistently overweight in some industry sectors relative to the benchmark weights of those sectors. Exhibit 1 shows the dividend yield for five of the FTSE 100 industry sectors: Utilities, Travel and Leisure, Energy (Oil and Gas), Mining, and Information Technology.

---

6 See Shefrin and Statman (1984).

Exhibit 1	Dividend Yield of Major FTSE 100 Industry Sectors June 2009 (Percent)

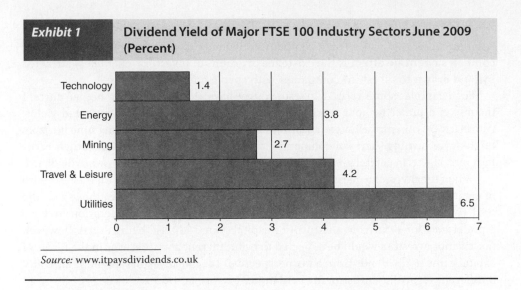

Source: www.itpaysdividends.co.uk

As is evident, there is a dramatic difference in dividend yields for these five industries, with Utilities having the highest yield and Technology having a relatively low one. This pattern in industry dividend yields appears to be global as shown in Exhibit 2 below.

Exhibit 2	Gross Dividend Yield on Selected FTSE All-World Sector Indices (Percent)

Industries	
Oil and Gas	3.1
Basic Materials	3.1
Consumer Goods	3.1
Health Care	2.8
Consumer Services	2.5
Financials	3.4
Utilities	5.0
Technology	1.6

Source: Financial Times, 5 June 2009, p. 19.

If the tax rates applied to dividends and capital gains are the same, then (all else being equal) the expected price drop when a share goes **ex-dividend** (i.e., first trades without the right to receive an upcoming dividend) is the amount of the dividend. When the ex-dividend day price change is consistently different from that amount, the discrepancy may carry information about the marginal tax rates of investors trading in the share on the **ex-dividend date** (the first date that the share trades without the right to receive an upcoming dividend). The point is worth developing in greater detail.

Suppose that a taxable investor purchases a share at price P_b (where b is for *buy*) and has marginal tax rates on dividends and capital gains of T_D and T_{CG}, respectively. Consider two trading strategies distinguished by whether a share is sold just before or just after the share goes ex-dividend:

- *Sell just before the share goes ex-dividend.* The share is sold at the end of the last trading day before the ex-dividend day at price P_w (where w is for *with right to receive the dividend*). By selling the share at that time the investor will *not* appear as a holder of record of the share as of the record date and will *not* be entitled to the dividend. (The purchaser of the share will be the owner of record.)

  The resulting cash flow is the sale price P_w minus the capital gains tax owed on the sale: $P_w - (P_w - P_b)(T_{CG})$

- *Sell just after the share goes ex-dividend.* The share is sold when it opens for trading on the ex-dividend day at price P_x (where x is for *ex-dividend*). The investor will receive the dividend.

  The resulting cash flow is the sale price P_x minus the capital gains tax owed on the sale plus the after-tax amount of the dividend:

$$P_x - (P_x - P_b)(T_{CG}) + D(1 - T_D)$$

A **marginal investor** in a given share is defined as an investor who is very likely to be part of the next trade in the share and who is therefore important in setting price. Suppose that the investor whose marginal tax rates we are describing is such an investor. The prices P_w and P_x represent an equilibrium if this marginal investor is indifferent about selling the share just before and just after it goes ex-dividend. For that to be the case, the two cash flows given must be equal:

$$P_w - (P_w - P_b)(T_{CG}) = P_x - (P_x - P_b)(T_{CG}) + D(1 - T_D)$$

This equation can be solved for the amount of the price decrease when the share goes ex-dividend, $P_w - P_x$:[7]

$$P_w - P_x = D\frac{1 - T_D}{1 - T_{CG}} \qquad (1)$$

Equation 1 implies three relationships. If the investor's marginal tax rate on dividends is equal to the marginal tax rate on capital gains, the share's price should drop by the amount of the dividend when the share goes ex-dividend. If the investor's marginal tax rate on dividends is higher than the marginal tax rate on capital gains, the share's price should drop by less than the amount of the dividend when the share goes ex-dividend. Finally, if the investor's marginal tax rate on dividends is less than the marginal tax rate on capital gains, the share's price should drop by more than the amount of the dividend when the share goes ex-dividend. For example, if the dividend is €12 and the marginal tax rate on dividends at 0.40 is higher than the marginal tax rate on capital gains at 0.20, we expect the price to drop by less than the amount of the dividend on the ex-dividend day. The expected price drop is calculated as (€12) $(1 - 0.40)/(1 - 0.20)$ = (€12)(0.75) = €9.

The ratio $(1 - T_D)/(1 - T_{CG})$ can be viewed as establishing an indifference relationship between dividends and capital gains. For example, assuming an investor pays taxes of 40 percent on the next unit of dividend income and taxes of 15 percent on the next unit of capital gains, €1 of dividend is worth as much as $(1 - 0.40)/(1 - 0.15)$ = €0.71 in capital gains.

---

7 See Elton and Gruber (1970), pp. 68–74. Technically, the expression does not take into account the time value of money and assumes investors are risk neutral (indifferent to risk).

The amount of the ex-dividend price drop may provide information on the tax rates applying to those trading in the stock. Example 1 shows details about this type of analysis.

EXAMPLE 1

Clienteles and Preferences for Dividends versus Capital Gains

1   An individual investor pays taxes of 28 percent on the next dollar of dividend income and taxes of 15 percent on the next dollar of capital gains. Which would she prefer: $1 in dividends or $0.87 in capital gains?

2   Suppose the tax rate on capital gains is 20 percent for all investors, but the tax rate on dividend income differs among investors. A share drops by 70 percent of the amount of the dividend, on average, when the share goes ex-dividend. Assume that any appropriate corrections for equity market price movements on ex-dividend days have been made. Calculate the marginal tax rate on dividend income applying to those who trade the issue around the ex-dividend day.

3   Consider a U.S. corporation with a corporate income tax rate of 40 percent. The corporation needs to report as taxable income only 30 percent of dividends received from other corporations—that is, it takes a 70 percent deduction on that type of dividend income in calculating taxes owed. Assume that both capital gains and reported dividends (dividends net of any deductible amount) are taxed at 40 percent. What is $1 of dividends worth in terms of capital gains for such a corporate investor?

4   Explain why the ex-dividend share price would be expected to drop by more than the amount of the dividend if such investors as the corporation described in question 3 are the marginal trader in the issue.

5   For a given share issue, the share price consistently drops by an amount very close to the amount of the dividend when the share goes ex-dividend. Describe the marginal investor in the shares.

Solution to 1:

For this investor, after taxes, $1 in dividends is worth $1(1 − 0.28)/(1 − 0.15) = $0.85 in capital gains. Because $0.87 exceeds $0.85, this investor would prefer $0.87 in capital gains to $1 in dividends. Viewed another way, the $0.87 in capital gains gives the investor $0.74 = ($0.87)(1 − 0.15) after tax, compared with $0.72 = ($1)(1 − 0.28) after tax for $1 of dividends.

Solution to 2:

The statement of the problem implies that $(P_w - P_x)/D = 0.70$. Thus, $0.70 = (1 - T_D)/(1 - T_{CG}) = (1 - T_D)/(1 - 0.20)$. So, $(0.80)(0.70) = 1 - T_D$ and $T_D = 1 - (0.80)(0.70) = 0.44$. The average ex-dividend day price movement reflects a 44 percent marginal tax rate on dividend income for those who trade around the ex-dividend day.

Solution to 3:

Because 70 percent of the dividend is excluded from taxation, the effective tax rate on dividends, T_D, is $0.4(1 - 0.7) = 0.12$. Thus, a $1 dividend is worth $(1 - 0.12)/(1 - 0.4) = $1.47 of capital gains for the corporate investor described.

Solution to 4:

Because 70 percent of the dividends received are excluded from taxation, the corporation has a tax-motivated preference for dividends over capital gains. Therefore, the ratio $(1 - T_D)/(1 - T_{CG})$ exceeds 1.0; that is, $(P_w - P_x) > D$. The ex-dividend day price decline is expected to exceed the amount of the dividend.

Solution to 5:

The marginal investor may be a tax-exempt investor. A taxable investor with the same marginal tax rate on dividends and capital gains is another possibility consistent with the data.

The existence of dividend clienteles does not contradict the hypothesis of dividend policy irrelevance. Example 2 addresses the point. In the example, **dividend payout ratio** refers to the percentage of total earnings paid out in dividends in a given year; in per-share terms, it is DPS/EPS.

EXAMPLE 2

Clienteles and Preferences for Dividends versus Capital Gains

Suppose it is established that about 70 percent of investors prefer a relatively high income stream from a given size position in shares. You are on the board of directors of a company with a dividend policy that specifies a particularly low dividend payout ratio. Give two reasons why having your company adopt a higher dividend payout ratio may not lead to an increase in shareholder wealth.

Solution:

First, even if the dividend payout ratio is not increased, individual shareholders may be able to manufacture their desired income stream by selling shares as needed (creating "homemade dividends"). Second, if there are tax clienteles, by adopting a higher dividend payout ratio the company may be merely exchanging one clientele (which it satisfies currently) for a different clientele.

2.4.2 The Information Content of Dividend Actions: Signaling

MM assumed that all investors—including outside investors—have the same information about the company: a situation of symmetric information. In reality, corporate managers typically have access to more detailed and extensive information about the company than do outside investors.

A situation of asymmetric information raises the possibility that dividend increases or decreases may affect share price because they may convey new information about the company. A company's board of directors and management, having more information than outside investors, may use dividends to signal to investors (i.e., convey information) how the company is *really* doing. A company's decision to initiate, maintain, increase, or cut a dividend may convey more credible information than positive words from management because cash is involved. For a signal to be effective it must be difficult or costly to mimic by another entity without the same attributes.

Dividend increases are costly to mimic because a company that does not expect its cash flows to increase will not be able to maintain the dividend at increasingly high levels in the long run.[8] (In the short run, a company can borrow to fund dividends.)

Empirical studies broadly support the thesis that dividend initiations or increases convey positive information and are associated with future earnings growth, whereas dividend omissions or reductions convey negative information and are associated with future earnings problems.[9] A dividend declaration can help resolve some of the information asymmetry between insiders and outsiders and help close any gap between the market price of shares and their intrinsic value.

Some researchers[10] have argued that a company's dividend initiation or increase tends to be associated with share price increases because it attracts more attention to the company. Managers have an incentive to increase the company's dividend if they believe the company to be undervalued because the increased scrutiny will lead to a positive price adjustment. In contrast, according to this line of reasoning, managers of overvalued companies have little reason to mimic such a signal because increased scrutiny would presumably result in a downward price adjustment to their shares.

EXAMPLE 3

Signaling with Dividends and the Costs of Mimicking

Suppose that the management of a company with poor future prospects recommends to the board of directors an increase in its dividend. Management explains to the board that investors may then believe that the company has positive future prospects, leading to an increase in share value and shareholder wealth.

1   State whether such imitation is likely to achieve the stated objective over the long term.

2   Justify your answer to Question 1.

Solution to 1:

No, such dividend increases are not likely to achieve the stated objective over the long term for the company described.

Solution to 2:

Dividend increases are costly to mimic because a company that does not expect its cash flows to increase will not be able to maintain the increased dividend. The company will have to either cut the dividend in the future or go to the market to obtain new equity funding to pay the dividend. Both these alternatives are costly for the company because they result in downward revisions to the stock price.

Many companies take pride in their record of consistently increasing dividends over a long period of time. Standard & Poor's, for example, identifies companies in its U.S.-based S&P 500 Index, Europe 350 Index, Pan Asia Index, and S&P/TSX Canadian Index that are "Dividend Aristocrats" in the sense that they have increased their dividend for a number of consecutive years (at least 25 years in the case of the S&P 500, at least 10 years in the case of the Europe 350, at least 7 years in the case of Pan Asia Index, and at least 5 years in the case of the S&P/TSX). These companies are in various

---

8 See, for example, Ross (1977) pp. 23–40, and Myers and Majluf (1984) pp. 187–221.
9 See Filbeck (2009) for a short summary of the evidence, including the evidence that does not support the thesis stated.
10 See Grinblatt, Masulis, and Titman (1984) pp. 461–490.

industries and include Procter & Gamble, Nestle, Novartis, Sanofi-Aventis, Wal-Mart, 3M, ExxonMobil, and Automatic Data Processing. When a company's earnings and cash flow outlook has been and continues to be positive, it often views a policy of increasing dividends as an important tool to convey that information to existing and potential shareholders. Companies that consistently increase their dividends seem to share certain characteristics:

- Dominant or niche positions in their industry;
- Global operations;
- Relatively high returns on assets; and
- Relatively low debt ratios (dividend payouts unlikely to be affected by restrictions in debt covenants).

Dividend cuts or omissions, in contrast, present powerful and often negative signals. For companies under financial or operating stress, the dividend declaration date may be viewed with more than usual interest. Will they cut the dividend? Will they omit the dividend altogether? In these instances, merely maintaining the dividend or not cutting it as much as expected is usually viewed as good news (i.e., that current difficulties are transitory and manageable), unless investors view managers as trying to convey erroneous information to the market.

In principle, management can attempt to send a positive signal by cutting the dividend, although that is difficult in practice. For example, IBM, long the giant of mainframe computers and a company with an enviable record of dividend increases over the years, announced in 1993 a more than 50 percent cut in its dividend. IBM explained that its intention was to use the funds conserved to shift its business into non-mainframe technology and consulting services for the purpose of improving future returns. Although the message was met with varying reactions, it was, in retrospect, a positive signal because IBM successfully used its cash flow to reorganize its business. IBM resumed its dividend increases again in 1996 and, as of the time of this writing, it has increased every year since.

EXAMPLE 4

Dividend Reductions and Price Increases

On 6 March 2003, the BBC reported that Royal & Sun Alliance Group, Britain's second largest insurer, had announced it would cut its dividend from 16 pence a share to 6 pence a share. The company also revealed that it had a shortfall of £406 million in its pension fund and was planning to increase contributions to the fund by about £30 million a year for the next 10 years.

All this was despite the fact that the company reported operating profits of £226 million at the end of 2002, up from just £16 million at the end of 2001. The insurer was in the process of reorganizing its business to focus on general insurance policies, and expanding into Australia and New Zealand, while replacing its chief executive. The interim chief executive told reporters that future dividends would depend on decisions made by the new leadership. As the market digested all this information, the insurance company's shares rose 2 percent.

Source: BBC News, http://news.bbc.co.uk/2/hi/business/2824527.stm.

Another even more complicated example of the signaling content of dividends can be found in Microsoft's initial dividend declaration. As Exhibit 1 showed, technology companies have among the lowest dividend yields and, it can be shown, below average dividend payout ratios. These facts make sense. Most technology companies have high R&D requirements and some (e.g., integrated circuit manufacturers) are capital intensive; those that are profitable often achieve returns on assets and owners' equity that are well above average. In addition, business risk is considerable as discoveries and unforeseen advances change the product landscape. All of these considerations would suggest a policy of low (or no) dividend payments, so that internally generated funds are directed for new product development and/or capital investment that will maintain high returns. Some companies in the technology sector, however, do mature. For example, in the mid-1990s, because of Microsoft's past phenomenal growth and its dominance of its industry, net cash grew to tens of billions of dollars. Many wondered if the company could effectively use its cash "hoard," and if it were time for Microsoft to pay a dividend.

In late 2003, Microsoft declared its first annual dividend of $0.06 a share, equaling about 7 percent of its yearly cash flow, less than 2 percent of its net cash position, and representing a yield of 0.3 percent. Then, in the summer of 2004, the company increased its annual dividend to $0.32 a share and announced a special year-end dividend of $3.00 a share. Clearly, the signaling effect was more important than the actual cash impact on either the company or its investors. Some investors viewed these declarations positively, whereas others viewed them negatively. On the one hand, some believed that Microsoft was signaling an interest in broadening its investor focus while refraining from undertaking unprofitable expansion. The clientele effect, discussed earlier, would suggest that Microsoft's dividend possibly attracted a new group of potential shareholders. On the other hand, others viewed the dividend declaration as an admission that it was becoming a mature company—that it could no longer reap high returns from reinvesting its earnings. The future growth prospects for the stock, they would argue, had been diminished, although a question was the extent to which the market already understood that. In any event, few could argue that the 2003–2004 dividend declarations by Microsoft were not corporate events of some importance.

2.4.3 *Agency Costs and Dividends as a Mechanism to Control Them*

In large, publicly traded corporations, there is typically a substantial separation between the professional managers who control the corporation's operations and the outside investors who largely own it. When agents (the managers) and owners (the shareholders) are different, managers may have an incentive to maximize their own welfare at the company's expense because they own none or relatively small percentages of the company for which they work and they do not bear all the costs of such actions. This incentive is ultimately also a problem of unequal (asymmetric) information between managers and outside investors because, if outside investors could perfectly observe managers, managers would be dissuaded from such actions. One managerial incentive of particular concern is investment in negative net present value (NPV) projects. Such projects may grow the size of the company (measured in sales or assets) and thus enlarge the manager's span of control, while they generate negative economic returns. This potential overinvestment agency problem might be alleviated by the payment of dividends. In particular, by paying out all free cash flow to equity in dividends, managers would be constrained in their ability to overinvest by undertaking negative NPV projects.[11] This concern or hypothesis that management may create an overinvestment agency cost is known as Jensen's free cash flow hypothesis.[12]

That management will squander free cash flow by undertaking unprofitable projects can be viewed as a possible concern to be evaluated case by case. For example, as discussed previously, Microsoft accumulated increasingly large cash positions but

---

11 Informally, free cash flow to equity is the cash flow available to be distributed as dividends after the company has accepted all positive NPV projects.
12 See Jensen (1986).

was not observed to squander monies on unprofitable projects. In some cases, such cash positions may provide financial flexibility to respond quickly to changes in the environment, to grasp unforeseen opportunities, or to survive periods of restricted credit, as in the case of Ford Motor Company's accumulation of cash during profitable years in the 1990s. Clearly, there are industry-specific and life-cycle conditions to consider. In general, it makes sense for growing companies in industries characterized by rapid change to hold cash and pay low or no dividends, but it does not make sense for large, mature companies in relatively non-cyclical industries. In general, there is empirical support for the market reaction to dividend change announcements to be stronger for companies with greater potential for overinvestment than for companies with lesser potential for overinvestment.[13]

There is another concern when a company is financed by debt as well as equity. Paying dividends can exacerbate the agency conflict between shareholders and bondholders. When a company has risky debt, the payment of dividends reduces the cash cushion available to the company for the disbursement of fixed payments to bondholders. The payment of large dividends, with the intention of transferring wealth from bondholders to shareholders, could lead to underinvestment in profitable projects. All else equal, both dividends and share repurchases increase the risk that the company will default on its debt. Reflecting bondholders' concern, the bond indenture (contract) often includes a covenant restricting distributions to shareholders that might impair the position of bondholders.[14] A typical form of this restriction is to define an amount that distributions to shareholders during the life of the bond may not exceed. This amount of funds is usually a positive function of the company's current and past earnings and issues of new equity, and a negative function of dividends paid since the bonds were issued. Dividends are not permitted if their payment would make the amount zero or if the amount is negative (e.g., because of negative earnings). Such covenants often do not really restrict the level of dividends as long as those dividends come from new earnings or from new issues of stock. What the covenant attempts to do is prevent the payment of dividends financed by the sale of the company's existing assets or by the issuance of new debt. Covenants that specify minimum levels of EBITDA and/or EBIT coverage of interest charges are frequently used as well. These covenants provide some assurance that operating earnings include a cushion for the payment of fixed charges.[15] Other covenants focus on balance sheet strength—for example, by specifying a maximum value for the ratio of debt to tangible net worth.

EXAMPLE 5

Agency Issues and Dividends

Two dividend-paying companies A and B directly compete with each other. Both companies are all-equity financed and have recent dividend payout ratios averaging 35 percent. The corporate governance practices at Company B are weaker than at Company A. For example, at B but not A, the chief executive officer is also chairperson of the board of directors. Recently, profitable investment opportunities for B have become fewer, although operating cash flow for A and B is strong.

---

13 For more information, see Mukherjee (2009).
14 This discussion draws on Smith and Warner (1979), pp. 117–161.
15 EBITDA and EBIT are earnings before interest, taxes, depreciation, and amortization and earnings before interest and taxes, respectively. Bond covenants typically indicate that EBITDA and EBIT are adjusted for nonrecurring items.

Based only on the information given, investors who own shares in both A and B are *most likely* to press for a dividend increase at:

A   Company A, because it has better growth prospects than Company B.

B   Company B, because a dividend increase may mitigate potential overinvestment agency problems.

C   Company B, because a dividend increase may mitigate potential underinvestment agency problems.

Solution:

B is correct. Company B's strong operating cash flow in an environment of fewer profitable growth opportunities may tempt Company B's management to overinvest. The concern is increased because of Company B's relatively weak corporate governance.

The final example in this section illustrates the complex agency considerations that may affect dividend policy.

EXAMPLE 6

Electric Utilities, Agency Costs, and Dividends

Electric utilities often have above average dividend yields. A distinctive characteristic of many utility companies is that they pay a high percentage of earnings as dividends, while periodically issuing new equity to invest in the many projects necessitated by the capital-intensive nature of their business. This practice of financing dividends with new equity appears unwise because new equity is expensive. Researchers[16] examining a set of U.S.-based electric utilities, however, have demonstrated that there may be a good reason for paying dividends and then issuing equity: the mitigation of the agency problems between managers and shareholders and between utility regulators and utility shareholders.

Because electric utilities are typically monopolies in the sense that they are usually the only providers of electricity in a given area, they are regulated so they are not able to set electricity rates at monopolistically high levels. The regulators are expected to set rates such that the company's operating expenses are met and investors are provided with a fair return. The regulators, however, are usually elected, or are political appointees, and view ratepayers as potential voters. Thus, utility shareholders, in addition to facing potential manager–shareholder agency issues because managers have incentives to consume perquisites or to overinvest, also face a regulator–shareholder conflict in which regulators set rates low to attract the votes of individuals being served by the utility.

In the utility industry, therefore, dividends and the subsequent equity issue are used as mechanisms to monitor managers and regulators. The company pays high dividends and then goes to the capital markets to issue new equity. If the market does not think that shareholders are getting a fair return because regulators are setting rates too low, or because managers are consuming too many perks, the price at which new equity can be sold will fall until the shareholder expectations for returns are met. As a result, the company may not be able to raise sufficient funds to expand its plant to meet increasing electricity demand—the electric utility industry is very capital intensive—and, in the extreme, the lights may go

---

16 See Hansen, Kumar, and Shome (1994), pp. 16–22.

out. Faced with this possibility, and potentially angry voters, regulators have incentives to set rates at a fair level. Thus, the equity market serves to monitor and arbitrate conflicts between shareholders and both managers and regulators.

2.5 Dividend Theory: Summary

What can we conclude about the link between dividends and valuation? In theory, in the absence of market imperfections, Miller and Modigliani (1961) find that dividend policy is irrelevant to the wealth of a company's investors. But in reality, the existence of market imperfections makes matters more complicated. In addition, some investors are led, by logic or custom, to prefer dividends.

Unfortunately, in the search for the link between dividend policy and value, the evidence is inconclusive. It is difficult to show an exact relationship between dividends and value because there are so many variables affecting value. We have presented factors that would seem to explain why some companies put emphasis on dividends and others do not. Financial theory predicts that reinvestment opportunities should be the dominant factor. Indeed, no matter where they are located in the world, smaller, fast-growing companies pay out little or none of their earnings. Regardless of jurisdiction, more mature companies with fewer reinvestment opportunities tend to pay dividends. For these mature companies, taxes, laws, tradition, signaling, ownership structure, and attempts to reconcile agency conflicts all seem to play a role in determining the dividend payout ratio. At a minimum, in looking at a company, an analyst should evaluate whether a given company's dividend policy matches its reinvestment opportunities, clientele preferences, and legal/financial environment.

FACTORS AFFECTING DIVIDEND POLICY

3

In Section 2 we discussed theories of dividend policy and value and concluded that the issue is, at best, unresolved. In this section we explore six factors that affect a company's **dividend policy** (decisions about whether and in what amount to pay dividends):

- Investment opportunities;
- The expected volatility of future earnings;
- Financial flexibility;
- Tax considerations;
- Flotation costs; and
- Contractual and legal restrictions.

Boards of directors and managers spend considerable time setting dividend policy despite the lack of clear guidance from theory to guide their deliberations. The factors listed are, however, often mentioned by managers themselves as relevant to dividend policy selection in practice. Some of the factors we explore, such as taxation, are not company-specific, whereas other factors, such as possible contractual restrictions on dividend payments and the expected volatility of future earnings, are more company-specific. The factors may be interrelated, and the presence of one may enhance or diminish the effect of another. Importantly, the independence between the investment, financing, and dividend decisions assumed by MM may no longer hold when such market imperfections as information effects, agency problems, and taxes are recognized.

3.1 Investment Opportunities

All else equal, a company with many profitable investment opportunities will tend to pay out less in dividends than a company with fewer opportunities because the former company will have more uses for internally generated cash flows. Internally generated cash flow is generally a cheaper source of equity funding than new equity issuance. Opportunities for new investments, and the speed with which a company needs to respond to them, are influenced by the industry in which the company operates. A company with the ability to delay the initiation of projects without penalty may be willing to pay out more in dividends than a company that needs to act immediately to exploit profitable investment opportunities. From Exhibit 1, we see that technology companies have the lowest dividend yields whereas utilities have the highest. The chief explanation may be the size and time horizon of profitable investment opportunities in relation to annual operating cash flow generated. For technology companies the pace of change is rapid, so having internally generated funds available to react to profitable opportunities affords such companies valuable flexibility. For utility companies, for which there are typically fewer such opportunities and for which change is much slower, higher dividend payouts are indicated.

3.2 The Expected Volatility of Future Earnings

In 1956, Lintner[17] published a survey of managers at 28 companies that identified several important factors in the dividend payout decision. Most managers

- had a target payout ratio based on long-run sustainable earnings;
- focused more on dividend changes (increases or decreases) than on dividend levels; and
- were reluctant to increase the dividend if the increase might soon need to be reversed.

More recently, Brav et al. (2005), in a survey of treasurers and chief financial officers, reported that managers are very reluctant to cut dividends and tend to smooth dividends.[18] All else equal, the more volatile earnings are, the greater the risk that a given dividend increase may not be covered by earnings in a future time period. Thus, when earnings are volatile, we expect companies to be more cautious in the size and frequency of dividend increases.

3.3 Financial Flexibility

Companies may not initiate, or may reduce or omit, dividends to obtain the financial flexibility associated with having substantial cash on hand. A company with substantial cash holdings is in a relatively strong position to meet unforeseen operating needs and to exploit investment opportunities with minimum delay. Having a strong cash position can be particularly valuable during economic contractions when the availability of credit may be reduced. Financial flexibility may be viewed as a tactical consideration that is of greater importance when access to liquidity is critical and when the company's dividend payout is relatively large.

---

17 Lintner, (1956), pp. 97–113.
18 Brav, Graham, Harvey, and Michaely, (2005), pp. 483–527.

A classic example of explaining a dividend decision in terms of the need to preserve financial flexibility occurred on 28 February 2009 when General Electric Company, which had not reduced its dividend at any time in the previous 71 years, announced that going forward it was cutting its quarterly dividend rate from US$0.31 to US$0.10. GE Chairman Jeffrey Immelt stated:

> We made the decision to cut the dividend because it is a prudent measure to further enhance our balance sheet and provide us with flexibility for potential future opportunities. It is the right, precautionary action to keep the company safe and secure in the difficult operating environment we see today. We believe it further strengthens our Company for the long-term, while still providing an attractive dividend.

> *Source*: www.gereports.com/jeff-immelt-talks-about-ges-dividend.

The cut was expected to conserve $9 billion on an annual basis. With approximately $50 billion of cash on hand at the time of the statement and with operating cash flow at least covering the previous dividend, the dividend reduction appeared to be accurately characterized as "precautionary." Nevertheless, the dividend cut was widely anticipated[19] despite the assurance in GE's February 2009 Investor Update (2 February 2009) that "We are committed to our plan for $1.24 per share dividend for 2009" (page 1). Furthermore, most analysts greeted GE's decision to cut the dividend favorably given the uncertainty about the magnitude of credit losses at its financing division, GE Capital, the duration of the economic contraction, and partially frozen credit markets.

When increasing financial flexibility is an important concern, a company may decide to distribute money to shareholders primarily by means of share repurchases rather than regular dividends. A program to repurchase shares in the open market does not involve a formal requirement that any repurchases be executed, and share repurchases in general do not establish the same expectations for continuation in the future as regular dividends.

3.4 Tax Considerations

Taxation is an important factor that affects investment decisions for taxable investors in particular, because it is the after-tax return that is most relevant to investors. Different countries tax corporate dividends in a wide variety of ways. Some tax both capital gains and dividend income. Others tax dividends but not capital gains. Hong Kong is an exception in that it levies no tax on either dividends or capital gains. Within a given country, tax policy can be quite complex. In addition, as a major fiscal policy tool that is subject to politics, governments have a tendency to "re-address" tax issues, sometimes with great frequency, thereby complicating the issue even more. As with other aspects of taxation, governments use the taxation of dividends to address a variety of goals: to encourage or discourage the retention or distribution of corporate earnings; to redistribute income; or to address other political, social, and/or investment goals.

For the global investor, foreign taxes can be just as important as domestic taxes. Foreign tax credits in the investor's home country also may figure importantly into the overall taxation issue. For example, France requires French companies to withhold 15 percent of dividends paid to foreign investors, but investors in the United States can claim a tax credit on their U.S. tax return for the amount of the French tax.

---

19 The precipitous decline in GE's share repurchases in the preceding quarter indicated to many investors an urgent concern for conserving cash.

3.4.1 *Taxation Methods*

We look at three main systems of taxation that impact dividends: double taxation, split-rate, and imputation. Other tax systems can be a combination of these.

In a **double taxation system**, corporate earnings are taxed at the corporate level and then taxed again at the shareholder level if they are distributed to taxable shareholders as dividends. Exhibit 3 illustrates double taxation. The United States is used as an example. In 2003, the individual tax rate on dividends was lowered from a maximum of 39.6 percent (the highest marginal income tax rate) to a maximum of 15 percent.[20] At the same time, the tax rate on long-term capital gains was also reduced from a 20 percent maximum rate to the same 15 percent. Exhibit 3 depicts the double taxation system using the highest marginal rate on dividends in the United States both before and after the 2003 tax law change.[21]

Exhibit 3	Double Taxation of Dividends at Different Personal Tax Rates (per $100)	
	39.6%	**15%**
Net income before taxes	$100	$100
Corporate tax rate	35%	35%
Net income after tax	$65	$65
Dividend assuming 100% payout	$65	$65
Shareholder tax on dividend	$25.74	$9.75
Net dividend to shareholder	$39.26	$55.25
Double tax rate on dividend distributions	60.7%	44.8%

Although there is still double taxation of dividends before and after the 2003 tax change, the net tax rate on a dollar of income distributed in dividends declined from 61 percent to 45 percent: a decline of about 26 percent. U.S. investors clearly prefer the lower tax rate on dividends, but it is not clear whether they would prefer a higher or lower payout because the current tax rate is the same on both dividends and long-term capital gains for most shareholders. Later we will discuss a company's decision with respect to the dividend payout ratio.

A second major taxation system is the **dividend imputation tax system**, which effectively ensures that corporate profits distributed as dividends are taxed just once, at the shareholder's tax rate. Australia, New Zealand, and France use a dividend imputation tax system, whereas the United Kingdom uses a modified dividend imputation system. Under this system, a corporation's earnings are first taxed at the corporate level. When those earnings are distributed to shareholders in the form of dividends, however, shareholders receive a tax credit, known as a **franking credit**, for the taxes that the corporation paid on those distributed earnings (i.e., corporate taxes paid are imputed to the individual shareholder). If the shareholder's marginal tax rate is higher than the company's, the shareholder pays the difference between the two rates.

---

20 For this 15 percent tax rate to apply, the dividends must meet certain criteria such that they are considered to be "qualified dividends." For dividends to be qualified for this tax rate, they must be out of accumulated taxable earnings of the corporation, and recipients of dividends must meet certain minimum holding periods during which they have not hedged away the economic risk of the security held.
21 Under U.S. tax law as of mid-2009, both dividend and capital gains tax rates are scheduled to return to pre-2003 levels in 2011.

Exhibit 4 shows one variation of a tax imputation system in which a shareholder with a lower marginal tax bracket than the company's actually receives a tax credit for the difference between the corporate rate and his own rate.

Exhibit 4	Taxation of Dividends Based on Tax Imputation System (Australian $)	

	Marginal Shareholder Tax Rate	
	15%	47%
Pretax income	$100	$100
Taxes at 30% corporate tax rate	30	30
Net income after tax	70	70
Dividend assuming 100% payout	70	70
Shareholder tax on pretax income	15	47
Less tax credit for corporate payment	30	30
Tax due from shareholder	(15) ← plug →	17
Effective tax rate on dividend	15/100	47/100
	= 15%	= 47%

A **split-rate tax system** is a third taxation system of greater historical than current importance. Under this system, corporate earnings that are distributed as dividends are taxed at a lower rate at the corporate level than earnings that are retained. At the level of the individual investor, dividends are taxed as ordinary income. Earnings distributed as dividends are still taxed twice, but the relatively low corporate tax rate on earnings mitigates that penalty. Exhibit 5 depicts this split-rate tax system for dividends.

Exhibit 5	Taxation of Dividends Based on Split-Rate System (per €100)
Pretax earnings	€200
Pretax earnings retained	100
35% tax on retained earnings	35
Pretax earnings allocated to dividends	100
20% tax on earnings allocated to dividends	20
Dividends distributed	80
Shareholder tax rate	35%
After tax dividend to shareholder	$[(1 - 0.35) \times 80] = 52$
Effective tax rate on dividend	$[20\% + (80 \times 0.35)\%] = 48\%$*

*Note that of every €100 allocated to dividends, the shareholder receives €52, which implies that the effective tax rate on dividends is $100 - 52 = 48\%$.

3.4.2 *Shareholder Preference for Current Income versus Capital Gains*

All other things being equal, one could expect that the lower an investor's tax rate on dividends relative to his or her tax rate on capital gains, the stronger the investor's preference for dividends. But other issues also impinge on this preference. The investor may buy high payout shares for a tax-exempt retirement account. Even if dividends are taxed at a lower rate than capital gains, it is not clear that shareholders will necessarily prefer higher dividends. After all, capital gains taxes do not have to be paid until the shares are sold, whereas taxes on dividends must be paid in the year received, even if reinvested. In addition, in some countries, such as the United States, shares held at the time of death benefit from a step-up valuation as of the death date.[22] Finally, tax-exempt institutions, such as pension funds and endowment funds, are major shareholders in most industrial countries. Such institutions are typically exempt from both taxes on dividends and taxes on capital gains. Hence, all other things being equal, they are indifferent as to whether their return comes in the form of current dividends or capital gains.

3.5 Flotation Costs

Another factor that affects a company's dividend policy is flotation costs. Flotation costs include 1) the fees that the company pays (to investment bankers, attorneys, securities regulators, auditors, and others) to issue shares and 2) the possible adverse market price impact from a rise in the supply of shares outstanding. Aggregate flotation costs are proportionally higher (in terms of percentage of gross proceeds) for smaller companies (who issue fewer shares) than for larger companies. Flotation costs make it more expensive for companies to raise new equity capital than to use their own internally generated funds. As a result, many companies try to avoid establishing a level of dividends that would create the need to raise new equity to finance positive NPV projects.[23]

EXAMPLE 7

A Company That Needs to Reinvest All Internally Generated Funds

Boar's Head Spirits Ltd., based in the United Kingdom, currently does not pay a dividend on its common shares. Boar's Head has an estimated operating cash flow of £500 million. The company's financial analyst has calculated its cost of capital as 12 percent. The same analyst has evaluated modernization and expansion projects with a positive NPV that would require £800 million. The cost of positive NPV projects exceeds estimated operating cash flow by £300 million (£800 million − £500 million). Having an above average debt ratio for its industry, Boar's Head is reluctant to increase its long-term debt in the next year. Discuss whether you would expect Boar's Head to initiate a dividend based on the above facts.

Solution:

One would expect Boar's Head not to initiate a dividend. As things stand, internally generated funds, as represented by operating cash flow, are not sufficient to fund positive NPV projects. So payment of a dividend would be at the expense of passing by positive NPV projects unless the balance of such projects and the dividend were both financed by debt. Given its concern about debt levels, the company would not be expected to pay a dividend that needs to be financed by

---

22 The tax basis of the shares received by the beneficiary from the decedent is stepped up to fair market value at the date of death of the decedent.
23 We mentioned this earlier. There are companies, however, that pay dividends and issue equity, mainly in the utility industry. For a further discussion, see Parrino and Kidwell (2009).

debt. Because the company has unfunded positive NPV projects, it could consider issuing new shares to fund those projects. The company, however, would not be expected to issue shares only for the purpose of paying dividends.

The solution to Example 7 can also be stated in terms of free cash flow to equity (FCFE). FCFE equals operating cash flow (OCF) minus fixed capital investment (FCInv) for the period (capital expenditures) plus net borrowing for the period. Conceptually, FCFE is the cash flow available for the payment of dividends, and in this case it is negative: FCFE = £500 million − £800 million + Net borrowing = − £300 million + Net borrowing, which is negative for values of net borrowing below £300 million.

3.6 Contractual and Legal Restrictions

The payment of dividends is often affected by legal or contractual restrictions or rules. In some countries, such as Brazil, the distribution of dividends is legally mandated (with certain exceptions).[24] In some countries (e.g., Canada and the United States) the payment of a dividend not specifically indicated to be a liquidating dividend may be restricted by an **impairment of capital rule**. Such a rule requires that the net value of the remaining assets as shown on the balance sheet be at least equal to some specified amount (related to the company's capital).

Contractual restrictions on the amount of dividends that can be paid are often imposed by bondholders in bond indentures.[25] These restrictions require that the company maintain certain ratios (interest coverage ratios, current ratio, etc.) or fulfill certain conditions before dividend payments can be made. Debt covenants in a bond indenture are a response to the agency problems that exist between shareholders and bondholders and are put in place to limit the ability of the shareholders to expropriate wealth from bondholders. As an extreme example, in the absence of covenants or legal restrictions,[26] management could liquidate the company's assets and pay the proceeds to the shareholders as a liquidating dividend, leaving the bondholders with nothing to settle their claims.

If a company has issued preference shares, dividends on common shares may not be paid until preference share dividends are paid. In addition, if the preference dividends are cumulative, then preference dividends that are in arrears must be paid before any common dividend can be paid.

3.7 Factors Affecting Dividend Policy: Summary

There are several factors of varying degrees of importance that can affect a company's dividend policy. In the following example, we explore how these factors affected Toyota Motor Company's dividend policy.

---

24 See www.mzweb.com.br/positivo/web/conteudo_en.asp?idioma=1&tipo=3667&conta=44#1.
25 An **indenture** is a written contract between a lender and borrower that specifies the terms of the loan, such as interest rate, interest payment schedule, maturity, etc.
26 An example of a legal restriction is a law against fraudulent transfer of assets.

EXAMPLE 8

Toyota Motor Company Cuts Its Dividend[27]

On 8 May 2009, Toyota Motor Company, the world's largest automobile manufacturer, announced that it was going to cut its dividend for the first time. Toyota, which pays dividends twice a year, said the dividend would be reduced to ¥35 a share from the ¥75 paid a year earlier. The 2008 total dividend was ¥140 a share. The dividend cut ends a 600 percent cumulative increase in the dividend over 10 years. Faced with plunging global demand for cars (Toyota's vehicle sales were forecasted to fall 14 percent) and ongoing turmoil in the auto industry, Toyota was expecting a loss as high as ¥550 billion (operating loss of ¥850 billion) for fiscal year ending March 2010, compared with the analyst forecast loss of ¥284 billion for the same period. The company already had a loss of ¥437 billion in fiscal year 2009 (the operating loss was ¥461 billion). Toyota is focused on aggressively cutting costs—it plans to cut production-related costs by ¥340 billion and fixed costs by ¥460 billion—and has said that the lower dividend is because of the difficulty of sustaining the dividend at its previous level. Board member bonuses have been eliminated and manager summer bonuses were reduced by 60 percent. Capital spending will be cut by 36 percent to ¥830 billion, and R&D spending will be cut by 9.3 percent to ¥820 billion.

The company announced plans to raise capital via a bond issue of as much as ¥700 billion. Standard & Poor's cut Toyota's bond rating from AA + to AA. Another problem facing Toyota and other Japanese automakers is the strong yen, which has gained 13 percent against the U.S. dollar in the preceding quarter. Toyota said that a one-yen gain against the dollar trims profits by about ¥30 billion and that a similar gain against the euro trims profits by ¥4 billion.

Discuss Toyota's decision to cut its dividend in light of the factors affecting dividend policy covered in this section.

Solution:

Of the six factors discussed in this section, the *volatility of future earnings* and preservation of *financial flexibility* are the major factors influencing Toyota's decision to cut its dividend. Paying the full dividend would have lowered Toyota's liquidity ratios and forced it to raise even more external capital. In addition, paying the full dividend probably would have resulted in a more severe downgrade in its bond rating, which would have increased its interest rate on its borrowed funds. Paying the full dividend when faced with huge, and larger than expected, operating losses might have also sent a signal to investors that Toyota was not serious about cutting costs and curtailing losses. *Flotation costs* could also play a role in Toyota's case. Flotation costs on new equity are typically higher than those on new debt, and it is possible that if it paid more than ¥35 a share it would have to issue new equity in addition to the ¥700 billion in debt.

---

27 *Source*: www.bloomberg.com/apps/news?pid=20601101&sid=aYuKh9k5NZGQ.

PAYOUT POLICIES

4

In this section, we categorize and discuss three types of dividend policy. **Dividend policy** is the strategy that a company follows to determine the amount and timing of dividend payments.

4.1 Types of Dividend Policies

In the following sections we discuss stable dividend, constant dividend payout ratio, and residual dividend policies. A **stable dividend policy** is one in which regular dividends are paid that generally do not reflect short-term volatility in earnings. This type of dividend policy is the most common because managers are very reluctant to cut dividends, as discussed earlier. A **constant dividend payout ratio policy** is the policy of paying out a constant percentage of net income in dividends. A **residual dividend policy** is based on paying out as dividends any internally generated funds remaining after such funds are used to finance positive NPV projects. This type of policy has often been mentioned in theoretical discussions of dividend policy but is rarely used in practice. In Section 4.2, we discuss share repurchases, which is as an alternative to the payment of cash dividends.

4.1.1 Stable Dividend Policy

This dividend policy is the most common. Companies that use a stable dividend policy base dividends on a long-term forecast of sustainable earnings, and increase dividends when earnings have increased to a sustainably higher level. Thus, if the long-term forecast for sustainable earnings is slow growth, the dividends would be expected to grow slowly over time, more or less independent of cyclical upward or downward spikes in earnings. If sustainable earnings were not expected to grow over time, however, the corresponding dividends would be level (i.e., not growing). Compared with the two other types of dividend policies that will be presented, a stable dividend policy typically involves less uncertainty for shareholders about the level of future dividends. This is so because the other types of policies reflect to a higher degree short-term volatility in earnings and/or in investment opportunities.

Many companies pride themselves on a long record of gradually and consistently increasing dividends. Exhibit 6 shows the recent record of E.ON AG, Europe's largest utility. Dividends per share (DPS) show an upward trajectory. The decline in earnings in 2008 was actually associated with an increase in dividends, underscoring the long-term perspective of a stable dividend policy. To explain further, the exhibit shows adjusted earnings per share (EPS) reported by E.ON that attempt to remove "special effects" (to use the language of the annual report), such as restructuring expenses, marking to market of derivatives, and so on. In 2008, earnings were severely affected by book losses on disposals. For the long term, E.ON management was obviously optimistic about earnings prospects.

Exhibit 6	E.ON AG Earnings and Dividends			
Year	**EPS (€)**	**EPS (adjusted)**	**DPS (€)**	**Dividend Payout Ratio (%)**	**Dividend Payout Ratio Using Adjusted EPS (%)**
2008	0.68	€3.01	1.50	221	50
2007	3.69	€2.62	1.37	37	52
2006	2.82	€2.22	1.12	40	50

(continued)

| | | | | Dividend | Dividend Payout Ratio |
Year	EPS (€)	EPS (adjusted)	DPS (€)	Payout Ratio (%)	Using Adjusted EPS (%)
2005	3.75	€1.84	0.92	25	50
2004	2.20	n/c	0.78	35	n/c

Exhibit 6   (Continued)

Source: www.eon.com/en/investoren/19886.jsp.

As the example shows, dividends over the period were fairly stable, even while earnings, affected by restructuring costs, experienced considerable variability.

A stable dividend policy can be modeled as a process of gradual adjustment towards a target payout ratio based on long-term sustainable earnings. A **target payout ratio** is a goal that represents the proportion of earnings that the company intends to distribute (pay out) to shareholders as dividends over the long term.

A model of gradual adjustment (which may be called a "target payout adjustment model") was developed by John Lintner.[28] The model reflects three basic conclusions from his study of dividend policy: 1) Companies have a target payout ratio, based on long-term, sustainable earnings; 2) managers are more concerned with dividend changes than with the level of the dividend; and 3) companies will cut or eliminate a dividend only in extreme circumstances or as a last resort.

A simplified version of Lintner's model can be used to show how a company can adjust its dividend.[29] For example, suppose that the payout ratio is below the target payout ratio and earnings are expected to increase. The expected increase in the dividend can be estimated as the product of three quantities: the expected increase in earnings next year, the target payout ratio, and the adjustment factor (one divided by the number of years over which the adjustment in dividends should take place). Suppose that the current dividend is $0.40, the target payout ratio is 50 percent, the adjustment factor is 0.2 (i.e., the adjustment is to occur over five years), and that the expected earnings increase is $0.50 (from earnings of $1.00 over the past year to earnings of $1.50 for the year ahead). The expected increase in dividends is

Increase in earnings × Target payout ratio × Adjustment factor

= $0.50 × 0.5 × 0.2

= $0.05 Increase in dividends

Therefore, even though earnings increased 50 percent from $1.00 to $1.50, the dividend would only incrementally increase by about 13 percent from $0.40 to $0.45.

By using this model, note that if in the following year earnings temporarily fell from $1.50 to $1.00, the dividend might well be increased by up to $0.05 a share, as the implied new dividend of $0.50 would still be moving the company toward its target payout ratio of 50 percent. Even if earnings were to fall further or even experience a loss, the company would be reluctant to cut or eliminate the dividend (unless its estimate of sustainable earnings or target payout ratio were lowered), but would rather opt to maintain the current dividend until future earnings increases justified an increase in the dividend.

---

28 Lintner (1956).
29 Lease et al. (2000), p. 124.

EXAMPLE 9

Determining Dividends by Using a Target Payout Adjustment Model

Last year Luna Inc. had earnings of $2.00 a share and paid a regular dividend of $0.40. For the current year, the company anticipates earnings of $2.80. It has a 30 percent target payout ratio and uses a 5-year period to adjust the dividend. Compute the expected dividend for the current year.

Solution:

$$\text{Expected dividend} = \text{Last dividend} + \big(\text{Expected increase in earnings}$$
$$\times \text{Target payout ratio} \times \text{Adjustment factor}\big)$$
$$= \$0.40 + \big[(\$2.80 - \$2.00) \times 0.3 \times (1/5)\big]$$
$$= \$0.40 + (\$0.80 \times 0.3 \times 0.2)$$
$$= \$0.45$$

Thus, although earnings are expected to increase by 40 percent, the increase in the dividend would be 12.5 percent.

4.1.2 *Constant Dividend Payout Ratio Policy*

In this type of policy, a dividend payout ratio decided on by the company is applied to current earnings to calculate the dividend. With this type of dividend policy, dividends fluctuate with earnings in the short term. Constant dividend payout ratio policies are infrequently adopted in practice. Example 10 illustrates this type of policy.

EXAMPLE 10

Cal-Maine Foods Changes from a Stable to a Constant Dividend Payout Ratio Policy

Cal-Maine Foods, Inc. (NASDAQ: CALM) is the leading egg producer in the United States. Cal-Maine's earnings tend to be highly volatile. Demand for eggs is seasonal, typically being higher in winter than in summer. On the supply side, costs are driven, to a great extent, by corn prices that are subject to business cycle influences and are thus very volatile. In consideration of earnings volatility, Cal-Maine might have difficulty sustaining a steadily rising dividend level. Probably in view of such considerations, Cal-Maine changed its dividend policy from a stable dividend policy to a constant dividend payout ratio policy (denoted a "variable dividend policy" by management) in its fiscal year 2008. The following is the explanation by the company:

> We have paid cash dividends on our Common Stock since 1998. The annual dividend rate of $0.05 per share of Common Stock, or $0.0125 per quarter, was paid in each of the fiscal quarters shown in the table above, through the second quarter of fiscal 2008. We have also paid cash dividends on our Class A Common Stock at a rate equal to 95 percent of the annual rate on our Common Stock.
>
> Effective 30 November 2007, the Company's Board of Directors approved the adoption of a variable dividend policy to replace the Company's fixed dividend policy. Commencing with the third quarter of fiscal 2008, Cal-Maine began to pay a dividend to shareholders of

its Common Stock and Class A Common Stock on a quarterly basis for each quarter for which the Company reports net income computed in accordance with generally accepted accounting principles in an amount equal to one-third (1/3) of such quarterly income. The amount of the dividend payable on each share of Class A Common Stock is in an amount equal to 95 percent of the amount paid on each share of Common Stock. Dividends are paid to shareholders of record as of the sixtieth day following the last day of such quarter, and are payable on the fifteenth day following the record date. Following a quarter for which the Company does not report net income, the Company shall not pay a dividend for a subsequent profitable quarter until the Company is profitable on a cumulative basis computed from the date of the last quarter for which a dividend was paid.

Management and Board of Directors of Cal-Maine believe the variable dividend policy will more accurately reflect the results of our operations while recognizing and allowing for the cyclicality of the egg industry.

Source: www.calmainefoods.com.

Exhibit 7 shows quarterly data for fiscal years 2009 and 2008.

Exhibit 7	Earnings per Share (EPS) and Dividends per Share (DPS) for Cal-Maine Foods (Fiscal Years End 31 or 30 May)	
Fiscal Period	**EPS($)**	**DPS($)**
2009:Q4	0.43	0.1438
2009:Q3	1.30	0.4322
2009:Q2	1.15	0.3817
2009:Q1	0.47	0.1570
2008:Q4	1.54	0.5138
2008:Q3	2.41	0.8038
2008:Q2	1.70	0.0125
2008:Q1	0.76	0.0125

Source: www.calmainefoods.com.

1   From the table above, identify the fiscal quarter when Cal-Maine first applied a constant dividend payout ratio policy.

2   Demonstrate that the dividend for 2009:Q4 reflects the stated current dividend policy.

Solution to 1:

Cal-Maine first used that policy in the third quarter of fiscal year 2008. Until then a quarterly dividend of $0.0125 was paid no matter what the quarterly earnings per share were. The payout ratios in all subsequent quarters round to approximately 33.3 percent.

> ### Solution to 2:
> (EPS $0.43)/3 = $0.1433, which differs only slightly from the reported dividend of $0.1438 (EPS are rounded to two decimal places so rounding error is expected).

4.1.3 Residual Dividend Policy

The **residual dividend policy** is an intuitively appealing dividend policy that is rarely used in practice because it typically results in highly volatile dividend payments. The residual dividend policy is based on paying out as dividends the full amount of any internally generated funds remaining after financing the current period's capital expenditures (investment in positive net present value projects) consistent with the target capital structure. A residual dividend policy presumes that equity financing comes from reinvested earnings rather than new share issuance, which is more expensive. Directing internally generated funds first to positive NPV projects is consistent with shareholder wealth maximization as is, typically, distributing to shareholders the balance that cannot be so invested. The residual dividend policy puts investment in positive NPV projects ahead of considerations of not reducing the dividend. Under a residual dividend policy, however, dividends may swing from low or zero when capital expenditure needs are high (relative to internally generated funds) to high when the reverse situation holds. The increased uncertainty about future dividends may lead investors to require a higher rate of return on equity investment as compensation, possibly offsetting any advantages to the policy.

Exhibit 8 provides an illustration of the residual dividend policy. The company has earnings of €100 million, a target capital structure of 30 percent debt and 70 percent equity, and three prospective capital expenditure levels of €50 million, €100 million, and €150 million. As Exhibit 8 shows, Dividend = Earnings − (Capital budget × Equity percent in capital structure) or zero, whichever is greater.

Exhibit 8	Residual Dividend Policy for a Target Capital Structure of 30 Percent Debt and 70 Percent Equity (€ Millions)		
	€50 Capital Budget	**€100 Capital Budget**	**€150 Capital Budget**
Earnings	€100	€100	€100
Capital spending	€50	€100	€150
Financed from new debt	0.3 × 50 = €15	0.3 × 100 = €30	0.3 × 150 = €45
Financed from retained earnings	0.7 × 50 = €35	0.7 × 100 = €70	(0.7 × 150 > 100) = €100
Financed from new equity or debt	€0	€0	€5
Residual cash flow = residual dividend	€100 − $35 = €65	€100 − $70 = €30	€100 − $100 = €0
Implied payout ratio	65/100 = 65%	30/100 = 30%	0/100 = 0%

In the final column of Exhibit 8, the €150 million in capital spending requires €105 million in equity (€150 million × 0.70), which is greater than the company's total earnings of €100 million. The company would probably finance the shortfall with debt, temporarily deviating from its target capital structure, rather than use more costly external equity financing.

As can be seen from Exhibit 8, various capital spending plans result in dramatically different implied dividend payments. Payout ratios, too, range from a zero payment of dividends under the highest capital spending plan, to a 65 percent payout ratio under the lowest capital spending plan.

To overcome the problem of volatile dividends, companies may use a longterm residual dividend approach to smooth their dividend payments. The approach would involve forecasting earnings and capital expenditures over the next 5 or 10 years, determining the resulting total amount of residual dividends for the period, which would then be paid out evenly over the forecast period. The company could also set a relatively low stable cash dividend based on the calculation and distribute a more flexible amount to shareholders in the form of share repurchases or even a special dividend as in the Microsoft case described earlier.

EXAMPLE 11

Determining Dividends

1 Suppose a company has €900 million in planned capital spending (representing positive NPV projects). The company's target capital structure is 60 percent debt and 40 percent equity. Given that the company follows a residual dividend policy, the company's indicated dividend with earnings of €500 million, is *closest* to:

   A €140 million.

   B €360 million.

   C €500 million.

2 Suppose a company has paid semiannual dividends of €3 a share over the prior two years and €2.75 for four years prior. During that six-year period, earnings and capital expenditure needs have shown considerable interim variability, and dividend payout ratios have ranged from 55 to 86 percent, with an average of 65 percent. In the current six-month period, suppose that 8 million shares are issued and outstanding and that earnings are anticipated to be €28 million. The company has €5 million in planned capital spending for the six-month period (representing positive NPV projects). The company's long-term target capital structure is 50 percent debt and 50 percent equity. Based on the facts given, the most likely dividend per share for the current six-month period is:

   A €2.28.

   B €3.00.

   C €3.19.

Solution to 1:

A is correct. To fund its €900 million in projects while maintaining its target debt ratio of 60 percent, the company will obtain €900 million × 0.60 = €540 million in new debt financing. The amount that needs to be financed by internally generated funds is €900 million – €540 million = €360 million. Netting that amount from earnings gives €500 million – €360 million = €140 million that can be paid out in dividends. The solution can also be obtained as €500 – €900 × 0.4 = €500 – €360 = €140 million.

> **Solution to 2:**
>
> B is correct. The historical description of the company's dividend payments is consistent with a stable dividend policy. The total cost of the dividend at 8 million shares × €3 a share = €24 million is covered by current earnings of €28 million. Just maintaining the current dividend implies a dividend payout ratio of (€24 million)/(€28 million) = 85.7 percent, which is at the high end of the historical range. No information is provided that points to increasing the dividend.
>
> Answer A at €2.28 ≈ €2.275 = (€28 million)(0.65)/(8 million shares) would be a possible value of the dividend under a target payout ratio policy, and answer C €3.19 ≈ €3.1875 = [€28 million − 0.5(€5 million)]/(8 million shares) would be a possible answer under a residual dividend policy.

4.2 The Dividend versus Share Repurchase Decision

Theory concerning the dividend–share repurchase decision generally concludes that share repurchases are equivalent to cash dividends of equal amount in their effect on shareholders' wealth, all other things being equal. Further discussion about the choice revolves around what might not "be equal" and what might cause one distribution mechanism to be preferred over the other. The use of share repurchases also may be legally restricted.[30]

In general, share repurchases can be considered part of a company's broad policy on distributing earnings to shareholders and a company may engage in share repurchases for reasons similar to those mentioned in connection with cash dividends—for example, to distribute free cash flow to equity to common shareholders. A number of additional reasons have been brought forward that apply to share repurchases, including:

- Potential tax advantages;
- Share price support/signaling that the company considers its shares a good investment;
- Added managerial flexibility;
- Offsetting dilution from employee stock options; and
- Increasing financial leverage.

Potential tax advantages. In jurisdictions that tax shareholder dividends at higher rates than capital gains, share repurchases have a tax advantage over cash dividends.

Share price support/signaling that the company considers its shares a good investment. Management of a company may view its own shares as undervalued in the marketplace and hence a good investment. Although management's stock market judgment can be just as good or bad as that of any other market participant, corporate management typically does have more information about the company's operation and future prospects than does any outside investor or analyst. Furthermore, share repurchases via open market purchase, the dominant repurchase mechanism, allow management to time share repurchases with respect to market price. The announcement of a share repurchase program is often understood as a positive signal about the company's prospects and attractiveness as an investment. An unexpected announcement of a meaningful share repurchase program can often have the same positive impact on

---

30 See Vermaelen (2005) for details.

share price as would a better-than-expected earnings report or similar positive event. In the days following the global stock market crash of October 1987, a number of prominent companies announced huge buybacks in an effort to halt the slide in the price of their shares and show confidence in the future. It may have been an important aspect in the stock market recovery that followed. Some investment analysts, however, take issue with the notion that initiation of share repurchases is a positive signal, because a repurchase program could mean that the company has no new profitable investment opportunities and is thus returning cash to shareholders.

Added managerial flexibility. Unlike regular cash dividends, share repurchase programs appear not to create the expectation among investors of continuance in the future. Furthermore, in contrast to an announced dividend, the announcement of a share repurchase by open market purchase does not typically create an obligation to follow through with repurchases. Additionally, the timing of share repurchases via open market activity is at managers' discretion. Share repurchases also afford shareholders flexibility because participation is optional, which is not the case with the receipt of cash dividends.

Offsetting dilution from employee stock options. For some companies, share repurchases are used to offset the possible dilution of earnings per share that may result from the exercise of employee stock options. Whether stated or not, many companies try to repurchase at least as many shares as were issued in the exercise of stock options—even though the options are typically exercised at lower prices than the repurchase price.

Increasing financial leverage. Another reason for repurchasing shares is to modify the company's capital structure, if greater leverage in the company's capital structure is viewed as efficient. Share repurchases increase leverage.

Among other reasons mentioned for share repurchases by corporate managers is the objective of increasing EPS. This objective is problematic for two reasons. First, even when share repurchases result in an EPS increase, the required rate of return will likely increase, reflecting higher leverage. Second, according to finance theory, changing EPS by changing the number of shares outstanding does not affect shareholder wealth given that total free cash flow is unchanged.

EXAMPLE 12

Share Repurchase to Increase Financial Leverage

Canadian Holdings Inc. (CHI), with debt and a debt ratio of C$30 million and 30 percent, respectively, plans a share repurchase program involving C$7 million or 10 percent of the market value of its common shares. What debt ratios would result from financing the repurchases using 1) cash on hand and 2) new debt?

Solution:

1) If CHI uses cash on hand to make the share repurchase, the debt ratio would rise to 32 percent. 2) If CHI uses debt to finance the share repurchases, the debt ratio would increase to 37 percent. Exhibit 9 shows the calculations. By either means of financing the share repurchase, it increases financial leverage.[31]

---

[31] Note that using a ratio of net debt to capital based on net debt (defined as debt net of cash) and capital (defined as net debt plus equity), the effect of using cash or using debt in the share repurchase would be the same. The initial ratio of net debt to capital is $(30 − 7)/(23 + 70) = 25$ percent. Using cash for the share repurchase, this ratio would become $(30)/(30 + 63) = 32$ percent, and using debt in the transaction, it would also be $(37 − 7)/(30 + 63) = 32$ percent.

| Exhibit 9 | Estimated Impact on Capital Structure (C$ Millions) |

	Before Buyback		After Buyback			
			All Cash		All Debt	
	C$	%	C$	%	C$	%
Debt	30	30	30	32	37	37
Equity (at market)	70	70	63	68	63	63
Total Cap	100	100	93	100	100	100

Canadian Holdings' beginning debt ratio was 30 percent. If Canadian Holdings uses borrowed funds to repurchase equity, the debt ratio at market will increase to 37 percent, which is significantly more than if it used excess cash (32 percent).

EXAMPLE 13

Siemens AG Announces Share Buyback to Achieve Target Capital Structure

On 7 November 2007, Siemens AG, a world leader in electrical and electronic equipment, reported that in order to optimize its capital structure it would repurchase shares by fiscal year end 2010 to achieve a target ratio of net industrial debt to EBITDA in the range 0.8x – 1.0x. Accordingly, Siemens said it could repurchase shares in the amount up to €10 billion in several tranches. Siemens repurchases in the first two tranches were as follows:

| Exhibit 10 | Share Buyback Activities, First Tranche (2008) |

Month	Shares Repurchased	Average Price (€)	Total Value (€)
January	1,829,000	84.6186	154,767,464.62
February	9,579,498	88.2335	845,232,489.97
March	9,943,030	75.4019	749,723,178.63
April	3,503,013	71.4466	250,278,201.67
Sum	24,854,541	80.4682	2,000,001,334.89

Share Buyback Activities, Second Tranche (2008)			
Month	Shares Repurchased	Average Price (€)	Total Value (€)
June	13,709,495	72.8857	999,225,910.57
July	14,207,169	70.3870	999,999,975.00
Sum	27,916,664	71.6141	1,999,225,885.57

Source: Siemens AG website, accessed November 2007.

> The company bought back about 52.77 million shares for approximately €4 billion. No further repurchases have been announced, and it is possible that Siemens has shelved the program to conserve cash in the economic downturn.

A company can use both special cash dividends and share repurchases as a supplement to regular cash dividends. These means of distributing cash are often used in years when there are large and extraordinary increases in cash flow that are not expected to continue in future years. In making these types of payments, the company essentially communicates that the distribution, like the increase in cash flow, should not be expected to continue in the future. In this context, a share repurchase is effectively an alternative to paying a special cash dividend.

Some companies initiate payouts to shareholders using share repurchases rather than cash dividends.[32] As with the case of a share repurchase substituting for a special cash dividend, the use of share repurchases is paid with the expectation that it will not be viewed as creating a fixed commitment.

Although all of the preceding can be the stated or unstated reasons for share repurchases, in general, share repurchases increase in volume when the economy is strong and companies have more cash. During recessions, when cash is often short, share repurchases typically fall. From the fourth quarter of 2004 to the fourth quarter of 2008, the 500 companies in the S&P 500 spent $1.8 trillion on share repurchases as compared with $2 trillion on capital expenditures and $1 trillion on cash dividends. In the market crash of 2008–2009, share repurchases plummeted.[33] Major companies (particularly in the global financial sector) that had made large share repurchases encountered challenges to their financial viability in 2008 and 2009.

Example 14, in which a company's board of directors initiates a cash dividend, integrates a number of themes related to cash dividends, stock dividends (in which additional shares are distributed to shareholders instead of cash), and share repurchases.

EXAMPLE 14

Scottsville Instruments' Dividend Policy Decision

Scottsville Instruments, Inc., (SCII) is a U.S.-based company emerging as a leader in providing medical testing equipment to the pharmaceutical and biotechnology industries. SCII's primary markets are growing and the company is spending $100 million a year on research and development to enhance its competitive position. SCII is highly profitable and has substantial positive free cash flow after funding positive NPV projects. During the past three years, SCII has made significant share repurchases. Subsequent to the reduction in the tax rate on cash dividends to 15 percent in the United States, the same tax rate as that on long-term capital gains, SCII management is proposing the initiation of a cash dividend. The first dividend is proposed to be an annual dividend of $0.40 a share to be paid during the next fiscal year. Based on estimated earnings per share of $3.20, this dividend would represent a payout ratio (DPS/EPS) of 0.125 or 12.5 percent. The proposal that will be brought before the board of directors is the following:

32　Grullon and Michaely (2002).
33　Grace and Curran (2009), p. C9.

"Proposed: Scottsville Instruments, Inc., will institute a program of cash dividends. The first dividend will be an annual dividend of $0.40 a share, to be paid at a time to be determined during the next fiscal year. Thereafter, an annual dividend will be paid consistent with retaining funds sufficient to finance profitable capital projects."

The company's board of directors will formally consider the dividend proposal at its next meeting in one month's time. Although some directors favor the dividend initiation proposal, other directors, led by William Marshall, are skeptical of it. Marshall has stated:

"The initiation of a cash dividend will suggest to investors that SCII is no longer a growth company."

As a counterproposal, Marshall has offered his support for the initiation of an annual 2 percent stock dividend. Elise Tashman, a director who is neutral to both the cash dividends and stock dividend ideas, has told Marshall the following:

"A 2 percent stock dividend will not affect the wealth of our shareholders."

Exhibit 11 presents selected *pro forma* financials of SCII, if the directors approve the initiation of a cash dividend.

Exhibit 11   Scottsville Instruments, Inc. Pro Forma Financial Data Assuming Cash Dividend ($ Millions)

Income Statement		Statement of Cash Flows	
Sales	1,200	Cash flow from operations	135
Earnings before taxes	155	Cash flow from investing activities	(84)
Taxes	35	Cash flow from financing activities:	
Net income	120	Debt repayment	(4)
		Share repurchase	(32)
		Proposed dividend	(15)
		Estimated change in cash	0

Ratios		Five-Year Forecasts	
Current ratio	2.1	Sales growth	8% annually
Debt/Equity (at market)	0.27	Earnings growth	11% annually
Interest coverage	10.8x	Projected cost of capital	10%
ROA	10.0%		
ROE	19.3%		
P/E	20x		
E/P	5.0%		

Using the information provided, address the following:

1 Critique Marshall's statement.

2 Justify Tashman's statement.

3 Identify and explain the dividend policy that the proposed $0.40 a share cash dividend reflects.

Solution to 1:

The following points argue against the thesis of Marshall's statement:

- As discussed in the text, dividend initiations and increases are on average associated with higher future earnings growth.

- Forecasted sales and earnings growth rates are relatively high.

- SCII still has considerable positive NPV projects available to it, as shown by the cash flow from investing activities of negative $84 million. This fact is consistent with SCII being a company with substantial current growth opportunities.

- For the past three years SCII has been making share repurchases, so investors are already cognizant that management is distributing cash to shareholders. The initiation of a dividend as a continuation of that policy is less likely to be interpreted as an information signaling event.

Solution to 2:

A stock dividend has no effect on shareholder wealth. A shareholder owns the same percentage of the company and its earnings as it did before the stock dividend. All other things being equal, the price of a stock will decline to reflect the stock dividend, but the decline will be exactly offset by the greater number of shares owned.

Solution to 3:

As shown in the statement of cash flows, the $0.40 a share annual dividend reflects a total amount of $15 million, fully using SCII's free cash flow after acceptance of positive NPV projects. The proposal brought before the board does not suggest a commitment to maintain the annual dividend at $0.40 a share (or greater), as a stable dividend policy would typically imply. Rather, the funding of profitable capital projects will first be considered. These facts taken together are most consistent with a residual dividend policy.

4.3 Global Trends in Payout Policy

An interesting question is whether corporations are changing their dividend policies in response to changes in the economic environment and in investor preferences. In 2001, Fama and French[34] investigated the case of disappearing dividends in the United States. They found a large decline in the number of U.S.-based industrial companies that paid dividends from 1978 to 1998. But the aggregate payout ratio in the 1990s was about 40 percent, within the 40–60 percent range typical of the 1960–1998 period. Fama and French argued that the decline in dividends was related to the large number of relatively unprofitable companies that were assuming prominence in the stock market. DeAngelo, DeAngelo, and Skinner[35] extended Fama and French's argument by showing that even though fewer corporations were paying dividends, the largest 100 companies in the United States increased their inflation-adjusted dividends by 23 percent from 1978 to 2000. What appeared to be happening was the formation of

---

34 Fama and French (2001).
35 DeAngelo, DeAngelo, and Skinner (2004).

two tiers of companies. The first tier is composed of approximately 100 large, extremely profitable companies that have a fairly stable payout ratio of around 42 percent. The second tier is composed of two types of non-dividend payers: financially troubled, marginally profitable or money-losing companies, and/or companies related to technology that typically use share repurchase as a substitute for dividends.

Dividend policy practices have international differences and change through time, even in one market, consistent with the catering theory of Baker and Wurgler (2004), which predicts that companies adapt their dividend policy over time to changing investor tastes.[36] Typically, a lower percentage of companies in a given U.S. stock market index have paid dividends than have companies in a comparable European stock market index. In addition, the following broad trends in dividend policy have been observed:

- The fraction of companies paying cash dividends has been in long-term decline in most developed markets (e.g., the United States, Canada, the European Union overall, the United Kingdom, and Japan).[37]

- Since the early 1980s in the United States[38] and the early 1990s in the United Kingdom and continental Europe,[39] the fraction of companies engaging in share repurchases has trended upward.

Ferris, Sen, and Unlu[40] study dividend behavior across 25 countries and conclude that both aggregate dividend amounts as well as payout ratios have generally increased over time, although the fraction of dividend payers has decreased (see Exhibit 12).[41]

Exhibit 12	Dividend Payout Ratios by Country and over Time[42]				
Country	**1994**	**1998**	**2001**	**2004**	**2007**
Australia	0.28	0.37	0.48	0.36	0.38
Austria	0.14	0.27	0.27	0.18	0.24
Canada	0.17	0.19	19.16	0.25	0.27
Denmark	0.07	0.15	0.25	0.13	0.13
Finland	0.06	0.19	0.29	0.41	0.35
France	0.10	0.14	0.31	0.24	0.26
Germany	0.20	0.30	0.48	0.20	0.26
Hong Kong	0.33	0.58	0.32	0.32	0.39
Indonesia	0.25	0.11	0.16	0.27	0.37
Ireland	0.12	0.14	0.28	0.27	0.11
Italy	0.04	0.14	0.45	0.49	0.25
Japan	0.13	0.13	0.13	0.10	0.13

(continued)

---

36 For the international evidence of catering and of international differences, see Ferris, Jayaraman, and Sabherwal (2009), pp. 1730–1738.
37 See Von Eije and Megginson (2008) and references therein.
38 Important in the United States was the adoption of Securities and Exchange Commission Rule 10b-18 in 1982, which relieved companies from concerns of stock manipulation in repurchasing shares as long as companies follow certain guidelines.
39 See Von Eije and Megginson (2008).
40 Ferris, Sen, and Unlu (2009).
41 Parrington (2009) has criticized the inter-comparability of the data behind the figures presented in Exhibit 12. The reader should be aware that the samples for each market shown generally represent different proportions of the total market and high proportions of large-cap stocks.
42 The data in Exhibit 12 are excerpted from Ferris et al. (2009), *ibid*, and appear as shown in the original document.

Exhibit 12	(Continued)				
Country	**1994**	**1998**	**2001**	**2004**	**2007**
South Korea	0.03	0.05	0.10	0.10	0.12
Malaysia	0.20	0.46	0.25	0.25	0.31
Mexico	0.35	0.21	0.10	0.16	0.18
Norway	0.09	0.25	0.12	0.19	0.21
Philippines	0.05	0.08	0.13	0.13	0.25
Portugal	0.11	0.25	0.30	0.22	0.31
Singapore	0.21	0.24	0.39	0.32	0.39
South Africa	0.23	0.19	0.27	0.23	0.25
Spain	0.19	0.20	0.19	0.33	0.26
Sweden	0.09	0.22	0.72	0.37	0.37
Switzerland	0.14	0.18	0.25	0.23	0.24
United Kingdom	0.27	0.38	0.49	0.38	0.29
United States	0.21	0.20	0.30	0.20	0.20

5   ANALYSIS OF DIVIDEND SAFETY

The Global Recession that began in late 2007 was predicted to give rise to the largest number of dividend cuts and suspensions since the Great Depression of the 1930s.[43] Global titans, such as GE, Toyota, Barclays, UBS, and Daimler AG, cut their dividend. By mid-2009, S&P 500 dividends for U.S. companies were down by 25 percent from the prior year, British investors were predicting a worst-case decline in dividends for UK companies of 35 percent, and market analysts forecast similar declines for the MSCI Global Index.[44] In this section, we discuss how an analyst can form a judgment on the likelihood that a company's cash dividend may be cut.

The traditional way of looking at dividend safety is the dividend payout ratio (dividends/net income) and its inverse, the **dividend coverage ratio** (net income/dividends). A higher dividend payout ratio or a lower dividend coverage ratio tends to indicate, all else equal, higher risk of a dividend cut. The logic is that with a relatively high dividend payout ratio, a relatively small percentage decline in earnings could cause the dividend not to be payable out of earnings.

EXAMPLE 15

Traditional Measures of Dividend Safety

Given the following data, calculate the dividend payout and coverage ratios:

Mature European SA	2010 FY
Net income available for common stock	EUR 100 mil.
Dividends paid	EUR 40 mil.

---

43 *The Economist*, 7 March 2009, p. 77.
44 FT.com, "Investors Fear New Flood of Dividend Cuts," 13 May 2009.

> **Solution:**
>
> | | |
> |---|---|
> | Dividend payout ratio | 40/100 = 40% |
> | Dividend coverage ratio | 100/40 = 2.5x |

In judging these ratios, various generalizations may be stated based on observed practice. In stating these generalizations, we emphasize that they should be confirmed for the particular market and time period being addressed.

Large mature companies typically target dividend payout ratios of 40 percent to 60 percent, so that dividend coverage ratios range from about 1.7x to 2.5x, excluding "extra" payments. Mature companies are expected to be in this range over the course of a 5- to 10-year business cycle. Higher dividend payout ratios (or lower dividend coverage ratios) often constitute a risk factor that a dividend may be cut if earnings decline. When a dividend coverage ratio drops to 1.0, the dividend is considered to be in jeopardy unless non-recurring events, such as an employee strike, or a typhoon, are responsible for a temporary decline in earnings. In judging safety, qualitative pluses are awarded for companies that have had stable or increasing dividends, while minuses accrue to companies that have reduced their dividend in the past. Indeed, concerning this issue, the 1962 edition of Graham, et al. stated that "[t]he absence of rate reduction in the past record is perhaps as important as the presence of numerous rate advances."[45]

Payout and coverage ratios are often compared on an industry basis when evaluating them. Fast-growing industries, often with relatively new companies, are associated with no or low dividend payouts, and mature and highly regulated companies have higher payouts. In the early 1990s, technology companies were regarded as quintessential growth companies with little concern for cash dividends. As the technology industry has matured, its dividend payout has become more significant.

Free cash flow to equity, defined earlier, represents the cash flow available for distribution as dividends after taking account of working and fixed capital expenditure needs. If those needs are ignored, distribution of dividends may be at cross-purposes with shareholder wealth maximization. Cash flow (specifically free cash flow to equity), not reported net income, should be viewed as the source of cash dividend payments from that perspective. Thus, analysis of dividend safety can properly include payout and coverage ratios based on FCFE rather than net income. Other cash flow definitions besides FCFE have also been used in such ratios. Examining the correlation of dividends with cash flow measures may also provide insights.

This reading has taken the position that payouts should be considered in terms of share repurchases as well as dividends because they both represent cash distributions to shareholders. Arguably, a comprehensive measure of dividend safety would relate FCFE to both cash dividends and share repurchases:[46]

FCFE coverage ratio = FCFE/[Dividends + Share repurchases]

If that ratio is 1, the company is returning all available cash to shareholders. If it is significantly greater than 1, the company is improving liquidity by using funds to increase cash and/or marketable securities. A ratio significantly less than 1 is not sustainable because the company is paying out more than it can afford by drawing down existing cash/marketable securities, thereby decreasing liquidity. At some point the company will have to raise new equity.

---

45 Graham, Dodd, Cottle, and Tatham (1962), p. 487.
46 See Damodaran (2001), pp. 689–704. Damodaran actually shows the inverse, the FCFE payout ratio.

Fundamental risk factors with regard to dividend safety include above-average financial leverage. Additional issuance of debt, whether to fund projects or to finance the dividend, may be restricted during business downturns.

Example 16 shows an analysis of the sustainability of the dividend of the iconic motorcycle company, Harley Davidson, Inc. The analysis includes the traditional earnings/dividend coverage approach and an alternative FCFE approach that considers total cash payouts to shareholders—dividends and share repurchases.

EXAMPLE 16

Harley Davidson's Coverage Ratios

Harley Davidson, Inc. (NYSE symbol HOG) produces and sells luxury motorcycles in the United States and Europe. The company has paid dividends since 1993.

Exhibit 13	Harley Davidson		
Years Ending 31 December (US$ Millions)	**2006**	**2007**	**2008**
Net income (earnings)	1,043	934	655
Cash flow from operations	762	798	(685)
FCInv (capital expenditures)	220	242	332
Net borrowing	493	352	1,845
Dividends paid	213	261	302
Stock repurchases	936	1,132	249

Source: Yahoo! Finance website, 24 July 2009.

1 Using the above information, calculate the following for 2006, 2007, and 2008:

   A Dividend/earnings payout ratio

   B Earnings/dividend coverage ratio

   C Free cash flow to equity (FCFE)

   D FCFE/[dividend + stock repurchase] coverage ratio

2 Discuss the trend in earnings/dividend coverage as compared with the trend in FCFE/[dividend + stock repurchase] coverage.

3 Comment on the sustainability of HOG's dividend and stocks repurchase policy after 2008.

Solution to 1:

A Dividend/earnings payout = $213/$1,043 = 0.20 or 20 percent in 2006, 0.28 or 28 percent in 2007, and 0.46 or 46 percent in 2008.

B Earnings/dividend coverage = $1,043/$213 = 4.9x in 2006, 3.6x in 2007, and 2.2x in 2008.

C FCFE = Cash flow from operations (CFO) – FCInv + Net borrowing = $762 – $220 + $493 = $1,035 in 2006, $798 – $242 + $352 = $908 in 2007, and $828 in 2008.

D FCFE coverage of dividends + share repurchases = FCFE/dividends + stock repurchases = $1,035/($213 + $936) = 0.90x in 2006. Similar calculations result in 0.65x in 2007 and 1.50x in 2008.

Solution to 2:

Earnings/dividend coverage declined over the three years. Still, even in 2008, accounting earnings were more than twice the amount necessary to pay the dividend. An analyst who looked at only this metric might not have suspected problems.

The FCFE coverage of both the dividend and stock repurchases was less than 1 in 2006 and 2007, indicating the company was reducing liquidity (and/or consciously electing to move to a more leveraged capital structure) by returning money to shareholders. The increase in this ratio to 1.5× in 2008 was the result of net borrowings. Harley was funding almost everything (negative CFO, capital expenditures, dividends, and share buyouts) with new borrowings. Analysis of FCFE generation in 2008, showing its reliance on net borrowing, was a better indicator of problems latent in Harley's payout policies than earnings/dividend coverage.

Solution to 3:

Funding dividends and stock repurchases with net borrowings is a short-term proposition and not a sustainable policy. Something has to give: cut the dividend and/or curtail share repurchases.

Update:

On 12 February 2009, Harley Davidson announced a cut in its quarterly dividend to $0.10 a share, a decline of 70 percent from its old rate of $0.33, and further announced that no stock repurchases would be made in the first quarter.

Whether based on a company's net income or free cash flow, past financial data do not always predict dividend safety. Surprise factors and other unexpected events can confound the most rigorous analysis of past data. Equity and debt markets were shaken in 2008–2009 by the losses taken by almost all U.S. and European banks. These losses led to the cutting and, in some cases, virtual elimination of cash dividends. Not all 21st century investors would agree with Graham and Dodd's 1962 assertion that "For the vast majority of common stocks, the dividend record and prospects have always been the most important factor controlling investment quality and value."[47] But most investors would agree that when the market even begins to suspect a decrease or suspension of a company's cash dividend, that expectation is likely to weigh unfavorably on that company's common stock valuation. Therefore, many analysts look for external stock market indicators of market expectations of dividend cuts.

Extremely high dividend yields compared with a company's past record and current bond yields is often another warning signal that investors are predicting a dividend cut. For example, the dividend yield on General Electric shares just prior to its 68 percent dividend cut in 2008 was nearly 14 percent.[48] After the dividend cut, GE shares still yielded about 4.7 percent, relatively high compared with its yields in

---

47 Graham, Dodd, Cottle, and Tatham (1962), p. 480.
48 Glader, Laise, and Browning (2009), p. A1.

recent years (generally under 3 percent) and the then current 10-year T-bond yield of about 3 percent. In such cases, investors bid down the price of shares such that, after the expected cut, the expected total return on the shares was still adequate.

The observations of Madden (2008) support an attitude of caution with respect to very high dividend yields. Madden examined yields for the 1,963 stocks in the MSCI World Index.[49] His company classified 865 companies out of the 1,963 companies as a "High Dividend Universe" (HDU). In the early months of the economic decline, Madden found that 78.6 percent of the companies in the HDU had questionable ability to maintain their dividend payments as compared with 30.7 percent of all the companies in the MCSI World Index.

SUMMARY

The dividend policy of a company affects the form in which shareholders receive the return on their investment and is a prominent decision of a company's board of directors. This reading has made the following points:

- There are three general theories on investor preference for dividends. The first, MM, argues that given perfect markets dividend policy is irrelevant. The "bird in hand" theory contends that investors value a dollar of dividends today more than uncertain capital gains in the future. The third theory argues that in countries in which dividends are taxed at higher rates than capital gains, taxable investors should prefer that companies reinvest earnings in growth opportunities or repurchase shares so they receive more of the return in the form of capital gains.

- An argument for dividend irrelevance given perfect markets is that corporate dividend policy is irrelevant because shareholders can create their preferred cash flow stream by selling any company's shares ("homemade dividends").

- The clientele effect suggests that different classes of investors have differing preferences for dividend income. Those who prefer dividends will tend to invest in higher yielding shares.

- Dividend declarations may provide information to current and prospective shareholders regarding the prospects of the company. Initiating a dividend or increasing a dividend sends a positive signal, whereas cutting a dividend or omitting a dividend typically sends a negative signal.

- Payment of dividends can help reduce the agency conflicts between managers and shareholders, but can worsen conflicts of interest between shareholders and debt holders.

- Empirically, several factors appear to influence dividend policy, including investment opportunities for the company, the volatility expected in its future earnings, financial flexibility, tax considerations, flotation costs, and contractual and legal restrictions.

- Under double taxation systems, dividends are taxed at both the corporate and shareholder level. Under tax imputation systems, a shareholder receives a credit on dividends for the tax paid on corporate profits. Under split-rate taxation systems, corporate profits are taxed at different rates depending on whether the profits are retained or paid out in dividends.

---

[49] Madden (2008), pp. 42–44.

- Companies with outstanding debt often are restricted in the amount of dividends they can pay because of debt covenants and legal restrictions. Some institutions require that a company pay a dividend to be on their "approved" list. If a company funds capital expenditures by borrowing while paying earnings out in dividends, it will incur flotation costs on new issues.

- Using a stable dividend policy, a company tries to align its dividend growth rate to the company's long-term earnings growth rate. Dividends may increase even in years when earnings decline, and dividends will increase at a lower rate than earnings in boom years.

- According to Lintner (1956), the stable dividend policy can be represented by a gradual adjustment process in which the expected dividend is equal to last year's dividend per share, plus [(this year's expected increase in earnings per share) × (the target payout ratio) × (an annual adjustment factor)].

- Using a constant dividend payout ratio policy, a company applies a target dividend payout ratio to current earnings; therefore, dividends are more volatile than with a stable dividend policy.

- In a residual dividend policy, the amount of the annual dividend is equal to annual earnings minus the capital budget times the percent of the capital budget to be financed through retained earnings or zero, whichever is greater. An advantage of this policy is that positive NPV opportunities have the first priority in the use of earnings.

- Companies can repurchase shares in lieu of increasing cash dividends. Share repurchases usually offer more flexibility than cash dividends by not establishing the expectation that a particular level of cash distribution will be maintained.

- Companies can pay regular cash dividends supplemented by share repurchases. In years of extraordinary increases in earnings, share repurchase can substitute for special cash dividends.

- Share repurchases can signal that company officials think their shares are undervalued. On the other hand, share repurchases could send a negative signal that the company has few positive NPV opportunities.

- The issue of dividend safety deals with how safe a company's dividend actually is, specifically whether the company's earnings and, more importantly, its cash flow are sufficient to sustain the payment of the dividend.

- Early warning signs of whether a company can sustain its dividend include the level of dividend yield, whether the company borrows to pay the dividend, and the company's past dividend record.

REFERENCES

Baker, Malcolm, and Jeffrey Wurgler. 2004. "A Catering Theory of Dividends." *Journal of Finance*, vol. 59, no. 3:1125–1165.

Brav, Alon, John Graham, Campbell Harvey, and Roni Michaely. 2005. "Payout Policy in the 21st Century." *Journal of Financial Economics*, vol. 77, no. 3:483–527.

Damodaran, Aswath. 2001. *Corporate Finance*. New York: John Wiley & Sons.

DeAngelo, Harry, Linda DeAngelo, and Douglas Skinner. 2004. "Are Dividends Disappearing? Dividend Concentration and the Consolidation of Earnings." *Journal of Financial Economics*, vol. 72, no. 3:425–456.

Elton, Edward, and Martin Gruber. 1970. "Marginal Tax Rates and the Clientele Effect." *Review of Economics and Statistics*, vol. 52, no. 1:68–74.

Fama, Eugene, and Kenneth French. 2001. "Disappearing Dividends: Changing Firm Characteristics or Lower Propensity to Pay?" *Journal of Financial Economics*, vol. 60, no. 1:3–43.

Ferris, Stephen, Narayanan Jayaraman, and Sanjiv Sabherwal. 2009. "Catering Effects in Corporate Dividend Policy: The International Evidence." *Journal of Banking & Finance*, vol. 33, no. 9:1730–1738.

Ferris, Stephen, Nilanjan Sen, and Emre Unlu. 2009. "An International Analysis of Dividend Payment Behavior." *Journal of Business Finance & Accounting*, vol. 36, no. 3-4:496–522.

Filbeck, Greg. 2009. "Asymmetric Information and Signaling Theory." *Dividends and Dividend Policy*, H. Kent Baker, ed. Hoboken, NJ: John Wiley & Sons.

Glader, Paul, Eleanor Laise, and E. S. Browning. 2009. "GE Joins Parade of Deep Dividend Cuts." *Wall Street Journal* (28 February 2009): A1.

Gordon, Myron J. 1963. "Optimal Investment and Financing Policy." *Journal of Finance*, vol. 18, no. 2:264–272.

Grace, Kerry, and Rob Curran. 2009. "Stock Buybacks Plummet." *Wall Street Journal* (27 March 2009): C9.

Graham, Benjamin, and David L. Dodd. 1934. *Security Analysis*. New York: McGraw-Hill.

Graham, Benjamin, David Dodd, Sidney Cottle, and Charles Tatham. 1962. *Security Analysis*, 4th edition. New York: McGraw-Hill.

Grinblatt, Mark, Ronald Masulis, and Sheridan Titman. 1984. "The Valuation Effects of Stock Splits and Stock Dividends." *Journal of Financial Economics*, vol. 13, no. 4:461–490.

Grullon, Gustavo, and Roni Michaely. 2002. "Dividends, Share Repurchases, and the Substitution Hypothesis." *Journal of Finance*, vol. 57, no. 4:1649–1684.

Hansen, Robert, Raman Kumar, and Dilip Shome. 1994. "Dividend Policy and Corporate Monitoring: Evidence from the Regulated Electric Utility Industry." *Financial Management*, vol. 23, no. 1:16–22.

Jensen, Michael C. 1986. "Agency Costs of Free Cash Flow, Corporate Finance, and Takeovers." *American Economic Review*, vol. 76, no. 2:323–329.

Lease, Ronald, Kose John, Avner Kalay, Uri Loewenstein, and Oded Sarig. 2000. *Dividend Policy: Its Impact on Firm Value.* Boston, MA: Harvard Business School Press.

Lintner, John. 1956. "Distribution of Incomes of Corporations among Dividends, Retained Earnings and Taxes." *American Economic Review*, vol. 46, no. 2:97–113.

Lintner, John. 1962. "Dividends, Earnings, Leverage, Stock Prices and the Supply of Capital to Corporations." *Review of Economics and Statistics*, vol. 44, no. 3:243–269.

Madden, Ian. 2008. "High Dividend Stocks: Proceed with Caution."

Miller, Merton H., and Franco Modigliani. 1961. "Dividend Policy, Growth, and the Valuation of Shares." *Journal of Business*, vol. 34, no. 4:411–433.

Mukherjee, Tarun. 2009. "Agency Costs and the Free Cash Flow Hypothesis." *Dividends and Dividend Policy*, H. Kent Baker, ed. Hoboken, NJ: John Wiley & Sons.

Myers, Stewart, and Nicholas Majluf. 1984. "Corporate Financing and Investment Decisions When Firms Have Information That Investors Do Not Have." *Journal of Financial Economics*, vol. 13, no. 2:187–221.

Parrino, Robert, and David Kidwell. 2009. *Fundamentals of Corporate Finance.* Hoboken, NJ: John Wiley and Sons.

Ross, Stephen. 1977. "The Determination of Financial Structure: The Incentive–Signaling Approach." *Bell Journal of Economics*, vol. 8, no. 1:23–40.

Shefrin, Hersh, and Meir Statman. 1984. "Explaining Investor Preference for Cash Dividends." *Journal of Financial Economics*, vol. 13, no. 2:253–282.

Smith, Clifford Jrand Jerold Warner. . 1979. "On Financial Contracting: An Analysis of Bond Covenants." *Journal of Financial Economics*, vol. 7, no. 2:117–161.

Vermaelen, Theo. 2005. *Share Repurchases.* Hanover, MA: now Publishers.

Von Eije, Henk, and William L. Megginson. 2008. "Dividends and Share Repurchases in the European Union." *Journal of Financial Economics*, vol. 89, no. 2:347–374.

PRACTICE PROBLEMS

1   Match the phrases in Column A with the corresponding dividend theory in Column B. Note that you may use the answers in Column B more than once.

Column A	Column B
1. Bird in the hand	a) Dividend policy matters
2. Homemade dividends	b) Dividend policy is irrelevant
3. High tax rates on dividends	

2   Which of the following assumptions is *not* required for Miller and Modigliani's (MM) dividend theory?

   A   Shareholders have no transaction costs when buying and selling shares.

   B   There are no taxes.

   C   Investors sort themselves into dividend clienteles.

3   The clientele effect implies that:

   A   investors prefer high dividend paying shares.

   B   investors have varying preferences regarding dividends.

   C   low tax bracket investors are indifferent to dividends.

4   Sophie Chan owns 100,000 shares of PAT Company. PAT is selling for €40 per share, so Chan's investment is worth €4,000,000. Chan reinvests the gross amount of all dividends received to purchase additional shares. Assume that the clientele for PAT shares consists of tax-exempt investors. If PAT pays a €1.50 dividend, Chan's new share ownership after reinvesting dividends at the ex-dividend price is *most* likely to be closest to:

   A   103,600.

   B   103,750.

   C   103,900.

5   Which of the following is *most* likely to signal negative information concerning a company?

   A   Share repurchase.

   B   Decrease in the quarterly dividend rate.

   C   A two-for-one stock split.

6   WL Corporation is located in a jurisdiction that has a 40 percent corporate tax rate on pretax income and a 30 percent personal tax rate on dividends. WL distributes all its after-tax income to shareholders. What is the effective tax rate on WL pretax income distributed in dividends?

   A   42 percent.

   B   58 percent.

   C   70 percent.

7   Which of the following factors would *not* tend to be associated with a company having a low dividend payout ratio?

   A   High flotation costs on new equity issues.

    B   High tax rates on dividends.

    C   Low growth prospects.

8 The dividend policy of Berkshire Gardens Inc. can be represented by a gradual adjustment to a target dividend payout ratio. Last year Berkshire had earnings per share of $3.00 and paid a dividend of $0.60 a share. This year it estimates earnings per share will be $4.00. Find its dividend per share for this year if it has a 25 percent target payout ratio and uses a five-year period to adjust its dividend.

    A $0.65.

    B $0.80.

    C $0.85.

9 The Apex Corp. has a target debt/equity ratio of 40/60. Its capital budget for next year is estimated to be $40 million. Estimated net income is $30 million. If Apex follows a residual dividend policy, its dividend is expected to be:

    A $6 million.

    B $12 million.

    C $18 million.

10 Beta Corporation is a manufacturer of inflatable furniture. Which of the following scenarios best reflects a stable dividend policy for Beta?

    A   Maintaining a constant dividend payout ratio of 40–50 percent.

    B   Maintaining the dividend at $1.00 a share for several years given no change in Beta's long-term prospects.

    C   Increasing the dividend 5 percent a year over several years to reflect the two years in which Beta recognized mark-to-market gains on derivative positions.

11 Investors may prefer companies that repurchase their shares instead of paying a cash dividend when:

    A   capital gains are taxed at lower rates than dividends.

    B   capital gains are taxed at the same rate as dividends.

    C   the company needs more equity to finance capital expenditures.

The following information relates to Questions 12–14

Janet Wu is treasurer of Wilson Paper Company, a manufacturer of paper products for the office and school markets. Wilson Paper is selling one of its divisions for $70 million cash. Wu is considering whether to recommend a special dividend of $70 million or a repurchase of 2 million shares of Wilson common stock in the open market. She is reviewing some possible effects of the buyback with the company's financial analyst. Wilson has a long-term record of gradually increasing earnings and dividends. Wilson's board has also approved capital spending of $15 million to be entirely funded out of this year's earnings.

Book value of equity	$750 million ($30 a share)
Shares outstanding	25 million
12-month trading range	$25–$35
Current share price	$35

After-tax cost of borrowing	7 percent
Estimated full year earnings	$25 million
Last year's dividends	$9 million
Target debt/equity (market value)	35/65

12 In investors' minds, Wilson's share buyback could be a signal that the company:

  A is decreasing its financial leverage.

  B views its shares as undervalued in the marketplace.

  C has more investment opportunities than it could fund internally.

13 Assume that Wilson Paper funds its capital spending out of its estimated full year earnings. If Wilson uses a residual dividend policy, determine Wilson's implied dividend payout ratio.

  A 36 percent.

  B 40 percent.

  C 60 percent.

14 The most likely tax environment in which Wilson Paper's shareholders would prefer that Wilson repurchase its shares (share buybacks) instead of paying dividends is one in which:

  A the tax rate on capital gains and dividends is the same.

  B capital gains tax rates are higher than dividend income tax rates.

  C capital gains tax rates are lower than dividend income tax rates.

SOLUTIONS

1 The appropriate matches are as follows:

Column A	Column B
1. Bird in the hand	a) Dividend policy matters
2. Homemade dividends	b) Dividend policy is irrelevant
3. High tax rates on dividends	a) Dividend policy matters

2 C is correct. The MM dividend theory assumes no taxes or transaction costs, but it does not assume a clientele effect.

3 B is correct. The clientele effect implies that there are varying preferences for dividends among distinct investor groups.

4 C is correct. Because the clientele for PAT investors has the same tax rate (zero) for dividends and capital gains, the ex-dividend stock price of PAT should decline by the amount of the dividend to €40 − €1.50 = €38.50. Chan will purchase €150,000/€38.50 = 3,896 additional shares. This increases her total shares owned to 103,896. Chan's new share ownership is closest to 103,900.

5 B is correct. A decrease in the quarterly dividend rate is likely to signal negative information. A decrease is typically understood as signaling poor future business prospects.

6 B is correct. The effective tax rate can be computed as 1 minus the fraction of 1 unit of earnings that investors retain after all taxes, or $1 - (1 - 0.40)(1 - 0.30) = 0.58$ or 58 percent effective tax rate. Another way to obtain the solution: Corporate taxes = $1.00 \times 0.40 = 0.40$ and Personal taxes = 0.60 in dividends × 0.30 = 0.18, so Total tax = 0.40 + 0.18 = 0.58, a 58 percent effective rate.

7 C is correct. With low growth prospects, a company would typically have a high payout ratio, returning funds to its shareholders rather than retaining funds.

8 A is correct. The estimated dividend per share is $0.65.

Previous DPS = $0.60

Expected increase in EPS = $4 − $3 = $1

Target payout ratio = 0.25

Five-year adjustment factor = 1/5 = 0.2

Expected DPS = Previous DPS + (Increase in EPS × Target payout ×Adjustment factor)

= $0.60 + ($1.00 × 0.25 × 0.2)

= $0.65

9 A is correct. Using the residual dividend policy, with a target debt/equity ratio of 40/60, 60 percent or $24 million of the $40 million in capital expenditures will be financed with equity; $30 million net income − $24 million retained earnings = $6 million for dividends.

10 B is correct. Choice A is consistent with a target payout ratio policy. Choice C is not correct because the earnings increases described are not sustainable long term.

11 A is correct. When capital gains are taxed at lower rates than dividends, investors may prefer companies that return cash to shareholders through share repurchases rather than dividends.

12 B is correct. Management sometimes undertakes share repurchases when it views shares as being undervalued in the marketplace.

13 B is correct. Earnings available for dividends = Earnings – Capital spending = $25 million – $15 million = $10 million; $10 million/$25 million = 40 percent dividend payout ratio.

14 C is correct. Shareholders would prefer that the company repurchase its shares instead of paying dividends when the tax rate on capital gains is lower than the tax rate on dividends.

Corporate Finance

Financing and Control Issues

This study session presents two major organizational topics of corporate finance. First, corporate governance covers the system of principles and policies used to manage conflicts of interest among various groups of stakeholders of a corporation. Second, mergers and acquisitions and corporate restructurings, which redistribute ownership and control, are analyzed.

READING ASSIGNMENTS

Reading 28	Corporate Governance *Corporate Finance: A Practical Approach,* by Michelle R. Clayman, CFA, Martin S. Fridson, CFA, and George H. Troughton, CFA
Reading 29	Mergers and Acquisitions *Corporate Finance: A Practical Approach,* by Michelle R. Clayman, CFA, Martin S. Fridson, CFA, and George H. Troughton, CFA

Corporate Governance

by Rebecca Todd McEnally, CFA, and Kenneth Kim

LEARNING OUTCOMES

Mastery	The candidate should be able to:
☐	**a.** describe objectives and core attributes of an effective corporate governance system, and evaluate whether a company's corporate governance has those attributes;
☐	**b.** compare major business forms, and describe the conflicts of interest associated with each;
☐	**c.** explain conflicts that arise in agency relationships, including manager–shareholder conflicts and director–shareholder conflicts;
☐	**d.** describe responsibilities of the board of directors, and explain qualifications and core competencies that an investment analyst should look for in the board of directors;
☐	**e.** explain effective corporate governance practice as it relates to the board of directors, and evaluate strengths and weaknesses of a company's corporate governance practice;
☐	**f.** describe elements of a company's statement of corporate governance policies that investment analysts should assess;
☐	**g.** describe environmental, social, and governance risk exposures;
☐	**h.** explain the valuation implications of corporate governance.

INTRODUCTION

1

The modern corporation is a very efficient and effective means of raising capital, obtaining needed resources, and generating products and services. These and other advantages have caused the corporate form of business to become the dominant one in many countries. The corporate form, in contrast to other business forms, frequently involves the separation of ownership and control of the assets of the business. The ownership of the modern, public corporation is typically diffuse; it has

Corporate Finance: A Practical Approach, by Michelle R. Clayman, CFA, Martin S. Fridson, CFA, and George H. Troughton, CFA. Copyright © 2008 by CFA Institute.

many owners, most with proportionally small stakes in the company, who are distant from, and often play no role in, corporate decisions. Professional managers control and deploy the assets of the corporation. This separation of ownership (shareholders) and control (managers) may result in a number of conflicts of interest between managers and shareholders. Conflicts of interest can also arise that affect creditors as well as other stakeholders such as employees and suppliers. In order to remove or at least minimize such conflicts of interest, corporate governance structures have been developed and implemented in corporations. Specifically, **corporate governance** is the system of principles, policies, procedures, and clearly defined responsibilities and accountabilities used by stakeholders to overcome the conflicts of interest inherent in the corporate form.

The failure of a company to establish an effective system of corporate governance represents a major operational risk to the company and its investors.[1] Corporate governance deficiencies may even imperil the continued existence of a company. Consequently, to understand the risks inherent in an investment in a company, it is essential to understand the quality of the company's corporate governance practices. It is also necessary to continually monitor a company's practices, because changes in management, the composition of its board of directors, the company's competitive and market conditions, or mergers and acquisitions, can affect them in important ways.

A series of major corporate collapses in North America, Europe, and Asia, nearly all of which involved the failure or direct override by managers of corporate governance systems, have made it clear that strong corporate governance structures are essential to the efficient and effective functioning of companies and the financial markets in which they operate. Investors lost great amounts of money in the failed companies. The collapses weakened the trust and confidence essential to the efficient functioning of financial markets worldwide.

Legislators and regulators responded to the erosion of trust by introducing strong new regulatory frameworks. These measures are intended to restore the faith of investors in companies and the markets, and, very importantly, to help prevent future collapses. Nevertheless, the new regulations did not address all outstanding corporate governance problems and were not uniform across capital markets. Thus, we may expect corporate governance-related laws and regulations to further evolve.

The reading is organized as follows: Section 2 presents the objectives of corporate governance systems and the key attributes of effective ones. Section 3 addresses forms of business and conflicts of interest, and Section 4 discusses two major sources of governance problems. In Section 5 we discuss standards and principles of corporate governance, providing three representative sets of principles from current practice. Section 6 addresses environmental, social, and governance factors, and Section 7 touches on the valuation implications of the quality of corporate governance.

---

1 An **operational risk** is the risk of loss from failures in a company's systems and procedures, or from external events.

CORPORATE GOVERNANCE: OBJECTIVES AND GUIDING PRINCIPLES

2

The modern corporation is subject to a variety of conflicts of interest. This fact leads to the following two major objectives of corporate governance:

- to eliminate or mitigate conflicts of interest, particularly those between managers and shareholders, and
- to ensure that the assets of the company are used efficiently and productively and in the best interests of its investors and other stakeholders.

How then can a company go about achieving those objectives? The first point is that it should have a set of principles and procedures sufficiently comprehensive to be called a corporate governance system. No single system of effective corporate governance applies to all firms in all industries worldwide. Different industries and economic systems, legal and regulatory environments, and cultural differences may affect the characteristics of an effective corporate governance system for a particular company. However, there are certain characteristics that are common to all sound corporate governance structures. The core attributes of an effective corporate governance system are:

- delineation of the *rights* of shareholders and other core stakeholders;
- clearly defined manager and director governance *responsibilities* to stakeholders;
- identifiable and measurable *accountabilities* for the performance of the responsibilities;
- *fairness* and equitable treatment in all dealings between managers, directors, and shareholders; and
- complete *transparency* and accuracy in disclosures regarding operations, performance, risk, and financial position.

These core attributes form the foundation for systems of good governance, as well as for the individual principles embodied in such systems. Investors and analysts should determine whether companies in which they may be interested have these core attributes.

FORMS OF BUSINESS AND CONFLICTS OF INTEREST

3

The goal of for-profit businesses in any society is simple and straightforward: to maximize their owners' wealth. This can be achieved through strategies that result in long-term growth in sales and profits. However, pursuing wealth maximization involves taking risks. A business itself is risky for a variety of reasons. For example, there may be demand uncertainty for its products and/or services, economic uncertainty, and competitive pressures. Financial risk is present when a business must use debt to finance operations. Thus, continued access to sufficient capital is an important consideration and risk for businesses. These risks, and the inherent conflicts of interests in businesses, increase the need for strong corporate governance.

A firm's ability to obtain capital and to control risk is perhaps most influenced by the manner in which it is organized. Three of the predominant forms of business globally are the sole proprietorship, the partnership, and the corporation. Hybrids of these three primary business forms also exist, but we do not discuss them here because they are simply combinations of the three main business forms. With regard to the three primary business forms, each has different advantages and disadvantages. We will discuss each of them, the conflicts of interest that can arise in each, and the relative need for strong corporate governance associated with each form. However, a summary of the characteristics is provided in Table 1.

Table 1	Comparison of Characteristics of Business Forms		
Characteristic	**Sole Proprietorship**	**Partnership**	**Corporation**
Ownership	Sole owner	Multiple owners	Unlimited ownership
Legal requirements and regulation	Few; entity easily formed	Few; entity easily formed	Numerous legal requirements
Legal distinction between owner and business	None	None	Legal separation between owners and business
Liability	Unlimited	Unlimited but shared among partners	Limited
Ability to raise capital	Very limited	Limited	Nearly unlimited
Transferability of ownership	Non-transferable (except by sale of entire business)	Non-transferable	Easily transferable
Owner expertise in business	Essential	Essential	Unnecessary

3.1 Sole Proprietorships

The **sole proprietorship** is a business *owned and operated* by a single person. The owner of the local cleaner, restaurant, beauty salon, or fruit stand is typically a sole proprietor. Generally, there are few, if any, legal formalities involved in establishing a sole proprietorship and they are relatively easy to start. In many jurisdictions, there are few, if any, legal distinctions between the sole proprietor and the business. For example, tax liabilities and related filing requirements for sole proprietorships are frequently set at the level of the sole proprietor. Legitimate business expenses are simply deducted from the sole proprietor's taxable income.

Sole proprietorships are the most numerous form of business worldwide, representing, for example, approximately 70 percent of all businesses in the United States, by number.[2] However, because they are usually small-scale operations, they represent the smallest amount of market capitalization in many markets. Indeed, the difficulties of the sole proprietor in raising large amounts of capital, coupled with unlimited liability and lack of transferability of ownership, are serious impediments to the growth of a sole proprietorship.

From the point of view of corporate governance, the sole proprietorship presents fewer risks than the corporation because the manager and the owner are one and the same. Indeed, the major corporate governance risks are those faced by creditors and suppliers of goods and services to the business. These stakeholders are in a position to be able to demand the types and quality of information that they need to evaluate

---

2 William J. Megginson, *Corporate Finance Theory* (Reading, MA: Addison-Wesley, 1997), p. 40.

risks before lending money to the business or providing goods and services to it. In addition, because they typically maintain direct, recurring business relations with the companies, they are better able to monitor the condition and risks of the business, and to control their own exposure to risk. Consequently, we will not consider sole proprietorships further in this reading.

3.2 Partnerships

A **partnership**, which is composed of more than one owner/manager, is similar to a sole proprietorship. For the most part, partnerships share many of the same advantages and disadvantages as the sole proprietorship. Two obvious advantages of a partnership over a sole proprietorship are the pooling together of financial capital of the partners and the sharing of business risk among them. However, even these advantages may not be as important as the pooling together of service-oriented expertise and skill, especially for larger partnerships. Some very large international partnerships operate in such fields as real estate, law, investment banking, architecture, engineering, advertising, and accounting. Note also that larger partnerships may enjoy competitive and economy-of-scale benefits over sole proprietorships.

Partners typically overcome conflicts of interest internally by engaging in partnership contracts specifying the rights and responsibilities of each partner. Conflicts of interest with those entities outside the partnership are similar to those for the sole proprietorship and are dealt with in the same way. Hence, we will not consider these conflicts further in this reading.

3.3 Corporations

Corporations represent less than 20 percent of all businesses in the United States but generate approximately 90 percent of the country's business revenue.[3] The percentage is lower elsewhere, but growing. The **corporation** is a legal entity, and has rights similar to those of a person. For example, a corporation is permitted to enter into contracts. The chief officers of the corporation, the executives or top managers, act as agents for the firm and are legally entitled to authorize corporate activities and to enter into contracts on behalf of the business.

There are several important and striking advantages of the corporate form of business. First, corporations can raise very large amounts of capital by issuing either stocks or bonds to the investing public. A corporation can grant ownership stakes, common stock, to individual investors in exchange for cash or other assets. Similarly, it can borrow money, for example, bonds or other debt from individual or institutional investors, in exchange for interest payments and a promise to pay back the principal of the loan. Shareholders are the owners of the corporation, and any profits that the corporation generates accrue to the shareholders.

A second advantage is that corporate owners need not be experts in the industry or management of the business, unlike the owners of sole proprietorships and partnerships where business expertise is essential to success. Any individual with sufficient money can own stock. This has benefits to both the business and the owners. The business can seek capital from millions of investors, not only in domestic markets but worldwide.

Among the most important advantages of the corporate form is that stock ownership is easily transferable. Transferability of shares allows corporations to have unlimited life. A final and extremely important advantage is that shareholders have limited liability. That is, they can lose only the money they have invested, nothing more.

---

3 Megginson, 1997.

The corporate form of business has a number of disadvantages, however. For example, because many corporations have thousands or even millions of nonmanager owners, they are subject to more regulation than are partnerships or sole proprietorships. While regulation serves to protect shareholders, it can also be costly to shareholders as well. For example, the corporation must hire accountants and lawyers to deal with accounting and other legal documents to comply with regulations. Perhaps the most significant disadvantage with the corporation (and the one most critical to corporate governance) is the difficulty that shareholders have in monitoring management and the firm's operations. As a sole proprietor of a small business, the owner will be able to directly oversee such day-to-day business concerns as inventory levels, product quality, expenses, and employees. However, it is impossible for a shareholder of a large corporation such as General Motors or International Business Machines to monitor business activities and personnel, and to exert any control rights over the firm. In fact, a shareholder of a large firm may not even feel like an owner in the usual sense, especially because corporations are owned by so many other shareholders, and because most owners of a large public corporation hold only a relatively small stake in it.

Agency relationships arise when someone, an agent, acts on behalf of another person, the principal. In a corporation, managers are the agents who act on behalf of the owners, the shareholders. If a corporation has in place a diligent management team that works in the best interests of its shareholders and other stakeholders, then the problem of passive shareholders and bondholders becomes a non-issue. In real life, unfortunately, management may not always work in the stakeholders' best interests. Managers may be tempted to see to their own well-being and wealth at the expense of their shareholders and others to whom they owe a fiduciary duty. This is known as an **agency problem**, or the **principal-agent problem**. The money of shareholders, the principals, is used and managed by agents, the managers, who promise that the firm will pursue wealth-maximizing business activities. However, there are potential problems with these relationships, which we will discuss next.

4 SPECIFIC SOURCES OF CONFLICT: AGENCY RELATIONSHIPS

Conflicts among the various constituencies in corporations have the potential to cause problems in the relationships among managers, directors, shareholders, creditors, employees, and suppliers. However, we will concentrate here on the relationships between 1) managers and shareholders, and 2) directors and shareholders. These two relationships are the primary focus of most systems of corporate governance. However, to the extent that strong corporate governance structures are in place and effective in companies, the agency conflicts among other stakeholders are mitigated as well. For example, managers are responsible for maximizing the wealth of the shareholders and minimizing waste (including excessive compensation and perquisite consumption). To the extent that managers do so, the interests of employees and suppliers are more likely to be met because the probability increases that sufficient funds will be available for payment of salaries and benefits, as well as for goods and services. In this section, we will describe these agency relationships, discuss the problems inherent in each, and we will illustrate these agency problems with real-world examples. An understanding of the nature of the conflicts in each relationship is essential to a full understanding of the importance of the provisions in codes of corporate governance.

4.1 Manager–Shareholder Conflicts

From the point of view of investors, the manager-shareholder relationship is the most critical one. It is important to recognize that firms and their managers, the shareholders' agents, obtain operating and investing capital from the shareholders, the owners, in two ways. First, although shareholders have a 100 percent claim on the firm's net income, the undistributed net income (the earnings remaining after the payment of dividends) is reinvested in the company. We normally term this reinvested income retained earnings. Second, the firm can issue stock to obtain the capital, either through an initial public offering (IPO) if the firm is currently privately owned, or through a seasoned equity offering (SEO) if the firm already has shares outstanding. By whatever means the firm obtains equity capital, shareholders entrust management to use the funds efficiently and effectively to generate profits and maximize investors' wealth.

However, although the manager is responsible for advancing the shareholder's best interests, this may not happen. For example, management may use funds to try to expand the size of the business to increase their job security, power, and salaries without consideration of the shareholders' interests. In addition, managers may also grant themselves numerous and expensive perquisites which are treated as ordinary business expenses. Managers enjoy these benefits, and shareholders bear the costs. This is a serious agency problem and, unfortunately, there are a number of recent real-world examples of their occurrence in corporations.

Managers also may make other business decisions, such as investing in highly risky ventures, that benefit themselves but that may not serve the company's investors well. For example, managers who hold substantial amounts of executive stock options will receive large benefits if risky ventures pay off, but will not suffer losses if the ventures fail. By contrast, managers whose wealth is closely tied to the company and who are therefore not well diversified may choose to not invest in projects with a positive expected net present value because of excessive risk aversion. The checks and balances in effective corporate governance systems are designed to reduce the probability of such practices.

The cases of Enron (bankruptcy filing: 2001, in the United States) and Tyco (resignation of CEO: 2002, in the United States) make clear that in the absence of the checks and balances of strong and effective corporate governance systems, investors and others cannot necessarily rely upon managers to serve as stewards of the resources entrusted to them. Example 1, dealing with Enron, illustrates the problems that can ensue from a lack of commitment to a corporate governance system. Example 2, dealing with Tyco, illustrates a case in which there were inadequate checks and balances to the power of a CEO.

EXAMPLE 1

Corporate Governance Failure (1)

Enron was one of the world's largest energy, commodities, and services companies. However, it is better known today as a classic example of how the conflicts of interest between shareholders and managers can harm even major corporations and their shareholders. Enron executives, with the approval of members of the board of directors, overrode provisions in Enron's code of ethics and corporate governance system that forbade any practices involving self-dealing by executives. Specifically, Enron's chief financial officer set up off-shore partnerships in which he served as general partner. As an Enron executive, he was able to make deals with these partnerships on behalf of Enron. As a general partner of the partnerships, he received the enormous fees that the deals generated.[4]

The partnerships served other useful purposes. For example, they made it possible to hide billions of dollars in Enron debt off of the company's balance sheet, and generated artificial profits for Enron. Thus, disclosure of the company's rapidly deteriorating financial condition was delayed, preventing investors and creditors from obtaining information critical to the valuation and riskiness of their securities. At the same time, Enron executives were selling their own stock in the company.

These egregious breaches of good governance harmed both Enron's outside shareholders and their creditors. The bonds were becoming riskier but the creditors were not informed of the deteriorating prospects. The exorbitant fees the executives paid themselves came out of the shareholders' earnings, earnings that were already overstated by the artificial profits. Investors did not receive full information about the problems in the company until well after the collapse and the company's bankruptcy filing, by which time their stock had lost essentially all of its value.

Most, if not all, of the core attributes of good governance were violated by Enron's managers, but especially the responsibility to deal fairly with all stakeholders, including investors and creditors, and to provide full transparency of all material information on a timely basis.

EXAMPLE 2

Corporate Governance Failure (2)

Tyco provides another well-known example of a corporate governance failure. The CEO of Tyco used corporate funds to buy home decorating items, including a $17,000 traveling toilette box, a $445 pin cushion, and a $15,000 umbrella stand. He also borrowed money from the company's employee loan program to buy $270 million dollars worth of yachts, art, jewelry, and vacation estates. Then, in his capacity as CEO, he forgave the loan. All told, the CEO may have looted the firm, and thereby its shareholders, of over $600 million.[5]

It is instructive that in court proceedings in the Tyco case, the CEO and his representatives have not argued that he did not do these things, but rather that it was not illegal for him to do so.

Tyco is a striking example of excessive perquisite consumption by a CEO.

The role of complete transparency in sound corporate governance, including understandable and accurate financial statements, cannot be overestimated. Without full information, investors and other stakeholders are unable to evaluate the company's financial position and riskiness, whether the condition is improving or deteriorating, and whether insiders are aggrandizing themselves, or making poor business decisions, to the detriment of long-term investors.

---

4 William C. Powers, Jr., Raymond S. Troubh, and Herbert S. Winokur, Jr., *Report of Investigation by the Special Investigative Committee of the Board of Directors of Enron Corp.*, February 1, 2002.
5 Mark Maremont and Laurie Cohen, "How Tyco's CEO Enriched Himself," the *Wall Street Journal*, August 7, 2002, p. A1.

Two additional cases illustrate how false, misleading, or incomplete corporate disclosure may harm investors and other stakeholders.

EXAMPLE 3

Corporate Governance Failure (3)

The Italian firm, Parmalat, was one of the world's largest dairy foods suppliers. The founders and top executives of Parmalat were accused of fictitiously reporting the existence of a $4.9 billion bank account so that the company's enormous liabilities would appear less daunting.[6] By hiding the true financial condition of the firm, the executives were able to continue borrowing. The fraud perpetrated by Parmalat's largest shareholders and executives hurt Parmalat's creditors as well as the shareholders. Parmalat eventually defaulted on a $185 million bond payment in November 2003 and the company collapsed shortly thereafter.

EXAMPLE 4

Corporate Governance Failure (4)

During the late 1990s, Adelphia, the fifth-largest provider of cable entertainment in the United States, and the company's founders embarked on an aggressive acquisition campaign to increase the size of the company. During this time, the size of Adelphia's debt more than tripled from $3.5 billion to $12.6 billion. However, the founders also arranged a $2.3 billion personal loan which Adelphia guaranteed, but this arrangement was not fully disclosed to Adelphia's other stakeholders.[7] In addition, it is alleged that fictitious transactions were recorded to boost accounting profits.[8] These actions by Adelphia's owners were harmful to all of Adelphia's non-founder stakeholders, including investors and creditors. The company collapsed in bankruptcy in 2002.

The severity of the agency problems of the companies discussed in Examples 1 through 4 does not represent the norm, although the potential for serious conflicts of interest between shareholders and managers is inherent in the modern corporation. Strong corporate governance systems provide mechanisms for monitoring managers' activities, rewarding good performance and disciplining those in a position of responsibility for the company to make sure they act in the interests of the company's stakeholders.

4.2 Director–Shareholder Conflicts

Corporate governance systems rely on a system of checks and balances between the managers and investors in which the board of directors plays a critical role. The purpose of boards of directors in modern corporations is to provide an intermediary between managers and the owners, the shareholders. Members of the board of directors serve as agents for the owners, the shareholders, a mechanism designed to represent the

---

6 Gail Edmondson, 2004, "How Parmalat Went Sour," *Business Week*, July 12, 2004.
7 John Nofsinger and Kenneth Kim, *Infectious Greed* (Prentice Hall Financial Times, 2003), pp. 60-61.
8 Jerry Markon and Robert Frank, 2002, "Five Adelphia Officials Arrested on Fraud Charges," the *Wall Street Journal*, July 25, page A3.

investors and to ensure that their interests are being well served. This intermediary generally is responsible for monitoring the activities of managers, approving strategies and policies and making certain that these serve investors' interests. The board is also responsible for approving mergers and acquisitions, approving audit contracts and reviewing the audit and financial statements, setting managers' compensation including any incentive or performance awards, and disciplining or replacing poorly performing managers.

The conflict between directors and shareholders arises when directors come to identify with the managers' interests rather than those of the shareholders. This can occur when the board is not independent, for example, or when the members of the board have business or personal relationships with the managers that bias their judgment or compromise their duties to the shareholders. If members of the board have consulting agreements with the company, serve as major lenders to the firm, are members of the manager's family, or are from the circle of close friends, their objectivity may be called into question. Many corporations have been found to have interlinked boards. For example, one or more senior managers from one firm may serve as directors in the companies of their own board members, frequently on compensation committees. Another ever-present problem is the frequently overly generous compensation paid to directors for their services. Excessive compensation may incline directors to accommodate the wishes of management rather than attend to the concerns of investors.

All of the examples cited in this section involve compliant or less than independent board members. In Section 5 we formulate the most important points to check in evaluating a company's corporate governance system.

5   CORPORATE GOVERNANCE EVALUATION

An essential component of the analysis of a company and its risk is a review of the quality of its corporate governance system. This evaluation requires an assessment of issues relating to the board of directors, managers, and shareholders. Ultimately, the long-term performance of a company is dependent upon the quality of managers' decisions and their commitment to applying sound management practice. However, as one group concerned with the issues observes, "by analyzing the state of corporate governance for a given company, an analyst or shareholder may ascertain whether the company is governed in a manner that produces better management practices, promotes higher returns on shareholder capital, or if there is a governance and/or management problem which may impair company performance."[9]

In the following sections we provide a set of guidelines for evaluating the quality of corporate governance in a company. We reiterate that there is no single system of governance that is appropriate for all companies in all industries worldwide. However, this core set of global best practices is being applied in financial markets in Europe, Asia, and North America. They represent a standard by which corporate practices may be evaluated.

The information and corporate disclosure available in a specific jurisdiction will vary widely. However, most large financial markets and, increasingly, smaller ones require a substantial amount of information be provided about companies' governance structures and practices. In addition, a few regulatory jurisdictions will require a subset of the criteria we shall give as part of registration, exchange listing, or other requirements.

---

9 New York Society of Securities Analysts, *Corporate Governance Handbook*, September 22, 2003. New York City. p. 1.

The analyst should begin by carefully reviewing the requirements in effect for the company. Information is generally available in the company's required filings with regulators. For example, in the United States, such information is provided in the 10-K report, the annual report, and the Proxy Statement (SEC Form DEF 14A). All of these are filed with the U.S. Securities and Exchange Commission (U.S. SEC), are available on the U.S. SEC website, usually are available on the company's website, and are provided by the company to current investors as well as on request. In Europe, the company's annual report provides some information. However, in an increasing number of EU countries, companies are required to provide a report on corporate governance. This report typically will provide information on board activities and decisions, whether the company has abided by its relevant national code, and explain why it departed from the code, if it has. In addition, the announcement of the company's annual general meeting should disclose the issues on the agenda that are subject to shareholder vote. The specific sources of information will differ by jurisdiction and company.

5.1 The Board of Directors

Boards of directors are a critical part of the system of checks and balances that lie at the heart of corporate governance systems. Board members, both individually and as a group, have the responsibility to:

- establish corporate values and governance structures for the company to ensure that the business is conducted in an ethical, competent, fair, and professional manner;

- ensure that all legal and regulatory requirements are met and complied with fully and in a timely fashion;

- establish long-term strategic objectives for the company with a goal of ensuring that the best interests of shareholders come first and that the company's obligations to others are met in a timely and complete manner;

- establish clear lines of responsibility and a strong system of accountability and performance measurement in all phases of a company's operations;

- hire the chief executive officer, determine the compensation package, and periodically evaluate the officer's performance;

- ensure that management has supplied the board with sufficient information for it to be fully informed and prepared to make the decisions that are its responsibility, and to be able to adequately monitor and oversee the company's management;

- meet frequently enough to adequately perform its duties, and meet in extraordinary session as required by events; and

- acquire adequate training so that members are able to adequately perform their duties.

Depending upon the nature of the company and the industries within which the company operates, these responsibilities will vary; however, these general obligations are common to all companies.

In summarizing the duties and needs of boards of directors, *The Corporate Governance of Listed Companies: A Manual for Investors*[10] states:

---

10 *The Corporate Governance of Listed Companies: A Manual for Investors*, Second Edition, CFA Institute, 2010, p. 8.

Board members have a duty to make decisions based on what ultimately is best for the long-term interests of shareowners. There has been much discussion in recent years about the needs for boards and management to balance the short-term operations of a company with a long-term sustainable strategic outlook. Although shareowners with a short holding period may indeed be interested in corporate governance, long-term shareowners (those that hold shares for years) are more likely to incorporate corporate governance factors into their investment analyses. The reason is that governance aspects often affect company value over a long time frame. To act in the best interests of shareowners, board members need a combination of four things: independence, experience, resources, and accurate information about the company's financial and operating position.

First, a board should be composed of at least a majority of independent board members with the autonomy to act independently from management. Rather than simply voting with management, board members should bring with them a commitment to take an unbiased approach in making decisions that will benefit the company and shareowners. **Second**, Board members who have appropriate experience and expertise relevant to the company's business are best able to evaluate what is in the best interests of shareowners. Depending on the nature of the business, specialized expertise by at least some board members may be required. **Third**, internal mechanisms are needed to support the independent work of the board. Such mechanisms include the authority to hire the external auditor and other outside consultants without management's intervention or approval. This mechanism alone provides the board with the ability to obtain expert help in specialized areas, helps it to circumvent potential areas of conflict with management, and overall, helps preserve the integrity of the board's independent oversight function. **Fourth**, Directors must have access to complete and accurate information about the financial position of the company and its underlying value drivers to enable them to steer the company in the best long-term interests of shareowners. [Emphasis added]

In the following sections we detail the attributes of the board that an investor or investment analyst must assess.

5.1.1 Board Composition and Independence

The board of directors of a corporation is established for the primary purpose of serving the best interests of the outside shareholders in the company. Other stakeholders including employees, creditors, and suppliers are usually in a more powerful position to oversee their interests in the company than are shareholders. The millions of outside investors cannot, individually or collectively, monitor, oversee, and approve management's strategies and policies, performance, and compensation and consumption of perquisites.

The objectives of the board are to see that company assets are used in the best long-term interests of shareholders and that management strategies, plans, policies, and practices are designed to achieve this objective. In a recent amendment to the *Investment Company Act of 1940* rules, the U.S. SEC argues that a board must be "an independent force in [company] affairs rather than a passive affiliate of management. Its independent directors must bring to the boardroom a high degree of rigor and skeptical objectivity to the evaluation of [company] managements and its plans and proposals, particularly when evaluating conflicts of interest."[11]

---

11 *Amendments to Rules Governing the Investment Company Act of 1940*, 17 CFR Part 270, July 2004, p. 3.

Similarly, the *Corporate Governance Handbook*[12] observes:

> Board independence is essential to a sound governance structure. Without independence there can be little accountability. In the words of Professor Jeffrey Sonnenfeld of Yale University, "The highest performing companies have extremely contentious boards that regard dissent as an obligation and that treat no subject as undiscussable."

Clearly, for members who are appointed to the board to be in a position to best perform their fiduciary responsibilities to shareholders, at a minimum a majority of the members must be independent of management. However, global best practice now recommends that *at least three-quarters* of the board members should be independent.

Some experts in corporate governance have argued that all members of the board should be independent, eliminating the possibility of any senior executives serving on the board. Those who hold this position argue that the presence of managers in board deliberations may work to the detriment of the best interests of investors and other shareholders by intimidating the board or otherwise limiting debate and full discussion of important matters. Others argue that with appropriate additional safeguards, such potential problems can be overcome to the benefit of all stakeholders.

Independence is difficult to evaluate. Factors that often indicate a lack of independence include:

- former employment with the company, including founders, executives, or other employees;
- business relationships, for example, prior or current service as outside counsel, auditors, or consultants, or business interests involving contractual commitments and obligations;
- personal relationships, whether familial, friendship, or other affiliations;
- interlocking directorships, a director of another company whose independence might be impaired by the relationship with the other board or company, particularly if the director serves on interlocking compensation committees; and
- ongoing banking or other creditor relationships.

Information on the business and other relationships of board members as well as nominees for the board may be obtained from regulatory filings in most jurisdictions. For example, in the United States, such information is required to be provided in the Proxy Statement, SEC Form DEF 14A, sent to shareholders and filed with the SEC prior to shareholder meetings.

5.1.2 *Independent Chairman of the Board*

Many, if not most, corporate boards now permit a senior executive of a corporation to serve as the chairman of the board of directors. However, corporate governance experts do not regard such an arrangement to be in the best interests of the shareholders of the company. As the U.S. SEC observes:

> This practice may contribute to the [company's] ability to dominate the actions of the board of directors. The chairman of a . . . board can largely control the board's agenda, which may include matters not welcomed by the [company's management] . . . Perhaps more important, the chairman of the board can have a substantial influence on the . . . boardroom's culture. The boardroom culture can foster (or suppress) the type of meaningful dialogue between . . . management and independent directors that is critical for healthy . . . governance. It can support (or diminish) the role

---

12 *Corporate Governance Handbook*, New York Society of Securities Analysts, September 2003, p. 3.

of the independent directors in the continuous, active engagement of . . . management necessary for them to fulfill their duties. A boardroom culture conducive to decisions favoring the long-term interest of . . . shareholders may be more likely to prevail when the chairman does not have the conflicts of interest inherent in his role as an executive of the [company]. Moreover, a . . . board may be more effective when negotiating with the [company] over matters such as the [compensation] if it were not at the same time led by an executive of the [company] with whom it is negotiating.[13]

Not all market participants agree with this view. Many corporate managers argue that it is essential for efficient and effective board functioning that the chairman be the senior executive in the company. They base their arguments on the proposition that only such an executive has the knowledge and experience necessary to provide needed information to the board on questions on strategy, policy, and the operational functioning of the company. Critics of this position counter that it is incumbent upon corporate management to provide all such necessary information to the board. Indeed, many argue that this obligation is the sole reason that one or more corporate managers serve as members of the board.

Whether the company has separate positions for the chief executive and chairman of the board can be determined readily from regulatory filings of the company. If the positions are not separate, an investor may doubt that the board is operating efficiently and effectively in its monitoring and oversight of corporate operations, and that decisions made are necessarily in the best interests of investors and other stakeholders.

Tradition and practice in many countries prescribe a so-called "unitary" board system, a single board of directors. However, some countries, notably Germany, have developed a formal system whose intent is to overcome such difficulties as lack of independence of board members and lack of independence of the chairman of the board from company management. The latter approach requires a tiered hierarchy of boards, a management board responsible for overseeing management's strategy, planning, and similar functions, and an independent supervisory board charged with monitoring and reviewing decisions of the management board, and making decisions in which conflicts of interest in the management board may impair their independence, for example, in determining managerial compensation.

Clearly, independence of the chairman of the board does not guarantee that the board will function properly. However, independence should be regarded as a necessary condition, even if it is not a sufficient one.

5.1.3 *Qualifications of Directors*

In addition to independence, directors need to bring sufficient skill and experience to the position to ensure that they will be able to fulfill their fiduciary responsibilities to investors and other stakeholders. Information on directors' prior business experience and other biographical material, including current and past business affiliations, can generally be found in regulatory filings.

Boards of directors require a variety of skills and experience in order to function properly. These skills will vary by industry, although such core skills as knowledge of finance, accounting, and legal matters are required by all boards. Evaluation of the members should include an assessment of whether needed skills are available among the board members. Among the qualifications and core competencies that an investor should look for in the board as a group, and in individual members or candidates for the board, are:

▪ independence (see factors to consider in Section 5.1.1);

---

13 *Amendments to Rules Governing the Investment Company Act of 1940*, 17 CFR Part 270, July 2004, p. 4.

- relevant expertise in the industry, including the principal technologies used in the business and in financial operations, legal matters, accounting and auditing; and managerial considerations such as the success of companies with which the director has been associated in the past;

- indications of ethical soundness, including public statements or writings of the director, problems in companies with which the director has been associated in the past such as legal or other regulatory violations involving ethical lapses;

- experience in strategic planning and risk management;

- other board experience with companies regarded as having sound governance practices and that are effective stewards of investors' capital as compared to serving management's interests;

- dedication and commitment to serving the board and investors' interests (board members with such qualities will not serve on more than a few boards, have an excellent record of attendance at board meetings, and will limit other business commitments that require large amounts of time); and

- commitment to the needs of investors as shown, for example, by significant personal investments in this or other companies for which he or she serves as a director, and by an absence of conflicts of interest.

Such attributes are essential to the sound functioning of a board of directors and should be carefully considered in any investment decision. Board members may be selected as much for their general stature and name recognition as for the specialized expertise they bring to their responsibilities. However, the skills, knowledge, and experience we have described are essential to effective corporate governance, oversight, and monitoring on behalf of shareholders.

5.1.4 Annual Election of Directors

Members of boards of directors may be elected either on an annual or a staggered basis. In annual votes, every member of the board stands for re-election every year. Such an approach ensures that shareholders are able to express their views on individual members' performance during the year, and to exercise their right to control who will represent them in corporate governance and oversight of the company. Opponents argue that subjecting members to annual re-election is disruptive to effective board oversight over the company.

Those who support election of board members on a staggered basis with re-election of only a portion of the board each year, argue that such a scheme is necessary to ensure continuity of the knowledge and experience in the company essential for good corporate governance. Critics express the view that such a practice diminishes the limited power that shareholders have to control who will serve on the board and ensure the responsiveness of board members to investor concerns, such as poor management performance and practices. They also argue that staggered boards better serve the interests of entrenched managers by making the board less responsive to the needs of shareholders, more likely to align their interests with those of managers, and more likely to resist takeover attempts that would benefit shareholders to the detriment of managers.

Corporate governance best practice generally supports the annual election of directors as being in the best interests of investors. When shareholders can express their views annually, either by casting a positive vote or by withholding their votes for poorly performing directors, directors are thought to be more likely to weigh their decisions carefully, to be better prepared and more attentive to the needs of investors, and to be more effective in their oversight of management.

Information on directors' terms and the frequency of elections may be obtained by examining the term structure of the board members in regulatory filings.

5.1.5 *Annual Board Self-Assessment*

Board members have a fiduciary duty to shareholders to oversee management's use of assets, to monitor and review strategies, policies and practices, and to take those actions necessary to fulfill their responsibilities to stakeholders. It is essential that a process be in place for periodically reviewing and evaluating their performance and making recommendations for improvement. Generally, this evaluation should occur at least once annually. The review should include:

■ an assessment of the board's effectiveness as a whole;

■ evaluations of the performance of individual board members, including assessments of the participation of each member, with regard to both attendance and the number and relevance of contributions made, and an assessment of the member's willingness to think independently of management and address challenging or controversial issues;

■ a review of board committee activities;

■ an assessment of the board's effectiveness in monitoring and overseeing their specific functions;

■ an evaluation of the qualities the company will need in its board in the future, along with a comparison of the qualities current board members currently have; and

■ a report of the board self-assessment, typically prepared by the nominations committee, and included in the proxy in the U.S. and in the corporate governance report in Europe.

The process of periodic self-assessment by directors can improve board and company performance by reminding directors of their role and responsibilities, improving their understanding of the role, improving communications between board members, and enhancing the cohesiveness of the board. Self-assessment allows directors to improve not only their own performance but to make needed changes in corporate governance structures. All of these will lead to greater efficiency and effectiveness in serving investors' and other stakeholders' interests.

The process of self-assessment should focus on board responsibilities and individual members' accountability for fulfilling these responsibilities. It should consider both substantive matters and procedural issues, for example, evaluations of the adequacy and effectiveness of the committee structure. The committees regarded as essential by corporate governance experts include the auditing, nominations, and compensation committees, all of which should be staffed by independent directors who are experts in the relevant areas. (The specific functions of these committees will be considered in later sections.)

The company, however, may need to establish additional committees. For example, for a mutual fund company, these might include a securities valuation committee responsible for setting policies for the pricing of securities, and monitoring the application of the policies by management. For a high-technology company, the committees might include one tasked with the valuation of intellectual property, or perhaps, management's success in creating new intellectual property through its investments in research and development.

In evaluating the effectiveness of the corporate governance system and specifically, the board of directors, an investment professional should consider the critical functions specific to a particular company and evaluate whether or not the board's structure and membership provides adequate oversight and control over management's strategic business decision-making and policy-making.

5.1.6 *Separate Sessions of Independent Directors*

Corporate governance best practice requires that independent directors of the board meet at least annually, and preferably quarterly, in separate sessions—that is, meetings without the presence of the management, other representatives, or interested persons (for example, retired founders of the company). The purpose of these sessions is to provide an opportunity for those entrusted with the best interests of the shareholders to engage in candid and frank discussions and debate regarding the management of the company, their strategies and policies, strengths and weaknesses, and other matters of concern. Such regular sessions would avoid the suggestion that directors are concerned with specific problems or threats to the company's well-being. Separate sessions could also enhance the board's effectiveness by improving the cooperation among board members, and their cohesiveness as a board, attributes that can strengthen the board in the fulfillment of its responsibilities to shareholders.

Regulatory filings should indicate how often boards have met, and which meetings were separate sessions of the independent directors. The investment professional should be concerned if such meetings appeared to be nonexistent, infrequent, or irregular in occurrence. These could suggest a variety of negative conclusions, including the presence of a "captive," that is, non-independent board, inattention or disinterest among board members, lack of cohesion and sense of purpose, or other conditions that can be detrimental to the interests of investors.

5.1.7 *Audit Committee and Audit Oversight*

The audit committee of the board is established to provide independent oversight of the company's financial reporting, non-financial corporate disclosure, and internal control systems. This function is essential for effective corporate governance and for seeing that their responsibilities to shareholders are fulfilled.

The primary responsibility for overseeing the design, maintenance, and continuing development of the control and compliance systems rests with this committee. At a minimum the audit committee must:

- include only independent directors;
- have sufficient expertise in financial, accounting, auditing, and legal matters to be able to adequately oversee and evaluate the control, risk management, and compliance systems, and the quality of the company's financial disclosure to shareholders and others. It is advisable for at least two members of the committee to have relevant accounting and auditing expertise;
- oversee the internal audit function; the internal audit staff should report directly and routinely to this committee of the board, and, when necessary report any concerns regarding the quality of controls or compliance issues;
- have sufficient resources to be able to properly fulfill their responsibilities;
- have full access to and the cooperation of management;
- have authority to investigate fully any matters within its purview;
- have the authority for the hiring of auditors, including the setting of contractual provisions, review of the cost-effectiveness of the audit, approving of non-audit services provided by the auditor, and assessing the auditors' independence;
- meet with auditors independently of management or other company interest parties periodically but at least once annually; and
- have the full authority to review the audit and financial statements, question auditors regarding audit findings, including the review of the system of internal controls, and to determine the quality and transparency of financial reporting choices.

Strong internal controls, risk management, and compliance systems are critical to a company's long-term success, the meeting of its business objectives, and enhancing the best interests of shareholders. Nearly all of the major corporate collapses have involved an absence of effective control systems, or the overriding of the systems by management to achieve their own interests and objectives to the detriment of those of investors.

The internal audit function should be entirely independent and separate from any of the activities being audited. Internal auditors should report directly to the chairman of the audit committee of the board of directors. The board should regularly meet with the internal audit supervisor and review the activities and address any concerns.

In evaluating the effectiveness of the board of directors, an investor should review the qualifications of the members of the audit committee, being alert to any conflicts of interest that individual members might have, for example, having previously been employed or otherwise associated with the current auditor or the company, determine the number of meetings held by the committee during the year and whether these meetings were held independent of management. A report on the activities of the audit committee, including a statement on whether the committee met independently and without the presence of management, should be included in the proxy in the U.S. and in the corporate governance report in Europe.

The audit committee should discuss in the regulatory filings the responsibilities and authority it has to evaluate and assess these functions, any findings or concerns the committee has with regard to the audit, internal control and compliance systems, and corrective action taken.

5.1.8 *Nominating Committee*

In most corporations, currently, nominations of members of the board of directors and for executive officers of the company are made by members of the board, most often at the recommendation of, or in consultation with, the management of the company. In such circumstances, the criteria for selection of nominees may favor management's best interests at the expense of the interests of shareholders. This is all the more important because in the usual case, shareholders have no authority to nominate slates of directors who might best represent them. Consequently, corporate governance best practice requires that nominees to the board be selected by a nominating committee comprising only independent directors. The responsibilities of the nominating committee are to:

▪ establish criteria for evaluating candidates for the board of directors;

▪ identify candidates for the general board and for all committees of the board;

▪ review the qualifications of the nominees to the board and for members of individual committees;

▪ establish criteria for evaluating nominees for senior management positions in the company;

▪ identify candidates for management positions;

▪ review the qualifications of the nominees for management positions; and

▪ document the reasons for the selection of candidates recommended to the board as a whole for consideration.

Given the pivotal role that the members of the nominating committee have in representing and protecting the interests of investors and other stakeholders, it is essential that the qualifications of these members be carefully reviewed in assessing the long-term investment prospects of a company. Particular attention should be paid to evaluating their independence, the qualities of those selected for senior management positions, and the success of businesses with which they've been associated. This information is available in the regulatory filings of the company.

5.1.9 *Compensation Committee*

Ideally, compensation should be a tool used by directors, acting on behalf of shareholders, to attract, retain, and motivate the highest quality and most experienced managers for the company. The compensation should include incentives to meet and exceed corporate *long-term* goals, rather than short-term performance targets.

Decisions regarding the amounts and types of compensation to be awarded to senior executives and directors of a company are thought by many corporate governance experts to be the most important decisions to be made by those in a position of trust. Reports abound of compensation that is excessive relative to corporate performance, awarded to executives by compliant boards. The problem has been particularly acute in the United States, but examples are found worldwide.

In recent years, a practice has developed of gauging levels of compensation awards based not upon company objectives and goals but rather by comparison to the highest levels of compensation awarded in other companies. This occurs whether the reference companies are relevant benchmarks or not, and has caused compensation packages in many cases to be unrelated to the performance of the company. Needless to say, such excessive compensation is highly detrimental to the interests of shareholders.

In one well-known case, that of the New York Stock Exchange, the compensation of the chief executive was a substantial proportion of the net earnings of the Exchange and considerably higher than the compensation awarded to senior executives of comparable companies. The facts that have come to light in the case suggest that the compensation committee of the board was not independent as measured by the usual criteria, was not expert in compensation matters and did not seek outside counsel, was not well-informed on the details of the compensation package, and acquiesced in management's proposal of its own compensation.[14] This case is currently the subject of extensive legal and regulatory action.

Several different types of compensation awards are in common use today:

- salary, generally set by contractual commitments between the company and the executive or director;

- perquisites, additional compensation in the form of benefits, such as insurance, use of company planes, cars, and apartments, services, ranging from investment advice, tax assistance, and financial planning advice to household services;

- bonus awards, normally based on performance as compared to company goals and objectives;

- stock options, options on future awards of company stock; and

- stock awards or restricted stock.

In general, shareholders would prefer that salary and perquisite awards constitute a relatively small portion of the total compensation award. That is, the fixed, non-performance-based portion of the award should be adequate, but not excessive. Because these fixed costs must be borne by shareholders regardless of corporate performance, executives should not be automatically rewarded by poor performance. Information on salaries and some perquisites can be found in regulatory filings of companies. For example, in the United States, this information is found in the Proxy Statement in

---

14 Landon Thomas Jr., "Saying Grasso Duped Big Board, Suit Seeks Return of $100 Million," the *New York Times*, May 25, 2004, and "Regulators Said to Be Focusing On Board's Vote For Grasso Pay," the *New York Times*, March 26, 2004.

tables and accompanying text. The investor should be alert to the fact that significant amounts of perquisites may not be fully disclosed, as has been shown to be the case in a number of corporate scandals recently in Europe and the United States.

Bonuses should be awarded based solely on exceeding expected performance. They should provide an incentive to motivate managers to achieve the highest and most stable long-term performance, rather than to reward short-term non-sustainable "growth" at the expense of the best interests of shareholders. To the extent that management controls the operations of the company as well as corporate disclosure, incentive-based awards require the most diligent monitoring by the members of the compensation committee. Directors must ascertain that management is not manipulating variables within its control, for example, accounting disclosure choices, to artificially achieve performance targets. The investor should examine the bonus awards carefully, evaluating the performance targets for reasonableness, and to make certain that the awards are consistent with the investor's best interests.

Stock options and stock awards have been argued to better align the interests of managers with those of shareholders by making a portion of the manager's compensation dependent on the value of the stock. Unfortunately, as recent events have made clear, stock options do not always result in such an alignment of interests. Indeed, until recently, the lack of appropriate accounting recognition of the expense of stock option awards has led to widespread abuse of this form of compensation. Large grants of stock options dilute shareholders' positions in the company and diminish the value of their holdings.

Appropriate accounting for stock options, that is, expensing in the income statement with assumed conversion to stock in the earnings-per-share calculation, has come to be seen as a litmus test for high-quality financial reporting and transparency.[15] Nevertheless, abusive practices involving information manipulation related to stock option grants and option exercise still occur.

In theory, grants of stock options to executives and other employees should be subject to shareholder approval. As a practical matter, however, there are loopholes that permit managers and directors to by-pass such approval, although some jurisdictions have closed some of these loopholes recently.

Stock options' potential dilutive effect on shareholders can be assessed by a measure known as the "share overhang." The overhang is simply the number of shares represented by the options, relative to the total amount of stock outstanding. Both of these numbers are readily available in company regulatory filings in most jurisdictions.

In addition, investors should be alert to any provisions permitting the so-called "repricing" of stock options. Repricing means that the company can, with approval of the board of directors, adjust the exercise price of outstanding option grants downward to the current price of the stock. This is done by some companies when the price of the stock has declined significantly and the options are **out-of-the-money**. As is readily apparent, such repricing is inconsistent with the argument that options should serve the interests of managers and shareholders and provide an incentive for managers to strive for excellent long-term corporate performance. The managers may have **at-the-money** options following repricing, but investors cannot recoup their losses so easily. Abuse in this area has been stemmed somewhat by accounting rule changes that now require that such repriced options be expensed in the income statement, although companies can still cancel the options and reissue them later at a time consistent with the rules, usually six months.

---

15 In 2003, the International Accounting Standards Board (IASB) issued a standard requiring the fair value expensing of stock options for all companies that use IASB standards. Some ninety countries worldwide adhere to IASB standards.

Stock grants by companies to executives can be an effective means of motivating them to achieve sustainable, long-term performance objectives. Restricted stock grants, that is, stock awards that cannot be sold or otherwise disposed of for a period of time, or that are contingent upon reaching certain performance goals, can be subject to the same abusive practices as stock option awards, depending upon the terms of the awards. Well-designed restricted stock awards are increasingly used by companies to reward executives for their performance as well as to remunerate lower-level employees. Most jurisdictions require companies to disclose such grants in regulatory filings.

5.1.10 Board's Independent Legal and Expert Counsel

The board of directors should have the ability and sufficient resources to hire such legal and other expert counsel as they require to fulfill their fiduciary duties. In most companies, for example, the corporate counsel also has the responsibility to advise the board of directors. Because the board of directors is charged with overseeing management on behalf of the shareholders, this represents a direct conflict of interest. That is, the corporate counsel cannot be wholly independent with regard to the advice provided to the directors if it also serves, and is paid by, corporate management.

Legal counsel will be needed to help the board assess the company's compliance with legal and regulatory requirements. Outside counsel becomes increasingly important for companies with global operations. Similarly, for example, in high-technology companies, the members of the board will likely require the assistance of experts in the particular specialized technologies employed or developed by the company. However, all boards, regardless of the industry, are likely to require additional counsel and should be able to obtain such services when they require it.

The investor should review regulatory filings carefully to determine if the board makes use of independent outside counsel. If the filings are silent on the issue, the analyst or investor should specifically inquire about the board's use of independent counsel. If satisfactory answers are not forthcoming, this should reflect negatively on the board's independence as well as its ability to perform its fiduciary duties.

5.1.11 Statement of Governance Policies

Companies that have a strong commitment to corporate governance frequently supply a statement of their corporate governance policies, variously in their regulatory filings, on their websites, or as part other investor information packets. Investors and investment analysts should assess the following elements of a statement of corporate governance policies:

- codes of ethics;
- statements of the oversight, monitoring, and review responsibilities of directors, including internal control, risk management, audit and accounting and disclosure policy, compliance assessment, nominations, compensation awards, and other responsibilities;
- statements of management's responsibilities to provide complete and timely information to the board members prior to board meetings, and to provide directors with free and unfettered access to control and compliance functions within the company;
- reports of directors' examinations, evaluations, and findings in their oversight and review function;
- board and committee performance self-assessments;
- management performance assessments; and
- training provided to directors prior to joining the board and periodically thereafter.

Obviously, one cannot rely solely on the corporate governance statement for assurance that the company has a sound corporate governance structure. Nevertheless, such disclosures provide investors with a comparison for evaluating company and director performance over time. For example, such disclosures should not be "boilerplate" statements that do not change over time and that provide no real content or information.

5.1.12 *Disclosure and Transparency*

The purpose of accounting and disclosure is to tell the company's economic story as it is, not as some might want it to be in order to achieve some personal objective. Investors depend critically on the quality, clarity, timeliness, and completeness of financial information in valuing securities and assessing risk. Attempts to hide or otherwise obfuscate essential information can result in the mispricing of securities and the misallocation of capital, reducing the efficiency and effectiveness of markets.

It is worth observing that nearly all of the major corporate collapses in recent years have involved equally massive attempts to hide, obfuscate, or falsify information that could have alerted investors to the seriousness of the financial problems and the impending implosions. Enron attempted to hide its massive and growing debt by moving it off the balance sheet and into "partnerships," run by insiders, for which no information was available. Tyco failed to report billions in "loans" to insiders. WorldCom not only hid $11 billion in operating expenses by recording them as assets in the balance sheet, but also failed to disclose hundreds of millions of dollars in loans to the chief executive. Parmalat staved off collapse for some time by reporting falsely that the company had nearly $5 billion in a corporate account with a major international financial institution.

The crisis of the loss of confidence and trust in the broad financial markets globally, rather than just the companies involved, signals the depths of the concern that investors have had about the quality and completeness of the disclosure they are receiving. Not surprisingly, the response has been a major overhaul of legislative, regulatory, and related criminal code provisions in countries in North America and Europe, as well as elsewhere. Such provisions as the requirements in the United States that the chief executive officer and chief financial officer certify the accuracy of financial statements and develop rigorous new systems of internal controls, backed up by new audit attestation requirements and stiffer criminal penalties, make clear the seriousness of the offenses and the public's response to such malfeasance.

However, such changes do not guarantee that those in a position of trust will not again willingly mislead and misinform their investors and others, particularly when they are faced with serious financial difficulties. Consequently, an evaluation of the quality and extent of financial information provided to investors is a crucial element in evaluating the corporate governance structure of a company and the risk borne by an investor in the company's securities. In assessing the quality of disclosure, some indicators of good quality financial reporting are:[16]

- conservative assumptions used for employee benefit plans;

- adequate provisions for lawsuits and other loss contingencies;

- minimal use of off-balance sheet financing techniques and full disclosure of assets, liabilities, revenues, and expenses associated with such activities;

- absence of nonrecurring gains;

- absence of noncash earnings;

- clear and adequate disclosure;

---

16 White, Gerald I., Ashwinpaul C. Sondhi, and Dov Fried, *The Analysis and Use of Financial Statements*, Third Edition, 2003, Wiley, p. 637 ff.

- conservative revenue and expense recognition methods;
- use of LIFO inventory accounting (during periods of generally rising prices);
- bad-debt reserves that are high relative to receivables and past credit losses;
- use of accelerated depreciation methods and short lives;
- rapid write-off of acquisition-related intangible assets;
- minimal capitalization of interest and overhead;
- minimal capitalization of computer software costs;
- expensing of startup costs of new operations; and
- use of the completed contract method of accounting for contracts.

One area of concern in recent years is the reporting by companies of so-called "pro forma" earnings numbers, earnings before non-cash or "non-recurring" charges. Pro forma earnings have occasionally been dubbed "earnings-before-the-bad-stuff." Such misleading disclosures have been widely used by companies with poor performance and poor prospects. Unfortunately, some analysts and investors have been willing to accept the deception as reflective of economic reality, frequently to their regret. To survive and flourish long-term, companies must be able to cover all of their costs.

In addition to high-quality financial disclosure, the company should make readily available in its regulatory filings clear and complete information on such items as:

- governance policies and procedures;
- reporting lines and organizational structure;
- corporate strategy, goals, and objectives;
- competitive threats and other risks and contingencies faced by the company and the potential effect of these on the company's operations;
- insider transactions involving executives or other senior employees, and directors;
- compensation policies and amounts of compensation awarded, including perquisites, for key executives and directors; and
- changes to governance structures, including the corporate charter and by-laws.

The investor should be alert particularly to references to off-balance sheet or insider transactions that are not accompanied by full disclosure of the effects of the items on the company. The investor should also consider the implications of a lack of disclosure. For example, many large companies maintain fleets of corporate jets for the use of executives and other employees. They routinely make such planes available to executives for their private use on holidays. A failure to mention such perquisites should raise questions, not only about this item but about other possible compensation that has not been disclosed.

5.1.13 *Insider or Related-Party Transactions*

The corporate collapse cases cited above involve egregious insider transactions by senior executives, frequently with the acquiescence of a compliant board of directors. The executives' objective was self-aggrandizement at the expense of shareholders and other stakeholders in the company. This is not a new problem. Indeed, audit standards have required for decades that auditors investigate such items and flag them for users of the statements. However, both the frequency and extent of the theft and fraud, and the losses incurred by investors, employees, and others recently have dismayed even the most seasoned professionals in the financial markets.

The analyst should assess the company's policies concerning related-party transactions, whether the company has entered into any such transactions, and, if so, what the effects are on the company's financial statements. Any related-party transaction should require the prior approval of the board of directors and a statement that such transactions are consistent with company policy. Financial disclosures and related notes in regulatory filings are a source for analysts in researching such transactions.

5.1.14 *Responsiveness of Board of Directors to Shareholder Proxy Votes*

A clear indicator of the extent to which directors and executives take seriously their fiduciary responsibility to shareholders is the response of the company to shareholder votes on proxy matters. A recent example involves the issue of expensing stock options, which has been put to proxy vote in a sizable number of companies. Shareholders in many of the companies have voted in the majority that the company begin expensing stock options. Very few company managers and directors have responded positively to the votes.

Directors cannot be expected to respond to trivial or frivolous shareholder initiatives, but few such issues carry a large portion of the vote of shareholders. However, when matters related to governance, executive compensation, mergers and acquisitions, or other matters of great importance to investors are put to a vote of the shareholders, and the results of the vote are ignored, the implications are abundantly clear: management and the board are not concerned for or motivated by the best interests of the company's shareholders. An analyst should review all such proxies put to the shareholders, determine the shareholders' consensus as reflected in the relative size of the affirmative vote, and determine the directors' response to the vote as reflected in the actions taken by the board and management. The responsiveness is a clear signal of the board's willingness to act in the best interests of the owners of the company.

5.2 Examples of Codes of Corporate Governance

We provide examples of three codes of corporate governance, one from General Electric, one from the Monetary Authority of Singapore, and a third from an international organization, the Organization for Economic Co-Operation and Development. The first code provides an example for one of the largest globally-diversified corporations. The second addresses corporate governance issues for financial institutions, specifically commercial banks and insurers operating in Singapore. The third has a much broader scope, addressing corporate governance issues in any type of firm in any industry, operating in a variety of countries that are members of the organization. Taken together, these three codes indicate the varying approaches to corporate governance worldwide while also illustrating how the core conflicts of interest between managers and owners are addressed.

5.2.1 *General Electric:* Governance Principles

General Electric's *Governance Principles* are a particularly good example of a company code of corporate governance. GE established the code to guide not only its managers and board of directors in their activities and decision-making, but to serve as a benchmark by which their performance may be evaluated. The company publishes their *Principles* in a prominent place on their website. A review of these principles will show that many of the major governance concerns discussed above are reflected here. The principles also explicitly address issues such as the company's policy on the adoption of "poison pills" and director education.

EXAMPLE 5

General Electric's *Governance Principles*

1 Role of Board and Management

GE's business is conducted by its employees, managers and officers, under the direction of the chief executive officer (CEO) and the oversight of the board, to enhance the long-term value of the company for its shareowners. The board of directors is elected by the shareowners to oversee management and to assure that the long-term interests of the shareowners are being served. Both the board of directors and management recognize that the long-term interests of shareowners are advanced by responsibly addressing the concerns of other stakeholders and interested parties including employees, recruits, customers, suppliers, GE communities, government officials and the public at large.

2 Functions of Board

The board of directors has eight scheduled meetings a year at which it reviews and discusses reports by management on the performance of the company, its plans and prospects, as well as immediate issues facing the company. Directors are expected to attend all scheduled board and committee meetings. In addition to its general oversight of management, the board also performs a number of specific functions, including:

- selecting, evaluating and compensating the CEO and overseeing CEO succession planning;
- providing counsel and oversight on the selection, evaluation, development and compensation of senior management;
- reviewing, monitoring and, where appropriate, approving fundamental financial and business strategies and major corporate actions;
- assessing major risks facing the company—and reviewing options for their mitigation; and
- ensuring processes are in place for maintaining the integrity of the company—the integrity of the financial statements, the integrity of compliance with law and ethics, the integrity of relationships with customers and suppliers, and the integrity of relationships with other stakeholders.

3 Qualifications

Directors should possess the highest personal and professional ethics, integrity and values, and be committed to representing the long-term interests of the shareowners. They must also have an inquisitive and objective perspective, practical wisdom and mature judgment. We endeavor to have a board representing diverse experience at policymaking levels in business, government, education and technology, and in areas that are relevant to the company's global activities. Directors must be willing to devote sufficient time to carrying out their duties and responsibilities effectively, and should be committed to serve on the board for an extended period of time. Directors should offer their resignation in the event of any significant change in their personal circumstances, including a change in their principal job responsibilities.

Directors who also serve as CEOs or in equivalent positions should not serve on more than two boards of public companies in addition to the GE board, and other directors should not serve on more than four other boards of public companies in addition to the GE board. Current positions in excess of these limits may be maintained unless the board determines that doing so would impair the director's service on the GE board.

The board does not believe that arbitrary term limits on directors' service are appropriate, nor does it believe that directors should expect to be renominated annually until they reach the mandatory retirement age. The board self-evaluation process described below will be an important determinant for board tenure. Directors will not be nominated for election to the board after their 73rd birthday, although the full board may nominate candidates over 73 for special circumstances.

4 Independence of Directors

A majority of the directors will be independent directors, as independence is determined by the board, based on the guidelines set forth below.

All future non-employee directors will be independent. GE seeks to have a minimum of ten independent directors at all times, and it is the board's goal that at least two-thirds of the directors will be independent. Directors who do not satisfy GE's independence guidelines also make valuable contributions to the board and to the company by reason of their experience and wisdom.

For a director to be considered independent, the board must determine that the director does not have any direct or indirect material relationship with GE. The board has established guidelines to assist it in determining director independence, which conform to or are more exacting than the independence requirements in the New York Stock Exchange listing requirements (NYSE rules). In addition to applying these guidelines, the board will consider all relevant facts and circumstances in making an independence determination, and not merely from the standpoint of the director, but also from that of persons or organizations with which the director has an affiliation.

The board will make and publicly disclose its independence determination for each director when the director is first elected to the board and annually thereafter for all nominees for election as directors. If the board determines that a director who satisfies the NYSE rules is independent even though he or she does not satisfy all of GE's independence guidelines, this determination will be disclosed and explained in the next proxy statement.

In accordance with the revised NYSE rules, independence determinations under the guidelines in section (a) below will be based upon a director's relationships with GE during the 36 months preceding the determination. Similarly, independence determinations under the guidelines in section (b) below will be based upon the extent of commercial relationships during the three completed fiscal years preceding the determination.

a   A director will not be independent if:

- the director is employed by GE, or an immediate family member is an executive officer of GE;

- the director receives any direct compensation from GE, other than director and committee fees and pension or other forms of deferred compensation for prior service (provided such compensation is not contingent in any way on continued service);

- an immediate family member who is a GE executive officer receives more than $100,000 per year in direct compensation from GE;

- the director is affiliated with or employed by GE's independent auditor, or an immediate family member is affiliated with or employed in a professional capacity by GE's independent auditor; or

- a GE executive officer is on the compensation committee of the board of directors of a company which employs the GE director or an immediate family member as an executive officer.

b A director will not be independent if, at the time of the independence determination, the director is an executive officer or employee, or if an immediate family member is an executive officer, of another company that does business with GE and the sales by that company to GE or purchases by that company from GE, in any single fiscal year during the evaluation period, are more than the greater of one percent of the annual revenues of that company or $1 million.

c A director will not be independent if, at the time of the independence determination, the director is an executive officer or employee, or an immediate family member is an executive officer, of another company which is indebted to GE, or to which GE is indebted, and the total amount of either company's indebtedness to the other at the end of the last completed fiscal year is more than one percent of the other company's total consolidated assets.

d A director will not be independent if, at the time of the independence determination, the director serves as an officer, director or trustee of a charitable organization, and GE's discretionary charitable contributions to the organization are more than one percent of that organization's total annual charitable receipts during its last completed fiscal year. (GE's automatic matching of employee charitable contributions will not be included in the amount of GE's contributions for this purpose.)

5 Size of Board and Selection Process

The directors are elected each year by the shareowners at the annual meeting of shareowners. Shareowners may propose nominees for consideration by the nominating and corporate governance committee by submitting the names and supporting information to: Secretary, General Electric Company, 3135 Easton Turnpike, Fairfield, CT 06828. The board proposes a slate of nominees to the shareowners for election to the board. The board also determines the number of directors on the board provided that there are at least 10. Between annual shareowner meetings, the board may elect directors to serve until the next annual meeting. The board believes that, given the size and breadth of GE and the need for diversity of board views, the size of the board should be in the range of 13 to 17 directors.

6 Board Committees

The board has established the following committees to assist the board in discharging its responsibilities: i) audit; ii) management development and compensation; iii) nominating and corporate governance; and iv) public responsibilities. The current charters and key practices of these committees are published on the GE website, and will be mailed to shareowners on written request. The committee chairs report the highlights of their meetings to the full board following each meeting of the respective committees. The committees occasionally hold meetings in conjunction with the full board. For example, it is the practice of the audit committee to meet in conjunction with the full board in February so that all directors may participate in the review of the annual financial statements and Management's Discussion and Analysis of Financial Condition and Results of Operations for the prior year and financial plans for the current year.

7 Independence of Committee Members

In addition to the requirement that a majority of the board satisfy the independence standards discussed in section 4 above, members of the audit committee must also satisfy an additional NYSE independence requirement. Specifically, they may not accept directly or indirectly any consulting, advisory or other compensatory fee from GE or any of its subsidiaries other than their directors' compensation. As a matter of policy, the board will also apply a separate and heightened independence standard to members of both the management development and compensation committee and the nominating and corporate governance committee. No member of either committee may be a partner, member or principal of a law firm, accounting firm or investment banking firm that accepts consulting or advisory fees from GE or any of its subsidiaries.

8 Meetings of Non-Employee Directors

The board will have at least three regularly scheduled meetings a year for the non-employee directors without management present. The directors have determined that the chairman of the management development and compensation committee will preside at such meetings, and will serve as the presiding director in performing such other functions as the board may direct, including advising on the selection of committee chairs and advising management on the agenda for board meetings. The non-employee directors may meet without management present at such other times as determined by the presiding director.

9 Self-Evaluation

As described more fully in the key practices of the nominating and corporate governance committee, the board and each of the committees will perform an annual self-evaluation. Each November, each director will provide to an independent governance expert his or her assessment of the effectiveness of the board and its committees, as well as director performance and board dynamics. The individual assessments will be organized and summarized by this independent governance expert for discussion with the board and the committees in December.

10 Setting Board Agenda

The board shall be responsible for its agenda. At the December board meeting, the CEO and the presiding director will propose for the board's approval key issues of strategy, risk and integrity to be scheduled and discussed during the course of the next calendar year. Before that meeting, the board will be invited to offer its suggestions. As a result of this process, a schedule of major discussion items for the following year will be established. Prior to each board meeting, the CEO will discuss the other specific agenda items for the meeting with the presiding director, who shall have authority to approve the agenda for the meeting. The CEO and the presiding director, or committee chair as appropriate, shall determine the nature and extent of information that shall be provided regularly to the directors before each scheduled board or committee meeting. Directors are urged to make suggestions for agenda items, or additional pre-meeting materials, to the CEO, the presiding director, or appropriate committee chair at any time.

11 Ethics and Conflicts of Interest

The board expects GE directors, as well as officers and employees, to act ethically at all times and to acknowledge their adherence to the policies comprising GE's code of conduct set forth in the company's integrity manual, "Integrity: The Spirit and the Letter of Our Commitment." GE will not make any personal loans or extensions of credit to directors or executive officers, other than consumer loans or credit card services on terms offered to the general public. No non-employee director may provide personal services for compensation to GE, other than in connection with serving as a GE director. The board will not permit any waiver of any ethics policy for any director or executive officer. If an actual or potential conflict of interest arises for a director, the director shall promptly inform the CEO and the presiding director. If a significant conflict exists and cannot be resolved, the director should resign. All directors will recuse themselves from any discussion or decision affecting their personal, business or professional interests. The board shall resolve any conflict of interest question involving the CEO, a vice chairman or a senior vice president, and the CEO shall resolve any conflict of interest issue involving any other officer of the company.

12 Reporting of Concerns to Non-Employee Directors or the Audit Committee

The audit committee and the non-employee directors have established the following procedures to enable anyone who has a concern about GE's conduct, or any employee who has a complaint about the company's accounting, internal accounting controls or auditing matters, to communicate that concern directly to the presiding director, to the non-employee directors or to the audit committee. Such communications may be confidential or anonymous, and may be e-mailed, submitted in writing or reported by phone to special addresses and a toll-free phone number that are published on the company's website. All such communications shall be promptly reviewed by GE's ombudsman, and any concerns relating to accounting, internal controls, auditing or officer conduct shall be sent immediately to the presiding director and to the chair of the audit committee. All concerns will be reviewed and addressed by GE's ombudsman in the same way that other concerns are addressed by the company. The status of all outstanding concerns addressed to the non-employee directors, the presiding director or the audit committee will be reported to the presiding director and the chair of the audit committee on a quarterly basis. The presiding director or the audit committee chair may direct that certain matters be presented to the audit committee or the full board and may direct special treatment, including the retention of outside advisors or counsel, for any concern addressed to them. The company's integrity manual prohibits any employee from retaliating or taking any adverse action against anyone for raising or helping to resolve an integrity concern.

13 Compensation of the Board

The nominating and corporate governance committee shall have the responsibility for recommending to the board compensation and benefits for non-employee directors. In discharging this duty, the committee shall be guided by three goals: compensation should fairly pay directors for work required in a company of GE's size and scope; compensation should align directors' interests with the long-term interests of shareowners; and the structure of the compensation should be simple, transparent and easy for shareowners to understand. As discussed more fully in the key practices of the nominating and corporate governance committee, the committee believes these goals will be served by providing 40% of non-employee director compensation in cash and 60% in deferred stock units. At the end of each year, the nominating and corporate governance committee shall review non-employee director compensation and benefits.

14 Succession Plan

The board shall approve and maintain a succession plan for the CEO and senior executives, based upon recommendations from the management development and compensation committee.

15 Annual Compensation Review of Senior Management

The management development and compensation committee shall annually approve the goals and objectives for compensating the CEO. That committee shall evaluate the CEO's performance in light of these goals before setting the CEO's salary, bonus and other incentive and equity compensation. The committee shall also annually approve the compensation structure for the company's officers, and shall evaluate the performance of the company's senior executive officers before approving their salary, bonus and other incentive and equity compensation.

16 Access to Senior Management

Non-employee directors are encouraged to contact senior managers of the company without senior corporate management present. To facilitate such contact, non-employee directors are expected to make two regularly scheduled visits to GE businesses a year without corporate management being present.

17 Access to Independent Advisors

The board and its committees shall have the right at any time to retain independent outside auditors and financial, legal or other advisors, and the company shall provide appropriate funding, as determined by the board or any committee, to compensate such independent outside auditors or advisors, as well as to cover the ordinary administrative expenses incurred by the board and its committees in carrying out their duties.

18 Director Education

The general counsel and the chief financial officer shall be responsible for providing an orientation for new directors. Each new director shall, within three months of election to the board, spend a day at corporate headquarters for personal briefing by senior management on the company's strategic plans, its financial statements, and its key policies and practices. In addition, directors shall be provided with continuing education on subjects that would assist them in discharging their duties, including regular programs on GE's financial planning and analysis, compliance and corporate governance developments; business-specific learning opportunities through site visits and Board meetings; and briefing sessions on topics that present special risks and opportunities to the company.

19 Policy on Poison Pills

The term "poison pill" refers to the type of shareowner rights plan that some companies adopt to make a hostile takeover of the company more difficult. GE does not have a poison pill and has no intention of adopting a poison pill because a hostile takeover of a company of our size is impractical and unrealistic. However, if GE were ever to adopt a poison pill, the board would seek prior shareowner approval unless, due to timing constraints or other reasons, a committee consisting solely of independent directors determines that it would be in the best interests of shareowners to adopt a poison pill before obtaining shareowner approval. If the GE board of directors were ever to adopt a poison pill without prior shareowner approval, the board would either submit the poison pill to shareowners for ratification, or would cause the poison pill to expire, without being renewed or replaced, within one year.

5.2.2 *Monetary Authority of Singapore:* Guidelines and Regulations on Corporate Governance

In February 2003, the Monetary Authority of Singapore (MAS) established principles of corporate governance for the banks and insurers that fall within its regulatory purview. The code, *Guidelines and Regulations on Corporate Governance,*[17] defines and explains corporate governance as:

> . . . The processes and structures by which the business and affairs of an Institution are directed, managed and controlled. [p. 6]

The MAS makes clear that the key element in an effective system of corporate governance rests with the board of directors, and that its primary duties are to shareholders and depositors, or, in the case of an insurer, the policyholders:

> The board of directors is responsible for directing the management of the Institution. Besides its obligations to the shareholders, the board of directors of an Institution has a duty to act in the best interest of the Institution and to ensure that the Institution has sufficient resources to meet its obligations to other stakeholders, in particular a bank's depositors or an insurer's policyholders.

The Monetary Authority of Singapore has the following thirteen principles to guide the banks and insurers within its regulatory authority in compliance with the corporate governance standards in its *Guidelines and Regulations on Corporate Governance*:

Principle 1	Every Institution should be headed by an effective Board.
Principle 2	There should be a strong and independent element on the Board which is able to exercise objective judgment on corporate affairs independently from management and substantial shareholders.
Principle 3	The Board should set and enforce clear lines of responsibility and accountability throughout the Institution.
Principle 4	There should be a formal and transparent process for the appointment of new directors to the Board.
Principle 5	There should be a formal assessment of the effectiveness of the Board as a whole and the contribution by each director to the effectiveness of the Board.
Principle 6	In order to fulfill their responsibilities, Board members should be provided with complete, adequate and timely information prior to board meetings and on an on-going basis by the management.
Principle 7	There should be a formal and transparent procedure for fixing the remuneration packages of individual directors. No director should be involved in deciding his own remuneration.
Principle 8	The level and composition of remuneration should be appropriate to attract, retain and motivate the directors to perform their roles and carry out their responsibilities.
Principle 9	The Board should establish an Audit Committee with a set of written terms of reference that clearly sets out its authority and duties.
Principle 10	The Board should ensure that there is an adequate risk management system and sound internal controls.

---

17 These guidelines expand and build upon the *Code of Corporate Governance,* issued in 2001 by the Corporate Governance Committee, established by the Ministry of Finance, the Authority and the Attorney-General's Chambers.

Principle 11   The Board should ensure that an internal audit function that is
              independent of the activities audited is established.

Principle 12   The Board should ensure that management formulates policies
              to ensure dealings with the public, the Institution's policyholders
              and claimants, depositors and other customers are conducted
              fairly, responsibly and professionally.

Principle 13   The Board should ensure that related party transactions with the
              Institution are made on an arm's length basis.

These principles are supported by requirements for extensive disclosures regarding companies' implementation and of the standards and their procedures for continuous monitoring of compliance. It is notable that the Monetary Authority does not require that a majority of the board members be independent, but only that one-third meet such a test.

5.2.3 *Organisation for Economic Co-Operation and Development:* OECD Principles of Corporate Governance

The Organisation for Economic Co-Operation and Development ("OECD")[18] issued its code, *OECD Principles of Corporate Governance* ("OECD Principles"), which applies to all Member countries. These countries comprise a number of different legislative, regulatory and market systems.

The OECD observes that its Principles "represent the first initiative by an inter-governmental organisation to develop the core elements of a good corporate governance regime. As such, the Principles can be used as a benchmark by governments as they evaluate and improve their laws and regulations." The Preface to the OECD Principles states:

> A good corporate governance regime helps to assure that corporations use their capital efficiently. Good corporate governance helps, too, to ensure that corporations take into account the interests of a wide range of constituencies as well as of the communities within which they operate, and that their boards are accountable to the company and the shareholders. This, in turn, helps to assure that corporations operate for the benefit of society as a whole. It helps to maintain the confidence of investors—both foreign and domestic—and to attract more "patient", long-term capital … **Common to all good corporate governance regimes, however, is a high degree of priority placed on the interests of shareholders, who place their trust in corporations to use their investment funds wisely and effectively.** [Emphasis added]

Despite the application of the OECD Principles to a wide variety of regimes, the OECD provides a special emphasis on the rights and fair treatment of shareholders. This characteristic, although considered to be a fundamental requirement for good systems of corporate governance, is not frequently found in either corporate codes or those of other business organizations. For example, the General Electric code is silent on shareholder rights, although it acknowledges in the first principle that managers and the directors have an obligation to attend to the interests of shareholders. The Monetary Authority of Singapore's code takes a similar approach.

---

18 Issued in 1999, and subsequently revised, the OECD Principles are intended to be adopted by each of the OECD Member countries, which include: Australia, Austria, Belgium, Canada, the Czech Republic, Denmark, Finland, France, Germany, Greece, Hungary, Iceland, Ireland, Italy, Japan, Korea, Luxembourg, Mexico, the Netherlands, New Zealand, Norway, Poland, Portugal, Spain, Sweden, Switzerland, Turkey, the United Kingdom, and the United States.

EXAMPLE 6

OECD Principles of Corporate Governance

I. The Rights of Shareholders

The corporate governance framework should protect shareholders' rights.

A Basic shareholder rights include the right to: 1) secure methods of ownership registration; 2) convey or transfer shares; 3) obtain relevant information on the corporation on a timely and regular basis; 4) participate and vote in general shareholder meetings; 5) elect members of the board; and 6) share in the profits of the corporation.

B Shareholders have the right to participate in, and to be sufficiently informed on, decisions concerning fundamental corporate changes such as:

   1 Amendments to the statutes, or articles of incorporation or similar governing documents of the company;

   2 The authorisation of additional shares; and

   3 Extraordinary transactions that in effect result in the sale of the company.

C Shareholders should have the opportunity to participate effectively and vote in general shareholder meetings and should be informed of the rules, including voting procedures, that govern general shareholder meetings:

   1 Shareholders should be furnished with sufficient and timely information concerning the date, location and agenda of general meetings, as well as full and timely information regarding the issues to be decided at the meeting.

   2 Opportunity should be provided for shareholders to ask questions of the board and to place items on the agenda at general meetings, subject to reasonable limitations.

   3 Shareholders should be able to vote in person or in absentia, and equal effect should be given to votes whether cast in person or in absentia.

D Capital structures and arrangements that enable certain shareholders to obtain a degree of control disproportionate to their equity ownership should be disclosed.

E Markets for corporate control should be allowed to function in an efficient and transparent manner.

   1 The rules and procedures governing the acquisition of corporate control in the capital markets, and extraordinary transactions such as mergers, and sales of substantial portions of corporate assets, should be clearly articulated and disclosed so that investors understand their rights and recourse. Transactions should occur at transparent prices and under fair conditions that protect the rights of all shareholders according to their class.

   2 Anti-take-over devices should not be used to shield management from accountability.

F Shareholders, including institutional investors, should consider the costs and benefits of exercising their voting rights.

II. The Equitable Treatment of Shareholders

The corporate governance framework should ensure the equitable treatment of all shareholders, including minority and foreign shareholders. All shareholders should have the opportunity to obtain effective redress for violation of their rights.

A All shareholders of the same class should be treated equally.

   1 Within any class, all shareholders should have the same voting rights. All investors should be able to obtain information about the voting rights attached to all classes of shares before they purchase. Any changes in voting rights should be subject to shareholder vote.

   2 Votes should be cast by custodians or nominees in a manner agreed upon with the beneficial owner of the shares.

   3 Processes and procedures for general shareholder meetings should allow for equitable treatment of all shareholders. Company procedures should not make it unduly difficult or expensive to cast votes.

B Insider trading and abusive self-dealing should be prohibited.

C Members of the board and managers should be required to disclose any material interests in transactions or matters affecting the corporation.

III. The Role of Stakeholders in Corporate Governance

The corporate governance framework should recognise the rights of stakeholders as established by law and encourage active co-operation between corporations and stakeholders in creating wealth, jobs, and the sustainability of financially sound enterprises.

A The corporate governance framework should assure that the rights of stakeholders that are protected by law are respected.

B Where stakeholder interests are protected by law, stakeholders should have the opportunity to obtain effective redress for violation of their rights.

C The corporate governance framework should permit performance-enhancing mechanisms for stakeholder participation.

D Where stakeholders participate in the corporate governance process, they should have access to relevant information.

IV. Disclosure and Transparency

The corporate governance framework should ensure that timely and accurate disclosure is made on all material matters regarding the corporation, including the financial situation, performance, ownership, and governance of the company.

A Disclosure should include, but not be limited to, material information on:

   1 The financial and operating results of the company.

   2 Company objectives.

   3 Major share ownership and voting rights.

   4 Members of the board and key executives, and their remuneration.

   5 Material foreseeable risk factors.

   6 Material issues regarding employees and other stakeholders.

   7 Governance structures and policies.

B Information should be prepared, audited, and disclosed in accordance with high quality standards of accounting, financial and non-financial disclosure, and audit.

C An annual audit should be conducted by an independent auditor in order to provide an external and objective assurance on the way in which financial statements have been prepared and presented.

D Channels for disseminating information should provide for fair, timely and cost-efficient access to relevant information by users.

V. The Responsibilities of the Board

The corporate governance framework should ensure the strategic guidance of the company, the effective monitoring of management by the board, and the board's accountability to the company and the shareholders.

A Board members should act on a fully informed basis, in good faith, with due diligence and care, and in the best interest of the company and the shareholders.

B Where board decisions may affect different shareholder groups differently, the board should treat all shareholders fairly.

C The board should ensure compliance with applicable law and take into account the interests of stakeholders.

D The board should fulfill certain key functions, including:

1 Reviewing and guiding corporate strategy, major plans of action, risk policy, annual budgets and business plans; setting performance objectives; monitoring implementation and corporate performance; and overseeing major capital expenditures, acquisitions and divestitures.

2 Selecting, compensating, monitoring and, when necessary, replacing key executives and overseeing succession planning.

3 Reviewing key executive and board remuneration, and ensuring a formal and transparent board nomination process.

4 Monitoring and managing potential conflicts of interest of management, board members and shareholders, including misuse of corporate assets and abuse in related party transactions.

5 Ensuring the integrity of the corporation's accounting and financial reporting systems, including the independent audit, and that appropriate systems of control are in place, in particular, systems for monitoring risk, financial control, and compliance with the law.

6 Monitoring the effectiveness of the governance practices under which it operates and making changes as needed.

7 Overseeing the process of disclosure and communications.

E The board should be able to exercise objective judgement on corporate affairs independent, in particular, from management.

1 Boards should consider assigning a sufficient number of non-executive board members capable of exercising independent judgement to tasks where there is a potential for conflict of interest. Examples of such key responsibilities are financial reporting, nomination and executive and board remuneration.

2 Board members should devote sufficient time to their responsibilities.

F In order to fulfill their responsibilities, board members should have access to accurate, relevant and timely information.

This code, and its predecessor variants, is not only among the earliest efforts to establish guidelines for good governance, but with its global reach has had wide influence on the development of other codes and regulatory frameworks.

6   ENVIRONMENTAL, SOCIAL, AND GOVERNANCE FACTORS

Investors now understand that nontraditional business factors—specifically, a company's environmental, social, and governance (ESG) risk exposures—may be as critical to the company's long-term sustainability as more traditional concerns. Indeed, many major financial institutions and portfolio managers routinely integrate ESG analyses into their equity valuations and other investment decisions.[19] Those analysts who fail to consider ESG factors in their valuations may well be assuming far greater long-term risks than they or their clients realize.[20]

ESG factors range from those associated with climate change (for example, carbon-based greenhouse gas emissions resulting from a company's operations) to labor rights, public and occupational health issues, and the soundness of the company's governance structures.[21]

The risks resulting from exposure to these various issues include the following:

▪ **Legislative and regulatory risk.** The risk that governmental laws and regulations directly or indirectly affecting a company's operations will change with potentially severe adverse effects on the company's continued profitability and even its long-term sustainability.

For example, in the United States, a law enacted in California in 2004 requires a 30 percent reduction in carbon dioxide emissions by 2016 for all new automobiles sold in the state. Other states, including Connecticut, Maine, Massachusetts, New Jersey, New York, Oregon, Pennsylvania, Rhode Island, Vermont, and Washington, are following California's example.[22] These states currently represent more than half of all U.S. automobile sales. Consequently, manufacturers that fail to meet the standards can expect to suffer a reduction in revenues and earnings as well as market power. Given strong industry competition, the effects of the changes in the laws on companies operating in the industry could be severe.

Other national and global efforts have brought rapid changes in operations for companies in affected countries. For example, the Kyoto Protocol is a 1997 amendment to the United Nations Framework Convention on Climate Change (UNFCCC). The Protocol now covers more than 160 countries, not including the United States and Australia, and over 60 percent of greenhouse gas emissions. The agreement calls for staged reductions in emissions of carbon dioxide and five other greenhouse gases for those countries that have ratified the agreement. The Protocol also provides for emissions credit trading for those signatories, principally in emerging countries, that could not otherwise afford the investment.

---

19 See, for example, Miranda Anderson and David Gardiner, *Climate Risk and Energy in the Auto Sector: Guidance for Investors and Analysts on Key Off-balance Sheet Drivers*, Ceres, Inc., 2006.
20 *The Materiality of Social, Environmental and Corporate Governance Issues to Equity Pricing: 11 Sector Studies by Brokerage House Analysts*, United Nations Environmental Programme Finance Initiative (UNEP FI), Asset Management Working Group. 2004.
21 Ibid.
22 Anderson et al., p. 7.

Companies in most industries are likely to be affected to at least some degree by these mandated changes, although the effects will vary widely across industries. Even within industries with the greatest exposures, companies that have invested in newer, more up-to-date technologies are likely to be affected less by the changes than their competitors. Thus, investors who consider ESG factors and who monitor regulatory and legislative developments for the companies they follow will be better equipped to make sound investment decisions.

- **Legal risk.** The risk that failures by company managers to effectively manage ESG factors will lead to lawsuits and other judicial remedies, resulting in potentially catastrophic losses for the company.

  All areas of ESG can, and sometimes do, lead to such lawsuits. The actions can be brought by employees for workplace issues and contractual defaults, by shareholders for management or director governance or other lapses that impair shareholder value, or by government attorneys for abridgement of federal or state laws.

  An investor can begin to analyze the potential for such risks in a particular company by reviewing regulatory filings for the particular jurisdictions in which the company operates. Many such filings, such as the U.S. SEC required disclosures in the Form 10-K Business, Risks, and Legal Proceedings sections, as well as the Management Discussion and Analysis of Financial Condition and Results of Operations, require substantial discussion of possible legal risk exposures. For those companies that provide them, the GRI reports may include useful insights.[23] However, an analyst should make an independent assessment of the company and carefully consider the nature of a company's operations to evaluate the possible scope of such exposures and their potential effects. The business press may also be a good source of information regarding such risks on both the company of immediate interest as well as other companies in the same industry.

- **Reputational risk.** This particular source of risk has risen in importance as ESG factors are increasingly recognized as a potentially major source of risk. Specifically, companies whose managers have demonstrated a lack of concern for managing ESG factors in the past, so as to eliminate or otherwise mitigate risk exposures, will suffer a diminution in market value relative to other companies in the same industry that may persist for a long period of time.

- **Operating risk.** The risk that a company's operations may be severely affected by ESG factors, even to the requirement that one or more product lines or possibly all operations might be shut down.

  An example of such a risk is that deriving from the industrial use of benzene, a powerful carcinogen and one of the most toxic chemicals known. Because of its use as both a building block in the plastics and rubber industry, as well as its more general use as an industrial solvent, benzene was widely used in industry and was dispersed into the air, drinking water, and soil. Billions of pounds of the chemical were produced and used annually.

  Once studies confirmed the harmful effects of the chemical, the U.S. Environmental Protection Agency (EPA) moved, for example, under the 1974 Safe Drinking Water Act to set targets for acceptable levels in water. The EPA Maximum Contaminant Level for benzene in drinking water was set at five parts per billion. Thus, companies that had previously relied on extensive use of

---

23 The Global Reporting Initiative (GRI) promotes systematic reporting of economic, environmental, and social performance. The website for the GRI is www.globalreporting.org.

benzene in their operations had either to modify their operations to ensure that no benzene escaped into the environment, or to cease those operations that used benzene altogether.

- **Financial risk.** The risk that ESG factors will result in significant costs or other losses to the company and its shareholders. Any of the above sources of risk can affect a company and its financial health, sometimes severely.

In summary, investors are well advised to consider the potential effects of ESG factors on companies in which they invest and to carefully analyze all sources of information relevant to such risk exposures. These analyses may alert the analyst to risk factors that should be incorporated into company valuations.

7   VALUATION IMPLICATIONS OF CORPORATE GOVERNANCE

The relative quality, strength and reliability of a company's corporate governance system have direct and profound implications for investors' assessments of investments and their valuations. As we have seen in the massive corporate collapses in recent years, most or all of an investor's capital can be lost suddenly if a company fails to establish an effective corporate governance system with the appropriate checks and balances.

Weak corporate governance systems pose the following risks to the value of investments in the company:

- **Accounting risk.** The risk that a company's financial statement recognition and related disclosures, upon which investors base their financial decisions, are incomplete, misleading, or materially misstated.

- **Asset risk.** The risk that the firm's assets, which belong to investors, will be misappropriated by managers or directors in the form of excessive compensation or other perquisites.

- **Liability risk.** The risk that management will enter into excessive obligations, committed to on behalf of shareholders, that effectively destroy the value of shareholders' equity; these frequently take the form of off-balance sheet obligations.

- **Strategic policy risk.** The risk that managers may enter into transactions, such as mergers and acquisitions, or incur other business risks that may not be in the best long-term interest of shareholders, but which may result in large payoffs for management or directors.

Not surprisingly, a growing body of evidence indicates that companies with sound corporate governance systems show higher profitability and investment performance measures, including returns, relative to those assessed to have weaker structures. For example, a joint study of Institutional Shareholder Services (ISS) and Georgia State University[24] found that the best-governed companies, as measured by the ISS Corporate Governance Quotient, generated returns on investment and equity over the period under study that were 18.7 percent and 23.8 percent, respectively, better than those of companies with poor governance. Similarly, a study of U.S. markets, conducted by

---

24 Brown, Lawrence D., and Caylor, Marcus, "Corporate Governance Study: The Correlation between Corporate Governance and Company Performance," Institutional Shareholder Services (2004).

researchers at Harvard University and the University of Pennsylvania,[25] found that portfolios of companies with strong shareholder-rights protections outperformed portfolios of companies with weaker protections by 8.5 percent per year. A study of European firms found annual mean return differences of 3.0 percent.[26]

This phenomenon is not limited to developed markets. Even before the collapse of Enron, a Malaysia-based analyst found that investors in emerging markets overwhelmingly preferred companies with good governance.[27] Of the 100 largest emerging markets companies his firm followed, those with the best governance, based on management discipline, transparency, independence, accountability, responsibility, fairness and social responsibility, generated three-year U.S. dollar returns of 267 percent, compared with average returns of 127 percent. The disparity in five-year returns was even greater, at 930 percent versus an average of 388 percent.

The conclusion from these and other studies is that good corporate governance leads to better results, both for companies and for investors. Therefore, investors and analysts should carefully evaluate the corporate governance structures of companies they are considering as investments and should continue to monitor the systems once the investments are made.

SUMMARY

Corporate governance is an essential concern for investors and investment analysts. This reading has presented the attributes of an effective corporate governance system and the types of practices that should raise investors' concerns. This reading has made the following points:

- Corporate governance is the system of principles, policies, procedures, and clearly defined responsibilities and accountabilities, used by stakeholders to eliminate or minimize conflicts of interest.

- The objectives of a corporate governance system are 1) to eliminate or mitigate conflicts of interest among stakeholders, particularly between managers and shareholders, and 2) to ensure that the assets of the company are used efficiently and productively and in the best interests of the investors and other stakeholders.

- The failure of a company to establish an effective system of corporate governance represents a major operational risk to the company and its investors. To understand the risks inherent in an investment in a company, it is essential to understand the quality of the company's corporate governance practices.

- The core attributes of an effective corporate governance system are:

  a delineation of the rights of shareholders and other core stakeholders;

  b clearly defined manager and director governance responsibilities to the stakeholders;

25 Gompers, Paul A., Joy L. Ishii, and Andrew Metrick, "Corporate Governance and Equity Prices," *Quarterly Journal of Economics*, 118(1) (February 2003), 107-155. The authors compared the investment performance of some 1,500 U.S.-listed companies against a corporate governance index the authors constructed from 24 distinct governance rules.
26 Bauer, Rod, and Nadja Guenster, "Good Corporate Governance Pays Off!: Well-Governed Companies Perform Better on the Stock Market," (2003). This study used Deminor Ratings as the basis for determining companies' relative corporate governance quality (www.deminor.org).
27 Gill, Amar, "Corporate Governance in Emerging Markets—Saints and Sinners: Who's Got Religion?," CLSA Emerging Markets, April 2001; Gill points out that CLSA assigned corporate governance ratings to 495 companies in 25 markets.

    c identifiable and measurable accountabilities for the performance of the responsibilities;

    d fairness and equitable treatment in all dealings between managers, directors and shareholders; and

    e complete transparency and accuracy in disclosures regarding operations, performance, risk and financial position.

■ The specific sources of conflict in corporate agency relationships are:

    a Manager–shareholder conflicts. Managers may, for example:

        ■ use funds to try to expand the size of a business even when this is not in the best interests of shareholders, and

        ■ grant themselves numerous expensive perquisites which are treated as ordinary business expenses.

    b Director–shareholder conflicts. Directors may, for example, identify with the managers' interests rather than those of the shareholders as a result of personal or business relationships with the manager.

■ The responsibilities of board members, both individually and as a group, are to:

    a establish corporate values and governance structures for the company to ensure that the business is conducted in an ethical, competent, fair, and professional manner;

    b ensure that all legal and regulatory requirements are met and complied with fully and in a timely fashion;

    c establish long-term strategic objectives for the company with a goal of ensuring that the best interests of shareholders come first and that the company's obligations to others are met in a timely and complete manner;

    d establish clear lines of responsibility and a strong system of accountability and performance measurement in all phases of a company's operations;

    e hire the chief executive officer, determine the compensation package, and periodically evaluate the officer's performance;

    f ensure that management has supplied the board with sufficient information for it to be fully informed and prepared to make the decisions that are its responsibility, and to be able to adequately monitor and oversee the company's management;

    g meet regularly to perform its duties and in extraordinary session as required by events; and

    h acquire adequate training so that members are able to adequately perform their duties.

■ An investor or investment analyst must assess:

    a board composition and independence;

    b whether the chairman of the board is independent;

    c the qualifications of the directors;

    d whether the board is elected on an annual or staggered basis;

    e board self-assessment practices;

    f the frequency of separate sessions of independent directors;

    g the audit committee and audit oversight;

    h the nominating committee;

    i the compensation committee and compensation awards to management; and

j the use (or not) of independent legal and expert counsel.

■ Companies committed to corporate governance often provide a statement of corporate governance policies. Analysts should assess the code of ethics; statements of the oversight, monitoring, and review responsibilities of directors; statements of management's responsibilities with respect to information and access of directors to internal company functions; reports of directors' examinations, evaluations, and findings; board and committee self-assessments; management self-assessments; and training policies for directors.

■ Weak corporate governance systems give rise to risks including accounting risk, asset risk, liability risk, and strategic policy risk. Such risks may compromise the value of investments in the company.

PRACTICE PROBLEMS

1 Which of the following *best* defines the concept of corporate governance?

A A system for monitoring managers' activities, rewarding performance, and disciplining misbehavior.

B Corporate values and governance structures that ensure the business is conducted in an ethical, competent, fair, and professional manner.

C A system of principles, policies, and procedures used to manage and control the activities of a corporation so as to overcome conflicts of interest inherent in the corporate form.

2 Which of the following is an example of a conflict of interest that an effective corporate governance system would mitigate or eliminate?

A A majority of the board is independent of management.

B Directors identify with the managers' interests rather than those of the shareholders.

C Directors have board experience with companies regarded as having sound governance practices.

3 Which of the following *best* describes the corporate governance responsibilities of members of the board of directors?

A Establish long-term strategic objectives for the company.

B Ensure that at board meetings no subject is undiscussable and dissent is regarded as an obligation.

C Ensure that the board negotiates with the company over all matters such as compensation.

4 Which of the following is *least likely* to be useful in evaluating a company's corporate governance system for investment analysis purposes?

A Assess issues related to the board, managers, and shareholders.

B Review the company's regulatory filings and financial information provided to shareholders.

C Flag items such as egregious use of insider transactions for users of the financial statements.

5 The objectives of an effective system of corporate governance include all of the following *except* to:

A ensure that the assets of the company are used efficiently and productively.

B eliminate or mitigate conflicts of interest among stakeholders.

C ensure complete transparency in disclosures regarding operations, performance, risk, and financial position.

6 All of the following are core attributes of an effective corporate governance system *except*:

A fairness and accuracy in identifying inherent conflicts of interest.

B clearly defined governance responsibilities for managers and directors.

C delineation of shareholders and other core stakeholders' rights.

7 All of the following are examples of conflicts of interest that an effective corporate governance system should address *except* relationships between:

A managers and shareholders.

    B   managers and directors.

    C   managers and institutional analysts.

8 All of the following are true of an effective system of corporate governance *except*:

    A   the system must be continually monitored, especially with changes in management and the board.

    B   a single system of effective corporate governance applies to all firms worldwide.

    C   there are a number of common characteristics of all sound corporate governance structures.

The following information relates to Questions 9–14

Jane Smith, CFA, has recently joined Zero Asset Management, Inc. (Zero) as a board member. Since Smith is also outside counsel for Zero, she is already very familiar with Zero's operations and expects to begin contributing good ideas right away. Zero is a publicly traded investment management firm that historically focused on mutual fund management. Although there is current market opportunity to add a new type of mutual fund, the board recently decided against adding the fund. Instead, the board decided to expand its business to include a hedge fund operation within the existing corporation.

Bill Week, CEO of Zero, has publicly stated that he is willing to bet the company's future on hedge fund management. Week is the founder of Zero, as well as Chairman of the board, and maintains a controlling interest in the company.

Like the rest of Zero, the firm's new hedge fund is quantitatively driven and index based. The fund has been set up in a separate office with new systems so that the analysts and managers can create a unique hedge fund culture. Trading and execution are the only operations that remain with Zero. The fund is run by one of Zero's most successful portfolio managers.

Smith learns that although none of the board members sit on other companies' boards, most have at one point or another worked at Zero and so they are very familiar with Zero's operations. A board member has attempted to make the health insurance and retirement concerns of the board members an agenda item, without success to date. Smith eagerly anticipates the next board meeting as they are always in a luxurious setting.

At the board meeting, Smith asks a number of questions about Zero's corporate governance system. The board becomes concerned by Smith's questions and decides to hire an independent consultant to review their corporate governance responsibilities. The consultant starts his analysis by stating that a corporate governance system relies upon checks and balances among managers, directors, and investors. Smith asks if Zero has the proper systems in place. The consultant says that he has looked at conflicts of interest and has one more area to review in order to verify that the board is meeting its major objectives. Concerned about the company's stock price, Smith asks the consultant what work he has done concerning Zero's corporate disclosures for investment professionals. The consultant indicates that he has reviewed Zero's regulatory filings for clear and complete information, as well as the company's policies regarding related party transactions.

9 All of the following indicate Zero's board's lack of independence *except*:

    A   personal relationships.

    B   service of the outside counsel as a board member.

    C   lack of interlocking directorships.

10 Which of the following is the most effective action for the board to take to address their oversight responsibilities concerning the hedge fund's proxy voting?

    A   Establish corporate values and governance structure for the company.

    B   Establish long-term strategic objectives that are met and fully complied with.

    C   Perform adequate training so that employees are able to perform their duties.

11 Which of the following omissions best describes a corporate governance short-coming of Zero's board of directors? The board's failure to:

    A   address the potential conflicts of interest between managing the firm's hedge fund and its mutual fund business.

    B   meet the market opportunity for a new kind of mutual fund.

    C   establish the hedge fund operation in a separate corporation.

12 Given that Zero's directors all previously worked at the company, which of the following would you recommend for a more effective system of corporate governance?

    A   Ensure that assets are used efficiently and productively and in the best interests of investors and stakeholders.

    B   Eliminate or mitigate conflicts of interest among stakeholders, particularly between managers and shareholders.

    C   Identify and measure accountabilities for the performance of the board's responsibilities.

13 Which of the following best describes the objectives of Zero's board that the consultant has not yet reviewed? The board should ensure:

    A   that the assets of the company are used efficiently and productively and in the best interests of the investors and other stakeholders.

    B   that material foreseeable risk factors are addressed and considered.

    C   compliance with applicable laws and take into account the interest of stakeholders.

14 Which of the following is the most critical activity that an analyst can engage in to assess the quality of the corporate governance system at Zero, among those that the consultant did not review?

    A   Look for vague references to off-balance sheet or insider information.

    B   Identify the responsiveness of the board to shareholder proxy votes.

    C   Evaluate the quality and extent of financial information provided to investors.

The following information relates to Questions 15–19

Shelley Newcome is the new CEO for a publicly traded financial services company, Asset Management Co. (AMC). Newcome is new to the corporate governance requirements of a publicly traded company, as she previously worked for a family office that invested in private equity.

At her first board meeting, the company's first in six months, she asks a director what the objectives of corporate governance should be. The director tells her that the most important objective he can think of is to eliminate or mitigate conflicts of interest among stakeholders.

One of Newcome's first steps as CEO is to fly to New York City in order to address a group of Wall Street analysts. Newcome is happy to discover that AMC provides her, and other senior management, with a company jet to attend such meetings.

At the opening of the meeting, Newcome is surprised to hear that most of the analysts are extremely interested in learning about AMC's corporate governance system. One analyst indicates that he has studied several of AMC's competitors and found that they share a set of critical and core attributes. The analyst goes on to note that like its competitors, AMC has included in its corporate governance system the following attributes: the rights of shareholders and other core stakeholders are clearly delineated; there is complete transparency and accuracy in disclosures regarding operations, performance, risk, and financial position; and identifiable and measurable accountabilities for the performance of responsibilities. The analyst also says that in order to verify that the board is meeting its major objectives he has looked at AMC's conflicts of interest and has one more area to review.

Newcome then asks the analyst why his corporate governance evaluation of AMC is so important. The analyst responds by saying that his decision whether or not to invest in AMC, and ultimately the long-term performance of the company, is dependent upon the quality of AMC's managers' decisions and the skill they use in applying sound management practices.

Closing the meeting, Newcome is delayed by one analyst who complains about the difficulties of flying these days and how he has to get to the airport hours ahead of time. The analyst goes on to say that he reviewed AMC's regulatory filings and was happy to see that the company does not spend its money on frivolous perquisites like executive jets.

15 Which of the following would *best* complete the objectives of corporate governance for the CEO?

   A Ensure that assets of the company are used efficiently and productively and in the best interests of investors and other stakeholders.

   B Clearly define governance responsibilities for both managers and directors.

   C Establish clear lines of responsibility and a strong system of accountability and performance measurement in all phases of a company's operations.

16 On the basis of the Wall Street analyst's comments about AMC's corporate governance system, which of the following would be most effective for AMC to attract investors' interest?

   A Implement a corporate governance system in which business activity is encouraged and rewarded, and that leads to innovation.

   B Establish a corporate governance system that overcomes inherent conflicts of interest since they represent a major operational risk to investors and the continued existence of the company.

    C Provide full transparency of all material information on a timely basis to all investment analysts.

17 Which of the following is a core attribute that the Wall Street analyst left out of his analysis of AMC?

    A Corporate governance systems rely on checks and balances among managers, directors, and investors.

    B Fairness in all dealings between managers, directors, and shareholders.

    C Complete, accurate, and transparent disclosure of loans to private equity funds.

18 Based on the information provided in the case, which of the following corporate disclosures could investment professionals use to evaluate the quality of the corporate governance system at AMC?

    A Inclusion of all vague references to off-balance sheet or insider transactions in board minutes.

    B Failure to disclose executive perquisites such as the use of corporate jets by senior management.

    C Provide other compensation that has not been disclosed to investment analysts.

19 Which of the following is an example of a corporate governance responsibility that AMC's board of directors has failed to meet?

    A Ensure that the board adequately monitors and oversees the company's management.

    B Ensure that management has supplied the board with sufficient information for it to be fully informed.

    C Meet regularly to perform its duties.

The following information relates to Questions 20–25 and is based on "Capital Structure" and this reading

Bobby Lee is an equity analyst for the U.S. investment management firm Larocque & Frères. Larocque & Frères has a substantial ownership stake in Skylark Industries, a U.S.-based company that operates in several business segments related to defense.

    Lee is reviewing the corporate governance standards at Skylark and how they may affect the firm's valuation. After extensive conversations with Skylark's chief financial officer, Doreen Miller, he summarizes the attributes of Skylark's governance system as:

    Attribute 1   Defining the rights of shareholders relative to bondholders, suppliers, customers, and employees.

    Attribute 2   Outlining specific responsibilities toward stakeholders that managers and directors must fulfill.

    Attribute 3   Separating the roles of chairman and chief executive officer.

    Lee is aware that weak corporate governance systems pose risks to the value of investments in the form of accounting risk, asset risk, liability risk, and strategic policy risk. He is considering whether Skylark's frequent acquisitions and extensive use of operating leases, respectively, represent examples of these risks.

Lee is also interested in determining whether Skylark's capital structure is optimal. He asks the director of research, "Does the 'optimal capital structure' result in the lowest beta, the lowest cost of equity, the highest earnings per share, or the lowest weighted average cost of capital?"

Using various sources, Lee estimates Skylark's costs of debt and equity for various capital structures, shown in Exhibit 1. Currently, Skylark has a market capitalization of $2 billion of debt and $8 billion of equity. The income tax rate is 36 percent.

During a shareholder conference call, Miller states that the company's objective is to minimize the weighted average cost of capital. She describes possible corporate actions. Use an amount equal to half of its net income to:

Corporate action 1   initiate a dividend

Corporate action 2   repurchase shares

Corporate action 3   reduce existing debt

After the conference call, Lee decides that Skylark should raise an additional $1 billion of debt and use the proceeds to repurchase common shares.

Lee also thinks that distributing an amount equal to half of its net income as a dividend may change Skylark's leading P/E. Miller responds, "Skylark's competitors that pay a dividend appear to benefit from a 100 basis point reduction in cost of equity, regardless of capital structure. I assume Skylark's cost of equity would decline by the same amount if it initiates a dividend." Lee estimates that Skylark's long-term earnings and dividend growth rate is 7.0 percent.

Exhibit 1	Skylark Industries Estimated Costs of Capital for Various Capital Structures			
Weight of Debt at Market Value (%)	Weight of Equity at Market Value (%)	Pretax Cost of Debt (%)	Cost of Equity (%)	Weighted Average Cost of Capital (%)
10	90	5.3	9.7	—
20	80	5.5	10.0	—
30	70	6.0	10.5	—
40	60	6.7	11.2	8.44
50	50	7.5	12.0	8.40
60	40	8.6	13.2	8.58
70	30	10.0	15.0	8.98

Note: Current capital structure (indicated in italics) is $2 billion of debt, $8 billion of equity.

20 Of the attributes summarized by Lee, which is *not* a requirement of an effective corporate governance system?

   A   Attribute 1.

   B   Attribute 2.

   C   Attribute 3.

21 Skylark's frequent acquisitions and extensive use of operating leases *best* represent which of the following risks?

	Frequent Acquisitions	Extensive Use of Operating Leases
A	Asset	Liability
B	Strategic Policy	Asset
C	Strategic Policy	Liability

22 The director of research's *best* response to Lee's question about the optimal capital structure is:

A lowest cost of equity.

B highest earnings per share.

C lowest weighted average cost of capital.

23 Given its objective and the three possible corporate actions, Skylark is *least likely* to select:

A Corporate action 1.

B Corporate action 2.

C Corporate action 3.

24 If Skylark implements Lee's proposal to issue $1 billion of debt and use the proceeds to repurchase common shares, its weighted average cost of capital following the buyback will *most likely*:

A increase to 8.50%.

B increase to 8.70%.

C decrease to 8.50%.

25 Given Skylark's current capital structure and Miller's assumption about the dividend's effect on the cost of equity, initiating a dividend will result in a price-to-earnings multiple *closest* to:

A 16.7.

B 20.0.

C 25.0.

SOLUTIONS

1 C is correct. Corporate governance is the system of principles, policies, procedures, and clearly defined responsibilities and accountabilities used by stakeholders to overcome the conflicts of interest inherent in the corporate form.

2 B is correct. Members of the board of directors serve as agents for the owners, the shareholders, a mechanism designed to represent the investors and to ensure that their interests are being well served. An effective corporate governance system helps ensure that directors are aligned with shareholders' interests rather than management's interests.

3 A is correct. The board of directors has the responsibility to establish long-term strategic objectives for the company with a goal of ensuring that the best interests of shareholders come first and that the company's obligations to others are met in a timely and complete manner.

4 C is correct. Flagging items such as egregious use of insider transactions is least likely to be useful in assessing the quality of the corporate governance system. While egregious use of insider transactions is problematic, financial disclosures and related notes in regulatory filings are the source for analysts in researching such transactions.

5 C is correct. The objectives of an effective corporate governance system do not include ensuring complete transparency in disclosures regarding operations, performance, risk, and financial position. This is an attribute of an effective corporate governance system, not an objective.

6 A is correct. Fairness and equitable treatment in all dealings between managers, directors, and shareholders is a core attribute of an effective corporate governance system, not fairness and accuracy in identifying inherent conflicts of interest.

7 C is correct. An effective corporate governance system does not address conflicts of interest between managers and institutional analysts.

8 B is correct. There is no single system of effective corporate governance that applies to all firms worldwide. Different industries and economic systems, legal and regulatory environments, and cultural differences may affect the characteristics of an effective corporate governance system for a particular company.

9 C is correct. Interlocking directorships may be indicative of lack of independence. The lack of interlocking directorships does not indicate lack of independence.

10 A is correct. By establishing corporate values and an effective governance structure, the board attempts to ensure that the hedge fund's proxy voting is in the best interest of the shareholders of Zero.

11 A is correct. The board has omitted to address the potential conflicts of interest between managing the firm's hedge fund and mutual fund businesses. A failure to address this potential conflict of interest is a corporate governance shortcoming.

12 B is correct. The issue is that the directors may identify with the managers' interests rather than those of the shareholders. By eliminating or mitigating the conflicts of interest between managers and shareholders, the impact of this potential misidentification by the board is eliminated or mitigated.

13 A is correct. The two major objectives of corporate governance are to eliminate or mitigate conflicts of interest and to ensure the efficient and productive use of assets. The consultant has not yet reviewed for the efficient and productive use of assets.

14 C is correct. The most critical activity not yet performed by the consultant is the review to evaluate the quality and extent of financial information provided to investors. The consultant has performed the preliminary step of reviewing regulatory filings but has not yet evaluated the quality and extent of financial information provided.

15 A is correct. The two major objectives of corporate governance are to eliminate or mitigate conflicts of interest, particularly between managers and shareholders, and to ensure the efficient and productive use of assets in the best interests of investors and other stakeholders.

16 B is correct. The Wall Street analyst is concerned with conflicts of interest. AMC should establish a corporate governance system that overcomes inherent conflicts of interest.

17 B is correct. The Wall Street analyst failed to consider the core attribute of fairness and equitable treatment in all dealings between managers, directors, and shareholders.

18 B is correct. The failure to disclose executive perquisites potentially reflects poor quality of the governance system.

19 C is correct. The board of directors has failed to meet regularly (meetings six months apart) to perform its duties.

20 C is correct. Separating the roles of chairman and chief executive officer is not a *required* attribute of an effective corporate governance policy. There is disagreement as to whether separating the roles of chairman and chief executive officer is an effective corporate governance attribute. The other attributes listed are part of an effective governance system.

21 C is correct. Transactions such as mergers and acquisitions that may not be in the best long-term interest of shareholders represent a strategic policy risk. Excessive obligations (frequently off-balance sheet) that may reduce the value of shareholder equity are classified as a liability risk.

22 C is correct. The capital structure that maximizes the company's stock value is also the capital structure that minimizes its WACC.

23 C is correct. At the current debt weight of 20%, the WACC is declining with increases in debt. If you calculate the WACC, it is currently 8.7% and would decline to 8.5% if the debt weight is 30%. Repurchasing shares or paying a dividend would increase the debt weight, which would reduce the WACC. Reducing debt would increase the WACC, so this is the corporate action that Skylark should be least likely to select.

24 C is correct. The WACC is the weight of debt times the after-tax cost of debt plus the weight of equity times the cost of equity. Skylark currently has a market value of $8 billion of equity and $2 billion of debt, for an 80/20 ratio. Using Exhibit 1, we find that this capital structure has a 5.5% pretax and 3.52% $[5.5 \times (1 - 0.36)]$ after-tax cost of debt and a 10.0% cost of equity. Thus the WACC equals $(0.2 \times 3.52) + (0.8 \times 10.0) = 0.70 + 8.0 = 8.7\%$. After the buyback,

Skylark's capital structure will be 70/30, which results in a 6.0% pretax cost of debt (3.84% after tax) and a 10.5% cost of equity. Thus, the new WACC will be $(0.3 \times 3.84) + (0.7 \times 10.5) = 1.15 + 7.35 = 8.5\%$, which is a decrease.

25 C is correct. The Gordon growth model can be used to calculate the P/E as the payout ratio divided by the difference between cost of equity and growth. In this case, the payout ratio would be 50%, cost of equity would drop from the current 10% (see table) to 9%, and the growth rate is 7%. The leading P/E is $0.5/(0.09 - 0.07) = 25\times$.

Mergers and Acquisitions

by Rosita P. Chang, CFA, and Keith M. Moore, CFA

LEARNING OUTCOMES

Mastery	The candidate should be able to:
☐	**a.** classify merger and acquisition (M&A) activities based on forms of integration and relatedness of business activities;
☐	**b.** explain common motivations behind M&A activity;
☐	**c.** explain bootstrapping of earnings per share (EPS) and calculate a company's postmerger EPS;
☐	**d.** explain, based on industry life cycles, the relation between merger motivations and types of mergers;
☐	**e.** contrast merger transaction characteristics by form of acquisition, method of payment, and attitude of target management;
☐	**f.** distinguish among pre-offer and post-offer takeover defense mechanisms;
☐	**g.** calculate and interpret the Herfindahl–Hirschman Index, and evaluate the likelihood of an antitrust challenge for a given business combination;
☐	**h.** compare the discounted cash flow, comparable company, and comparable transaction analyses for valuing a target company, including the advantages and disadvantages of each;
☐	**i.** calculate free cash flows for a target company, and estimate the company's intrinsic value based on discounted cash flow analysis;
☐	**j.** estimate the value of a target company using comparable company and comparable transaction analyses;
☐	**k.** evaluate a takeover bid, and calculate the estimated post-acquisition value of an acquirer and the gains accrued to the target shareholders versus the acquirer shareholders;
☐	**l.** explain how price and payment method affect the distribution of risks and benefits in M&A transactions;
☐	**m.** describe characteristics of M&A transactions that create value;

(continued)

Corporate Finance: A Practical Approach, by Michelle R. Clayman, CFA, Martin S. Fridson, CFA, and George H. Troughton, CFA. Copyright © 2008 by CFA Institute.

LEARNING OUTCOMES

Mastery	The candidate should be able to:
☐	**n.** distinguish among equity carve-outs, spin-offs, split-offs, and liquidation;
☐	**o.** explain common reasons for restructuring.

1   INTRODUCTION

Companies enter into merger and acquisition activities for a variety of reasons. Many companies use mergers as a means to achieve growth. Others seek to diversify their businesses. In all cases, it is important for corporate executives and analysts to understand both the motives for mergers and their financial and operational consequences.

Merger and acquisition (M&A) activities involve a variety of complexities and risks. For the case described in Example 1, corporate managers, investors, regulators, and a bevy of advisers—including investment bankers, financial analysts, lawyers, and accountants—each evaluated the various offers from a variety of perspectives.

EXAMPLE 1

Guidant–Boston Scientific Merger

On 15 December 2004, Guidant Corporation (GDT), a manufacturer of heart defibrillators and other specialized medical equipment, agreed to merge with Johnson & Johnson (JNJ), a large, multinational producer of medical products and equipment. Guidant shareholders were to receive $30.40 in cash and $45.60 in JNJ stock (subject to conditions) per share of Guidant stock held. Although a merger such as the combination between GDT and JNJ normally would take about four months to complete, unanticipated events caused the planned merger transaction to become a year-long saga.

While the companies worked to obtain the required regulatory clearances, a number of investigative articles exposing problems with GDT's defibrillators appeared in the *New York Times* in the spring of 2005. The company issued notices to physicians who prescribed the company's products warning them of potential problems with various defibrillator models. During the summer of 2005, GDT removed some defibrillators from the market as it tried to correct the technical problems. Meanwhile, numerous liability suits were filed against the company, and GDT subsequently lost a significant portion of its sales. Because of these negative developments, JNJ sought to renegotiate the terms of the transaction, claiming that the "material adverse change" clause in the merger agreement had been violated.[1]

GDT held that the loss of business did not violate the "material adverse change" clause. After initially filing a lawsuit in the U.S. District Court in an attempt to force JNJ to adhere to the original agreement, GDT later decided to enter into negotiations with JNJ to see if the two companies could agree on an acceptable modified agreement. In November 2005, the two companies agreed to modify the consideration that JNJ would pay GDT shareholders. In the new

---

[1] Many merger and acquisition agreements include provisions for renegotiation or cancellation following events that have a significant negative effect on the company's value or business operations.

agreement, GDT shareholders were to receive $33.25 in cash and 0.493 shares of JNJ stock for each share of GDT held. With JNJ stock trading at a price of about $62.00 in November 2005, the total value of the deal to GDT shareholders was about $63.82 per share of GDT held, which was a significantly lower merger price than in the original agreement.

Shortly after the modified merger agreement was announced, the chairman of another medical device manufacturer, Boston Scientific Corporation (BSX), contacted the chairman of GDT and indicated an interest in pursuing a business combination as an alternative to the JNJ merger. Because of the existing GDT–JNJ merger agreement, Guidant's legal advisers reminded the company's managers that they were prevented from entering into any competing merger discussions unless there was a merger proposal that could be deemed "superior" to the JNJ offer. As a result, on 5 December 2005, BSX communicated an offer to acquire GDT for $36 in cash and $36 in BSX common stock (subject to various conditions).

Although JNJ had fought for many months to acquire GDT at a reduced price, within a month, it improved the price it was willing to pay for GDT. A bidding war was under way. On 11 January 2006, JNJ's offer was for $37.25 in cash and 0.493 shares of JNJ stock—an increase of $4 in cash. The following day, BSX responded by increasing its offer to a total of $73—$36.50 in cash and $36.50 in stock plus $0.012 interest per day for every day after 1 April that the merger was not completed. By offering compensation for any delay past 1 April, BSX sought to reassure any shareholders who might otherwise decline the offer out of concerns that antitrust objections might delay completion of the merger.

JNJ responded the next day, on 13 January, by increasing its offer to $40.52 in cash and 0.493 shares of JNJ stock. Although some believed that the auction was over, BSX was not done. On 15 January 2006, BSX increased its offer to $42 in cash and $38 in BSX stock for a total of $80. The two companies entered into a definitive merger agreement, the agreement with JNJ was terminated, and the GDT–BSX merger was ultimately completed in April 2006.

Despite all the legal issues and product liability problems, a competitive bidding war resulted in a more lucrative merger consideration for Guidant shareholders, who ultimately received $4.00 more than the original JNJ merger proposal.

This reading will discuss many of the issues brought forth in Example 1, such as the forms of payment in a merger, legal and contractual issues, and the necessity for regulatory approval. More importantly, this reading aims to equip you with the basic tools for analyzing M&A deals and the companies behind them. In subsequent sections, we will discuss the motives behind business combinations, various transaction characteristics of M&A deals, the regulations governing M&A activity, and how to evaluate a target company and a proposed merger. Section 2 discusses the basic types of mergers. Section 3 examines the common motives that drive merger activities. In Section 4, we consider various transaction characteristics and their impact on different facets of M&A deals. Section 5 focuses on takeovers and the common defenses used to defeat unwelcome takeover attempts. In Section 6, we outline the various regulations that apply to M&A activity. Section 7 explores methods for analyzing a target company and provides a framework for analyzing merger bids. In Section 8, we review the empirical evidence related to the distribution of gains in mergers. Section 9 provides a brief introduction to corporate restructuring activities, and we conclude the reading with a summary.

2 MERGERS AND ACQUISITIONS: DEFINITIONS AND CLASSIFICATIONS

Business combinations come in different forms. A distinction can be made between acquisitions and mergers. In the context of M&A, an **acquisition** is the purchase of some portion of one company by another. An acquisition might refer to the purchase of assets from another company, the purchase of a definable segment of another entity, such as a subsidiary, or the purchase of an entire company, in which case the acquisition would be known as a merger. A **merger** represents the absorption of one company by another. That is, one of the companies remains and the other ceases to exist as a separate entity. Typically, the smaller of the two entities is merged into the larger, but that is not always the case.

Mergers can be classified by the form of integration. In a **statutory merger**, one of the companies ceases to exist as an identifiable entity and all its assets and liabilities become part of the purchasing company. In a **subsidiary merger**, the company being purchased becomes a subsidiary of the purchaser, which is often done in cases where the company being purchased has a strong brand or good image among consumers that the acquiring company wants to retain. A **consolidation** is similar to a statutory merger except that in a consolidation, *both* companies terminate their previous legal existence and become part of a newly formed company. A consolidation is common in mergers where both companies are approximately the same size.

The parties to a merger are often identified as the target company and the acquiring company. The company that is being acquired is the **target company**, or simply the **target**. The company acquiring the target is called the **acquiring company**, or the **acquirer**. We will use this terminology throughout the reading.

In practice, many of the terms used to describe various types of transactions are used loosely such that the distinctions between them are blurred. For example, the term "consolidation" is often applied to transactions where the entities are about the same size, even if the transaction is technically a statutory merger. Similarly, mergers are often described more generally as **takeovers**, although that term is often reserved to describe **hostile transactions**, which are attempts to acquire a company against the wishes of its managers and board of directors. A **friendly transaction**, in contrast, describes a potential business combination that is endorsed by the managers of both companies, although that is certainly no guarantee that the merger will ultimately occur.

An additional way that mergers are classified is based on the relatedness of the merging companies' business activities. Considered this way, there are three basic types of mergers: horizontal, vertical, and conglomerate.

A **horizontal merger** is one in which the merging companies are in the same kind of business, usually as competitors. The Vodafone AirTouch acquisition of telecommunications competitor Mannesmann AG in 2000 is one example of a horizontal merger. Another example is the merger of Mobil and Exxon in 1999. One of the great motivators behind horizontal mergers is the pursuit of **economies of scale**, which are savings achieved through the consolidation of operations and elimination of duplicate resources. Another common reason for horizontal mergers is to increase market power, because the merger results in a reduction of the number of industry competitors and an increase in the size of the acquiring company.

In a **vertical merger**, the acquirer buys another company in the same production chain, for example, a supplier or a distributor. In addition to cost savings, a vertical merger may provide greater control over the production process in terms of quality or procurement of resources or greater control over the distribution of the acquirer's finished goods. If the acquirer purchases a target that is ahead of it in the value chain (a supplier), it is called **backward integration**. An example of backward integration is if a steel manufacturer purchases an iron ore mining company. When an acquirer purchases a company that is further down the value chain (a distributor), it is called **forward integration**. An example of forward integration is Merck & Co.'s 1993 acquisition of Medco Containment Services, a marketer of discount prescription medicines. The merger brought together the production and distribution of pharmaceuticals into one integrated company.

When an acquirer purchases another company that is unrelated to its core business, it may be called a **conglomerate merger**. General Electric is an example of a conglomerate, having purchased companies in a wide range of industries, including media, finance, home appliances, aircraft parts, and medical equipment. Conglomerate mergers were particularly popular from the 1960s through the 1980s. The concept of company-level diversification was commonly used as a rationale for inter-industry mergers during this period. By investing in companies from a variety of industries, companies hoped to reduce the volatility of the conglomerate's total cash flows. As we will discuss in the section on merger motivations, company-level diversification is not necessarily in the shareholders' best interests.

EXAMPLE 2

History of U.S. Merger Activity

The history of merger activity in the United States illustrates the various types of M&A combinations. Merger and acquisition activities have historically been clustered in waves. The predominant types of mergers and the structures of merger deals have varied with each wave, typically as a result of differences in the regulatory environment. Similarly, the industries involved tend to vary by wave. Merger activity is apt to be concentrated in a relatively small number of industries, usually those going through dramatic changes, such as deregulation or rapid technological advancement.

First Wave (1897–1904)

At the close of the 1800s, growth in the railroads linked regional markets and created an environment conducive to larger companies that could capitalize on the emerging national U.S. economy, particularly within the mining and manufacturing industries. A relatively lax regulatory environment contributed to the situation, and many horizontal mergers resulted in near monopolistic conditions in several industries. The wave ended in 1904 as a result of a landmark decision by the U.S. Supreme Court limiting horizontal mergers among large competitors.

Second Wave (1916–1929)

In the 1920s, motor vehicles and radio coupled with improved railroad infrastructure further bolstered the U.S. economy. Like the previous wave, the second wave was accompanied by a sharp increase in stock prices. This time, however, the regulatory environment was less friendly to horizontal combinations and more sensitive to market power. Because market power was already concentrated among a few companies and further horizontal integration was difficult, companies sought to integrate backward into supply and forward into distribution through vertical mergers. Consequently, business combinations in this wave tended to create oligopolies. This second wave came to a conclusion with the 1929 stock market crash.

Third Wave (1965–1969)

The third wave occurred in a regulatory environment that strongly discouraged any merger—horizontal or vertical—that would reduce competition within an industry. Companies seeking to expand thus looked outside their own industries and began forming conglomerates. Many of the conglomerates created during this period subsequently underperformed the market. The third merger wave ended in 1969 as antitrust enforcement curtailed the rise of conglomerates.

Fourth Wave (1981–1989)

The regulatory environment in the 1980s was friendlier to both horizontal and vertical mergers than it had been in the 1960s, but what really fueled business combinations during this period was the development of the high-yield bond market, which benefited as falling interest rates and rising stock prices created an environment conducive to the greater use of leverage.

Although hostile takeovers were nothing new, increased ability to tap the high-yield bond market put the capacity to finance a takeover in the hands of people and companies that otherwise might not have had access to the necessary capital. This period was marked by the rise of the corporate raider and increasingly sophisticated takeover attempts (and defenses). A **corporate raider** is a person or organization seeking to profit by acquiring a company and reselling it.[2] As the 1980s came to a close, the stock market and economy softened, bringing the fourth wave to its conclusion.

Fifth Wave (1992–2001)

Following the 1990–91 recession, merger activity increased in 1992 and intensified throughout the decade. A strong and long-running bull market created many companies with high market valuations, which were then more easily able to use their equity to purchase other companies; thus, stock-swap mergers became more common during this wave. Additionally, during the latter half of the 1990s, U.S. regulators were more open to industry consolidation as merger waves in Europe and Asia created larger international competitors. Deregulation and technological advancement further fueled merger activity, particularly in banking, health care, defense, and telecommunications. The fifth wave ended with a dramatic decline in transactions in 2001 as the market and the economy waned following the end of the internet bubble of the late 1990s.

Sixth Wave (2003–Present)

Based on M&A industry statistics, such as M&A deal volume, it appears that we are in the midst of a sixth wave that began in 2003. After a sharp decline in the number of M&A deals directly following the conclusion of the fifth wave in 2001, the market began to pick up again in 2003 and strengthened rapidly through 2004. The number of transactions increased again in 2005 and surpassed the transaction volume records set at the height of the internet bubble to reach a new all-time high. As in the fifth wave, there has been much industry consolidation in the sixth wave, which is producing larger companies that are better able to compete globally.

---

2 As we will point out later in the section on takeover defenses, in some circumstances a corporate raider can profit from an unsuccessful takeover attempt. It was common during this merger wave for companies to pay raiders a premium in exchange for the raider terminating the attempted takeover, a tactic commonly referred to as "greenmail." Indeed, many raiders initiated takeover attempts without expecting to complete the acquisition.

MOTIVES FOR MERGER

3

In the previous section, we mentioned some of the basic motives behind mergers, such as the search for economies of scale (in a horizontal merger) or cost savings through integration (in a vertical merger). In this section, we will expand on this topic and survey some of the reasons companies merge—the motives or rationales for merger.

The topic is important because in assessing a proposed combination, investors and analysts need to carefully evaluate the rationale behind the merger. Does the stated rationale make sense? Is the merger likely to create value? What is the probability that each of the stated goals for the merger will be attained? Keep in mind that many motives are interrelated and that there are typically several motives, both acknowledged and tacit, behind any given merger.

3.1 Synergy

Among the most common motivations for a merger is the creation of synergy, in which the whole of the combined company will be worth more than the sum of its parts. Generally speaking, synergies created through a merger will either reduce costs or enhance revenues. Cost synergies are typically achieved through economies of scale in research and development, procurement, manufacturing, sales and marketing, distribution, and administration. Revenue synergies are created through the cross-selling of products, expanded market share, or higher prices arising from reduced competition. For example, a bank that acquires its competitors can both increase its market share and realize operating efficiencies by closing duplicate branches and integrating back-office operations.

3.2 Growth

Corporate managers are under constant pressure to grow their companies' revenues, and they often turn to M&A activity to achieve that growth. Companies can grow either by making investments internally (i.e., **organic growth**) or by buying the necessary resources externally (i.e., **external growth**). It is typically faster for companies to grow externally. Growth through M&A activity is common when a company is in a mature industry. For example, the global oil industry is a mature industry, and BP, ExxonMobil, and Chevron Corporation have increased their reserves and output by acquiring smaller competitors.

External growth can also mitigate risk. It is considered less risky to merge with an existing company than to enter an unfamiliar market and establish the resources internally. The last several years of the fifth merger wave in the 1990s were characterized by a surge in cross-border M&A transactions, many of which were motivated by the desire to establish footholds in international markets.

3.3 Increasing Market Power

In industries where there are few competitors or where market share is sufficiently concentrated, horizontal integration may be a means by which to increase market power. When a company increases its market power through horizontal mergers, it may have a greater ability to influence market prices. Taken to an extreme, horizontal integration results in a monopoly.

Vertical integration may also result in increased market power. Vertical mergers can lock in a company's sources of critical supplies or create captive markets for its products. Imagine, for example, an industry in which one company supplies raw materials to two separate manufacturing companies. If one of the manufacturers were to acquire the raw materials provider, the acquirer would be in a position to influence industry output and ultimately prices. As we will discuss further in the section on antitrust regulation, government regulators routinely block both horizontal and vertical mergers that sufficiently reduce competition in an industry and concentrate market power in the hands of too few companies.

3.4 Acquiring Unique Capabilities and Resources

Many companies undertake a merger or an acquisition either to pursue competitive advantages or to shore up lacking resources. When a company cannot cost-effectively create internally the capabilities needed to sustain its future success, it may seek to acquire them elsewhere. For example, a company may engage in M&A activity in order to acquire specific competencies or resources it lacks, such as a strong research department, nimble sales force, intellectual capital, or creative talent.

3.5 Diversification

Companies sometimes cite diversification as one of the motives behind a merger. Indeed, this was an especially popular motive for conglomerates during the third merger wave. The idea behind company-level diversification is that the company can be treated as a portfolio of investments in other companies. If a conglomerate invests in companies from a variety of industries, then the variability of the conglomerate's total cash flows should be reduced, at least to the extent that the industries are uncorrelated.

Although this may seem like a rational motive, typically, it is not in the best interests of the conglomerate's shareholders. In a well-functioning capital market, investors can diversify their own portfolios more easily and at less expense. Additionally, the desire to diversify has led some companies to lose sight of their major competitive strengths and to expand into businesses where they lack comparative advantages.

3.6 Bootstrapping Earnings

Even when there are no reasons to believe that synergies or growth would result from a merger, it is possible to create the illusion of synergies or growth. When a company's earnings increase as a consequence of the merger transaction itself (rather than because of resulting economic benefits of the combination), it is referred to as the "bootstrap effect" or "bootstrapping earnings." The bootstrap effect occurs when the shares of the acquirer trade at a higher price–earnings ratio (P/E) than those of the target and the acquirer's P/E does not decline following the merger.

EXAMPLE 3

Bootstrapping Earnings

Assume two companies are planning a merger. Company A is the acquirer, Company T is the target, and Company A* is the post-merger combination of the two companies. The companies' stock prices and earnings per share are as shown below. Note that the acquirer has a P/E of 25.0 and the target has a P/E of 20.0:

	A	T	A*
Stock price	$100.00	$50.00	
EPS	$4.00	$2.50	$4.20
P/E	25.0	20.0	
Total shares outstanding	100,000	50,000	125,000

	A	T	A*
Total earnings	$400,000	$125,000	$525,000
Market value of equity	$10,000,000	$2,500,000	

Given its stock price, the acquirer can issue 25,000 of its own shares and use the proceeds to buy the target company. This amount is determined by dividing the target's market value by the acquirer's stock price ($2,500,000/$100 = 25,000). The total shares outstanding of the merged company will be 125,000—the acquirer's initial 100,000 shares plus the 25,000 shares that the acquirer issued to purchase the target. After the merger, the company's combined earnings are divided by the number of shares outstanding to determine the new EPS ($525,000/125,000 = $4.20), which is $0.20 higher per share than the acquirer would have reported without the merger.

If the acquirer's pre-merger stock price had been $80 instead of $100, then A's pre-merger P/E would have been 20.0 ($80/$4.00). Under that scenario, the acquirer would have issued 31,250 shares to purchase the target. The EPS of the merged company would then have been $525,000/131,250 = $4.00, thus illustrating that for bootstrapping to work, the acquirer's P/E must be higher than the target's P/E.

If the market is efficient, the post-merger P/E should adjust to the weighted average of the two companies' contributions to the merged company's earnings. In the previous example, the P/E of the merged company would be about 23.8, which implies that the acquirer's stock price would remain at $100. If, however, the acquiring company's P/E is higher than the target's and management can convince investors to value the merged company using the acquirer's pre-merger P/E, then the stock price of the new company should rise. If the acquirer bootstraps earnings to $4.20 per share as shown in the example above, then the share price should increase to $105 if investors apply the pre-merger P/E of 25.0 times earnings ($4.20 × 25.0 = $105). When there are no expected gains from synergy or other factors, such share price increases are not expected.

The market usually recognizes the bootstrapping effect, and post-merger P/Es adjust accordingly. But there have been periods when bootstrapping seemed to pay off for managers, at least in the short run. During the third merger wave, many conglomerates benefited from bootstrapping as investors grappled with how to value these diversified corporate behemoths. Likewise, during the internet bubble of the late 1990s, many high P/E companies bootstrapped their earnings and showed continuous EPS growth through a constant string of mergers with lower P/E companies.

3.7 Managers' Personal Incentives

Various managerial-related theories for mergers have been developed over the years based on evidence of agency problems. **Managerialism theories** posit that because executive compensation is highly correlated with company size, corporate executives are motivated to engage in mergers to maximize the size of their company rather than shareholder value. Additionally, corporate executives may be motivated by self-aggrandizement. For example, being the senior executive of a large company conveys greater power and more prestige.

3.8 Tax Considerations

It is possible for a profitable acquirer to benefit from merging with a target that has accumulated a large amount of tax losses. Instead of carrying the tax losses forward, the merged company would use the tax losses to immediately lower its tax liability. In many countries, the taxing authority disallows an offset in cases where the primary reason for the merger is tax avoidance. Mergers are typically conducted for a variety of reasons, however, and it is difficult for regulatory authorities to prove that tax considerations are a primary motivator.

3.9 Unlocking Hidden Value

A potential target company may be uncompetitive over a sustained period for a host of reasons, including poor management, lack of resources, high legacy costs, or poor organizational structure. In those instances, when a potential target is underperforming, an acquirer may believe it can acquire the company cheaply and then unlock hidden value through reorganization, better management, or synergy. If the target has been underperforming significantly, the acquirer may even believe it can obtain the company for less than its breakup value. A company's **breakup value** is the value that can be achieved if a company's assets are divided and sold separately.

Sometimes mergers are conducted because the acquirer believes that it is purchasing assets for below their replacement cost. For example, a pharmaceutical company may believe it can acquire another company's research more cheaply than to undergo a lengthy development process of its own. Or, an oil company may believe it will be less expensive to acquire another oil company's assets than to find and develop additional reserves of its own.

3.10 Cross-Border Motivations

The growth of cross-border deals was high during the 1990s, and foreign M&A became a popular strategic tool for multinational companies seeking to extend their market reach, acquire new manufacturing facilities, develop new sources of raw materials, and tap into the capital markets. Given the increasing international privatization trends, reduction in cumbersome industry regulations and bureaucracy, and development of uniform accounting standards, cross-border mergers and acquisitions will likely intensify in the future. In addition to the various factors that drive domestic mergers, cross-border mergers can provide an efficient way of achieving other international business goals.

3.10.1 *Exploiting Market Imperfections*

Cross-border transactions can enable companies to more fully exploit market imperfections. For example, to take advantage of differences in the relative cost of labor, a manufacturer may purchase a company in a country where the relative cost of labor is lower.

3.10.2 *Overcoming Adverse Government Policy*

Cross-border mergers can be a means by which to overcome disadvantageous government policy, for example, to circumvent protective tariffs, quotas, or other barriers to free trade.

3.10.3 *Technology Transfer*

Companies that possess a new or superior technology may make acquisitions abroad in order to open new markets or otherwise more fully exploit their business advantage. Conversely, it is common for a company to purchase a foreign company that possesses a new or superior technology in order to enhance the acquirer's competitive position both at home and abroad.

3.10.4 *Product Differentiation*

Companies often purchase foreign companies to exploit the advantages of having a highly differentiated line of products. Similarly, buying certain intangibles, such as a good reputation, helps to ensure success in the global market. Lenovo's (China) acquisition of IBM's (United States) personal computer line is one example of this strategy.

3.10.5 *Following Clients*

Companies may engage in a cross-border merger to follow and support domestic clients more effectively. As an example, many German banks have established cross-border presences to provide services abroad to their domestic clients.

EXAMPLE 4

Mergers and the Industry Life Cycle

The types of mergers (e.g., horizontal, vertical, or conglomerate) occurring in an industry and the motivations behind those mergers will vary over time as an industry proceeds through its life cycle. The stages in an industry life cycle are normally categorized by their rates of growth in sales; growth stages can vary in length.

Mergers and Industry Life Cycles

Industry Life Cycle Stage	Industry Description	Motives for Merger	Types of Mergers
Pioneering development	■ Industry exhibits substantial development costs and has low, but slowly increasing, sales growth.	■ Younger, smaller companies may sell themselves to larger companies in mature or declining industries and look for ways to enter into a new growth industry. ■ Young companies may look to merge with companies that allow them to pool management and capital resources.	■ Conglomerate ■ Horizontal
Rapid accelerating growth	■ Industry exhibits high profit margins caused by few participants in the market.	■ Explosive growth in sales may require large capital requirements to expand existing capacity.	■ Conglomerate ■ Horizontal
Mature growth	■ Industry experiences a drop in the entry of new competitors, but growth potential remains.	■ Mergers may be undertaken to achieve economies of scale, savings, and operational efficiencies.	■ Horizontal ■ Vertical

(continued)

(Continued)

Industry Life Cycle Stage	Industry Description	Motives for Merger	Types of Mergers
Stabilization and market maturity	■ Industry faces increasing competition and capacity constraints.	■ Mergers may be undertaken to achieve economies of scale in research, production, and marketing to match the low cost and price performance of other companies (domestic and foreign). ■ Large companies may acquire smaller companies to improve management and provide a broader financial base.	■ Horizontal
Deceleration of growth and decline	■ Industry faces overcapacity and eroding profit margins.	■ Horizontal mergers may be undertaken to ensure survival. ■ Vertical mergers may be carried out to increase efficiency and profit margins. ■ Companies in related industries may merge to exploit synergy. ■ Companies in this industry may acquire companies in young industries.	■ Horizontal ■ Vertical ■ Conglomerate

Source: Adapted from J. Fred Weston, Kwang S. Chung, and Susan E. Hoag, *Mergers, Restructuring, and Corporate Control* (New York: Prentice Hall, 1990, p. 102) and Bruno Solnik and Dennis McLeavey, *International Investments,* 5th edition (Boston: Addison Wesley, 2004, pp. 264–265).

4 TRANSACTION CHARACTERISTICS

The specifics of M&A transactions can vary along many dimensions, including the form of acquisition, financing, timing, control and governance, accounting choices, and numerous details ranging from the post-merger board composition to the location of the new headquarters. In this section, we will focus on the form of acquisition, method of payment, and mind-set of target management. These three characteristics play a large role in determining how the transaction will occur, which regulatory rules might apply, how the transaction will be valued, and how it will be taxed.

4.1 Form of Acquisition

There are two basic forms of acquisition: An acquirer can purchase the target's stock or its assets. The decision will have several consequences, as summarized in Exhibit 1.

Stock purchases are the most common form of acquisition. A **stock purchase** occurs when the acquirer gives the target company's shareholders some combination of cash and securities in exchange for shares of the target company's stock. For a stock purchase to proceed, it must be approved by at least 50 percent of the target company's shareholders and sometimes more depending on the legal jurisdiction.

Although it can be difficult and time consuming to win shareholder approval, it also stands as an opportunity to circumvent the target company's management in cases where management opposes the merger.

In an **asset purchase**, the acquirer purchases the target company's assets and payment is made directly to the target company. One advantage of this type of transaction is that it can be conducted more quickly and easily than a stock purchase because shareholder approval is not normally required unless a substantial proportion of the assets are being sold, usually more than 50 percent. Another advantage is that an acquirer can focus on buying the parts of a company of particular interest, such as a specific division, rather than the entire company.

Exhibit 1	**Major Differences of Stock versus Asset Purchases**	
	Stock Purchase	**Asset Purchase**
Payment	Target shareholders receive compensation in exchange for their shares.	Payment is made to the selling company rather than directly to the shareholders.
Approval	Shareholder approval required.	Shareholder approval might not be required.
Tax: Corporate	No corporate-level taxes.	Target company pays taxes on any capital gains.
Tax: Shareholder	Target company's shareholders are taxed on their capital gain.	No direct tax consequence for target company's shareholders.
Liabilities	Acquirer assumes the target's liabilities.	Acquirer generally avoids the assumption of liabilities.

Some of the more dramatic consequences of the decision to pursue one form of acquisition versus another concern taxation. In a stock purchase, the target company's shareholders exchange their shares for compensation and must pay tax on their gains, but there are no tax consequences at the corporate level.[3] For an asset purchase, in contrast, there are no direct tax consequences for the target company's shareholders, but the target company itself may be subject to corporate taxes.

In addition to shifting the basic tax burden, the form-of-acquisition decision plays a role in determining how tax rules are applied in accounting for the merger. For example, use of a target's accumulated tax losses is allowable in the United States for stock purchases, but not for asset purchases.

Another key difference between stock and asset purchases relates to the assumption of liabilities. In stock purchases, the acquiring company assumes the target company's liabilities. Acquiring companies must thus be on guard to avoid assuming unexpected or undisclosed liabilities. With asset purchases, acquiring companies generally avoid assuming the target's liabilities. However, purchasing substantially all of a company's assets instead of conducting a stock purchase so as to specifically avoid assuming liabilities is fraught with legal risk because courts have tended to hold acquirers responsible for the liabilities in these cases.

---

3 Keep in mind throughout this discussion of taxation that we are speaking in generalities and that the complexity of M&A deals, coupled with the complexity and variability of tax laws in different jurisdictions, can generate a host of exceptions.

4.2 Method of Payment

The acquirer can pay for the merger with cash, securities, or some combination of the two in what is called a **mixed offering**. In a **cash offering**, the cash might come from the acquiring company's existing assets or from a debt issue. In the most general case of a **securities offering**, the target shareholders receive shares of the acquirer's common stock as compensation.[4] Instead of common stock, however, the acquirer might offer other securities, such as preferred shares or even debt securities.

In a stock offering, the **exchange ratio** determines the number of shares that stockholders in the target company receive in exchange for each of their shares in the target company. Because share prices are constantly fluctuating, exchange ratios are typically negotiated in advance for a range of stock prices. The acquirer's cost is the product of the exchange ratio, the number of outstanding shares of the target company, and the value of the stock given to target shareholders. Each shareholder of the target company receives new shares based on the number of target shares he or she owns multiplied by the exchange ratio.

EXAMPLE 5

Stock Offering

Discount Books, a Canadian bookseller, has announced its intended acquisition of Premier Marketing Corporation, a small marketing company specializing in print media. In a press release, Discount Books outlines the terms of the merger, which specify that Premier Marketing's shareholders will each receive 0.90 shares of Discount Books for every share of Premier Marketing owned. Premier Marketing has 1 million shares outstanding. On the day of the merger announcement, Discount Books' stock closed at C\$20.00 and Premier Marketing's stock closed at C\$15.00. Catherine Willis is an individual investor who owns 500 shares of Premier Marketing, currently worth C\$7,500 (500 × C\$15.00).

1 Based on the current share prices, what is the cost of the acquisition for Discount Books?

2 How many shares of Discount Books will Catherine Willis receive, and what is the value of those shares (based on current share prices)?

Solution to 1:

Because there are 1 million shares of Premier Marketing outstanding and the exchange ratio is 0.90 shares, Discount Books will need to issue 0.90 × 1 million = 900,000 shares of Discount Books stock to complete the transaction. Because the cost per share of Discount Books stock is currently C\$20.00, the cost of the transaction to Discount Books will be C\$20.00 × 900,000 = C\$18 million.

Solution to 2:

Catherine Willis will turn over her 500 shares of Premier Marketing stock. As compensation, she will receive 0.90 × 500 = 450 shares of stock in Discount Books. With each share of Discount Books being worth C\$20.00, the value of those shares to Catherine is C\$9,000.

Note that the value of Willis's Premier Marketing shares was C\$7,500. The C\$1,500 difference in value is a premium paid by Discount Books for control of Premier Marketing. The pre-merger value of Premier Marketing was C\$15 million,

---

4 In the case of a consolidation, the target company's shareholders may receive new shares in the surviving entity.

> but Discount Books' total cost to purchase the company was C$18 million. The 20 percent or C$3 million difference is the total-control premium paid by Discount Books.

A variety of factors influence a company's decision to negotiate for one method of payment versus another. As we shall explore in more detail later, the form of payment has an impact on the distribution of risk and reward between acquirer and target shareholders. In a stock offering, target company shareholders assume a portion of the reward as well as a portion of the risk related to the estimated synergies and the target company's value. Consequently, when an acquiring company's management is highly confident both in their ability to complete the merger and in the value to be created by the merger, they are more inclined to negotiate for a cash offering rather than a stock offering.

Another factor in the decision relates to the relative valuations of the companies involved in the transaction. When an acquirer's shares are considered overvalued by the market relative to the target company's shares, stock financing is more appropriate. In effect, the shares are more valuable as a currency. In fact, investors sometimes interpret an acquirer's stock offering as a signal that the company's shares may be overvalued. This effect is similar to the negative market reaction observed in seasoned equity offerings. Indeed, during the stock market bubble in the late 1990s, stock financing of mergers was quite popular.

Another important consideration when deciding on the payment method is the accompanying change in capital structure. The costs and benefits of different payment structures reflect how the offer will affect the acquirer's capital structure. For instance, on the one hand, borrowing to raise funds for a cash offering increases the acquirer's financial leverage and risk. On the other hand, issuing a significant number of new common shares for a stock offering can dilute the ownership interests of existing shareholders.

Preferences in the use of cash versus stock vary over time, but the proportions in 2005 are characteristic of the past several years. According to *Mergerstat Review 2006*, cash payment accounted for 54 percent of merger transactions in 2005, pure stock exchanges accounted for about 19 percent, and mixed offerings represented 25 percent.[5] A very small portion of deals, about 2 percent, were completed with other securities, such as debt, options, or warrants.

4.3 Mind-Set of Target Management

Mergers are referred to as either friendly or hostile depending on how the target company's senior managers and board of directors view the offer. The distinction is not trivial because an enormous amount of time and resources can be expended by both acquirer and target when the takeover is hostile. Whether a merger is friendly or hostile has an impact on how it is completed, what regulations must be followed, how long the transaction takes, and possibly how much value is created (or destroyed) as a result of the combination.

4.3.1 *Friendly Mergers*

Unless there is cause to think the target will be hostile to a merger, the acquirer will generally start the process by approaching target management directly. The target could approach the acquirer, although this method is much less common. If both management teams are amenable to a potential deal, then the two companies enter

---

5 *Mergerstat Review 2006*. FactSet Mergerstat, LLC (www.mergerstat.com).

into merger discussions. The negotiations revolve around the consideration to be received by the target company's shareholders and the terms of the transaction as well as other aspects, such as the post-merger management structure.

Before negotiations can culminate in a formal deal, each of the parties examines the others' books and records in a process called due diligence. The purpose of due diligence is to protect the companies' respective shareholders by attempting to confirm the accuracy of representations made during negotiations. For example, an acquirer would want to ensure that the target's assets exist and are worth approximately what was claimed by the target. Likewise, a target might want to examine an acquirer's financial records to gauge the likelihood that the acquirer has the capacity to pay for the acquisition as outlined in negotiations. Any deficiencies or problems uncovered during the due diligence process could have an impact on negotiations, resulting in adjustments to the terms or price of the deal. If the issue is large enough, the business combination might be called off entirely.

Once due diligence and negotiations have been completed, the companies enter into a definitive merger agreement. The **definitive merger agreement** is a contract written by both companies' attorneys and is ultimately signed by each party to the transaction. The agreement contains the details of the transaction, including the terms, warranties, conditions, termination details, and the rights of all parties.

Common industry practice has evolved such that companies typically discuss potential transactions in private and maintain secrecy until the definitive merger agreement is reached. This trend may have been influenced by shifts in securities laws toward more stringent rules related to the disclosure of material developments to the public. Additionally, news of a merger can cause dramatic changes in the stock prices of the parties to the transaction. Premature announcement of a deal can cause volatile swings in the stock prices of the companies as they proceed through negotiations.

After the definitive merger agreement has been signed, the transaction is generally announced to the public through a joint press release by the companies. In a friendly merger, the target company's management endorses the merger and recommends that its stockholders approve the transaction. In cases where a shareholder vote is needed, whether it is the target shareholders approving the stock purchase or the acquirer shareholders approving the issuance of a significant number of new shares, the material facts are provided to the appropriate shareholders in a public document called a **proxy statement**, which is given to shareholders in anticipation of their vote.

After all the necessary approvals have been obtained—from shareholders as well as any other parties, such as regulatory bodies—the attorneys file the required documentation with securities regulators and the merger is officially completed. Target shareholders receive the consideration agreed upon under the terms of the transaction, and the companies are officially and legally combined.

4.3.2 *Hostile Mergers*

In a hostile merger, which is a merger that is opposed by the target company's management, the acquirer may decide to circumvent the target management's objections by submitting a merger proposal directly to the target company's board of directors and bypassing the CEO. This tactic is known as a **bear hug**.

Because bear hugs are not formal offers and have not been mutually agreed upon, there are no standard procedures in these cases. If the offer is high enough to warrant serious consideration, then the board may appoint a special committee to negotiate a sale of the target.

Although unlikely in practice, it is possible that target management will capitulate after a bear hug and enter into negotiations, which may ultimately lead to a friendly merger. If the bear hug is not successful, then the hopeful acquirer will attempt to appeal more directly to the target company's shareholders.

One method for taking a merger appeal directly to shareholders is through a **tender offer**, whereby the acquirer invites target shareholders to submit ("tender") their shares in return for the proposed payment.[6] It is up to the individual shareholders to physically tender shares to the acquiring company's agent in order to receive payment. A tender offer can be made with cash, shares of the acquirer's own stock, other securities, or some combination of securities and cash. Because a cash tender offer can be completed in less time than a cash merger, some acquiring companies use this type of transaction to gain control of a target company quickly.

Another method of taking over a target company involves the use of a proxy fight. In a **proxy fight**, a company or individual seeks to take control of a company through a shareholder vote. Proxy solicitation is approved by regulators and then mailed directly to target company shareholders. The shareholders are asked to vote for the acquirer's proposed slate of directors. If the acquirer's slate is elected to the target's board, then it is able to replace the target company's management. At this point, the transaction may evolve into a friendly merger.

Regardless of how an acquirer seeks to establish control, target managers have a variety of alternatives available for defending the company against unwanted overtures. In these cases, the target usually retains the services of law firms and investment bankers to design a defense against the unwanted takeover attempt. As we will discuss in the next section, target company managers may use a variety of legal and financial defensive maneuvers to ward off a takeover attempt.

TAKEOVERS

5

When a target company is faced with a hostile tender offer (takeover) attempt, the target managers and board of directors face a basic choice. They can decide to negotiate and sell the company, either to the hostile bidder or a third party, or they can attempt to remain independent. Aside from the strength of the company's defenses and target management's resolve to stay independent, the premium over the market price offered by the acquirer for the target company's shares is the major driving factor in the decision to support or resist any given takeover.

If the target management decides to resist the unwanted overture, they have a variety of takeover defense mechanisms at their disposal. Once the decision has been reached, the target company generally seeks the counsel of investment bankers and lawyers to explore the fairness of the hostile offer and to advise the board of the alternatives.

A target might use defensive measures to delay, negotiate a better deal for shareholders, or attempt to keep the company independent. Defensive measures can be implemented either before or after a takeover attempt has begun. Most law firms specializing in takeovers recommend that defenses be set up before a company receives or expects any takeover activity.

5.1 Pre-Offer Takeover Defense Mechanisms

In the United States, most hostile takeover attempts result in litigation. The courts generally bless legal pre-offer defense mechanisms but tend to scrutinize post-offer defenses very closely. The target usually assumes the burden of proof in showing that the recently enacted defenses are not simply intended to perpetuate management's

---

6 Tender offers are often associated with hostile mergers, but they also occur in a friendly context. Tender offers are considered hostile only when the offer is opposed by the target company's management and board of directors.

tenure at the target company. It is for this reason that most attorneys recommend that target companies put defenses in place prior to any takeover action. Following this policy gives the target more flexibility when defending against a takeover bid.

With different twists in takeover strategy come new innovations and variations in takeover defenses. Given the many possible variations, the following is not an exhaustive list but an overview of the more well known anti-takeover strategies. The two broad varieties of pre-offer defenses are rights-based defenses, such as poison pills and poison puts, and a variety of changes to the corporate charter (e.g., staggered boards of directors and supermajority provisions) that are sometimes collectively referred to as **shark repellents**.

5.1.1 *Poison Pills*

The **poison pill** is a legal device that makes it prohibitively costly for an acquirer to take control of a target without the prior approval of the target's board of directors. Most poison pills make the target company less attractive by creating rights that allow for the issuance of shares of the target company's stock at a substantial discount to market value.

There are two basic types of poison pills: the **flip-in pill** and the **flip-over pill**. When the common shareholder of the target company has the right to buy its shares at a discount, the pill is known as a flip-in. The pill is triggered when a specific level of ownership is exceeded. Because the acquiring company is generally prohibited from participating in the purchase through the pill, the acquirer is subject to a significant level of dilution. Most plans give the target's board of directors the right to redeem the pill prior to any triggering event. If the takeover becomes friendly, the board generally exercises this waiver.

In the case of a flip-over pill, the target company's common shareholders receive the right to purchase shares of the acquiring company at a significant discount from the market price, which has the effect of causing dilution to all existing acquiring company shareholders. Again, the board of the target generally retains the right to redeem the pill should the transaction become friendly.

Another possible aspect of the poison pill is the **"dead-hand" provision**. This provision allows the board of the target to redeem or cancel the poison pill only by a vote of the continuing directors. Because continuing directors are generally defined as directors who were on the target company's board prior to the takeover attempt, this provision has the effect of making it much more difficult to take over a target without prior board approval.

5.1.2 *Poison Puts*

Whereas poison pills grant common shareholders certain rights in a hostile takeover attempt, **poison puts** give rights to the target company's bondholders. In the event of a takeover, poison puts allow bondholders to put the bonds to the company. In other words, if the provision is triggered by a hostile takeover attempt, then bondholders have the right to sell their bonds back to the target at a redemption price that is pre-specified in the bond indenture, typically at or above par value. The effect of a poison put defense is to require that an acquirer be prepared to refinance the target's debt immediately after the takeover. This defense increases the need for cash and raises the cost of the acquisition.

5.1.3 *Incorporation in a State with Restrictive Takeover Laws (United States)*

In the United States, many states have adopted laws that specifically address unfriendly takeover attempts. These laws are designed to provide target companies with flexibility in dealing with unwanted suitors. Some states have designed their laws to give the company maximum protection and leeway in defending against an offer. As a result, companies that anticipate the possibility of a hostile takeover attempt may find it attractive to reincorporate in a jurisdiction that has enacted strict anti-takeover laws. Ohio and Pennsylvania are examples of two U.S. states that have been regarded historically as "target friendly" states; their state laws tend to give target companies the most power in defending against hostile takeover attempts.[7]

5.1.4 Staggered Board of Directors

Instead of electing the entire board of directors each year at the company's annual meeting, a company may arrange to stagger the terms for board members so that only a portion of the board seats are due for election each year. For example, if the company has a board consisting of nine directors, members could be elected for three-year terms with only three directors coming up for election each year. The effect of this staggered board is that it would take at least two years to elect enough directors to take control of the board.

5.1.5 Restricted Voting Rights

Some target companies adopt a mechanism that restricts stockholders who have recently acquired large blocks of stock from voting their shares. Usually, there is a trigger stockholding level, such as 15 or 20 percent. Shareholders who meet or exceed this trigger point are no longer able to exercise their voting rights without the target company's board releasing the shareholder from the constraint. The possibility of owning a controlling position in the target without being able to vote the shares serves as a deterrent.

5.1.6 Supermajority Voting Provisions

Many target companies change their charter and bylaws to provide for a higher percentage approval by shareholders for mergers than normally is required. A typical provision might require a vote of 80 percent of the outstanding shares of the target company (as opposed to a simple 51 percent majority). This supermajority requirement is triggered by a hostile takeover attempt and is frequently accompanied by a provision that prevents the hostile acquirer from voting its shares. Thus, even if an acquirer is able to accumulate a substantial portion of the target's shares, it may have great difficulty accumulating enough votes to approve a merger.

5.1.7 Fair Price Amendments

Fair price amendments are changes to the corporate charter and bylaws that disallow mergers for which the offer is below some threshold. For example, a fair price amendment might require an acquirer to pay at least as much as the highest stock price at which the target has traded in the public market over a specified period. Fair price amendments protect targets against temporary declines in their share prices by setting a floor value bid. Additionally, fair price amendments protect against two-tiered tender offers where the acquirer offers a higher bid in a first step tender offer with the threat of a lower bid in a second step tender offer for those who do not tender right away.

---

7 Delaware has historically been the most popular state for corporations to domicile their legal entities. To protect this status, the state has found it necessary to toughen its laws regarding takeover attempts. In the past, as some states adopted strict takeover laws, some corporations left Delaware and reincorporated in these "friendly" states. In order to compete, Delaware has changed its own laws to make it more difficult to take over a Delaware corporation on a hostile basis.

5.1.8 *Golden Parachutes*

Golden parachutes are compensation agreements between the target company and its senior managers. These employment contracts allow the executives to receive lucrative payouts, usually several years' worth of salary, if they leave the target company following a change in corporate control. In practice, golden parachutes do not offer much deterrent, especially for large deals where the managers' compensation is small relative to the overall takeover price. One reason they persist is that they help alleviate target management's concerns about job loss. Golden parachutes may encourage key executives to stay with the target as the takeover progresses and the target explores all options to generate shareholder value. Without a golden parachute, some contend that target company executives might be quicker to seek employment offers from other companies to secure their financial future. Whether this is actually the case and whether golden parachutes are fair and in the best interest of shareholders is the subject of considerable debate among shareholder rights activists and senior managers.

5.2 Post-Offer Takeover Defense Mechanisms

A target also has several defensive mechanisms that can be used once a takeover has already been initiated. Because they may not be as successful when used in isolation and because they have historically been subject to greater scrutiny by the courts, post-offer defenses are typically used in conjunction with pre-offer defenses.

5.2.1 *"Just Say No" Defense*

Probably the simplest place for a target company to start when confronted with a hostile takeover bid is to rely on pre-takeover defenses and to decline the offer. If the acquirer attempts a bear hug or tender offer, then target management typically lobbies the board of directors and shareholders to decline and build a case for why the offering price is inadequate or why the offer is otherwise not in the shareholders' best interests. This strategy forces the hopeful acquirer to adjust its bid or further reveal its own strategy in order to advance the takeover attempt.

5.2.2 *Litigation*

A popular technique used by many target companies is to file a lawsuit against the acquiring company based on alleged violations of securities or antitrust laws. In the United States, these suits may be filed in either state or federal courts. Unless there is a serious antitrust violation, these suits rarely stop a takeover bid. Instead, lawsuits often serve as a delaying tactic to create additional time for target management to develop other responses to the unwanted offer. Generally, any securities law violations, even if upheld, can be corrected with additional public disclosures. In the United States, most antitrust claims that eventually prevent takeover attempts are initiated by either antitrust or securities regulators rather than by the target company.

5.2.3 *Greenmail*

This technique involves an agreement allowing the target to repurchase its own shares back from the acquiring company, usually at a premium to the market price. Greenmail is usually accompanied by an agreement that the acquirer will not pursue another hostile takeover attempt of the target for a set period. In effect, greenmail is the termination of a hostile takeover through a payoff to the acquirer. The shareholders of the target company do not receive any compensation for their shares. Greenmail was popular in the United States during the 1980s, but its use has been extremely restricted since 1986 when the U.S. Internal Revenue Code was amended to add a 50 percent tax on profits realized by acquirers through greenmail.

5.2.4 Share Repurchase

Rather than repurchasing only the shares held by the acquiring company, as in green-mail, a target might use a share repurchase to acquire shares from any shareholder. For example, a target may initiate a cash tender offer for its own outstanding shares. An effective repurchase can increase the potential cost for an acquirer by either increasing the stock's price outright or by causing the acquirer to increase its bid to remain competitive with the target company's tender offer for its own shares. Additionally, a share repurchase often has the effect of increasing the target company's use of leverage because borrowing is typically required to purchase the shares. This additional debt makes the target less attractive as a takeover candidate.

In some cases, a target company buys all of its shares and converts to a privately held company in a transaction called a leveraged buyout. In a **leveraged buyout** (LBO), the management team generally partners with a private equity firm that specializes in buyouts. The new entity borrows a high proportion of the overall purchase price; the financial firm contributes a certain amount of capital; and the management team provides the management expertise to run the business. In exchange for their expertise, management generally receives a payout percentage based on the profitability and success of the company after the LBO is completed. This strategy may allow the target to defend against a hostile bid provided that the LBO provides target shareholders with a level of value that exceeds the would-be acquirer's offer.

5.2.5 Leveraged Recapitalization

A technique somewhat related to the leveraged buyout is the leveraged recapitalization. A **leveraged recapitalization** involves the assumption of a large amount of debt that is then used to finance share repurchases (but in contrast to a leveraged buyout, in a recapitalization, some shares remain in public hands). The effect is to dramatically change the company's capital structure while attempting to deliver a value to target shareholders in excess of the hostile bid.

5.2.6 "Crown Jewel" Defense

After a hostile takeover is announced, a target may decide to sell off a subsidiary or asset to a third party. If the acquisition of this subsidiary or asset was one of the acquirer's major motivations for the proposed merger, then this strategy could cause the acquirer to abandon its takeover effort. When a target initiates such a sale after a hostile takeover bid is announced, there is a good chance that the courts will declare this strategy illegal.

5.2.7 "Pac-Man" Defense

The target can defend itself by making a counteroffer to acquire the hostile bidder. This technique is rarely used because, in most cases, it means that a smaller company (the target) is making a bid for a larger entity. Additionally, once a target uses a Pac-Man defense, it forgoes the ability to use a number of other defensive strategies. For instance, after making a counteroffer, a target cannot very well take the acquirer to court claiming an antitrust violation.

5.2.8 White Knight Defense

Often the best outcome for target shareholders is for the target company's board to seek a third party to purchase the company in lieu of the hostile bidder. This third party is called a **white knight** because it is coming to the aid of the target. A target usually initiates this technique by seeking out another company that has a strategic fit with the target. Based on a good strategic fit, the third party can often justify a higher price for the target than what the hostile bidder is offering.

Once a white knight bid is made public, it may elicit an additional higher bid from the hostile bidder. This can help kick off a competitive bidding situation. In some cases, because of the competitive nature of the bidders, the winner's curse can prevail and the target company shareholders may receive a very good deal. **Winner's curse** is the tendency for the winner in certain competitive bidding situations to overpay, whether because of overestimation of intrinsic value, emotion, or information asymmetries.[8]

5.2.9 *White Squire Defense*

In the **white squire** defense, the target seeks a friendly party to buy a substantial minority stake in the target—enough to block the hostile takeover without selling the entire company. Although the white squire may pay a significant premium for a substantial number of the target's shares, these shares may be purchased directly from the target company and the target shareholders may not receive any of the proceeds.[9]

The use of the white squire defense may carry a high litigation risk depending on the details of the transaction and local regulations. Additionally, stock exchange listing requirements sometimes require that target shareholders vote to approve these types of transactions, and shareholders may not endorse any transaction that does not provide an adequate premium to them directly.

EXAMPLE 6

Engelhard Takeover Defenses

On 14 December 2005, BASF, a worldwide producer of chemicals and high-performance products, offered to acquire Engelhard Corporation for $37 cash per share. Engelhard, a manufacturer and developer of value-added technologies, determined that the $37 offer was inadequate and decided to defend itself against the unwanted takeover attempt.

Prior to the BASF takeover offer, Engelhard had participating preferred stock purchase rights in place.[10] These rights acted as a poison pill by allowing Engelhard to issue shares at a discount if triggered by a takeover that was unsupported by Engelhard's board of directors. Additionally, in advance of the takeover attempt, Engelhard restated its certificate of incorporation to include a supermajority provision. It stated that business combinations with a holder of more than 5 percent of Engelhard's outstanding shares would require an affirmative vote of both the holders of 80 percent of the outstanding shares and at least 50 percent of the outstanding shares not held by the acquirer unless the board of directors approved the business combination.

After the tender offer was commenced by BASF, Engelhard also pursued a recapitalization plan that involved the repurchase of approximately 20 percent of Engelhard's outstanding shares through a tender offer at $45 per share, a price superior to BASF's tender offer. Together these pre- and post-offer defenses made it very difficult for BASF to succeed with its $37 cash tender offer.

Although Engelhard did not complete the tender for its own shares, the recapitalization plan was incentive enough for BASF to increase its offer. Takeover targets frequently use their takeover defenses to negotiate a better deal for their shareholders. After much negotiation, BASF increased its tender offer

---

8 The winner's curse is most likely to occur when the target company has roughly the same value to all bidders but the target's true value is hard to ascertain. The average bid in such cases may represent the best estimate of the target's intrinsic value, and the high (winning), an overestimate of its intrinsic value.
9 For example, the white squire may purchase shares of convertible preferred stock instead of common stock.
10 Shares of participating preferred stock offer the possibility of a higher dividend when the dividend on common shares reaches a pre-specified threshold.

and Engelhard withdrew all takeover defenses. On 30 May 2006, the companies announced a definitive merger agreement under which BASF would acquire all outstanding shares of Engelhard for $39 per share in cash.

REGULATION

6

Even when a merger has been accepted by the target company's senior managers, the board of directors, and shareholders, the combination must still be approved by regulatory authorities. Additionally, there are a variety of rules that companies must follow when initiating and completing the merger transaction itself. This section provides an overview of the key rules and issues that arise from M&A activity.

The two major bodies of jurisprudence relating to mergers are antitrust law and securities law. Antitrust laws are intended to ensure that markets remain competitive; the securities laws we will discuss are concerned largely with maintaining both fairness in merger activities and confidence in the financial markets.

6.1 Antitrust

Most countries have antitrust laws, which prohibit mergers and acquisitions that impede competition. Antitrust legislation began in the United States with the Sherman Antitrust Act of 1890, which made contracts, combinations, and conspiracies in restraint of trade or attempts to monopolize an industry illegal. The Sherman Antitrust Act was not effective at deterring antitrust activity partly because the U.S. Department of Justice at the time lacked the resources necessary to enforce the law rigorously. Within a few years of its passage, the law was challenged in the courts and rendered unenforceable because of ambiguous aspects of its wording.

To resurrect antitrust law, the U.S. Congress passed the Clayton Antitrust Act in 1914, which clarified and strengthened the Sherman Antitrust Act by detailing the specific business practices that the U.S. Congress wished to outlaw. In order to ensure that the law could be effectively enforced, the legislature also passed the Federal Trade Commission Act of 1914, which established the Federal Trade Commission (FTC) as a regulatory agency to work in tandem with the Department of Justice to enforce antitrust law.

During the ensuing years, additional weaknesses and loopholes in antitrust legislation became apparent. For instance, the Clayton Act regulated only the acquisition of shares of stock, not the acquisition of assets. The Celler–Kefauver Act was passed in 1950 to close this loophole; the law also addressed vertical and conglomerate mergers, whereas previous legislation had focused primarily on horizontal combinations.

The last major piece of U.S. antitrust legislation was the Hart–Scott–Rodino Antitrust Improvements Act of 1976, which required that the FTC and Department of Justice have the opportunity to review and approve mergers in advance. A key benefit of the Hart–Scott–Rodino Act is that it gives regulators an opportunity to halt a merger prior to its completion rather than having to disassemble a company after a merger is later deemed to be anticompetitive.

Just as U.S. transactions are reviewed by the FTC and the Department of Justice, the European Commission (EC) has the authority to review the antitrust implications of transactions among companies that generate significant revenues within the European Union. Although the European Commission's member states have jurisdiction on mergers within their respective national borders, mergers with significant cross-border effects are subject to EC review. Similar to the requirements in the United States, pre-merger notification is required.

In addition to regulatory watchdogs, such as the FTC and the European Commission, approval may be needed from other regulatory agencies. For example, in the United States, a merger involving banks requires approvals from state banking authorities as well as the Federal Reserve Bank and possibly the Federal Deposit Insurance Corporation (FDIC). Insurance mergers require the approval of state insurance commissioners. In some cases where one of the company's businesses is deemed to be of strategic national interest, additional government approvals may be necessary. Each merger must be analyzed by legal experts to determine the specific regulatory approvals required to comply with the relevant rules and laws. This is a very specialized area and can cause significant delays in the closing of some transactions.

The situation can become further complicated when the merging companies have a global presence that falls within multiple jurisdictions of regulatory control. For example, a large trans-Atlantic merger would require approval of both the United States regulatory bodies and the European Commission. Global companies often face dozens of regulatory agencies with different standards and filing requirements. For example, Coca-Cola Company's 1999 acquisition of the Cadbury Schweppes beverage brands involved sales and production in more than 160 countries, requiring antitrust approval in more than 40 jurisdictions around the world.

Prior to 1982, the FTC and Department of Justice used market share as a measure of market power when determining potential antitrust violations among peer competitors in an industry. Using a simple measure of industry concentration and the market shares of the acquirer and the target, companies contemplating a horizontal merger could determine in advance whether the combination would likely be challenged. The transparency and predictability of the measure was advantageous, but the approach proved to be too simplistic and rigid in practice.

In 1982, the agencies shifted toward using a new measure of market power called the **Herfindahl–Hirschman Index (HHI)**. By summing the squares of the market shares for each company in an industry, the HHI does a better job of modeling market concentration while remaining relatively easy to calculate and interpret. To calculate the HHI, the market shares for competing companies are squared and then summed:

$$\text{HHI} = \sum_{i}^{n} \left(\frac{\text{Sales or output of firm } i}{\text{Total sales or output of market}} \times 100 \right)^2 \qquad \textbf{(1)}$$

Regulators initially calculate the HHI based on *post-merger* market shares. If post-merger market shares result in an HHI of less than 1,000, the market is not considered to be concentrated and a challenge is unlikely unless other anticompetitive issues arise. A moderately concentrated HHI measure of between 1,000 and 1,800, or a highly concentrated measure of more than 1,800, requires a comparison of post-merger and pre-merger HHI. A merger resulting in an increase of 100 points in a moderately concentrated market or 50 points in a highly concentrated market is likely to evoke antitrust concerns; smaller increases are less likely to pose a problem.[11] Exhibit 2 summarizes HHI ranges and the corresponding probability for regulatory action:

---

11 See the U.S. Department of Justice and the Federal Trade Commission's Horizontal Merger Guidelines, issued 2 April 1992 and revised 8 April 1997.

Exhibit 2	HHI Concentration Level and Possible Government Action

HHI Concentration Level

Post-Merger HHI	Concentration	Change in HHI	Government Action
Less than 1,000	Not concentrated	Any amount	No action
Between 1,000 and 1,800	Moderately concentrated	100 or more	Possible challenge
More than 1,800	Highly concentrated	50 or more	Challenge

EXAMPLE 7

Herfindahl–Hirschman Index

Given an industry with 10 competitors and the following market shares, calculate the pre-merger HHI. How would the HHI change if Companies 2 and 3 merged? How would it change if Companies 9 and 10 merged instead? Would either set of mergers be likely to evoke an antitrust challenge?

Company	1	2	3	4	5	6	7	8	9	10
Market Share (%)	25	20	10	10	10	5	5	5	5	5

Solution:

To calculate the pre-merger HHI, first square the market share for each company. Then add together the squared market shares to obtain an HHI of 1,450, which indicates that this is a moderately concentrated industry. If Companies 2 and 3 were to merge, the HHI would jump 400 points to 1,850. The large change in the HHI combined with the high post-merger HHI value indicates that this merger would likely evoke antitrust objections. If Companies 9 and 10 were to merge instead of Companies 2 and 3, the HHI would climb only 50 points to 1,500. Although the post-merger HHI indicates a moderately concentrated industry, the combination is unlikely to raise antitrust concerns because the post-merger HHI is only 50 points higher than the pre-merger HHI.

	Pre-Merger			Post-Merger: Companies 2 and 3			Post-Merger: Companies 9 and 10	
Company	Market Share (%)	Market Share Squared	Company	Market Share (%)	Market Share Squared	Company	Market Share (%)	Market Share Squared
1	25	625	1	25	625	1	25	625
2	20	400	2 + 3	30	900	2	20	400
3	10	100	4	10	100	3	10	100
4	10	100	5	10	100	4	10	100
5	10	100	6	5	25	5	10	100
6	5	25	7	5	25	6	5	25
7	5	25	8	5	25	7	5	25
8	5	25	9	5	25	8	5	25
9	5	25	10	5	25	9 + 10	10	100
10	5	25						

(continued)

	Pre-Merger			Post-Merger: Companies 2 and 3			Post-Merger: Companies 9 and 10	
Company	Market Share (%)	Market Share Squared	Company	Market Share (%)	Market Share Squared	Company	Market Share (%)	Market Share Squared
	HHI:	1,450		HHI:	1,850		HHI:	1,500
				HHI Change:	400		HHI Change:	50

Although the introduction of the Herfindahl–Hirschman Index was an improvement, regulators still found it to be too mechanical and inflexible. Thus, by 1984, the Department of Justice sought to increase the flexibility of its policies through the inclusion of additional information, such as market power measured by the responsiveness of consumers to price changes, as well as qualitative information, such as the efficiency of companies in the industry, the financial viability of potential merger candidates, and the ability of U.S. companies to compete in foreign markets.[12]

When reviewing quantitative and qualitative data, one should note that merger guidelines are just that—guidelines. It is possible that under unusual circumstances the government may not challenge one merger that does violate the guidelines and may challenge another merger that does not. Each transaction must be analyzed carefully to fully explore all potential antitrust issues.

When conflicts between companies and regulators arise, it is often because of disagreements about how the markets are defined. Regulators must consider the market in terms of both geography and product. When considering the industry's geography, regulators must decide whether the relevant competitors are global, national, regional, or local. When considering product offerings, there may be one or multiple relevant product market overlaps. In some cases the overlap may be clear, and in other transactions it may not be obvious.

Parties to the transaction are usually counseled by attorneys who have relevant experience in the antitrust area. Most companies try to complete their analyses prior to signing a merger agreement in order to avoid entering into a long period of uncertainty while the government decides whether to challenge the transaction. Not only do delays increase costs, but they may also cause the companies to lose other important strategic opportunities.

6.2 Securities Laws

As we discussed in the section covering pre-offer takeover defense mechanisms, in the United States individual states regulate M&A activities to varying degrees. But companies must also comply with federal U.S. securities regulations. In the United States, the cornerstone of securities legislation regulating merger and acquisition activities is the Williams Amendment to the Securities Exchange Act of 1934 (also known as the Williams Act), which was passed in 1968 near the end of the third merger wave.

During the 1960s, tender offers became a popular means to execute hostile takeovers. Acquirers often announced tender offers that expired in short time frames or threatened lower bids and less desirable terms for those shareholders who waited

12 Patrick A. Gaughan, *Mergers, Acquisitions, and Corporate Restructurings*, 3rd ed. (New York: John Wiley & Sons, 2002), p. 95.

to tender. In addition to giving shareholders little time to evaluate the fairness of an offer, it gave target management little time to respond. The Williams Act sought to remedy these problems in two keys ways: disclosure requirements and a formal process for tender offers.

Section 13(d) of the Williams Act requires public disclosure whenever a party acquires 5 percent or more of a target's outstanding common stock. As part of this disclosure, the company acquiring the stake must provide a variety of details, including self-identification, the purpose of the transaction, and the source of the funds used to finance the stock purchases. This disclosure requirement calls target managers' and shareholders' attention to large share purchases, which keeps acquirers from gaining too large a toehold before the target is aware of the acquirer's interest.

Section 14 of the Williams Act creates a tender offer process by setting forth various rules and restrictions that companies must observe. For example, as part of initiating a tender offer, an acquirer must file a public statement that contains the details of the offer and information about the acquirer. Target management must then respond through a formal statement containing their opinion and advice to accept or reject the offer; target management can abstain from offering an opinion as long as they provide the reasons for doing so.

Other important provisions of Section 14 are that the tender offer period be at least 20 business days, that the acquirer must accept all shares tendered, that all tendered shares must receive the same price, and that target shareholders can withdraw tendered shares during the offer period. These provisions ensure that target shareholders receive equitable treatment and that they have adequate time to investigate and evaluate a tender offer without the risk of receiving a lower price. Section 14 also gives target management the time and opportunity to adequately respond to a hostile tender offer.

MERGER ANALYSIS   **7**

In this section, we will examine the analysis of merger activity from two perspectives. First, we will discuss valuation of the target company, something of key importance for analysts on both sides of the deal as well as for shareholders as they all grapple to determine the fairness and adequacy of an offer. Then, we will discuss the analysis of the bid. Analysts can estimate the distribution of benefits in a merger based on expected synergies relative to the premium paid for the target in excess of its intrinsic value.

7.1 Target Company Valuation

The three basic valuation techniques that companies and their advisers use to value companies in an M&A context are discounted cash flow analysis, comparable company analysis, and comparable transaction analysis. An analyst is likely to use some combination of these primary techniques, and possibly others, when gauging a company's fair value.

7.1.1 *Discounted Cash Flow Analysis*

Discounted cash flow (DCF) analysis, as it is generally applied in this context, discounts the company's expected future free cash flows to the present in order to derive an estimate for the value of the company. **Free cash flow** (FCF) is the relevant measure in this context because it represents the actual cash that would be available to the company's investors after making all investments necessary to maintain the company as an ongoing enterprise.[13] Free cash flows are the internally generated funds that can be distributed to the company's investors (e.g., shareholders and bondholders) without impairing the value of the company.

There are several variations to the models an analyst might use to estimate and discount free cash flows. In the following, we will develop an approximation to free cash flow and illustrate its use in valuation using a two-stage model.[14] Estimating a company's free cash flows begins with the creation of pro forma financial statements. The first step is to select an appropriate time horizon for the first stage. The first stage should include only those years over which the analyst feels capable of generating reasonably accurate estimates of the company's free cash flows. These free cash flow estimates are then discounted to their present value.

To incorporate value deriving from years beyond the first stage, the analyst estimates the value of expected second-stage free cash flows as of the end of the first stage. The result is the so-called terminal value (or continuing value) of the company. The analyst then discounts the terminal value back to the present. The sum of the two pieces (the present value of first-stage expected free cash flows plus the present value of the company's terminal value) is the estimated value of the company.

There is no standard approach for creating pro forma financial statements. The art of financial analysis involves an ability to use the appropriate tools and to exercise good judgment in order to produce the best possible estimates for each financial statement item. In the process, analysts make adjustments to their prior projections based on proposed synergies and the announced plans for the merged company. For example, duplicated resources might result in the sale of one of the target's divisions. Or, the operating costs might be adjusted downward in anticipation of economies of scale. These adjustments are easier to estimate in friendly mergers where the analyst has access to detailed financial data about the target than in hostile mergers. But even in a hostile merger scenario, an analyst with experience in the appropriate industry can still make reasonably good estimates.

Once pro forma financial statements have been generated, the analyst can begin the conversion from pro forma net income to pro forma free cash flow for each year of the first stage. To demonstrate this process, we will use the pro forma financial statements and FCF calculations provided in Exhibit 3. The perspective is that of a valuation being done at the beginning of 2007.

| Exhibit 3 | Sample Pro Forma Financial Statements and FCF Calculations |

	Historical	Pro Forma				
	2006	2007	2008	2009	2010	2011
Income Statement (*Thousands of Dollars*)						
Revenues	$ 14,451	$ 15,752	$ 17,327	$ 19,060	$ 20,966	$ 23,063
Cost of goods sold	7,948	8,664	9,530	10,483	11,531	12,685
Gross profit	$ 6,503	$ 7,088	$ 7,797	$ 8,577	$ 9,435	$ 10,378
Selling, general, and administrative expenses	2,168	2,363	2,599	2,859	3,145	3,459

---

13 Free cash flow as used here is also called **free cash flow to the firm**, particularly when a distinction is being made between free cash flows accruing to all providers of capital and those accruing only to equityholders (**free cash flow to equity**).

14 See Stowe, Robinson, Pinto, and McLeavey (2002) for details of estimating free cash flow (free cash flow to the firm) more precisely.

Exhibit 3 (Continued)

	Historical	Pro Forma				
	2006	2007	2008	2009	2010	2011
Depreciation	506	551	606	667	734	807
Earnings before interest and taxes	$ 3,829	$ 4,174	$ 4,592	$ 5,051	$ 5,556	$ 6,112
Net interest expense	674	642	616	583	543	495
Earnings before taxes	$ 3,155	$ 3,532	$ 3,976	$ 4,468	$ 5,013	$ 5,617
Income tax	1,104	1,236	1,392	1,564	1,755	1,966
Net income	$ 2,051	$ 2,296	$ 2,584	$ 2,904	$ 3,258	$ 3,651
Balance Sheet (*Thousands of Dollars*)						
Current assets	$ 8,671	$ 9,451	$ 10,396	$ 11,436	$ 12,580	$ 13,838
Net property, plant, and equipment	10,116	11,026	12,129	13,342	14,676	16,144
Total assets	$ 18,787	$ 20,477	$ 22,525	$ 24,778	$ 27,256	$ 29,982
Current liabilities	$ 3,613	$ 3,938	$ 4,332	$ 4,765	$ 5,242	$ 5,766
Deferred income taxes	92	111	132	155	181	209
Long-term debt	7,924	7,548	7,243	6,862	6,394	5,830
Total liabilities	$ 11,629	$ 11,597	$ 11,707	$ 11,782	$ 11,817	$ 11,805
Common stock and paid-in capital	1,200	1,200	1,200	1,200	1,200	1,200
Retained earnings	5,958	7,680	9,618	11,796	14,239	16,977
Shareholders' equity	$ 7,158	$ 8,880	$ 10,818	$ 12,996	$ 15,439	$ 18,177
Total liabilities and shareholders' equity	$ 18,787	$ 20,477	$ 22,525	$ 24,778	$ 27,256	$ 29,982
Selected Pro Forma Cash Flow Data (*Thousands of Dollars*)						
Change in net working capital		$ 455	$ 551	$ 607	$ 667	$ 734
Capital expenditures		$ 1,461	$ 1,709	$ 1,880	$ 2,068	$ 2,275

	Pro Forma				
	2007	2008	2009	2010	2011
FCF Calculations					
Net income	$ 2,296	$ 2,584	$ 2,904	$ 3,258	$ 3,651
Plus: Net interest after tax	417	400	379	353	322
Unlevered net income	$ 2,713	$ 2,984	$ 3,283	$ 3,611	$ 3,973
Plus: Change in deferred taxes	19	21	23	26	28
Net op. profit less adj. taxes (NOPLAT)	$ 2,732	$ 3,005	$ 3,306	$ 3,637	$ 4,001
Plus: Depreciation	551	606	667	734	807
Less: Change in net working capital	455	551	607	667	734
Less: Capital expenditures	1,461	1,709	1,880	2,068	2,275
Free cash flow	$ 1,367	$ 1,351	$ 1,486	$ 1,636	$ 1,799
Valuation Calculations					
WACC	9.41%				

(continued)

		Pro Forma			
	2007	2008	2009	2010	2011
PV of FCF		$ 5,802			
Terminal growth rate	6.0%				
Terminal value, 2011	$ 55,922				
Terminal value, 2006		$ 35,670			
Enterprise Value, 2006		$ 41,471			

The calculation of FCF involves first making adjustments to net income to convert it to **net operating profit less adjusted taxes (NOPLAT)**. This adjustment is made so that the resulting estimate of FCF represents the after-tax cash flows available to all providers of capital to the company. The first step in this process is to add net interest after tax to net income. This step removes the tax shield from interest payments and puts the cash flows on common footing with other cash flows that are available to all capital providers of the company.[15] This is referred to as unlevered net income.[16] For the year 2007 in Exhibit 3, pro forma net income for the year is $2.296 million. There is no reported interest income, so net interest expense is simply $642,000. The company's estimated tax rate is 35 percent, found by dividing the previous year's income tax by the company's earnings before tax.

Step 1:

$$\text{Unlevered net income} = \text{Net income} + \text{Net interest after tax}$$

$$\text{Net interest after tax} = (\text{Interest expense} - \text{Interest income}) \times (1 - \text{Tax rate}) \qquad (2)$$

For 2007,

$$\text{Unlevered net income} = \$2,296 + 642(1 - 0.35) = \$2,713$$
$$= \$2.713 \text{ million}$$

To convert unlevered net income to NOPLAT, we must account for differences in depreciation for financial reporting purposes versus depreciation for tax purposes, which has an impact on cash flows. Companies typically report depreciation for property, plant, and equipment at a faster rate for tax purposes (higher depreciation shields more income from taxes) than for financial reporting purposes (lower depreciation results in higher net income). The differences in depreciation result in different taxes. This difference is accounted for as a liability on the balance sheet—deferred income taxes. To account for this impact on cash flow, we add the change in deferred taxes to unlevered net income (an increase in deferred taxes increases cash flow; a decrease in deferred taxes reduces cash flow).[17]

---

[15] The tax deductibility of interest will be accounted for later in the calculation when we discount free cash flows by the weighted average cost of capital (WACC).

[16] It is also possible to calculate unlevered net income as earnings before interest and taxes (EBIT) × (1 − tax rate).

[17] Some analysts also estimate and subtract the value of after-tax nonoperating income to obtain an estimate more closely reflecting operating results only. See Copeland, Koller, Murrin (2000), Chapter 9, for more details on NOPLAT.

Step 2:

$$\text{NOPLAT} = \text{Unlevered net income}$$
$$+ \text{Change in deferred taxes} \quad\quad (3)$$

For 2007,

$$\text{NOPLAT} = \$2,713 + (111 - 92) = \$2,732$$
$$= \$2.732 \text{ million}$$

At this point, NOPLAT is adjusted to add back net noncash charges (NCC), which prominently include depreciation (of tangible assets) and amortization and impairment (of intangible assets); noncash charges affect net income but do not represent cash expenditures. To estimate free cash flow, we then subtract the value of necessary or otherwise planned investments in working capital and property, plant, and equipment.[18] They are recorded as the change in net working capital and capital expenditures (capex), respectively.

Step 3:

$$\text{FCF} = \text{NOPLAT} + \text{NCC}$$
$$- \text{Change in net working capital} - \text{Capex} \quad\quad (4)$$

For 2007,

$$\text{FCF} = \$2,732 + 551 - 455 - 1,461 = \$1,367 = \$1.367 \text{ million}$$

(The only NCC in this example is depreciation)

Summarizing, FCF is approximated by:

	Net income
+	Net interest after tax
	Unlevered net income
+	Change in deferred taxes
	Net operating profit less adjusted taxes (NOPLAT)
+	Net noncash charges
–	Change in net working capital
–	Capital expenditures (capex)
	Free cash flow (FCF)

Once free cash flow has been estimated for each year in the first stage (2007–2011 in Exhibit 3), the free cash flows are discounted back to present at the company's weighted average cost of capital (WACC).[19] When evaluating the target from a non-control perspective, we would use the target's WACC, which reflects that company's existing business risk and operating environment. In anticipation of a merger, however, we would adjust that WACC to reflect any anticipated changes in the target's risk from such actions as a redeployment of assets or change in capital structure.

For the company in Exhibit 3, we will assume that the appropriate discount rate is 9.41 percent. Discounting free cash flow for the years 2007 through 2011 at 9.41 percent results in a present value of $5.802 million. That is the portion of the company's current value that can be attributed to the free cash flows that occur over the first

---

18 Working capital is defined in this use as current assets (excluding cash and equivalents) minus current liabilities (excluding short-term debt).

19 For details on the estimation of WACC, see the reading on cost of capital.

stage. Next, we must determine the portion of the present value attributable to the company's terminal value, which arises from those cash flows occurring from the end of the first stage to **perpetuity**.

There are two standard methods for calculating a terminal value. The first method makes use of the constant growth formula. To apply the constant growth formula, an analyst must select a terminal growth rate, which is the long-term equilibrium growth rate that the company can expect to achieve in perpetuity, accounting for both inflation and real growth. The terminal growth rate is often lower than the growth rate applied during the first stage because any advantages from synergies, new opportunities, or cost reductions are transitory as competitors adjust and the industry evolves over time. The constant growth formula can be applied whenever the terminal growth rate is less than the WACC.

$$\text{Terminal value}_T = \frac{\text{FCF}_T(1+g)}{(\text{WACC}-g)} \tag{5}$$

where

FCF$_T$ = free cash flow produced during the final year of the first stage

g = terminal growth rate

For the company in Exhibit 3, we will assume a terminal growth rate of 6.0 percent:

$$\text{Terminal value}_{2011} = \frac{\$1,799(1+0.06)}{(0.0941-0.06)} = \$55,922 = \$55.922 \text{ million}$$

A second method for estimating the terminal value involves applying a multiple at which the analyst expects the average company to sell at the end of the first stage. The analyst might use a free cash flow or other multiple that reflects the expected risk, growth, and economic conditions in the terminal year. Market multiples are rules of thumb applied by analysts, investment bankers, and venture capitalists to produce rough estimates of a company's value. Multiples tend to vary by industry. They can be based on anything applicable to the industry and correlated with market prices. Some service industries tend to be priced as multiples of EBITDA (earnings before interest, taxes, depreciation, and amortization). In contrast, retail stores in some industries might be priced based on multiples applied to floor space. In these cases, the respective multiples can be used directly to produce a terminal value, or they can be incorporated into a pro forma analysis to convert the multiple into a consistent value for free cash flow.

If the company in Exhibit 3 is in an industry where the typical company sells for about 20 times its free cash flow, then the company's terminal value estimate would be:

$$\text{Terminal value}_{2011} = 20 \times \$1,799 = \$35,980 = \$36.0 \text{ million}$$

Having established an estimate for the terminal value, the analyst must discount it back from the end of the estimate horizon to present. The discount rate used is the same WACC estimate that was previously applied to discount the free cash flows. If we decide that the terminal value found using the constant growth method is more accurate than a market multiple, we would discount that value back five years (2011 back to the present):

$$\text{Terminal value}_{2006} = \frac{\$55,922}{(1+0.0941)^5} = \$35,670 = \$35.670 \text{ million}$$

Adding the present value of the free cash flows ($5.802 million) to the present value of the terminal value ($35.670 million), we can estimate the value of the company to be $41.471 million.[20] Note that a large proportion of the company's value is attributable to its terminal value (more than 85 percent in our example). The assumed terminal growth rate and WACC estimate can have a dramatic impact on the terminal value calculation: The final estimate of the company's value will only be as accurate as the estimates used in the model.

Advantages of Using Discounted Cash Flow Analysis

- Expected changes in the target company's cash flows (e.g., from operating synergies and cost structure changes) can be readily modeled.

- An estimate of intrinsic value based on forecast fundamentals is provided by the model.

- Changes in assumptions and estimates can be incorporated by customizing and modifying the model.

Disadvantages of Using Discounted Cash Flow Analysis

- It is difficult to apply when free cash flows do not align with profitability within the first stage. For example, a rapidly expanding company may be profitable but have negative free cash flows because of heavy capital expenditures to the horizon that can be forecast with confidence. The free cash flow value of the company will then derive from a later and harder to estimate period when free cash flow turns positive.

- Estimating cash flows and earnings far into the future is not an exact science. There is a great deal of uncertainty in estimates for the following year, and even greater uncertainty in perpetuity.

- Estimates of discount rates can change over time because of capital market developments or changes that specifically affect the companies in question. These changes can also significantly affect acquisition estimates.

- Terminal value estimates often subject the acquisition value calculations to a disproportionate degree of estimate error. The estimate of terminal value can differ depending on the specific technique used. Additionally, the range of estimates can be affected dramatically by small changes in the assumed growth and WACC estimates.

7.1.2 *Comparable Company Analysis*

A second approach that investment bankers use to estimate acquisition values is called "comparable company analysis." In this approach, the analyst first defines a set of other companies that are similar to the target company under review. This set may include companies within the target's primary industry as well as companies in similar industries. The sample should be formed to include as many companies as possible that have similar size and capital structure to the target.

Once a set of comparable companies is defined, the next step is to calculate various relative value measures based on the current market prices of the comparable companies in the sample. Such valuation is often based on enterprise multiples. A company's enterprise value is the market value of its debt and equity minus the value of its cash and investments. Examples include enterprise value to free cash flow,

---

20 The estimate differs slightly from the sum due to rounding.

enterprise value to EBITDA, enterprise value to EBIT, and enterprise value to sales. Because the denominator in such ratios is pre-interest, they may be preferred when the companies being compared have differences in leverage. The equity can also be valued directly using equity multiples, such as price to cash flow per share (P/CF), price to sales per share (P/S), price to earnings per share (P/E), and price to book value per share (P/BV).

The specific ratios that the analyst selects are determined by the industry under observation. Often, in addition to common market multiples, analysts will include industry-specific multiples. For instance, in the oil and gas industry, in addition to looking at price paid to earnings and cash flow ratios, many analysts evaluate the price paid per barrel of oil or per thousand cubic feet of natural gas reserves.

Analysts typically review the mean, median, and range for whichever metrics are chosen, and then they apply those values to corresponding estimates for the target to develop an estimated company value. This is quite similar to the approach we discussed earlier for using multiples to produce a terminal value estimate. In this case, however, we are calculating various relative value metrics rather than using an industry rule of thumb.

Each metric (P/E, P/CF, etc.) is likely to produce a different estimate for the target's value. Analysts hope that these values converge because that increases confidence in the overall estimate. To the extent that they diverge, analysts must apply judgment and experience to decide which estimates are producing the most accurate market values.

It should be noted that the value determined up to this point in the process yields an estimate of where the target company should trade as a stock in the marketplace relative to the companies in the sample. In order to calculate an acquisition value, the analyst must also estimate a takeover premium. The **takeover premium** is the amount by which the takeover price for each share of stock must exceed the current stock price in order to entice shareholders to relinquish control of the company to an acquirer. This premium is usually expressed as a percentage of the stock price and is calculated as:

$$PRM = \frac{(DP - SP)}{SP} \tag{6}$$

where

PRM = takeover premium (as a percentage of stock price)
 DP = deal price per share of the target company
 SP = stock price of the target company[21]

To calculate the relevant takeover premium for a transaction, analysts usually compile a list of the takeover premiums paid for companies similar to the target. Preferably, the calculations will be from the recent past because acquisition values and premiums tend to vary over time and economic cycles.

EXAMPLE 8

Comparable Company Analysis

Sam Jones, an investment banker, has been retained by the Big Box Company to estimate the price that should be paid to acquire New Life Books Inc. Jones decides to use comparable company analysis to find a fair value for New Life, and has gathered the following information about three comparable companies:

---

[21] The analyst must be careful to note any pre-deal jump in the price that may have occurred because of takeover speculation in the market. In these cases, the analyst should apply the takeover premium to a selected representative price from before any speculative influences on the stock price.

Valuation Variables	Company 1	Company 2	Company 3
Current stock price ($)	20.00	32.00	16.00
Earnings per share ($)	1.00	1.82	0.93
Cash flow per share ($)	2.55	3.90	2.25
Book value per share ($)	6.87	12.80	5.35
Sales per share ($)	12.62	18.82	7.62

First, Jones calculates valuation metrics using the data he gathered. For each metric, he also calculates the mean.

Relative Valuation Ratio	Company 1	Company 2	Company 3	Mean
P/E	20.00	17.58	17.20	18.26
P/CF	7.84	8.21	7.11	7.72
P/BV	2.91	2.50	2.99	2.80
P/S	1.58	1.70	2.10	1.79

Jones then applies the mean relative valuation ratios to the corresponding data for New Life Books to estimate the comparable *stock* price. Because the four valuation metrics produce estimates that are all relatively close, he decides he is comfortable using an average of the four estimates to produce the estimated stock value.

Target Company Valuation Variables	Target Company (a)	Comparable Companies' Valuation Variables	Mean Multiples for Comparable Companies (b)	Estimated Stock Value Based on Comparables (a × b)
Earnings per share	1.95	P/E	18.26	$35.61
Cash flow per share	4.12	P/CF	7.72	$31.81
Book value per share	12.15	P/BV	2.80	$34.02
Sales per share	18.11	P/S	1.79	$32.42
Estimated stock value				Mean: $33.47

To determine the proper acquisition or takeover value, Jones must now estimate the relevant takeover premium. Using five of the most recent takeovers of companies that are similar to the target, he has compiled the following estimates:

Target Company	Stock Price Prior to Takeover ($)	Takeover Price ($)	Takeover Premium (%)
Target 1	23.00	28.50	23.9
Target 2	17.25	22.65	31.3
Target 3	86.75	102.00	17.6
Target 4	45.00	53.75	19.4

(continued)

Target Company	Stock Price Prior to Takeover ($)	Takeover Price ($)	Takeover Premium (%)
Target 5	36.75	45.00	22.4
Mean premium			22.9

After examining the data, Jones decides that the mean estimated premium is reasonable. His next step is to apply the takeover premium to his mean estimate of the stock price for New Life Books:

Target's estimated stock value	$33.47
Estimated takeover premium	22.9%
Estimated takeover price of target	($33.47)(1.229) = $41.14

From all the calculations and estimates above, Jones concludes that a fair takeover price for the Big Box Company to pay for each share of New Life Books would be $41.14.[22]

Advantages of Using Comparable Company Analysis

▪ This method provides a reasonable approximation of a target company's value relative to similar companies in the market. This assumes that "like" assets should be valued on a similar basis in the market.

▪ With this method, most of the required data are readily available.

▪ The estimates of value are derived directly from the market. This is unlike the discounted cash flow method where the takeover value is determined based on many assumptions and estimates.

Disadvantages of Using Comparable Company Analysis

▪ The method is sensitive to market mispricing. To illustrate the issue, suppose that the comparable companies are overvalued. A valuation relative to those companies may suggest a value that is too high in the sense that values would be revised downward when the market corrects.

▪ Using this approach yields a market-estimated fair *stock* price for the target company. In order to estimate a fair *takeover* price, analysts must additionally estimate a fair takeover premium and use that information to adjust the estimated stock price.

▪ The analysis may be inaccurate because it is difficult for the analyst to incorporate any specific plans for the target (e.g., changing capital structure or eliminating duplicate resources) in the analysis.

▪ The data available for past premiums may not be timely or accurate for the particular target company under consideration.

---

22 As we shall discuss in Section 7.2 (covering bid evaluation), the analysis in Example 8 is not quite complete because the acquirer must evaluate the estimated takeover price relative to any expected synergies.

7.1.3 *Comparable Transaction Analysis*

A third common approach to value target companies is known as "comparable transaction analysis." This approach is closely related to comparable company analysis except that the analyst uses details from recent takeover transactions for comparable companies to make direct estimates of the target company's takeover value.

The first step in comparable transaction analysis is to collect a relevant sample of recent takeover transactions. The sample should be as broad as possible but limited to companies in the same industry as the target, or at least closely related. Once the transactions are identified, the analyst can look at the same types of relative value multiples that were used in comparable company analysis (P/E, P/CF, other industry-specific multiples, etc.). In this case, however, we are not comparing the target against market multiples. For this approach we compare the multiples actually paid for similar companies in other M&A deals. As before, analysts typically look at **descriptive statistics**, such as the mean, median, and range for the multiples, and apply judgment and experience when applying that information to estimate the target's value.

EXAMPLE 9

Comparable Transaction Analysis

Joel Hofer, an analyst with an investment banking firm, has been asked to estimate a fair price for the General Health Company's proposed acquisition of Medical Services, Inc. He has already taken the initial step and assembled a sample containing companies involved in acquisitions within the same industry in which Medical Services operates. These companies have all been acquired in the past two years. Details on the acquisition prices and relevant pricing variables are shown below.

Valuation Variables	Acquired Company 1	Acquired Company 2	Acquired Company 3
Acquisition share price ($)	35.00	16.50	87.00
Earnings per share ($)	2.12	0.89	4.37
Cash flow per share ($)	3.06	1.98	7.95
Book value per share ($)	9.62	4.90	21.62
Sales per share ($)	15.26	7.61	32.66

The next step in the process is for Hofer to calculate the multiples at which each company was acquired:

Relative Valuation Ratio	Comparable Company 1	Comparable Company 2	Comparable Company 3	Mean
P/E	16.5	18.5	19.9	18.3
P/CF	11.4	8.3	10.9	10.2
P/BV	3.6	3.4	4.0	3.7
P/S	2.3	2.2	2.7	2.4

After reviewing the distribution of the various values around their respective means, Hofer is confident about using the mean value for each ratio because the range in values above and below the mean is reasonably small. Based on his experience with this particular industry, Hofer believes that cash flows are a particularly important predictor of value for these types of companies. Consequently, instead of finding an equally weighted average, Hofer has decided to apply the weights shown below for calculating a weighted average estimated price.

Target Company Valuation Variables	Target Company (a)	Comparable Companies' Valuation Multiples	Mean Multiple Paid for Comparable Companies (b)	Estimated Takeover Value Based on Comparables (c = a × b)	Weight (d)	Weighted Estimates (e = c × d)
Earnings per share	$ 2.62	P/E	18.3	$47.95	20%	$ 9.59
Cash flow per share	$ 4.33	P/CF	10.2	$44.17	40%	$17.67
Book value per share	$12.65	P/BV	3.7	$46.81	20%	$ 9.36
Sales per share	$22.98	P/S	2.4	$55.15	20%	$11.03
Weighted average estimate						$47.65

In sum, Hofer multiplied each valuation multiple by the corresponding variable for the target company to produce an estimated takeover value based on each comparable. He then decided to overweight cash flow per share and calculated a weighted average to determine an overall takeover value estimate of $47.65 per share for Medical Services, Inc. The same procedure could be repeated using the median, high, and low valuations for each of the valuation variables. This would generate a range of takeover values for Medical Services, Inc.

Advantages of Comparable Transaction Approach

■ It is not necessary to separately estimate a takeover premium. The takeover premium is derived directly from the comparable transactions.

■ The takeover value estimates come directly from values that were recently established in the market. This is unlike the discounted cash flow method where the takeover value is determined based on many assumptions and estimates.

■ The use of prices established through other recent transactions reduces litigation risk for both companies' board of directors and managers regarding the merger transaction's pricing.

Disadvantages of Comparable Transaction Approach

■ Because the value estimates assume that the M&A market has properly determined the intrinsic value of the target companies, there is a risk that the real takeover values in past transactions were not accurate. If true, these inaccurate takeover values are imputed in the estimates based on them.

■ There may not be any, or an adequate number of, comparable transactions to use for calculating the takeover value. In these cases, analysts may try to use data from related industries. These derived values may not be accurate for the specific industry under study.

■ The analysis may be inaccurate because it is difficult for the analyst to incorporate any specific plans for the target (e.g., changing capital structure or eliminating duplicate resources) in the analysis.

7.2 Bid Evaluation

Assessing the target's value is important, but it is insufficient for an assessment of the deal. Even if both the acquirer and the target separately agree on the target company's underlying value, the acquirer will obviously want to pay the lowest price possible while the target will negotiate for the highest price possible. Both the price and form of payment in a merger will determine the distribution of risks and benefits between the counterparties to the deal.

Acquirers must typically pay a premium to induce the owners of the target company to relinquish control. In an M&A transaction, the premium is the portion of the compensation received by the target company's shareholders that is in excess of the pre-merger market value of their shares. The target company's managers will attempt to negotiate the highest possible premium relative to the value of the target company.[23]

$$\text{Target shareholders' gain} = \text{Premium} = P_T - V_T \tag{7}$$

where

P_T = price paid for the target company

V_T = pre-merger value of the target company

The acquirer is willing to pay in excess of the target company's value in anticipation of reaping its own gains. The acquirer's gains are derived from the synergies generated by the transaction—usually from some combination of cost reductions and revenue enhancements. All else constant, synergies increase the value of the acquiring company by the value of the synergies minus the premium paid to target shareholders:

$$\text{Acquirer's gain} = \text{Synergies} - \text{Premium} = S - \left(P_T - V_T\right) \tag{8}$$

where

S = synergies created by the business combination

The post-merger value of the combined company is a function of the pre-merger values of the two companies, the synergies created by the merger, and any cash paid to the target shareholders as part of the transaction:

$$V_{A*} = V_A + V_T + S - C \tag{9}$$

where

V_{A*} = post-merger value of the combined companies

V_A = pre-merger value of the acquirer

C = cash paid to target shareholders

When evaluating a bid, the pre-merger value of the target company is the absolute minimum bid that target shareholders should accept. Individual shareholders could sell their shares in the open market for that much instead of tendering their shares for a lower bid. At the other extreme, unless there are mitigating circumstances or other economic justifications, the acquirer's shareholders would not want to pay more than the pre-merger value of the target company plus the value of any expected synergies. If the acquirer were to pay more than that, then the acquirer's post-merger value would be lower than its pre-merger value—therefore, a reduction in shareholder value.

---

23 A burst of speculative stock activity typically accompanies merger negotiations. This activity typically results in a higher share price for the target company in anticipation of a takeover premium. When conducting a bid evaluation, the analyst should use some combination of an assessment of the company's intrinsic value and a representative stock price from before any merger speculation.

Bidding should thus generally be confined to a range dictated by the synergies expected from the transaction, with each side of the transaction negotiating to capture as much of the synergies as possible. Consequently, analysis of a merger depends not only on an assessment of the target company's value but also on estimates of the value of any synergies that the merged company is expected to attain.

Confidence in synergy estimates will have implications not only for the bid price but also for the method of payment. The reason for this is that different methods of payment for the merger—cash offer, stock offer, or mixed offer—inherently provide varying degrees of risk shifting with respect to misestimating the value of merger synergies. To see why this is the case, we will first walk through the evaluation of an offer for each method of payment.

EXAMPLE 10

Adagio Software Offer

Adagio Software, Inc., and Tantalus Software Solutions, Inc., are negotiating a friendly acquisition of Tantalus by Adagio. The management teams at both companies have informally agreed upon a transaction value of about €12.00 per share of Tantalus Software Solutions stock but are presently negotiating alternative forms of payment. Sunil Agrawal, CFA, works for Tantalus Software Solutions' investment banking team and is evaluating three alternative offers presented by Adagio Software:

1 Cash Offer: Adagio will pay €12.00 per share of Tantalus stock.

2 Stock Offer: Adagio will give Tantalus shareholders 0.80 shares of Adagio stock per share of Tantalus stock.

3 Mixed offer: Adagio will pay €6.00 plus 0.40 shares of Adagio stock per share of Tantalus stock.

Agrawal estimates that the merger of the two companies will result in economies of scale with a net present value of €90 million. To aid in the analysis, Agrawal has also compiled the following data:

	Adagio	Tantalus
Pre-merger stock price	€ 15.00	€ 10.00
Number of shares outstanding (millions)	75	30
Pre-merger market value (millions)	€ 1,125	€ 300

Based only on the information given, which of the three offers should Agrawal recommend to the Tantalus Software Solutions management team?

Solution:

Alternative 1:

Cash offer of €12.00 per share of Tantalus stock. A cash offer is the most straightforward and easiest to evaluate. The price paid for the target company, P_T, is equal to cash price per share times the number of target shares: €12.00 × 30 million = €360 million. Because Tantalus' value, V_T, is €300 million, the premium is the difference between the two: €360 million − €300 million = €60 million.

Adagio's gain in this transaction is €30 million, which equals the value of the synergies minus the premium paid to Tantalus shareholders. A longer way to get to the same conclusion is to remember that the value of the post-merger combined company equals the pre-merger values of both companies plus the value of created synergies less the cash paid to target shareholders: $V_{A^*} = V_A + V_T + S - C$ = €1,125 + 300 + 90 − 360 = €1,155 million. Adagio's pre-merger market value was €1,125 million, and Adagio's gain from the transaction is thus €1,155 − 1,125 = €30 million. Agrawal can divide the post-merger market value of €1,155 by the number of shares outstanding to determine Adagio's post-merger stock price. Under a cash offer, Adagio will not issue additional shares of stock, so Agrawal divides €1,155 by 75 million shares to see that, all else constant, Adagio's stock price after the merger should rise to €15.40.

In an all cash offer, Tantalus shareholders receive €60 million—the premium. Adagio's gain from the transaction equals the expected synergies (€90 million) less the premium paid to Tantalus shareholders (€60 million), which equals €30 million.

Alternative 2:

Stock offer of 0.80 shares of Adagio stock per share of Tantalus stock. A stock offer of 0.80 shares might seem at first glance to be equivalent to a cash offer of €12.00 because Adagio's share price is €15.00 (0.80 × €15 = €12). The results are actually slightly different, however, because Agrawal must account for the dilution that occurs when Adagio issues new shares to Tantalus stockholders. Because there are 30 million shares of the target outstanding, Adagio must issue: 30 million × 0.80 = 24 million shares.

To calculate the price paid for Tantalus, Agrawal starts by ascertaining the post-merger value of the combined company. Agrawal uses the same formula as before while using a value of zero for C because this is a stock offer and no cash is changing hands: $V_{A^*} = V_A + V_T + S - C$ = €1,125 + 300 + 90 − 0 = €1,515 million. Next, Agrawal divides Adagio's post-merger value by the post-merger number of shares outstanding. Because Adagio issued 24 million shares to complete the transaction, Agrawal adds 24 million to the original 75 million shares outstanding and arrives at 99 million. Dividing the post-merger market value by the post-merger number of shares outstanding, Agrawal determines that the value of each share given to Tantalus shareholders is actually worth €1,515 million/99 million = €15.30 and that the total value paid to Tantalus shareholders is €15.30 × 24 million = €367 million.

The premium is thus €367 − 300 = €67 million, which is €7 million higher than it was for the cash offer. Because the target shareholders receive €7 million more than in the cash offer, the acquirer's gain is correspondingly less. Because the synergies are valued at €90 million and the premium is €67 million, the acquirer's gain under a stock transaction with these terms is €23 million.

Alternative 3:

Mixed offer of €6.00 plus 0.40 shares of Adagio stock per share of Tantalus stock. A mixed offer will still result in some dilution, although not as much as a pure stock offer. Agrawal begins by calculating Adagio's post-merger value. Agrawal inserts €180 million for C because the company is paying €6 per share for 30 million shares: $V_{A^*} = V_A + V_T + S - C$ = €1,125 + 300 + 90 − 180 = €1,335 million.

Next, Agrawal determines that Adagio must issue 12 million shares to complete the transaction: 0.40 × 30 million = 12 million. Combined with the original 75 million shares outstanding, Adagio's post-merger number of shares outstanding will be 87 million. Agrawal divides €1,335 million by 87 million and finds that each share given to the Tantalus shareholders is worth €15.35.

The total value paid to Tantalus shareholders includes a cash component, €6.00 × 30 million = €180 million, and a stock component, 12 million shares issued with a value of €15.35 each equaling €184 million. Added together, the total value is €180 + 184 = €364 million, and the premium is therefore €364 million − 300 million = €64 million. The acquirer's gain is $26 million.

> *Conclusion:*
>
> Agrawal should recommend that the Tantalus Software Solutions management team opt for the all stock offer because that alternative provides Tantalus shareholders the most value (the highest premium).

In Example 10, Adagio's gain ranged from €30 million in the pure cash offer to €26 million in the mixed offer and €23 million in the pure stock offer. If the dilution of a stock offer reduces the acquirer's gains from the transaction, why would an acquirer ever pay stock in a merger? The answer brings us back to the beginning of the section where we pointed out that the price and form of payment in a merger determine the distribution of risks and benefits. The choice of payment method is influenced by both parties' confidence in the estimated synergies and the relative value of the acquirer's shares.

The more confident the managers are that the estimated synergies will be realized, the more the acquiring managers will prefer to pay with cash and the more the target managers will prefer to receive stock. And the more the merger is paid for with the acquirer's stock, the more that the risks and benefits of realizing synergies will be passed on to the target shareholders. For example, in the cash offer we analyzed in Example 10, if the synergies later turned out to be worth €60 million rather than the originally estimated €90 million, then the Tantalus shareholders' premium would be unaffected but Adagio's gain would completely evaporate. In contrast, if the synergies were greater than estimated, then Tantalus shareholders' premium would still be unchanged but Adagio's gain would increase.

When stock is used as payment, the target shareholders become part owners of the acquiring company. In the Adagio stock offer, Tantalus shareholders would receive 24 million shares and thus own 24/99 (24.2 percent) of the post-merger acquirer. Thus, Tantalus shareholders would participate by that proportion in any deviation of synergies from pre-merger estimates. If synergies were worth only €60 million, Adagio would lose its €23 million gain and Tantalus shareholders' gain from the transaction would fall by €7 million.

The other factor affecting the method of payment decision relates to the counterparties' confidence in the companies' relative values. The more confident managers are in estimates of the target company's value, the more the acquirer would prefer cash and the more the target would prefer stock. For example, what if Adagio estimates that Tantalus is worth more than €10 per share and consequently offers €12.50 per share in cash instead of €12.00? In that case, Tantalus shareholders would receive a premium that is €15 million higher and Adagio's gain from the transaction would be reduced by €15 million to €15 million.

8   WHO BENEFITS FROM MERGERS?

What does the empirical evidence say about who actually gains in business combinations? Studies on the performance of mergers fall into two categories: short-term performance studies, which examine stock returns surrounding merger announcement dates, and long-term performance studies of post-merger companies. The empirical evidence suggests that merger transactions create value for target company shareholders in the short run. On average, target shareholders reap 30 percent premiums over the stock's pre-announcement market price, and the acquirer's stock price falls, on average, between 1 and 3 percent.[24] Moreover, on average, both the acquirer and target tend to see higher stock returns surrounding cash acquisition offers than around share offers.[25]

The high average premiums paid to target shareholders may be attributed, at least partly, to the winner's curse—the tendency for competitive bidding to result in overpayment. Even if the average bidding company accurately estimates the target company's value, some bidders will overestimate the target's value and other potential buyers will underestimate its value. Unless the winner can exploit some strong synergies that are not available to other bidders, the winning bidder is likely to be the one who most overestimates the value.

Roll argues that high takeover bids may stem from hubris, from "the over-bearing presumption of bidders that their valuations are correct."[26] Implied in this behavior is that these executives are somehow smarter than everyone else and can see value where others cannot. Even if there were no synergies from a merger, managerial hubris would still lead to higher-than-market bids and a transfer of wealth from the acquiring company's shareholders to the target's shareholders. The empirical evidence is consistent with Roll's hubris hypothesis.

When examining a longer period, empirical evidence shows that acquirers tend to underperform comparable companies during the three years following an acquisition. This implies a general post-merger operational failure to capture synergies. Average returns to acquiring companies subsequent to merger transactions are negative 4.3 percent with about 61 percent of acquirers lagging their industry peers.[27] This finding suggests that financial analysts would be well served to thoroughly scrutinize estimates of synergy and post-merger value creation.

Analysts must attempt to distinguish those deals that create value and those that do not. Too often, companies with surplus cash but few new investment opportunities are prone to make acquisitions rather than distribute excess cash to shareholders. When distinguishing value-creating deals, analysts must examine the operational strengths possessed by the acquirer and the target to discern the likelihood that post-merger synergies will be achieved.

Based on past empirical results, the following are characteristics of M&A deals that create value:[28]

- **The buyer is strong**. Acquirers whose earnings and share prices grow at a rate above the industry average for three years before the acquisition earn statistically significant positive returns on announcement.

- **The transaction premiums are relatively low**. Acquirers earn negative returns on announcement when paying a high premium.

- **The number of bidders is low**. Acquirer stock returns are negatively related to the number of bidders.

- **The initial market reaction is favorable**. Initial market reaction is an important barometer for the value investors place on the gains from merging as well as an indication of future returns. If the acquiring company's stock price falls when the deal is announced, investors are sending a message that the merger benefits are doubtful or that the acquirer is paying too much.

---

24 J. Fred Weston and Samuel C. Weaver, *Mergers & Acquisitions* (New York: McGraw-Hill, 2001), pp. 93 – 116.

25 Robert F. Bruner, *Deals from Hell: M&A Lessons That Rise above the Ashes* (New York: John Wiley & Sons, 2005), p. 33.

26 Richard Roll, "The Hubris Hypothesis on Corporate Takeovers," *Journal of Business*, vol. 59 (April 1986), pp. 176 – 216.

27 T. Koller, M. Goedhart, and D. Wessels, *Valuation: Measuring and Managing the Value of Companies*, 4th ed. (Hoboken, NJ: John Wiley & Sons, 2005), p. 439, footnotes 3 and 4.

28 J. Fred Weston and Samuel C. Weaver, *Mergers & Acquisitions* (New York: McGraw-Hill, 2001), Chapter 5.

9   CORPORATE RESTRUCTURING

Just as mergers and acquisitions are a means by which companies get bigger, a corporate restructuring is usually used in reference to ways that companies get smaller—by selling, splitting off, or otherwise shedding operating assets. When a company decides to sell, liquidate, or spin off a division or a subsidiary, it is referred to as a **divestiture**.

Given, as we have discussed, that many companies have great difficulty actually achieving the planned synergies of a business combination, it is not surprising that many companies seek to undo previous mergers. Indeed, periods of intense merger activity are often followed by periods of heightened restructuring activity. Of course, previous mergers that did not work out as planned are not the only reason companies may choose to divest assets. Some of the common reasons for restructuring follow:

- **Change in strategic focus**. Either through acquisitions or other investments over time, companies often become engaged in multiple markets. Management may hope to improve performance by eliminating divisions or subsidiaries that are outside the company's core strategic focus.

- **Poor fit**. Sometimes a company will decide that a particular division is a poor fit within the overall company. For example, the company may not have the expertise or resources to fully exploit opportunities pursued by the division and may decide to sell the segment to another company that does have the necessary resources. Or, the division might simply not be profitable enough to justify continued investment based on the company's cost of capital.

- **Reverse synergy**. Managers may feel that a segment of the company is undervalued by the market, sometimes because of poor performance of the overall company or because the division is not a good strategic fit. In these cases, it is possible that the division and the company will be worth more separately than combined.

- **Financial or cash flow needs**. If times are tough, managers may decide to sell off portions of the company as a means by which to raise cash or cut expenses.

Restructuring can take many forms, but the three basic ways that a company divests assets are a sale to another company, a spin-off to shareholders, or liquidation. As part of a sale to another company, a company might offer to sell the assets of a division or may offer an equity carve-out. An **equity carve-out** involves the creation of a new legal entity and sales of equity in it to outsiders.

In a **spin-off**, shareholders of the parent company receive a proportional number of shares in a new, separate entity. Whereas the sale of a division results in an inflow of cash to the parent company, a spin-off does not. A spin-off simply results in shareholders owning stock in two different companies where there used to be one. A similar type of transaction is called a **split-off**, where some of the parent company's shareholders are given shares in a newly created entity in exchange for their shares of the parent company. **Liquidation** involves breaking up a company, division, or subsidiary and selling off its assets piecemeal. For a company, liquidation is typically associated with bankruptcy.

SUMMARY

Mergers and acquisitions are complex transactions. The process often involves not only the acquiring and target companies but also a variety of other stakeholders, including securities antitrust regulatory agencies. To fully evaluate a merger, analysts must ask two fundamental questions: First, will the transaction create value; and second, does the acquisition price outweigh the potential benefit? This reading has made the following important points.

- An acquisition is the purchase of some portion of one company by another. A merger represents the absorption of one company by another such that only one entity survives following the transaction.

- Mergers can be categorized by the form of integration. In a statutory merger, one company is merged into another; in a subsidiary merger, the target becomes a subsidiary of the acquirer; and in a consolidation, both the acquirer and target become part of a newly formed company.

- Horizontal mergers occur among peer companies engaged in the same kind of business. Vertical mergers occur among companies along a given value chain. Conglomerates are formed by companies in unrelated businesses.

- Merger activity has historically occurred in waves. These waves have typically coincided with a strong economy and buoyant stock market activity. Merger activity tends to be concentrated in a few industries, usually those undergoing changes, such as deregulation or technological advancement.

- The motives for M&A activity include synergy, growth, market power, the acquisition of unique capabilities and resources, diversification, increased earnings, management's personal incentives, tax considerations, and the possibilities of uncovering hidden value. Cross-border motivations may involve technology transfer, product differentiation, government policy, and the opportunities to serve existing clients abroad.

- A merger transaction may take the form of a stock purchase (when the acquirer gives the target company's shareholders some combination of cash or securities in exchange for shares of the target company's stock) or an asset purchase (when the acquirer purchases the target company's assets and payment is made directly to the target company). The decision of which approach to take will affect other aspects of the transaction, such as how approval is obtained, which laws apply, how the liabilities are treated, and how the shareholders and the company are taxed.

- The method of payment for a merger can be cash, securities, or a mixed offering with some of both. The exchange ratio in a stock or mixed offering determines the number of shares that stockholders in the target company will receive in exchange for each of their shares in the target company.

- Hostile transactions are those opposed by target managers, whereas friendly transactions are endorsed by the target company's managers. There are a variety of both pre- and post-offer defenses a target can use to ward off an unwanted takeover bid.

- Examples of pre-offer defense mechanisms include poison pills and puts, incorporation in a jurisdiction with restrictive takeover laws, staggered boards of directors, restricted voting rights, supermajority voting provisions, fair price amendments, and golden parachutes.

- Examples of post-offer defenses include "just say no" defense, litigation, greenmail, share repurchases, leveraged recapitalization, "crown jewel" defense, "Pac-Man" defense, or finding a white knight or a white squire.

- Antitrust legislation prohibits mergers and acquisitions that impede competition. Major U.S. antitrust legislation includes the Sherman Antitrust Act, the Clayton Act, the Celler–Kefauver Act, and the Hart–Scott–Rodino Act.

■ The Federal Trade Commission and Department of Justice review mergers for antitrust concerns in the United States. The European Commission reviews transactions in the European Union.

■ The Herfindahl–Hirschman Index (HHI) is a measure of market power based on the sum of the squared market shares for each company in an industry. Higher index values or combinations that result in a large jump in the index are more likely to meet regulatory challenges.

■ The Williams Act is the cornerstone of securities legislation for M&A activities in the United States. The Williams Act ensures a fair tender offer process through the establishment of disclosure requirements and formal tender offer procedures.

■ Three major tools for valuing a target company are discounted cash flow analysis (which involves discounting free cash flows estimated with pro forma financial statements), comparable company analysis (which estimates a company's intrinsic value based on relative valuation metrics for similar companies), and comparable transaction analysis (which derives valuation from details of recent takeover transactions for comparable companies).

■ In a merger bid, the gain to target shareholders is measured as the control premium, which equals the price paid for the target company in excess of its value. The acquirer gains equal the value of any synergies created by the merger minus the premium paid to target shareholders. Together, the bid and the method of payment determine the distribution of risks and returns among acquirer and target shareholders with regard to realization of synergies as well as correct estimation of the target company's value.

■ The empirical evidence suggests that merger transactions create value for target company shareholders. Acquirers, in contrast, tend to accrue value in the years following a merger. This finding suggests that synergies are often overestimated or difficult to achieve.

■ When a company decides to sell, liquidate, or spin off a division or a subsidiary, it is referred to as a divestiture. Companies may divest assets for a variety of reasons, including a change in strategic focus, poor fit of the asset within the corporation, reverse synergy, or cash flow needs.

■ The three basic ways that a company divests assets are a sale to another company, a spin-off to shareholders, and liquidation.

PRACTICE PROBLEMS

The following information relates to Questions 1–6

Modern Auto, an automobile parts supplier, has made an offer to acquire Sky Systems, creator of software for the airline industry. The offer is to pay Sky Systems' shareholders the current market value of their stock in Modern Auto's stock. The relevant information it used in those calculations is given below:

	Modern Auto	Sky Systems
Share price	$40	$25
Number of outstanding shares (millions)	40	15
Earnings (millions)	$100	$30

Although the total earnings of the combined company will not increase and are estimated to be $130 million, Charles Wilhelm (treasurer of Modern Auto) argues that there are two attractive reasons to merge. First, Wilhelm says, "The merger of Modern Auto and Sky Systems will result in lower risk for our shareholders because of the diversification effect." Second, Wilhelm also says, "If our EPS increases, our stock price will increase in line with the EPS increase because our P/E will stay the same."

Sky Systems managers are not interested in the offer by Modern Auto. The managers, instead, approach HiFly, Inc., which is in the same industry as Sky Systems, to see if it would be interested in acquiring Sky Systems. HiFly is interested, and both companies believe there will be synergies from this acquisition. If HiFly were to acquire Sky Systems, it would do so by paying $400 million in cash.

HiFly is somewhat concerned whether antitrust regulators would consider the acquisition of Sky Systems an antitrust violation. The market in which the two companies operate consists of eight competitors. The largest company has a 25 percent market share. HiFly has the second largest market share of 20 percent. Five companies, including Sky Systems, each have a market share of 10 percent. The smallest company has a 5 percent market share.

1 The acquisition of Sky Systems by Modern Auto and the acquisition of Sky Systems by HiFly, respectively, would be examples of a:

   A vertical merger and a horizontal merger.

   B conglomerate merger and a vertical merger.

   C conglomerate merger and a horizontal merger.

2 If Sky Systems were to be acquired by Modern Auto under the terms of the original offer, the post-merger EPS of the new company would be *closest* to:

   A $2.00.

   B $2.32.

   C $2.63.

3 Are Wilhelm's two statements about his shareholders benefiting from the diversification effect of the merger and about the increase in the stock price, respectively, correct?

	The Merger Will Result in Lower Risk for Shareholders	Stock Price Will Increase in Line with the EPS Increase
A	No	No
B	No	Yes
C	Yes	No

4 Which of the following defenses *best* describes the role of HiFly in the acquisition scenario?

  A Crown jewel.

  B Pac-Man.

  C White knight.

5 Suppose HiFly acquires Sky Systems for the stated terms. The gain to Sky Systems shareholders resulting from the merger transaction would be *closest* to:

  A $25 million.

  B $160 million.

  C $375 million.

6 If HiFly and Sky Systems attempt to merge, the increase in the Herfindahl–Hirschman Index (HHI) and the probable action by the Department of Justice and the FTC, respectively, in response to the merger announcement are:

	Increase in the HHI	Probable Response of Department of Justice and FTC
A	290	To challenge the merger
B	290	To investigate the merger
C	400	To challenge the merger

The following information relates to Questions 7–12

Kinetic Corporation is considering acquiring High Tech Systems. Jim Smith, the vice president of finance at Kinetic, has been assigned the task of estimating a fair acquisition price for High Tech. Smith is aware of several approaches that could be used for this purpose. He plans to estimate the acquisition price based on each of these approaches, and has collected or estimated the necessary financial data.

High Tech has 10 million shares of common stock outstanding and no debt. Smith has estimated that the post-merger free cash flows from High Tech, in millions of dollars, would be 15, 17, 20, and 23 at the end of the following four years. After Year 4, he projects the free cash flow to grow at a constant rate of 6.5 percent a year. He determines that the appropriate rate for discounting these estimated cash flows is 11 percent. He also estimates that after four years High Tech would be worth 23 times its free cash flow at the end of the fourth year.

Smith has determined that three companies—Alpha, Neutron, and Techno—are comparable to High Tech. He has also identified three recent takeover transactions—Quadrant, ProTech, and Automator—that are similar to the takeover of High Tech under consideration. He believes that price-to-earnings, price-to-sales, and price-to-book value per share of these companies could be used to estimate the value of High Tech. The relevant data for the three comparable companies and for High Tech are as follows:

Valuation Variables	Alpha	Neutron	Techno	High Tech
Current stock price ($)	44.00	23.00	51.00	31.00
Earnings/share ($)	3.01	1.68	2.52	1.98
Sales/share ($)	20.16	14.22	18.15	17.23
Book value/share ($)	15.16	7.18	11.15	10.02

The relevant data for the three recently acquired companies are given below:

Valuation Variables	Quadrant	ProTech	Automator
Stock price pre-takeover ($)	24.90	43.20	29.00
Acquisition stock price ($)	28.00	52.00	34.50
Earnings/share ($)	1.40	2.10	2.35
Sales/share ($)	10.58	20.41	15.93
Book value/share ($)	8.29	10.14	9.17

While discussing his analysis with a colleague, Smith makes two comments. Smith's first comment is: "If there were a pre-announcement run-up in Quadrant's price because of speculation, the takeover premium should be computed based on the price prior to the run-up." His second comment is: "Because the comparable transaction approach is based on the acquisition price, the takeover premium is implicitly recognized in this approach."

7   What is the present value per share of High Tech stock using the discounted cash flow approach if the terminal value of High Tech is based on using the constant growth model to determine terminal value?

   A $39.38.

   B $40.56.

   C $41.57.

8   What is the value per share of High Tech stock using the discounted cash flow approach if the terminal value of High Tech is based on using the cash flow multiple method to determine terminal value?

   A $35.22.

   B $40.56.

   C $41.57.

9   The average stock price of High Tech for the three relative valuation ratios (if it is traded at the mean of the three valuations) is *closest* to:

   A $35.21.

   B $39.38.

   C $40.56.

10 Taking into account the mean takeover premium on recent comparable take-overs, what would be the estimate of the fair acquisition price of High Tech based on the comparable company approach?

  A $35.22.

  B $40.83.

  C $41.29.

11 The fair acquisition price of High Tech using the comparable transaction approach is *closest* to:

  A $35.22.

  B $40.86.

  C $41.31.

12 Are Smith's two comments about his analysis correct?

  A Both of his comments are correct.

  B Both of his comments are incorrect.

  C His first comment is correct, and his second comment is incorrect.

The following information relates to Questions 13–18 and is based on "Corporate Governance" and this reading

Mark Zin and Stella Lee are CEO and CFO, respectively, of Moonbase Corporation. They are concerned that Moonbase is undervalued and subject to a hostile takeover bid. To assess the value of their own firm, they are reviewing current financial data for Jupiter PLC, Saturn Corporation, and Voyager Corporation, three firms they believe are comparable to Moonbase.

Relative Valuation Ratio	Jupiter	Saturn	Voyager
P/E	23.00	19.50	21.50
P/B	4.24	5.25	4.91
P/CF	12.60	11.40	13.30

Zin believes Moonbase should trade at similar multiples to these firms and that each valuation ratio measure is equally valid. Moonbase has a current stock price of $34.00 per share, earnings of $1.75 per share, book value of $8.50 per share, and cash flow of $3.20 per share. Using the average of each of the three multiples for the three comparable firms, Zin finds that Moonbase is undervalued.

Lee states that the low valuation reflects current poor performance of a subsidiary of Moonbase. She recommends that the board of directors consider divesting the subsidiary in a manner that would provide cash inflow to Moonbase.

Zin proposes that some action should be taken before a hostile takeover bid is made. He asks Lee if changes can be made to the corporate governance structure in order to make it more difficult for an unwanted suitor to succeed.

In response, Lee makes two comments of actions that would make a hostile takeover more difficult. Lee's first comment is "Moonbase can institute a poison pill that allows our shareholders, other than the hostile bidder, to purchase shares at a substantial discount to current market value." Lee's second comment is: "Moonbase can instead institute a poison put. The put allows shareholders the opportunity to redeem their shares at a substantial premium to current market value."

Zin is also concerned about the general attitude of outside investors with the governance of Moonbase. He has read brokerage reports indicating that the Moonbase governance ratings are generally low. Zin believes the following statements describe characteristics that should provide Moonbase with a strong governance rating.

Statement 1   Moonbase's directors obtain advice from the corporate counsel to aid them in assessing the firm's compliance with regulatory requirements.

Statement 2   Five of the ten members of the board of directors are not employed by Moonbase and are considered independent. Though not employed by the company, two of the independent directors are former executives of the company and thus can contribute useful expertise relevant for the business.

Statement 3   The audit committee of the board is organized so as to have sufficient resources to carry out its task, with an internal staff that reports routinely and directly to the audit committee.

Zin is particularly proud of the fact that Moonbase has begun drafting a "Statement of Corporate Governance" (SCG) that would be available on the company website for viewing by shareholders, investment analysts, and any interested stakeholders. In particular, the SCG pays special attention to policies that ensure effective contributions from the board of directors. These policies include:

Policy 1   Training is provided to directors prior to joining the board and periodically thereafter.

Policy 2   Statements are provided of management's assessment of the board's performance of its fiduciary responsibilities.

Policy 3   Statements are provided of directors' responsibilities regarding oversight and monitoring of the firm's risk management and compliance functions.

Zin concludes the discussion by announcing that Johann Steris, a highly regarded ex-CFO of a major corporation, is under consideration as a member of an expanded board of directors. Zin states that Steris meets all the requirements as an independent director including the fact that he will not violate the interlocking directorship requirement. Steris also will bring experience as a member of the compensation committee of the board of another firm. He also comments that Steris desires to serve on either the audit or compensation committee of the Moonbase board and that good governance practice suggests that Steris would not be prohibited from serving on either committee.

13 The value the CEO estimated based on comparable company analysis is *closest* to:

A $37.33.

B $39.30.

C $40.80.

14 The divestiture technique that Lee is recommending is *most likely*:

A   a spin-off.

B   a split-off.

C   an equity carve-out.

15 With regard to poison pills and puts, Lee's comments are:

    A correct.

    B incorrect with regard to the poison put.

    C incorrect with regard to the poison pill.

16 Which statement by Zin provides the *most* support for a strong governance rating?

    A Statement 1.

    B Statement 2.

    C Statement 3.

17 Which policy of the Statement of Corporate Governance is *least likely* to ensure effective contributions from the board of directors?

    A Policy 1.

    B Policy 2.

    C Policy 3.

18 Is Zin's comment that good governance practice does not preclude Steris from serving on either of the two committees of the Moonbase board correct?

    A Yes.

    B No, good governance practice precludes Steris from serving on the audit committee.

    C No, good governance practice precludes Steris from serving on the compensation committee.

The following information relates to Questions 19–24

Josh Logan is a buy-side equity analyst who follows Durtech. Logan's supervisor believes that Durtech is a likely takeover candidate and has asked Logan to estimate the company's value per share in the event of an "all stock" takeover bid. Logan plans to estimate Durtech's value per share using three approaches: discounted cash flow, comparable company analysis, and comparable transaction analysis.

Durtech has 1.2 million common shares outstanding and no outstanding long-term debt or preferred stock. Logan estimates that Durtech's free cash flows at the end of the next three years will be $5.0 million, $6.0 million, and $7.0 million, respectively. After Year 3, he projects that free cash flow will grow at 5 percent per year. He determines the appropriate discount rate for this free cash flow stream is 15 percent per year.

Applying discounted cash flow analysis to the information above, Logan determines that Durtech's fair enterprise value is $61.8 million. In a separate analysis based on ratios, Logan estimates that at the end of the third year, Durtech will be worth ten times its Year 3 free cash flow.

Logan's supervisor is troubled by the sensitivity of his enterprise value calculation to the terminal growth rate assumption. She asks Logan:

> "What is the percentage change in your fair enterprise value of $61.8 million if you use a terminal growth rate of zero percent rather than 5 percent?"

Logan gathers data on two companies comparable to Durtech: Alphatech and Betatech. He believes that price-to-earnings, price-to-sales, and price-to-book-value per share of these companies should be used to value Durtech. The relevant data for the three companies are given in Exhibit 1.

Exhibit 1	Valuation Variables for Durtech and Comparable Companies		
Valuation Variables	**Alphatech**	**Betatech**	**Durtech**
Current stock price ($)	72.00	45.00	24.00
Earnings per share ($)	2.00	1.50	1.00
Sales per share ($)	32.00	22.50	16.00
Book value per share ($)	18.00	10.00	8.00

Logan also identifies one recent takeover transaction and analyzes its takeover premium (the amount by which its takeover price per share exceeds its current stock price). Omegatech is comparable to the possible transaction on Durtech. Omegatech had a stock price of $44.40 per share prior to a newspaper report of a takeover rumor. After the takeover rumor was reported, the price rose immediately to $60.30 per share. Eventually, the takeover offer was accepted by Omegatech's shareholders for $55.00 per share. One-year trailing earnings per share for Omegatech immediately prior to the takeover were $1.25 per share.

In order to evaluate the risk of government antitrust action, Logan computes the Herfindahl–Hirschman Index (HHI) for the industry group that includes Durtech. He computes the pre-merger value of the HHI to be 1400. As shown in Exhibit 2, Logan also computes the post-merger industry HHI assuming three possible merger scenarios with Durtech.

Exhibit 2	Post-Merger Industry HHI (Assuming Merger with Durtech)	
	Durtech Merger Partner	**Post-Merger Industry HHI**
	Alphatech	1500
	Betatech	1510
	Gammatech	1520

Based upon this analysis, Logan concludes that the industry is moderately concentrated and that a merger of Durtech (with any of the companies listed in Exhibit 2) will face a possible government challenge.

19 Using the discounted cash flow approach and assuming that Durtech's terminal value is based upon the cash flow multiple method, Logan's best estimate of Durtech's current value per share is *closest* to:

   A $49.60.

   B $51.50.

   C $53.51.

20 Logan's best response to the supervisor's question concerning the sensitivity of the enterprise value to the terminal growth rate assumption, is *closest* to:

   A −36.5%.

   B −28.5%.

   C −24.8%.

21 Based on Exhibit 1 and the mean of each of the valuation ratios, Logan's estimate of Durtech's value per share should be *closest* to:

A $30.44.

B $33.67.

C $34.67.

22 Based upon the premium on a recent comparable transaction, Logan's best estimate of the takeover premium for Durtech is *closest* to:

A 19.9%.

B 23.9%.

C 35.8%.

23 Using comparable transaction analysis, Logan's estimate of the fair acquisition value per share for Durtech is *closest* to:

A $35.52.

B $42.59.

C $44.00.

24 The best justification for Logan's conclusion concerning possible government antitrust action is that:

A the post- and pre-merger HHI are both between 1000 and 1800.

B the change in the HHI is 100 or more and the post-merger HHI is between 1000 and 1800.

C the change in the HHI is 100 or more and the pre-merger HHI is between 1000 and 1800.

SOLUTIONS

1 C is correct. These are conglomerate and horizontal mergers, respectively.

2 C is correct. EPS is $2.63.

Because Modern Auto's stock price is $40 and Sky Systems' stock price is $25, Modern Auto will acquire Sky Systems by exchanging 1 of its shares for 40/25 = 1.60 shares of Sky Systems. There are 15 million shares of Sky Systems. Their acquisition will take 15/1.60 = 9.375 million shares of Modern Auto. The total number of shares after the merger = 49.375 million. The EPS after the merger = 130/49.375 = $2.63.

3 A is correct. Both of the statements by Wilhelm are wrong.

The first statement is wrong because diversification by itself does not lower risk for shareholders. Investors can diversify very cheaply on their own by purchasing stocks of different companies (for example, a Modern Auto shareholder could purchase stocks of Sky Systems).

The second statement is also wrong. The P/E ratio will not necessarily remain the same following the merger and is more likely to decline. The pre-merger P/E for Modern Auto is 40/2.50 = 16. After the merger, the EPS would be $130 million/49.375 million shares, or 2.6329. The post-merger P/E will probably fall to 40/2.6329 = 15.19.

4 C is correct. HiFly is a white knight.

5 A is correct.

Target shareholders' gain = Premium = $P_T - V_T$,

P_T = Price paid for the target company = $400 million as provided in the vignette

V_T = Pre-merger value of the target = $25 share price × 15 million shares = $375 million

$400 million − $375 million = $25 million

6 C is correct. The pre- and post-merger HHI measures are 1,550 and 1,950, respectively. Not only is the HHI increasing by 400 points, but the industry concentration level also moves from moderately to highly concentrated. The probable action by the regulatory authorities is thus a challenge.

	Pre-Merger			Post-Merger	
Company	Market Share (%)	Market Share Squared	Company	Market Share (%)	Market Share Squared
1	25	625	1	25	625
2 (HiFly)	20	400	2 & 3	30	900
3 (Sky)	10	100	4	10	100
4	10	100	5	10	100
5	10	100	6	10	100
6	10	100	7	10	100
7	10	100	8	5	25

(continued)

	Pre-Merger			**Post-Merger**	
Company	**Market Share (%)**	**Market Share Squared**	**Company**	**Market Share (%)**	**Market Share Squared**
8	5	25			
	HHI =	1,550		HHI =	1,950

7 C is correct. The estimated stock value is $41.57.

The value of High Tech = Total PV (present value) of free cash flows during the first four years + PV of the terminal value of High Tech at the end of the fourth year using the constant growth model.

Total PV of free cash flows during the first four years = $15/1.11 + 17/1.11^2 + 20/1.11^3 + 23/1.11^4$ = $57.09 million.

Based on the constant growth model, the terminal value (TV) of High Tech at the end of the fourth year is TV = FCF at the end of the fifth year/$(k - g)$ = $(23 \times 1.065)/(0.11 - 0.065)$ = $544.33 million.

PV of the terminal value = $544.33/1.11^4$ = $358.57 million.

Estimated value of High Tech = 57.09 + 358.57 = $415.66 million.

Estimated stock price = 415.66 million/10 million shares = $41.57.

8 B is correct. The estimated stock price is $40.56.

Total PV of free cash flows during the first four years = $15/1.11 + 17/1.11^2 + 20/1.11^3 + 23/1.11^4$ = $57.09 million.

Based on the cash flow multiple method, the terminal value of High Tech four years later = 23×23 = $529 million.

PV of the terminal value = $529/1.11^4$ = $348.47 million.

Estimated value of High Tech = Total PV of free cash flows during the first four years + PV of the terminal value at the end of the fourth year = 57.09 + 348.47 = $405.55 million.

Estimated stock price = 405.55 million/10 million shares = $40.56.

9 A is correct. The estimated value is $35.21.

First, calculate the relative valuation ratios for the three comparable companies and their means.

Relative Valuation Ratio	**Alpha**	**Neutron**	**Techno**	**Mean**
P/E	14.62	13.69	20.24	16.18
P/S	2.18	1.62	2.81	2.20
P/BV	2.90	3.20	4.57	3.56

Then apply the means to the valuation variables for High Tech to get the estimated stock price for High Tech based on the comparable companies.

Valuation Variables	High Tech	Mean Multiple for Comparables	Estimated Stock Price
Current stock price	31.00		
Earnings/share	1.98	16.18	32.04
Sales/share	17.23	2.20	37.91
Book value/share	10.02	3.56	35.67

The mean estimated stock price is (32.04 + 37.91 + 35.67)/3 = $35.21.

10 C is correct. The price is $41.29.

The takeover premiums on three recent comparable takeovers are:

(28.00 − 24.90)/24.90 = 12.45%
(52.00 − 43.20)/43.20 = 20.37%
(34.50 − 29.00)/29.00 = 18.97%
Mean takeover premium = 17.26%

Using the comparable company approach, the stock price of High Tech if it is traded at the mean of the comparable company valuations is $35.21. Considering the mean takeover premium, the estimated fair acquisition price for High Tech is 35.21 × 1.1726 = $41.29.

11 B is correct. The fair acquisition price is $40.86. First, calculate the relative valuation ratios based on the acquisition price for the three comparable transactions and their means.

Relative Valuation Ratio	Quadrant	ProTech	Automator	Mean
P/E	20.00	24.76	14.68	19.81
P/S	2.65	2.55	2.17	2.46
P/BV	3.38	5.13	3.76	4.09

Then apply the means to the valuation variables for High Tech to get the estimated acquisition price for High Tech based on the comparable transactions.

Valuation Variables	High Tech	Mean Multiple Paid for Comparables	Estimated Acquisition Price
Earnings/share	1.98	19.81	39.22
Sales/share	17.23	2.46	42.39
Book value/share	10.02	4.09	40.98

The mean estimated acquisition stock price is (39.22 + 42.39 + 40.98)/3 = $40.86.

12 A is correct. Both of Smith's statements are correct.

If there was a pre-announcement run-up in Quadrant's price because of speculation, the takeover premium should be computed based on the price prior to the run-up. Because the comparable transaction approach is based on the acquisition price, the takeover premium is implicitly recognized in this approach.

13 B is correct. Value is $39.30.

Average P/E ratio is 21.33 = (23.00 + 19.50 + 21.50)/3

Value based on P/E ratio = 21.33 (1.75) = 37.33

Average P/B ratio is 4.80 = (4.24 + 5.25 + 4.91)/3

Value based on P/B ratio = 4.80 (8.50) = 40.80

Average P/CF ratio is 12.43 = (12.60 + 11.40 + 13.30)/3

Value based on P/CF ratio = 12.43 (3.20) = 39.79

Since Zin believes each valuation ratio is equally valid, value is a simple average of the three values.

Value = (37.33 + 40.80 + 39.79)/3 = 39.30

14 C is correct. An equity carve-out involves sale of equity in a new legal entity to outsiders, and would thus result in a cash inflow for Moonbase. A spin-off or a split-off does not generate a cash flow to the firm.

15 B is correct. The first comment about the poison pill is correct, but the second comment is incorrect. Shareholders do not "put" their shares to the company; rather bondholders can exercise the put in the event of a hostile takeover. Bondholders have the right to sell their bonds back to the target at a redemption price that is pre-specified in the bond indenture, typically at or above par value.

16 C is correct. Statement 3 provides the most support for a strong governance rating. The statement describes the manner in which the audit committee should work. The other two statements do not support a strong governance rating as each casts doubt about the independence of the board from management's control.

17 B is correct. The second policy is least likely to ensure effective contributions from the board. The board through self-assessment, and not management, should assess the board's performance.

18 A is correct. As an independent director, without an interlocking relationship and with the expertise required, Steris would be eligible to serve on either of the two committees.

19 A is correct.

PV of first three cash flows: $5/1.15 + 6/1.15^2 + 7/1.15^3 = 13.49$

Terminal value: $7 \times 10 = 70$

PV of terminal value: $= 70/1.15^3 = 46.03$

Value = 13.49 + 46.03 = 59.52

Value per share = 59.52/1.2 = 49.60

20 B is correct.

Terminal value at 5 percent: $7(1.05)/(.15 - .05) = 73.50M$

Terminal value at 0 percent: $7/.15 = 46.67M$

Change in present value: $(46.67 - 73.50)/1.15^3 = -17.64$

Percentage change: $-17.64/61.8 = -28.5\%$

21 B is correct.

Step 1. Compute Valuation Ratios

Valuation Ratio	Alphatech	Betatech	Mean
P/E	36.00	30.00	33.00
P/S	2.25	2.00	2.125
P/BV	4.00	4.50	4.25

Step 2. Apply to Durtech's Variables

Valuation Ratio	Durtech	Mean Multiple	Estimated Stock Price
Earnings per share	1.00	33.00	33.00
Sales per share	16.00	2.125	34.00
Book value per share	8.00	4.25	34.00

Step 3. Determine Mean Value: (33 + 34 + 34)/3 = $33.67 per share

22 B is correct. A comparable transaction sells for premium of 55/44.4 − 1 = 23.9%.

23 C is correct. Omegatech's transaction P/E ratio: 55/1.25 = 44. So estimated fair acquisition value per share is 44 × 1 = $44.00.

24 B is correct. Possible government action is based upon the change in the HHI and the post-merger HHI.

Glossary

Abandonment option The ability to terminate a project at some future time if the financial results are disappointing.

Abnormal earnings See *residual income.*

Abnormal return The return on an asset in excess of the asset's required rate of return; the risk-adjusted return.

Absolute convergence The idea that developing countries, regardless of their particular characteristics, will eventually catch up with the developed countries and match them in per capita output.

Absolute valuation model A model that specifies an asset's intrinsic value.

Absolute version of PPP The extension of the law of one price to the broad range of goods and services that are consumed in different countries.

Accounting estimates Estimates of items such as the useful lives of assets, warranty costs, and the amount of uncollectible receivables.

Accrual basis Method of accounting in which the effect of transactions on financial condition and income are recorded when they occur, not when they are settled in cash.

Acquirer The company in a merger or acquisition that is acquiring the target.

Acquiring company The company in a merger or acquisition that is acquiring the target.

Acquisition The purchase of some portion of one company by another; the purchase may be for assets, a definable segment of another entity, or the purchase of an entire company.

Active factor risk The contribution to active risk squared resulting from the portfolio's different-than-benchmark exposures relative to factors specified in the risk model.

Active return The return on a portfolio minus the return on the portfolio's benchmark.

Active risk The standard deviation of active returns.

Active risk squared The variance of active returns; active risk raised to the second power.

Active specific risk The contribution to active risk squared resulting from the portfolio's active weights on individual assets as those weights interact with assets' residual risk.

Add-on interest A procedure for determining the interest on a bond or loan in which the interest is added onto the face value of a contract.

Adjusted R^2 A measure of goodness-of-fit of a regression that is adjusted for degrees of freedom and hence does not automatically increase when another independent variable is added to a regression.

Adjusted beta Historical beta adjusted to reflect the tendency of beta to be mean reverting.

Adjusted funds from operations Funds from operations (FFO) adjusted to remove any non-cash rent reported under straight-line rent accounting and to subtract maintenance-type capital expenditures and leasing costs, including leasing agents' commissions and tenants' improvement allowances.

Adjusted present value (APV) As an approach to valuing a company, the sum of the value of the company, assuming no use of debt, and the net present value of any effects of debt on company value.

Administrative regulations or administrative law Rules issued by government agencies or other regulators.

Agency costs Costs associated with the conflict of interest present when a company is managed by non-owners. Agency costs result from the inherent conflicts of interest between managers and equity owners.

Agency costs of equity The smaller the stake that managers have in the company, the less is their share in bearing the cost of excessive perquisite consumption or not giving their best efforts in running the company.

Agency issues Conflicts of interest that arise when the agent in an agency relationship has goals and incentives that differ from the principal to whom the agent owes a fiduciary duty. Also called *agency problems* or *principal–agent problems.*

Agency problem A conflict of interest that arises when the agent in an agency relationship has goals and incentives that differ from the principal to whom the agent owes a fiduciary duty.

Alpha The return on an asset in excess of the asset's required rate of return; the risk-adjusted return.

American Depositary Receipt A negotiable certificate issued by a depositary bank that represents ownership in a non--U.S. company's deposited equity (i.e., equity held in custody by the depositary bank in the company's home market).

American option An option that can be exercised at any time until its expiration date.

Amortizing and accreting swaps A swap in which the notional principal changes according to a formula related to changes in the underlying.

Analysis of variance (ANOVA) The analysis of the total variability of a dataset (such as observations on the dependent variable in a regression) into components representing different sources of variation; with reference to regression, ANOVA provides the inputs for an F-test of the significance of the regression as a whole.

Arbitrage 1) The simultaneous purchase of an undervalued asset or portfolio and sale of an overvalued but equivalent asset or portfolio, in order to obtain a riskless profit on the price differential. Taking advantage of a market inefficiency in a risk-free manner. 2) The condition in a financial market in which equivalent assets or combinations of assets sell for two different prices, creating an opportunity to profit at no risk with no commitment of money. In a well-functioning financial market, few arbitrage opportunities are possible. 3) A risk-free operation that earns an expected positive net profit but requires no net investment of money.

Arbitrage opportunity An opportunity to conduct an arbitrage; an opportunity to earn an expected positive net profit without risk and with no net investment of money.

Arbitrage portfolio The portfolio that exploits an arbitrage opportunity.

Arrears swap A type of interest rate swap in which the floating payment is set at the end of the period and the interest is paid at that same time.

Asset beta The unlevered beta; reflects the business risk of the assets; the asset's systematic risk.

Asset purchase An acquisition in which the acquirer purchases the target company's assets and payment is made directly to the target company.

Asset selection risk The contribution to active risk squared resulting from the portfolio's active weights on individual assets as those weights interact with assets' residual risk.

Asset-backed securities A type of bond issued by a legal entity called a *special purpose vehicle* (SPV), on a collection of assets that the SPV owns. Also, securities backed by receivables and loans other than mortgage loans.

Asset-based approach Approach that values a private company based on the values of the underlying assets of the entity less the value of any related liabilities.

Asset-based valuation An approach to valuing natural resource companies that estimates company value on the basis of the market value of the natural resources the company controls.

Asymmetric information The differential of information between corporate insiders and outsiders regarding the company's performance and prospects. Managers typically have more information about the company's performance and prospects than owners and creditors.

At-the-money An option in which the underlying value equals the exercise price.

Autocorrelation The correlation of a time series with its own past values.

Autoregressive model (AR) A time series regressed on its own past values, in which the independent variable is a lagged value of the dependent variable.

Available-for-sale investments Debt and equity securities not classified as either held-to-maturity or fair value through profit or loss securities. The investor is willing to sell but not actively planning to sell. In general, available-for-sale securities are reported at fair value on the balance sheet.

Backward integration A merger involving the purchase of a target ahead of the acquirer in the value or production chain; for example, to acquire a supplier.

Backwardation A condition in the futures markets in which the benefits of holding an asset exceed the costs, leaving the futures price less than the spot price.

Balance-sheet-based accruals ratio The difference between net operating assets at the end and the beginning of the period compared to the average net operating assets over the period.

Balance-sheet-based aggregate accruals The difference between net operating assets at the end and the beginning of the period.

Bankruptcy A declaration provided for by a country's laws that typically involves the establishment of a legal procedure that forces creditors to defer their claims.

Basic earnings per share (EPS) Net earnings available to common shareholders (i.e., net income minus preferred dividends) divided by the weighted average number of common shares outstanding during the period.

Basis swap 1) An interest rate swap involving two floating rates. 2) A swap in which both parties pay a floating rate.

Basis trade A trade based on the pricing of credit in the bond market versus the price of the same credit in the CDS market. To execute a basis trade, go long the "underpriced" credit and short the "overpriced" credit. A profit is realized when the price of credit between the short and long position converges.

Bear hug A tactic used by acquirers to circumvent target management's objections to a proposed merger by submitting the proposal directly to the target company's board of directors.

Benchmark A comparison portfolio; a point of reference or comparison.

Benchmark value of the multiple In using the method of comparables, the value of a price multiple for the comparison asset; when we have comparison assets (a group), the mean or median value of the multiple for the group of assets.

Bill-and-hold basis Sales on a bill-and-hold basis involve selling products but not delivering those products until a later date.

Binomial model A model for pricing options in which the underlying price can move to only one of two possible new prices.

Binomial tree The graphical representation of a model of asset price dynamics in which, at each period, the asset moves up with probability p or down with probability $(1 - p)$.

Blockage factor An illiquidity discount that occurs when an investor sells a large amount of stock relative to its trading volume (assuming it is not large enough to constitute a controlling ownership).

Bond indenture A legal contract specifying the terms of a bond issue.

Bond option An option in which the underlying is a bond; primarily traded in over-the-counter markets.

Bond yield plus risk premium method An estimate of the cost of common equity that is produced by summing the before-tax cost of debt and a risk premium that captures the additional yield on a company's stock relative to its bonds. The additional yield is often estimated using historical spreads between bond yields and stock yields.

Bond-equivalent yield The yield to maturity on a basis that ignores compounding.

Bonding costs Costs borne by management to assure owners that they are working in the owners' best interest (e.g., implicit cost of non-compete agreements).

Book value Shareholders' equity (total assets minus total liabilities) minus the value of preferred stock; common shareholders' equity.

Book value of equity Shareholders' equity (total assets minus total liabilities) minus the value of preferred stock; common shareholders' equity.

Book value per share The amount of book value (also called carrying value) of common equity per share of common stock, calculated by dividing the book value of shareholders' equity by the number of shares of common stock outstanding.

Bottom-up approach With respect to forecasting, an approach that usually begins at the level of the individual company or a unit within the company.

Bottom-up investing An approach to investing that focuses on the individual characteristics of securities rather than on macroeconomic or overall market forecasts.

Breakup value The value derived using a sum-of-the-parts valuation.

Breusch–Pagan test A test for conditional heteroskedasticity in the error term of a regression.

Broker 1) An agent who executes orders to buy or sell securities on behalf of a client in exchange for a commission. 2) *See* Futures commission merchants.

Brokerage The business of acting as agents for buyers or sellers, usually in return for commissions.

Buy-side analysts Analysts who work for investment management firms, trusts, and bank trust departments, and similar institutions.

CDS spread A periodic premium paid by the buyer to the seller that serves as a return over LIBOR required to protect against credit risk.

Call An option that gives the holder the right to buy an underlying asset from another party at a fixed price over a specific period of time.

Cannibalization Cannibalization occurs when an investment takes customers and sales away from another part of the company.

Cap 1) A contract on an interest rate, whereby at periodic payment dates, the writer of the cap pays the difference between the market interest rate and a specified cap rate if, and only if, this difference is positive. This is equivalent to a stream of call options on the interest rate. 2) A combination of interest rate call options designed to hedge a borrower against rate increases on a floating-rate loan.

Cap rate See *capitalization rate.*

Capital allocation line (CAL) A graph line that describes the combinations of expected return and standard deviation of return available to an investor from combining the optimal portfolio of risky assets with the risk-free asset.

Capital asset pricing model (CAPM) An equation describing the expected return on any asset (or portfolio) as a linear function of its beta relative to the market portfolio.

Capital charge The company's total cost of capital in money terms.

Capital deepening An increase in the capital-to-labor ratio.

Capital market line (CML) The line with an intercept point equal to the risk-free rate that is tangent to the efficient frontier of risky assets; represents the efficient frontier when a risk-free asset is available for investment.

Capital rationing A capital rationing environment assumes that the company has a fixed amount of funds to invest.

Capital structure The mix of debt and equity that a company uses to finance its business; a company's specific mixture of long-term financing.

Capitalization of earnings method In the context of private company valuation, valuation model based on an assumption of a constant growth rate of free cash flow to the firm or a constant growth rate of free cash flow to equity.

Capitalization rate The divisor in the expression for the value of perpetuity. In the context of real estate, the divisor in the direct capitalization method of estimating value. The cap rate equals net operating income divided by value.

Capitalized cash flow method In the context of private company valuation, valuation model based on an assumption of a constant growth rate of free cash flow to the firm or a constant growth rate of free cash flow to equity. Also called *capitalized cash flow model.*

Capitalized cash flow model In the context of private company valuation, valuation model based on an assumption of a constant growth rate of free cash flow to the firm or a constant growth rate of free cash flow to equity. Also called *capitalized cash flow method.*

Capitalized income method In the context of private company valuation, valuation model based on an assumption of a constant growth rate of free cash flow to the firm or a constant growth rate of free cash flow to equity.

Caplet Each component call option in a cap.

Capped swap A swap in which the floating payments have an upper limit.

Carried interest A share of any profits that is paid to the general partner (manager) of an investment partnership, such as a private equity or hedge fund, as a form of compensation designed to be an incentive to the manager to maximize performance of the investment fund.

Carrying costs The costs of holding an asset, generally a function of the physical characteristics of the underlying asset.

Cash available for distribution Funds from operations (FFO) adjusted to remove any non-cash rent reported under straight-line rent accounting and to subtract maintenance-type capital expenditures and leasing costs, including leasing agents' commissions and tenants' improvement allowances.

Cash basis Accounting method in which the only relevant transactions for the financial statements are those that involve cash.

Cash offering A merger or acquisition that is to be paid for with cash; the cash for the merger might come from the acquiring company's existing assets or from a debt issue.

Cash settlement A procedure used in certain derivative transactions that specifies that the long and short parties engage in the equivalent cash value of a delivery transaction.

Cash-flow-statement-based accruals ratio The difference between reported net income on an accrual basis and the cash flows from operating and investing activities compared to the average net operating assets over the period.

Cash-flow-statement-based aggregate accruals The difference between reported net income on an accrual basis and the cash flows from operating and investing activities.

Cash-generating unit The smallest identifiable group of assets that generates cash inflows that are largely independent of the cash inflows of other assets or groups of assets.

Catalyst An event or piece of information that causes the marketplace to re-evaluate the prospects of a company.

Chain rule of forecasting A forecasting process in which the next period's value as predicted by the forecasting equation is substituted into the right-hand side of the equation to give a predicted value two periods ahead.

Cheapest-to-deliver The debt instrument that can be purchased and delivered at the lowest cost yet has the same seniority as the reference obligation.

Clean surplus accounting Accounting that satisfies the condition that all changes in the book value of equity other than transactions with owners are reflected in income. The bottom-line income reflects all changes in shareholders' equity arising from other than owner transactions. In the absence of owner transactions, the change in shareholders' equity should equal net income. No adjustments such as translation adjustments bypass the income statement and go directly to shareholders equity.

Clean surplus relation The relationship between earnings, dividends, and book value in which ending book value is equal to the beginning book value plus earnings less dividends, apart from ownership transactions.

Clientele effect The preference some investors have for shares that exhibit certain characteristics.

Club convergence The idea that only rich and middle-income countries sharing a set of favorable attributes (i.e., are members of the "club") will converge to the income level of the richest countries.

Cobb–Douglas production function A function of the form $Y = K^\alpha L^{1-\alpha}$ relating output (Y) to labor (L) and capital (K) inputs.

Cointegrated Describes two time series that have a long-term financial or economic relationship such that they do not diverge from each other without bound in the long run.

Commercial mortgage-backed securities Securities backed by commercial mortgage loans.

Commercial real estate properties Income-producing real estate properties, properties purchased with the intent to let, lease, or rent (in other words, produce income).

Common size statements Financial statements in which all elements (accounts) are stated as a percentage of a key figure such as revenue for an income statement or total assets for a balance sheet.

Company fundamental factors Factors related to the company's internal performance, such as factors relating to earnings growth, earnings variability, earnings momentum, and financial leverage.

Company share-related factors Valuation measures and other factors related to share price or the trading characteristics of the shares, such as earnings yield, dividend yield, and book-to-market value.

Comparables Assets used as benchmarks when applying the method of comparables to value an asset. Also called *comps*, *guideline assets*, or *guideline companies*.

Compiled financial statements Financial statements that are not accompanied by an auditor's opinion letter.

Comprehensive income All changes in equity other than contributions by, and distributions to, owners; income under clean surplus accounting; includes all changes in equity during a period except those resulting from investments by owners and distributions to owners; comprehensive income equals net income plus other comprehensive income.

Comps Assets used as benchmarks when applying the method of comparables to value an asset.

Conditional convergence The idea that convergence of per capita income is conditional on the countries having the same savings rate, population growth rate, and production function.

Conditional heteroskedasticity Heteroskedasticity in the error variance that is correlated with the values of the independent variable(s) in the regression.

Conglomerate discount The discount possibly applied by the market to the stock of a company operating in multiple, unrelated businesses.

Conglomerate merger A merger involving companies that are in unrelated businesses.

Consolidation The combining of the results of operations of subsidiaries with the parent company to present financial statements as if they were a single economic unit. The assets, liabilities, revenues and expenses of the subsidiaries are combined with those of the parent company, eliminating intercompany transactions.

Constant dividend payout ratio policy A policy in which a constant percentage of net income is paid out in dividends.

Constant maturity swap A swap in which the floating rate is the rate on a security known as a constant maturity treasury or CMT security.

Constant maturity treasury (CMT) A hypothetical U.S. Treasury note with a constant maturity. A CMT exists for various years in the range of 2 to 10.

Constant returns to scale The condition that if all inputs into the production process are increased by a given percentage, then output rises by that same percentage.

Contango A situation in a futures market where the current futures price is greater than the current spot price for the underlying asset.

Contingent consideration Potential future payments to the seller that are contingent on the achievement of certain agreed on occurrences.

Continuing earnings Earnings excluding nonrecurring components.

Continuing residual income Residual income after the forecast horizon.

Continuing value The analyst's estimate of a stock's value at a particular point in the future.

Continuous time Time thought of as advancing in extremely small increments.

Control premium An increment or premium to value associated with a controlling ownership interest in a company.

Convenience yield The nonmonetary return offered by an asset when the asset is in short supply, often associated with assets with seasonal production processes.

Conventional cash flow A conventional cash flow pattern is one with an initial outflow followed by a series of inflows.

Conversion factor An adjustment used to facilitate delivery on bond futures contracts in which any of a number of bonds with different characteristics are eligible for delivery.

Core earnings Earnings excluding nonrecurring components.

Corporate governance The system of principles, policies, procedures, and clearly defined responsibilities and accountabilities used by stakeholders to overcome the conflicts of interest inherent in the corporate form.

Corporate raider A person or organization seeking to profit by acquiring a company and reselling it, or seeking to profit from the takeover attempt itself (e.g., greenmail).

Corporation A legal entity with rights similar to those of a person. The chief officers, executives, or top managers act as agents for the firm and are legally entitled to authorize corporate activities and to enter into contracts on behalf of the business.

Correlation analysis The analysis of the strength of the linear relationship between two data series.

Cost approach Approach that values a private company based on the values of the underlying assets of the entity less the value of any related liabilities. In the context of real estate, this approach estimates the value of a property based on what it would cost to buy the land and construct a new property on the site that has the same utility or functionality as the property being appraised.

Cost of carry The cost associated with holding some asset, including financing, storage, and insurance costs. Any yield received on the asset is treated as a negative carrying cost.

Cost of debt The cost of debt financing to a company, such as when it issues a bond or takes out a bank loan.

Cost of equity The required rate of return on common stock.

Cost-of-carry model A model for pricing futures contracts in which the futures price is determined by adding the cost of carry to the spot price.

Covariance stationary Describes a time series when its expected value and variance are constant and finite in all periods and when its covariance with itself for a fixed number of periods in the past or future is constant and finite in all periods.

Covered interest arbitrage A transaction executed in the foreign exchange market in which a currency is purchased (sold) and a forward contract is sold (purchased) to lock in the exchange rate for future delivery of the currency. This transaction should earn the risk-free rate of the investor's home country.

Covered interest rate parity Relationship among the spot exchange rate, forward exchange rate, and the interest rates in two currencies that ensures that the return on a hedged (i.e., covered) foreign risk-free investment is the same as the return on a domestic risk-free investment.

Credit correlation The correlation of credits contained in an index CDS.

Credit curve The credit spreads for a range of maturities of a company's debt; applies to non-government borrowers and incorporates credit risk into each rate.

Credit default swap A derivative contract between two parties in which the buyer makes a series of cash payments to the seller and receives a promise of compensation for credit losses resulting from the default.

Credit derivative A derivative instrument in which the underlying is a measure of the credit quality of a borrower.

Credit event The outcome that triggers a payment from the credit protection seller to the credit protection buyer.

Credit protection buyer One party to a credit default swap; the buyer makes a series of cash payments to the seller and receives a promise of compensation for credit losses resulting from the default.

Credit protection seller One party to a credit default swap; the buyer makes a series of cash payments to the seller and receives a promise of compensation for credit losses resulting from the default.

Credit ratings Ordinal rankings of the credit risk of a company, government (sovereign), quasi-government, or asset-backed security.

Credit risk The risk that the borrower will not repay principal and interest. Also called *default risk*.

Credit scoring Ordinal rankings of a retail borrower's credit riskiness. It is called an *ordinal ranking* because it only orders borrowers' riskiness from highest to lowest.

Credit spreads The difference between the yields on default-free and credit risky zero-coupon bonds.

Currency option An option that allows the holder to buy (if a call) or sell (if a put) an underlying currency at a fixed exercise rate, expressed as an exchange rate.

Current credit risk The risk associated with the possibility that a payment currently due will not be made.

Current exchange rate For accounting purposes, the spot exchange rate on the balance sheet date.

Current rate method Approach to translating foreign currency financial statements for consolidation in which all assets and liabilities are translated at the current exchange rate. The current rate method is the prevalent method of translation.

Curve trade Buying a CDS of one maturity and selling a CDS on the same reference entity with a different maturity.

Cyclical businesses Businesses with high sensitivity to business- or industry-cycle influences.

DOWNREIT A variation of the UPREIT structure under which the REIT owns more than one partnership and may own properties at both the REIT level and the partnership level.

Daily settlement See *marking to market*.

Data mining The practice of determining a model by extensive searching through a dataset for statistically significant patterns.

Day trader A trader holding a position open somewhat longer than a scalper but closing all positions at the end of the day.

"Dead-hand" provision A poison pill provision that allows for the redemption or cancellation of a poison pill provision only by a vote of continuing directors (generally directors who were on the target company's board prior to the takeover attempt).

Debt covenants Agreements between the company as borrower and its creditors.

Debt ratings An objective measure of the quality and safety of a company's debt based upon an analysis of the company's ability to pay the promised cash flows, as well as an analysis of any indentures.

Decision rule With respect to hypothesis testing, the rule according to which the null hypothesis will be rejected or not rejected; involves the comparison of the test statistic to rejection point(s).

Deep-in-the-money Options that are far in-the-money.

Deep-out-of-the-money Options that are far out-of-the-money.

Default intensity Gives the probability of default over the next instant $[t, t + \Delta]$ when the economy is in state X_t.

Default probability See *probability of default*.

Default risk See *credit risk*.

Deferred revenue A liability account for money that has been collected for goods or services that have not yet been delivered; payment received in advance of providing a good or service.

Definition of value A specification of how "value" is to be understood in the context of a specific valuation.

Definitive merger agreement A contract signed by both parties to a merger that clarifies the details of the transaction, including the terms, warranties, conditions, termination details, and the rights of all parties.

Delivery A process used in a deliverable forward contract in which the long pays the agreed-upon price to the short, which in turn delivers the underlying asset to the long.

Delivery option The feature of a futures contract giving the short the right to make decisions about what, when, and where to deliver.

Delta The relationship between the option price and the underlying price, which reflects the sensitivity of the price of the option to changes in the price of the underlying.

Dependent variable The variable whose variation about its mean is to be explained by the regression; the left-hand-side variable in a regression equation.

Depository Trust and Clearinghouse Corporation A U.S.-headquartered entity providing post-trade clearing, settlement, and information services.

Depreciated replacement cost In the context of real estate, the replacement cost of a building adjusted different types of depreciation.

Derivative A financial instrument whose value depends on the value of some underlying asset or factor (e.g., a stock price, an interest rate, or exchange rate).

Descriptive statistics The study of how data can be summarized effectively.

Diff swaps A swap in which the payments are based on the difference between interest rates in two countries but payments are made in only a single currency.

Diluted earnings per share (diluted EPS) Net income, minus preferred dividends, divided by the number of common shares outstanding considering all dilutive securities (e.g., convertible debt and options); the EPS that would result if all dilutive securities were converted into common shares.

Dilution A reduction in proportional ownership interest as a result of the issuance of new shares.

Diminishing marginal productivity When each additional unit of an input, keeping the other inputs unchanged, increases output by a smaller increment.

Direct capitalization method In the context of real estate, this method estimates the value of an income-producing property based on the level and quality of its net operating income.

Direct financing leases A type of finance lease, from a lessor perspective, where the present value of the lease payments (lease receivable) equals the carrying value of the leased asset. The revenues earned by the lessor are financing in nature.

Discount To reduce the value of a future payment in allowance for how far away it is in time; to calculate the present value of some future amount. Also, the amount by which an instrument is priced below its face value.

Discount for lack of control An amount or percentage deducted from the pro rata share of 100 percent of the value of an equity interest in a business to reflect the absence of some or all of the powers of control.

Discount for lack of marketability An amount of percentage deducted from the value of an ownership interest to reflect the relative absence of marketability.

Discount interest A procedure for determining the interest on a loan or bond in which the interest is deducted from the face value in advance.

Discount rate Any rate used in finding the present value of a future cash flow.

Discounted abnormal earnings model A model of stock valuation that views intrinsic value of stock as the sum of book value per share plus the present value of the stock's expected future residual income per share.

Discounted cash flow (DCF) analysis In the context of merger analysis, it is an estimate of a target company's value found by discounting the company's expected future free cash flows to the present.

Discounted cash flow method Income approach that values an asset based on estimates of future cash flows discounted to present value by using a discount rate reflective of the risks associated with the cash flows. In the context of real estate, this method estimates the value of an income-producing property based by discounting future projected cash flows.

Discounted cash flow model A model of intrinsic value that views the value of an asset as the present value of the asset's expected future cash flows.

Discrete time Time thought of as advancing in distinct finite increments.

Discriminant analysis A multivariate classification technique used to discriminate between groups, such as companies that either will or will not become bankrupt during some time frame.

Diversified REITs REITs that own and operate in more than one type of property; they are more common in Europe and Asia than in the United States.

Divestiture The sale, liquidation, or spin-off of a division or subsidiary.

Dividend coverage ratio The ratio of net income to dividends.

Dividend discount model (DDM) A present value model of stock value that views the intrinsic value of a stock as present value of the stock's expected future dividends.

Dividend displacement of earnings The concept that dividends paid now displace earnings in all future periods.

Dividend imputation tax system A taxation system which effectively assures that corporate profits distributed as dividends are taxed just once, at the shareholder's tax rate.

Dividend payout ratio The ratio of cash dividends paid to earnings for a period.

Dividend policy The strategy a company follows with regard to the amount and timing of dividend payments.

Dividend rate The most recent quarterly dividend multiplied by four.

Double taxation system Corporate earnings are taxed twice when paid out as dividends. First, corporate earnings are taxed regardless of whether they will be distributed as dividends or retained at the G-13 corporate level, and second, dividends are taxed again at the individual shareholder level.

Downstream A transaction between two related companies, an investor company (or a parent company) and an associate company (or a subsidiary) such that the investor company records a profit on its income statement. An example is a sale of inventory by the investor company to the associate or by a parent to a subsidiary company.

Due diligence Investigation and analysis in support of a recommendation; the failure to exercise due diligence may sometimes result in liability according to various securities laws.

Dummy variable A type of qualitative variable that takes on a value of 1 if a particular condition is true and 0 if that condition is false.

Duration A measure of an option-free bond's average maturity. Specifically, the weighted average maturity of all future cash flows paid by a security, in which the weights are the present value of these cash flows as a fraction of the bond's price. A measure of a bond's price sensitivity to interest rate movements.

Dutch disease A situation in which currency appreciation driven by strong export demand for resources makes other segments of the economy (particularly manufacturing) globally uncompetitive.

Dynamic hedging A strategy in which a position is hedged by making frequent adjustments to the quantity of the instrument used for hedging in relation to the instrument being hedged.

Earnings expectations management Attempts by management to encourage analysts to forecast a slightly lower number for expected earnings than the analysts would otherwise forecast.

Earnings game Management's focus on reporting earnings that meet consensus estimates.

Earnings management activity Deliberate activity aimed at influencing reporting earnings numbers, often with the goal of placing management in a favorable light; the opportunistic use of accruals to manage earnings.

Earnings surprise The difference between reported earnings per share and expected earnings per share.

Earnings yield Earnings per share divided by price; the reciprocal of the P/E ratio.

Economic growth The expansion of production possibilities that results from capital accumulation and technological change.

Economic obsolescence In the context of real estate, a reduction in value due to current economic conditions.

Economic profit See *residual income*.

Economic sectors Large industry groupings.

Economic value added (EVA®) A commercial implementation of the residual income concept; the computation of EVA® is the net operating profit after taxes minus the cost of capital, where these inputs are adjusted for a number of items.

Economies of scale A situation in which average costs per unit of good or service produced fall as volume rises. In reference to mergers, the savings achieved through the consolidation of operations and elimination of duplicate resources.

Edwards–Bell–Ohlson model A model of stock valuation that views intrinsic value of stock as the sum of book value per share plus the present value of the stock's expected future residual income per share.

Efficient frontier The portion of the minimum-variance frontier beginning with the global minimum-variance portfolio and continuing above it; the graph of the set of portfolios offering the maximum expected return for their level of variance of return.

Efficient portfolio A portfolio offering the highest expected return for a given level of risk as measured by variance or standard deviation of return.

Enterprise value (EV) Total company value (the market value of debt, common equity, and preferred equity) minus the value of cash and investments.

Enterprise value multiple A valuation multiple that relates the total market value of all sources of a company's capital (net of cash) to a measure of fundamental value for the entire company (such as a pre-interest earnings measure).

Entry price The price paid to buy an asset.

Equilibrium The condition in which supply equals demand.

Equity REIT A REIT that owns, operates, and/or selectively develops income-producing real estate.

Equity carve-out A form of restructuring that involves the creation of a new legal entity and the sale of equity in it to outsiders.

Equity charge The estimated cost of equity capital in money terms.

Equity forward A contract calling for the purchase of an individual stock, a stock portfolio, or a stock index at a later date at an agreed-upon price.

Equity options Options on individual stocks; also known as stock options.

Error autocorrelation The autocorrelation of the error term.

Error term The portion of the dependent variable that is not explained by the independent variable(s) in the regression.

Estimated parameters With reference to a regression analysis, the estimated values of the population intercept and population slope coefficient(s) in a regression.

Eurodollar A dollar deposited outside the United States.

European option An option that can only be exercised on its expiration date.

Ex ante version of PPP Hypothesis that expected changes in the spot exchange rate are equal to expected differences in national inflation rates. An extension of relative purchasing power parity to expected future changes in the exchange rate.

Ex-dividend Trading ex-dividend refers to shares that no longer carry the right to the next dividend payment.

Ex-dividend date The first date that a share trades without (i.e., "ex") the dividend.

Ex-dividend price The price at which a share first trades without (i.e., "ex") the right to receive an upcoming dividend.

Excess earnings method Income approach that estimates the value of all intangible assets of the business by capitalizing future earnings in excess of the estimated return requirements associated with working capital and fixed assets.

Exchange for physicals (EFP) A permissible delivery procedure used by futures market participants, in which the long and short arrange a delivery procedure other than the normal procedures stipulated by the futures exchange.

Exchange ratio The number of shares that target stockholders are to receive in exchange for each of their shares in the target company.

Exercise The process of using an option to buy or sell the underlying. Also called *exercising the option*.

Exercise price The fixed price at which an option holder can buy or sell the underlying. Also called *strike price, striking price*, or *strike*.

Exercise rate The fixed rate at which the holder of an interest rate option can buy or sell the underlying. Also called *strike rate*.

Exercise value The value of an asset given a hypothetically complete understanding of the asset's investment characteristics; the value obtained if an option is exercised based on current conditions. Also called *intrinsic value*.

Exercising the option The process of using an option to buy or sell the underlying. Also called *exercise*.

Exit price The price received to sell an asset or transfer a liability.

Expanded CAPM An adaptation of the CAPM that adds to the CAPM a premium for small size and company-specific risk.

Expected holding-period return The expected total return on an asset over a stated holding period; for stocks, the sum of the expected dividend yield and the expected price appreciation over the holding period.

Expected loss The probability of default multiplied by the loss given default; the full amount owed minus the expected recovery.

Expenses Outflows of economic resources or increases in liabilities that result in decreases in equity (other than decreases because of distributions to owners); reductions in net assets associated with the creation of revenues.

Expiration date The date on which a derivative contract expires.

Exposure to foreign exchange risk The risk of a change in value of an asset or liability denominated in a foreign currency due to a change in exchange rates.

External growth Company growth in output or sales that is achieved by buying the necessary resources externally (i.e., achieved through mergers and acquisitions).

External sustainability approach An approach to assessing the equilibrium exchange rate that focuses on exchange rate adjustments required to ensure that a country's net foreign-asset/GDP ratio or net foreign-liability/GDP ratio stabilizes at a sustainable level.

Externalities Spillover effects of production and consumption activities onto others who did not consent to participate in the activity.

FX carry trade   An investment strategy that involves taking on long positions in high-yield currencies and short positions in low-yield currencies.

Factor   A common or underlying element with which several variables are correlated.

Factor betas   An asset's sensitivity to a particular factor; a measure of the response of return to each unit of increase in a factor, holding all other factors constant.

Factor loadings   See *factor betas*.

Factor price   The expected return in excess of the risk-free rate for a portfolio with a sensitivity of 1 to one factor and a sensitivity of 0 to all other factors.

Factor risk premium   The expected return in excess of the risk-free rate for a portfolio with a sensitivity of 1 to one factor and a sensitivity of 0 to all other factors. Also called *factor price*.

Factor sensitivity   See *factor betas*.

Failure to pay   When a borrower does not make a scheduled payment of principal or interest on any outstanding obligations after a grace period.

Fair market value   The market price of an asset or liability that trades regularly.

Fair value   The amount at which an asset (or liability) could be bought (or incurred) or sold (or settled) in a current transaction between willing parties, that is, other than in a forced or liquidation sale; the price that would be received to sell an asset or paid to transfer a liability in an orderly transaction between market participants at the measurement date.

Fiduciary call   A combination of a European call and a risk-free bond that matures on the option expiration day and has a face value equal to the exercise price of the call.

Finance lease   Essentially, the purchase of some asset by the buyer (lessee) that is directly financed by the seller (lessor). Also called *capital lease*.

Financial contagion   A situation where financial shocks spread from their place of origin to other locales; in essence, a faltering economy infects other, healthier economies.

Financial distress   Heightened uncertainty regarding a company's ability to meet its various obligations because of lower or negative earnings.

Financial futures   Futures contracts in which the underlying is a stock, bond, or currency.

Financial reporting quality   The accuracy with which a company's reported financials reflect its operating performance and their usefulness for forecasting future cash flows.

Financial risk   The risk that environmental, social, or governance risk factors will result in significant costs or other losses to a company and its shareholders; the risk arising from a company's obligation to meet required payments under its financing agreements.

Financial transaction   A purchase involving a buyer having essentially no material synergies with the target (e.g., the purchase of a private company by a company in an unrelated industry or by a private equity firm would typically be a financial transaction).

First-differencing   A transformation that subtracts the value of the time series in period $t-1$ from its value in period t.

First-in, first-out (FIFO)   The first in, first out, method of accounting for inventory, which matches sales against the costs of items of inventory in the order in which they were placed in inventory.

First-order serial correlation   Correlation between adjacent observations in a time series.

Fitted parameters   With reference to a regression analysis, the estimated values of the population intercept and population slope coefficient(s) in a regression.

Fixed-rate perpetual preferred stock   Nonconvertible, noncallable preferred stock with a specified dividend rate that has a claim on earnings senior to the claim of common stock, and no maturity date.

Flip-in pill   A poison pill takeover defense that dilutes an acquirer's ownership in a target by giving other existing target company shareholders the right to buy additional target company shares at a discount.

Flip-over pill   A poison pill takeover defense that gives target company shareholders the right to purchase shares of the acquirer at a significant discount to the market price, which has the effect of causing dilution to all existing acquiring company shareholders.

Floor   A combination of interest rate put options designed to hedge a lender against lower rates on a floating-rate loan.

Floor traders   Market makers that buy and sell by quoting a bid and an ask price. They are the primary providers of liquidity to the market.

Floored swap   A swap in which the floating payments have a lower limit.

Floorlet   Each component put option in a floor.

Flotation cost   Fees charged to companies by investment bankers and other costs associated with raising new capital.

Foreign currency transactions   Transactions that are denominated in a currency other than a company's functional currency.

Forward P/E   A P/E calculated on the basis of a forecast of EPS; a stock's current price divided by next year's expected earnings.

Forward contract   An agreement between two parties in which one party, the buyer, agrees to buy from the other party, the seller, an underlying asset at a later date for a price established at the start of the contract.

Forward dividend yield   A dividend yield based on the anticipated dividend during the next 12 months.

Forward integration   A merger involving the purchase of a target that is farther along the value or production chain; for example, to acquire a distributor.

Forward price or forward rate   The fixed price or rate at which the transaction scheduled to occur at the expiration of a forward contract will take place. This price is agreed on at the initiation date of the contract.

Forward rate agreement (FRA)   A forward contract calling for one party to make a fixed interest payment and the other to make an interest payment at a rate to be determined at the contract expiration.

Forward swap   A forward contract to enter into a swap.

Franking credit   A tax credit received by shareholders for the taxes that a corporation paid on its distributed earnings.

Free cash flow   The actual cash that would be available to the company's investors after making all investments necessary to maintain the company as an ongoing enterprise (also referred to as free cash flow to the firm); the internally generated funds that can be distributed to the company's investors (e.g., shareholders and bondholders) without impairing the value of the company.

Free cash flow hypothesis   The hypothesis that higher debt levels discipline managers by forcing them to make fixed debt service payments and by reducing the company's free cash flow.

Free cash flow method   Income approach that values an asset based on estimates of future cash flows discounted to present value by using a discount rate reflective of the risks associated with the cash flows.

Free cash flow to equity   The cash flow available to a company's common shareholders after all operating expenses, interest, and principal payments have been made, and necessary investments in working and fixed capital have been made.

Free cash flow to equity model   A model of stock valuation that views a stock's intrinsic value as the present value of expected future free cash flows to equity.

Free cash flow to the firm   The cash flow available to the company's suppliers of capital after all operating expenses (including taxes) have been paid and necessary investments in working and fixed capital have been made.

Free cash flow to the firm model   A model of stock valuation that views the value of a firm as the present value of expected future free cash flows to the firm.

Friendly transaction   A potential business combination that is endorsed by the managers of both companies.

Functional currency   The currency of the primary economic environment in which an entity operates.

Functional obsolescence   In the context of real estate, a reduction in value due to a design that differs from that of a new building constructed for the intended use of the property.

Fundamental beta   A beta that is based at least in part on fundamental data for a company.

Fundamental factor models   A multifactor model in which the factors are attributes of stocks or companies that are important in explaining cross-sectional differences in stock prices.

Fundamentals   Economic characteristics of a business such as profitability, financial strength, and risk.

Funds available for distribution   Funds from operations (FFO) adjusted to remove any non-cash rent reported under straight-line rent accounting and to subtract maintenance-type capital expenditures and leasing costs, including leasing agents' commissions and tenants' improvement allowances.

Funds from operations   Accounting net earnings excluding (1) depreciation charges on real estate, (2) deferred tax charges, and (3) gains or losses from sales of property and debt restructuring.

Futures commission merchants (FCMs)   Individuals or companies that execute futures transactions for other parties off the exchange.

Futures contract   A variation of a forward contract that has essentially the same basic definition but with some additional features, such as a clearinghouse guarantee against credit losses, a daily settlement of gains and losses, and an organized electronic or floor trading facility.

Gamma   A numerical measure of how sensitive an option's delta is to a change in the underlying.

Generalized least squares   A regression estimation technique that addresses heteroskedasticity of the error term.

Going-concern assumption   The assumption that the business will maintain its business activities into the foreseeable future.

Going-concern value   A business's value under a going-concern assumption.

Goodwill   An intangible asset that represents the excess of the purchase price of an acquired company over the value of the net assets acquired.

Gross domestic product   A money measure of the goods and services produced within a country's borders over a stated time period.

Gross lease   A lease under which the tenant pays a gross rent to the landlord who is responsible for all operating costs, utilities, maintenance expenses, and real estate taxes relating to the property.

Growth accounting equation   The production function written in the form of growth rates. For the basic Cobb–Douglas production function, it states that the growth rate of output equals the rate of technological change plus α times the growth rate of capital plus $(1 - \alpha)$ times the growth rate of labor.

Growth capital expenditures   Capital expenditures needed for expansion.

Growth option   The ability to make additional investments in a project at some future time if the financial results are strong. Also called *expansion option*.

Guideline assets   Assets used as benchmarks when applying the method of comparables to value an asset.

Guideline companies   Assets used as benchmarks when applying the method of comparables to value an asset.

Guideline public companies   Public-company comparables for the company being valued.

Guideline public company method   A variation of the market approach; establishes a value estimate based on the observed multiples from trading activity in the shares of public companies viewed as reasonably comparable to the subject private company.

Guideline transactions method   A variation of the market approach; establishes a value estimate based on pricing multiples derived from the acquisition of control of entire public or private companies that were acquired.

Harmonic mean   A type of weighted mean computed by averaging the reciprocals of the observations, then taking the reciprocal of that average.

Hazard rate   The probability that an event will occur, given that it has not already occurred.

Hazard rate estimation   A technique for estimating the probability of a binary event, such as default/no default, mortality/no mortality, and prepay/no prepay.

Health care REITs   REITs that invest in skilled nursing facilities (nursing homes), assisted living and independent residential facilities for retired persons, hospitals, medical office buildings, or rehabilitation centers.

Hedge ratio   The relationship of the quantity of an asset being hedged to the quantity of the derivative used for hedging.

Hedging   A general strategy usually thought of as reducing, if not eliminating, risk.

Held for trading investments   Debt or equity securities acquired with the intent to sell them in the near term.

Held-to-maturity investments   Debt (fixed-income) securities that a company intends to hold to maturity; these are presented at their original cost, updated for any amortization of discounts or premiums.

Herfindahl–Hirschman Index (HHI)   A measure of market concentration that is calculated by summing the squared market shares for competing companies in an industry; high HHI readings or mergers that would result in large HHI increases are more likely to result in regulatory challenges.

Heteroskedastic   With reference to the error term of regression, having a variance that differs across observations.

Heteroskedasticity   The property of having a nonconstant variance; refers to an error term with the property that its variance differs across observations.

Heteroskedasticity-consistent standard errors   Standard errors of the estimated parameters of a regression that correct for the presence of heteroskedasticity in the regression's error term.

Historical exchange rates   For accounting purposes, the exchange rates that existed when the assets and liabilities were initially recorded.

Holding period return   The return that an investor earns during a specified holding period; a synonym for total return.

Homoskedasticity   The property of having a constant variance; refers to an error term that is constant across observations.

Horizontal merger   A merger involving companies in the same line of business, usually as competitors.

Hostile transaction   An attempt to acquire a company against the wishes of the target's managers.

Hotel REITs   REITs that own hotel properties but, similar to health care REITs, in many countries they must refrain from operating their properties themselves to maintain their tax-advantaged REIT status.

Human capital   The accumulated knowledge and skill that workers acquire from education, training, or life experience.

Hybrid REITs   REITs that own and operate income-producing real estate and invest in mortgages as well; REITs that have positions in both real estate assets and real estate debt.

Hybrid approach   With respect to forecasting, an approach that combines elements of both top-down and bottom-up analysis.

ISDA Master Agreement   A standard or "master" agreement published by the International Swaps and Derivatives Association. The master agreement establishes the terms for each party involved in the transaction.

Illiquidity discount   A reduction or discount to value that reflects the lack of depth of trading or liquidity in that asset's market.

Impairment   Diminishment in value as a result of carrying (book) value exceeding fair value and/or recoverable value.

Impairment of capital rule   A legal restriction that dividends cannot exceed retained earnings.

Implied repo rate   The rate of return from a cash-and-carry transaction implied by the futures price relative to the spot price.

Implied volatility   The volatility that option traders use to price an option, implied by the price of the option and a particular option-pricing model.

In-process research and development   Research and development costs relating to projects that are not yet completed, such as have been incurred by a company that is being acquired.

In-sample forecast errors   The residuals from a fitted time-series model within the sample period used to fit the model.

In-the-money   Options that, if exercised, would result in the value received being worth more than the payment required to exercise.

Income approach   Valuation approach that values an asset as the present discounted value of the income expected from it. In the context of real estate, this approach estimates the value of a property based on an expected rate of return; the estimated value is the present value of the expected future income from the property, including proceeds from resale at the end of a typical investment holding period.

Incremental cash flow   The cash flow that is realized because of a decision; the changes or increments to cash flows resulting from a decision or action.

Indenture   A written contract between a lender and borrower that specifies the terms of the loan, such as interest rate, interest payment schedule, maturity, etc.

Independent projects   Independent projects are projects whose cash flows are independent of each other.

Independent regulators   Regulators recognized and granted authority by a government body or agency. They are not government agencies per se and typically do not rely on government funding.

Independent variable   A variable used to explain the dependent variable in a regression; a right-hand-side variable in a regression equation.

Index CDS   A type of credit default swap that involves a combination of borrowers.

Index amortizing swap   An interest rate swap in which the notional principal is indexed to the level of interest rates and declines with the level of interest rates according to a predefined schedule. This type of swap is frequently used to hedge securities that are prepaid as interest rates decline, such as mortgage-backed securities.

Indexing   An investment strategy in which an investor constructs a portfolio to mirror the performance of a specified index.

Industrial REITs   REITs that hold portfolios of single-tenant or multi-tenant industrial properties that are used as warehouses, distribution centers, light manufacturing facilities, and small office or "flex" space.

Industry structure   An industry's underlying economic and technical characteristics.

Information ratio   (IR) Mean active return divided by active risk; or alpha divided by the standard deviation of diversifiable risk.

Informational frictions   Forces that restrict availability, quality, and/or flow of information and its use.

Initial margin requirement   The margin requirement on the first day of a transaction as well as on any day in which additional margin funds must be deposited.

Initial public offering   (IPO) The initial issuance of common stock registered for public trading by a formerly private corporation.

Instability in the minimum-variance frontier   The characteristic of minimum-variance frontiers that they are sensitive to small changes in inputs.

Interest rate call   An option in which the holder has the right to make a known interest payment and receive an unknown interest payment.

Interest rate cap   A series of call options on an interest rate, with each option expiring at the date on which the floating loan rate will be reset, and with each option having the same exercise rate. A cap in general can have an underlying other than an interest rate.

Interest rate collar   A combination of a long cap and a short floor, or a short cap and a long floor. A collar in general can have an underlying other than an interest rate.

Interest rate floor   A series of put options on an interest rate, with each option expiring at the date on which the floating loan rate will be reset, and with each option having the same exercise rate. A floor in general can have an underlying other than the interest rate. Also called *floor*.

Interest rate option   An option in which the underlying is an interest rate.

Interest rate parity A formula that expresses the equivalence or parity of spot and forward rates, after adjusting for differences in the interest rates.

Interest rate put An option in which the holder has the right to make an unknown interest payment and receive a known interest payment.

Interest rate risk Risk that interest rates will change such that the return earned is not commensurate with returns on comparable instruments in the marketplace.

Internal rate of return (IRR) Rate of return that discounts future cash flows from an investment to the exact amount of the investment; the discount rate that makes the present value of an investment's costs (outflows) equal to the present value of the investment's benefits (inflows).

Internal ratings Credit ratings developed internally and used by financial institutions or other entities to manage risk.

International Fisher effect Proposition that nominal interest rate differentials across currencies are determined by expected inflation differentials.

Intrinsic value The value of an asset given a hypothetically complete understanding of the asset's investment characteristics; the value obtained if an option is exercised based on current conditions. The difference between the spot exchange rate and the strike price of a currency.

Inverse price ratio The reciprocal of a price multiple, e.g., in the case of a P/E ratio, the "earnings yield" E/P (where P is share price and E is earnings per share).

Investment objectives Desired investment outcomes; includes risk objectives and return objectives.

Investment strategy An approach to investment analysis and security selection.

Investment value The value to a specific buyer, taking account of potential synergies based on the investor's requirements and expectations.

Judicial law Interpretations of courts.

Justified (fundamental) P/E The price-to-earnings ratio that is fair, warranted, or justified on the basis of forecasted fundamentals.

Justified price multiple The estimated fair value of the price multiple, usually based on forecasted fundamentals or comparables.

kth order autocorrelation The correlation between observations in a time series separated by k periods.

Labor force Everyone of working age (ages 16 to 64) that either is employed or is available for work but not working.

Labor force participation rate The percentage of the working age population that is in the labor force.

Labor productivity The quantity of real GDP produced by an hour of labor. More generally, output per unit of labor input.

Labor productivity growth accounting equation States that potential GDP growth equals the growth rate of the labor input plus the growth rate of labor productivity.

Lack of marketability discount An extra return to investors to compensate for lack of a public market or lack of marketability.

Last-in, first-out (LIFO) The last in, first out, method of accounting for inventory, which matches sales against the costs of items of inventory in the reverse order the items were placed in inventory (i.e., inventory produced or acquired last are assumed to be sold first).

Law of one price Hypothesis that (1) identical goods should trade at the same price across countries when valued in terms of a common currency, or (2) two equivalent financial instruments or combinations of financial instruments can sell for only one price. The latter form is equivalent to the principle that no arbitrage opportunities are possible.

Leading P/E A P/E calculated on the basis of a forecast of EPS; a stock's current price divided by next year's expected earnings.

Leading dividend yield Forecasted dividends per share over the next year divided by current stock price.

Legal risk The risk that failures by company managers to effectively manage a company's environmental, social, and governance risk exposures will lead to lawsuits and other judicial remedies, resulting in potentially catastrophic losses for the company; the risk that the legal system will not enforce a contract in case of dispute or fraud.

Legislative and regulatory risk The risk that governmental laws and regulations directly or indirectly affecting a company's operations will change with potentially severe adverse effects on the company's continued profitability and even its long-term sustainability.

Lessee The party obtaining the use of an asset through a lease.

Lessor The owner of an asset that grants the right to use the asset to another party.

Leveraged buyout (LBO) A transaction whereby the target company management team converts the target to a privately held company by using heavy borrowing to finance the purchase of the target company's outstanding shares.

Leveraged recapitalization A post-offer takeover defense mechanism that involves the assumption of a large amount of debt that is then used to finance share repurchases; the effect is to dramatically change the company's capital structure while attempting to deliver a value to target shareholders in excess of a hostile bid.

Limit down A limit move in the futures market in which the price at which a transaction would be made is at or below the lower limit.

Limit move A condition in the futures markets in which the price at which a transaction would be made is at or beyond the price limits.

Limit up A limit move in the futures market in which the price at which a transaction would be made is at or above the upper limit.

Linear association A straight-line relationship, as opposed to a relationship that cannot be graphed as a straight line.

Linear regression Regression that models the straight-line relationship between the dependent and independent variable(s).

Linear trend A trend in which the dependent variable changes at a constant rate with time.

Liquidation To sell the assets of a company, division, or subsidiary piecemeal, typically because of bankruptcy; the form of bankruptcy that allows for the orderly satisfaction of creditors' claims after which the company ceases to exist.

Liquidation value The value of a company if the company were dissolved and its assets sold individually.

Liquidity risk The risk that a financial instrument cannot be purchased or sold without a significant concession in price due to the size of the market.

Local currency The currency of the country where a company is located.

Locals Market makers that buy and sell by quoting a bid and an ask price. They are the primary providers of liquidity to the market.

Locational obsolescence In the context of real estate, a reduction in value due to decreased desirability of the location of the building.

Locked limit A condition in the futures markets in which a transaction cannot take place because the price would be beyond the limits.

Log-linear model With reference to time-series models, a model in which the growth rate of the time series as a function of time is constant.

Log-log regression model A regression that expresses the dependent and independent variables as natural logarithms.

Logit model A qualitative-dependent-variable multiple regression model based on the logistic probability distribution.

London interbank offered rate (Libor or LIBOR) Collective name for multiple rates at which a select set of banks believe they could borrow unsecured funds from other banks in the London interbank market for different currencies and different borrowing periods ranging from overnight to one year.

Long The buyer of a derivative contract. Also refers to the position of owning a derivative.

Long-term equity anticipatory securities (LEAPS) Options originally created with expirations of several years.

Long/short trade A long position in one CDS and a short position in another.

Look-ahead bias A bias caused by using information that was not available on the test date.

Loss given default The amount that will be lost if a default occurs.

Lower bound The lowest possible value of an option.

Macroeconomic balance approach An approach to assessing the equilibrium exchange rate that focuses on exchange rate adjustments needed to close the gap between the medium-term expectation for a country's current account balance and that country's normal (or sustainable) current account balance.

Macroeconomic factor A factor related to the economy, such as the inflation rate, industrial production, or economic sector membership.

Macroeconomic factor model A multifactor model in which the factors are surprises in macroeconomic variables that significantly explain equity returns.

Maintenance capital expenditures Capital expenditures needed to maintain operations at the current level.

Maintenance margin requirement The margin requirement on any day other than the first day of a transaction.

Managerialism theories Theories that posit that corporate executives are motivated to engage in mergers to maximize the size of their company rather than shareholder value.

Margin The amount of money that a trader deposits in a margin account. The term is derived from the stock market practice in which an investor borrows a portion of the money required to purchase a certain amount of stock. In futures markets, there is no borrowing so the margin is more of a down payment or performance bond.

Marginal investor An investor in a given share who is very likely to be part of the next trade in the share and who is therefore important in setting price.

Mark-to-market The revaluation of a financial asset or liability to its current market value or fair value.

Market approach Valuation approach that values an asset based on pricing multiples from sales of assets viewed as similar to the subject asset.

Market efficiency A finance perspective on capital markets that deals with the relationship of price to intrinsic value. The **traditional efficient markets formulation** asserts that an asset's price is the best available estimate of its intrinsic value. The **rational efficient markets formulation** asserts that investors should expect to be rewarded for the costs of information gathering and analysis by higher gross returns.

Market price of risk The slope of the capital market line, indicating the market risk premium for each unit of market risk.

Market risk premium The expected excess return on the market over the risk-free rate.

Market timing Asset allocation in which the investment in the market is increased if one forecasts that the market will outperform T-bills.

Market value The estimated amount for which a property should exchange on the date of valuation between a willing buyer and a willing seller in an arm's-length transaction after proper marketing wherein the parties had each acted knowledgeably, prudently, and without compulsion.

Market value of invested capital The market value of debt and equity.

Marking to market A procedure used primarily in futures markets in which the parties to a contract settle the amount owed daily. Also known as the *daily settlement*.

Markowitz decision rule A decision rule for choosing between two investments based on their means and variances.

Mature growth rate The earnings growth rate in a company's mature phase; an earnings growth rate that can be sustained long term.

Mean reversion The tendency of a time series to fall when its level is above its mean and rise when its level is below its mean; a mean-reverting time series tends to return to its long-term mean.

Mean–variance analysis An approach to portfolio analysis using expected means, variances, and covariances of asset returns.

Merger The absorption of one company by another; two companies become one entity and one or both of the pre-merger companies ceases to exist as a separate entity.

Method based on forecasted fundamentals An approach to using price multiples that relates a price multiple to forecasts of fundamentals through a discounted cash flow model.

Method of comparables An approach to valuation that involves using a price multiple to evaluate whether an asset is relatively fairly valued, relatively undervalued, or relatively overvalued when compared to a benchmark value of the multiple.

Minimum-variance frontier The graph of the set of portfolios that have minimum variance for their level of expected return.

Minimum-variance portfolio The portfolio with the minimum variance for each given level of expected return.

Minority Interest The proportion of the ownership of a subsidiary not held by the parent (controlling) company.

Mispricing Any departure of the market price of an asset from the asset's estimated intrinsic value.

Mixed factor models Factor models that combine features of more than one type of factor model.

Mixed offering A merger or acquisition that is to be paid for with cash, securities, or some combination of the two.

Model specification With reference to regression, the set of variables included in the regression and the regression equation's functional form.

Modified duration   A measure of a bond's price sensitivity to interest rate movements. Equal to the Macaulay duration of a bond divided by one plus its yield to maturity.

Molodovsky effect   The observation that P/Es tend to be high on depressed EPS at the bottom of a business cycle, and tend to be low on unusually high EPS at the top of a business cycle.

Momentum indicators   Valuation indicators that relate either price or a fundamental (such as earnings) to the time series of their own past values (or in some cases to their expected value).

Monetary assets and liabilities   Assets and liabilities with value equal to the amount of currency contracted for, a fixed amount of currency. Examples are cash, accounts receivable, accounts payable, bonds payable, and mortgages payable. Inventory is not a monetary asset. Most liabilities are monetary.

Monetary/non-monetary method   Approach to translating foreign currency financial statements for consolidation in which monetary assets and liabilities are translated at the current exchange rate. Non-monetary assets and liabilities are translated at historical exchange rates (the exchange rates that existed when the assets and liabilities were acquired).

Monetizing   The conversion of the value of a financial transaction into currency.

Moneyness   The relationship between the price of the underlying and an option's exercise price.

Monitoring costs   Costs borne by owners to monitor the management of the company (e.g., board of director expenses).

Mortgage REITs   REITs that invest the bulk of their assets in interest-bearing mortgages, mortgage securities, or short-term loans secured by real estate.

Mortgage sector   The mortgage-backed securities sector.

Mortgage-backed securities   Asset-backed securitized debt obligations that represent rights to receive cash flows from portfolios of mortgage loans.

Mortgages   Loans with real estate serving as collateral for the loans.

Multi-family/residential REITs   REITs that invest in and manage rental apartments for lease to individual tenants, typically using one-year leases.

Multicollinearity   A regression assumption violation that occurs when two or more independent variables (or combinations of independent variables) are highly but not perfectly correlated with each other.

Multiple linear regression   Linear regression involving two or more independent variables.

Multiple linear regression model   A linear regression model with two or more independent variables.

Mutually exclusive projects   Mutually exclusive projects compete directly with each other. For example, if Projects A and B are mutually exclusive, you can choose A or B, but you cannot choose both.

NTM P/E   Next twelve months P/E: current market price divided by an estimated next twelve months EPS.

Naked credit default swap   A position where the owner of the CDS does not have a position in the underlying credit.

Negative serial correlation   Serial correlation in which a positive error for one observation increases the chance of a negative error for another observation, and vice versa.

Net asset balance sheet exposure   When assets translated at the current exchange rate are greater in amount than liabilities translated at the current exchange rate. Assets exposed to translation gains or losses exceed the exposed liabilities.

Net asset value   The difference between assets and liabilities, all taken at current market values instead of accounting book values.

Net asset value per share   Net asset value divided by the number of shares outstanding.

Net lease   A lease under which the tenant pays a net rent to the landlord as well as an additional amount based on the tenant's pro rata share of the operating costs, utilities, maintenance expenses, and real estate taxes relating to the property.

Net liability balance sheet exposure   When liabilities translated at the current exchange rate are greater assets translated at the current exchange rate. Liabilities exposed to translation gains or losses exceed the exposed assets.

Net operating assets   The difference between operating assets (total assets less cash) and operating liabilities (total liabilities less total debt).

Net operating income   Gross rental revenue minus operating costs, but before deducting depreciation, corporate overhead, and interest expense. In the context of real estate, a measure of the income from the property after deducting operating expenses for such items as property taxes, insurance, maintenance, utilities, repairs, and insurance but before deducting any costs associated with financing and before deducting federal income taxes. It is similar to earnings before interest, taxes, depreciation, and amortization (EBITDA) in a financial reporting context.

Net operating profit less adjusted taxes (NOPLAT)   A company's operating profit with adjustments to normalize the effects of capital structure.

Net present value (NPV)   The present value of an investment's cash inflows (benefits) minus the present value of its cash outflows (costs).

Net realisable value   Estimated selling price in the ordinary course of business less the estimated costs necessary to make the sale.

Net regulatory burden   The private costs of regulation less the private benefits of regulation.

Net rent   A rent that consists of a stipulated rent to the landlord and a further amount based on their share of common area costs for utilities, maintenance, and property taxes.

Netting   When parties agree to exchange only the net amount owed from one party to the other.

Network externalities   The impact that users of a good, a service, or a technology have on other users of that product; it can be positive (e.g., a critical mass of users makes a product more useful) or negative (e.g., congestion makes the product less useful).

No-growth company   A company without positive expected net present value projects.

No-growth value per share   The value per share of a no-growth company, equal to the expected level amount of earnings divided by the stock's required rate of return.

Node   Each value on a binomial tree from which successive moves or outcomes branch.

Non-cash rent   An amount equal to the difference between the average contractual rent over a lease term (the straight-line rent) and the cash rent actually paid during a period. This figure is one of the deductions made from FFO to calculate AFFO.

Non-convergence trap   A situation in which a country remains relative poor, or even falls further behind, because it fails to t implement necessary institutional reforms and/or adopt leading technologies.

Non-monetary assets and liabilities   Assets and liabilities that are not monetary assets and liabilities. Non-monetary assets include inventory, fixed assets, and intangibles, and non-monetary liabilities include deferred revenue.

Non-renewable resources   Finite resources that are depleted once they are consumed; oil and coal are examples.

Nonconventional cash flow   In a nonconventional cash flow pattern, the initial outflow is not followed by inflows only, but the cash flows can flip from positive (inflows) to negative (outflows) again (or even change signs several times).

Nondeliverable forwards (NDFs)   Cash-settled forward contracts, used predominately with respect to foreign exchange forwards.

Nonearning assets   Cash and investments (specifically cash, cash equivalents, and short-term investments).

Nonlinear relation   An association or relationship between variables that cannot be graphed as a straight line.

Nonstationarity   With reference to a random variable, the property of having characteristics such as mean and variance that are not constant through time.

Normal EPS   The earnings per share that a business could achieve currently under mid-cyclical conditions.

Normal backwardation   The condition in futures markets in which futures prices are lower than expected spot prices.

Normal contango   The condition in futures markets in which futures prices are higher than expected spot prices.

Normalized EPS   The earnings per share that a business could achieve currently under mid-cyclical conditions.

Normalized P/E   P/Es based on normalized EPS data.

Normalized earnings   The expected level of mid-cycle earnings for a company in the absence of any unusual or temporary factors that affect profitability (either positively or negatively).

Notional amount   The amount of protection being purchased in a CDS.

n-Period moving average   The average of the current and immediately prior $n - 1$ values of a time series.

Off-market FRA   A contract in which the initial value is intentionally set at a value other than zero and therefore requires a cash payment at the start from one party to the other.

Off-the-run   A series of securities or indexes that were issued/created prior to the most recently issued/created series.

Office REITs   REITs that invest in and manage multi-tenanted office properties in central business districts of cities and suburban markets.

Offsetting   A transaction in exchange-listed derivative markets in which a party re-enters the market to close out a position.

On-the-run   The most recently issued/created series of securities or indexes.

Operating lease   An agreement allowing the lessee to use some asset for a period of time; essentially a rental.

Operating risk   The risk attributed to the operating cost structure, in particular the use of fixed costs in operations; the risk arising from the mix of fixed and variable costs; the risk that a company's operations may be severely affected by environmental, social, and governance risk factors.

Operational risk   The risk of loss from failures in a company's systems and procedures, or from external events.

Opportunity cost   The value that investors forgo by choosing a particular course of action; the value of something in its best alternative use.

Opportunity set   The set of assets available for investment.

Optimal capital structure   The capital structure at which the value of the company is maximized.

Optimizer   A specialized computer program or a spreadsheet that solves for the portfolio weights that will result in the lowest risk for a specified level of expected return.

Option   A financial instrument that gives one party the right, but not the obligation, to buy or sell an underlying asset from or to another party at a fixed price over a specific period of time. Also referred to as contingent claims.

Option premium   The amount of money a buyer pays and seller receives to engage in an option transaction.

Option price   The amount of money a buyer pays and seller receives to engage in an option transaction.

Orderly liquidation value   The estimated gross amount of money that could be realized from the liquidation sale of an asset or assets, given a reasonable amount of time to find a purchaser or purchasers.

Organic growth   Company growth in output or sales that is achieved by making investments internally (i.e., excludes growth achieved through mergers and acquisitions).

Orthogonal   Uncorrelated; at a right angle.

Other comprehensive income   Changes to equity that bypass (are not reported in) the income statement; the difference between comprehensive income and net income.

Out-of-sample forecast errors   The differences between actual and predicted value of time series outside the sample period used to fit the model.

Out-of-the-money   Options that, if exercised, would require the payment of more money than the value received and therefore would not be currently exercised.

Overnight index swap (OIS)   A swap in which the floating rate is the cumulative value of a single unit of currency invested at an overnight rate during the settlement period.

PEG   The P/E-to-growth ratio, calculated as the stock's P/E divided by the expected earnings growth rate.

Pairs trading   An approach to trading that uses pairs of closely related stocks, buying the relatively undervalued stock and selling short the relatively overvalued stock.

Parameter instability   The problem or issue of population regression parameters that have changed over time.

Partial regression coefficients   The slope coefficients in a multiple regression. Also called *partial slope coefficients*.

Partial slope coefficients   The slope coefficients in a multiple regression. Also called *partial regression coefficients*.

Partnership   A business owned and operated by more than one individual.

Payer swaption   A swaption that allows the holder to enter into a swap as the fixed-rate payer and floating-rate receiver.

Payoff   The value of an option at expiration.

Payout amount   The payout ratio times the notional.

Payout policy   The principles by which a company distributes cash to common shareholders by means of cash dividends and/or share repurchases.

Payout ratio An estimate of the expected credit loss.

Pecking order theory The theory that managers take into account how their actions might be interpreted by outsiders and thus order their preferences for various forms of corporate financing. Forms of financing that are least visible to outsiders (e.g., internally generated funds) are most preferable to managers and those that are most visible (e.g., equity) are least preferable.

Perfect capital markets Markets in which, by assumption, there are no taxes, transactions costs, or bankruptcy costs, and in which all investors have equal ("symmetric") information.

Performance appraisal The evaluation of risk-adjusted performance; the evaluation of investment skill.

Periodic inventory system An inventory accounting system in which inventory values and costs of sales are determined at the end of the accounting period.

Perpetual inventory system An inventory accounting system in which inventory values and costs of sales are continuously updated to reflect purchases and sales.

Perpetuity A perpetual annuity, or a set of never-ending level sequential cash flows, with the first cash flow occurring one period from now.

Persistent earnings Earnings excluding nonrecurring components.

Pet projects Projects in which influential managers want the corporation to invest. Often, unfortunately, pet projects are selected without undergoing normal capital budgeting analysis.

Physical deterioration In the context of real estate, a reduction in value due to wear and tear.

Physical settlement Involves actual delivery of the debt instrument in exchange for a payment by the credit protection seller of the notional amount of the contract.

Plain vanilla swap An interest rate swap in which one party pays a fixed rate and the other pays a floating rate, with both sets of payments in the same currency.

Poison pill A pre-offer takeover defense mechanism that makes it prohibitively costly for an acquirer to take control of a target without the prior approval of the target's board of directors.

Poison puts A pre-offer takeover defense mechanism that gives target company bondholders the right to sell their bonds back to the target at a pre-specified redemption price, typically at or above par value; this defense increases the need for cash and raises the cost of the acquisition.

Pooling of interests method A method of accounting in which combined companies were portrayed as if they had always operated as a single economic entity. Called pooling of interests under U.S. GAAP and uniting of interests under IFRS. (No longer allowed under U.S. GAAP or IFRS).

Portfolio balance approach A theory of exchange rate determination that emphasizes the portfolio investment decisions of global investors and the requirement that global investors willingly hold all outstanding securities denominated in each currency at prevailing prices and exchange rates.

Portfolio performance attribution The analysis of portfolio performance in terms of the contributions from various sources of risk.

Portfolio possibilities curve A graphical representation of the expected return and risk of all portfolios that can be formed using two assets.

Position trader A trader who typically holds positions open overnight.

Positive serial correlation Serial correlation in which a positive error for one observation increases the chance of a positive error for another observation, and a negative error for one observation increases the chance of a negative error for another observation.

Potential GDP The maximum amount of output an economy can sustainably produce without inducing an increase in the inflation rate. The output level that corresponds to full employment with consistent wage and price expectations.

Potential credit risk The risk associated with the possibility that a payment due at a later date will not be made.

Premise of value The status of a company in the sense of whether it is assumed to be a going concern or not.

Premium The amount of money a buyer pays and seller receives to engage in an option transaction.

Premium leg The series of payments the credit protection buyer promises to make to the credit protection seller.

Present value model A model of intrinsic value that views the value of an asset as the present value of the asset's expected future cash flows.

Present value of growth opportunities The difference between the actual value per share and the nogrowth value per share. Also called *value of growth*.

Present value of the expected loss Conceptually, the largest price one would be willing to pay on a bond to a third party (e.g., an insurer) to entirely remove the credit risk of purchasing and holding the bond.

Presentation currency The currency in which financial statement amounts are presented.

Price limits Limits imposed by a futures exchange on the price change that can occur from one day to the next.

Price momentum A valuation indicator based on past price movement.

Price multiples The ratio of a stock's market price to some measure of value per share.

Price-setting option The operational flexibility to adjust prices when demand varies from forecast. For example, when demand exceeds capacity, the company could benefit from the excess demand by increasing prices.

Priced risk Risk for which investors demand compensation for bearing (e.g., equity risk, company-specific factors, macroeconomic factors).

Principal-agent problem A conflict of interest that arises when the agent in an agency relationship has goals and incentives that differ from the principal to whom the agent owes a fiduciary duty.

Prior transaction method A variation of the market approach; considers actual transactions in the stock of the subject private company.

Private market value The value derived using a sum-of-the-parts valuation.

Probability of default The probability that a bond issuer will not meet its contractual obligations on schedule.

Probability of survival The probability that a bond issuer will meet its contractual obligations on schedule.

Probit model A qualitative-dependent-variable multiple regression model based on the normal distribution.

Procedural law The body of law that focuses on the protection and enforcement of the substantive laws.

Production-flexibility The operational flexibility to alter production when demand varies from forecast. For example, if demand is strong, a company may profit from employees working overtime or from adding additional shifts.

Project sequencing To defer the decision to invest in a future project until the outcome of some or all of a current project is known. Projects are sequenced through time, so that investing in a project creates the option to invest in future projects.

Prospective P/E A P/E calculated on the basis of a forecast of EPS; a stock's current price divided by next year's expected earnings.

Protection leg The contingent payment that the credit protection seller may have to make to the credit protection buyer.

Protective put An option strategy in which a long position in an asset is combined with a long position in a put.

Proxy fight An attempt to take control of a company through a shareholder vote.

Proxy statement A public document that provides the material facts concerning matters on which shareholders will vote.

Prudential supervision Regulation and monitoring of the safety and soundness of financial institutions to promote financial stability, reduce system-wide risks, and protect customers of financial institutions.

Purchased in-process research and development costs Costs of research and development in progress at an acquired company; often, part of the purchase price of an acquired company is allocated to such costs.

Purchasing power gain A gain in value caused by changes in price levels. Monetary liabilities experience purchasing power gains during periods of inflation.

Purchasing power loss A loss in value caused by changes in price levels. Monetary assets experience purchasing power loss during periods of inflation.

Purchasing power parity (PPP) The idea that exchange rates move to equalize the purchasing power of different currencies.

Pure factor portfolio A portfolio with sensitivity of 1 to the factor in question and a sensitivity of 0 to all other factors.

Put An option that gives the holder the right to sell an underlying asset to another party at a fixed price over a specific period of time.

Put–call parity An equation expressing the equivalence (parity) of a portfolio of a call and a bond with a portfolio of a put and the underlying, which leads to the relationship between put and call prices.

Put–call–forward parity The relationship among puts, calls, and forward contracts.

Qualitative dependent variables Dummy variables used as dependent variables rather than as independent variables.

Quality of earnings analysis The investigation of issues relating to the accuracy of reported accounting results as reflections of economic performance; quality of earnings analysis is broadly understood to include not only earnings management, but also balance sheet management.

Random walk A time series in which the value of the series in one period is the value of the series in the previous period plus an unpredictable random error.

Rational efficient markets formulation See *market efficiency.*

Real estate investment trusts (REITS) Tax-advantaged entities (companies or trusts) that typically own, operate, and—to a limited extent—develop income-producing real estate property.

Real estate operating companies Regular taxable real estate ownership companies that operate in the real estate industry in countries that do not have a tax-advantaged REIT regime in place or are engaged in real estate activities of a kind and to an extent that do not fit within their country's REIT framework.

Real exchange rate The relative purchasing power of two currencies, defined in terms of the *real* goods and services that each can buy at prevailing national price levels and nominal exchange rates. Measured as the ratio of national price levels expressed in a common currency.

Real interest rate parity The proposition that real interest rates will converge to the same level across different markets.

Real options Options that relate to investment decisions such as the option to time the start of a project, the option to adjust its scale, or the option to abandon a project that has begun.

Receiver swaption A swaption that allows the holder to enter into a swap as the fixed-rate receiver and floating-rate payer.

Recovery rate The percentage of the loss recovered.

Reduced form models Models of credit analysis based on the outputs of a structural model but with different assumptions. The model's credit risk measures reflect changing economic conditions.

Reference entity The borrower on a single-name CDS.

Reference obligation A particular debt instrument issued by the borrower that is the designated instrument being covered.

Regime With reference to a time series, the underlying model generating the times series.

Regression coefficients The intercept and slope coefficient(s) of a regression.

Regulatory arbitrage Entities identify and use some aspect of regulations that allows them to exploit differences in economic substance and regulatory interpretation or in foreign and domestic regulatory regimes to their (the entities) advantage.

Regulatory burden The costs of regulation for the regulated entity.

Regulatory capture Theory that regulation often arises to enhance the interests of the regulated.

Regulatory competition Regulators may compete to provide a regulatory environment designed to attract certain entities.

Relative valuation models A model that specifies an asset's value relative to the value of another asset.

Relative version of PPP Hypothesis that changes in (nominal) exchange rates over time are equal to national inflation rate differentials.

Relative-strength indicators Valuation indicators that compare a stock's performance during a period either to its own past performance or to the performance of some group of stocks.

Renewable resources Resources that can be replenished, such as a forest.

Rental price of capital The cost per unit of time to rent a unit of capital.

Replacement cost In the context of real estate, the value of a building assuming it was built today using current construction costs and standards.

Replacement value The market value of a swap.

Reporting unit An operating segment or one level below an operating segment (referred to as a component).

Reputational risk The risk that a company will suffer an extended diminution in market value relative to other companies in the same industry due to a demonstrated lack of concern for environmental, social, and governance risk factors.

Required rate of return The minimum rate of return required by an investor to invest in an asset, given the asset's riskiness.

Residential mortgage-backed securities Securities backed by residential mortgage loans.

Residential properties Properties that provide housing for individuals or families. Single-family properties may be owner-occupied or rental properties, whereas multi-family properties are rental properties even if the owner or manager occupies one of the units.

Residual autocorrelations The sample autocorrelations of the residuals.

Residual dividend policy A policy in which dividends are paid from any internally generated funds remaining after such funds are used to finance positive NPV projects.

Residual income Earnings for a given time period, minus a deduction for common shareholders' opportunity cost in generating the earnings. Also called *economic profit* or *abnormal earnings*.

Residual income method Income approach that estimates the value of all intangible assets of the business by capitalizing future earnings in excess of the estimated return requirements associated with working capital and fixed assets.

Residual income model (RIM) A model of stock valuation that views intrinsic value of stock as the sum of book value per share plus the present value of the stock's expected future residual income per share. Also called *discounted abnormal earnings model* or *Edwards–Bell–Ohlson model*.

Residual loss Agency costs that are incurred despite adequate monitoring and bonding of management.

Restructuring Reorganizing the financial structure of a firm.

Retail REITs REITs that invest in such retail properties as regional shopping malls or community/neighborhood shopping centers.

Return on capital employed Operating profit divided by capital employed (debt and equity capital).

Return on invested capital A measure of the after-tax profitability of the capital invested by the company's shareholders and debt holders.

Revenue The amount charged for the delivery of goods or services in the ordinary activities of a business over a stated period; the inflows of economic resources to a company over a stated period.

Reviewed financial statements A type of non-audited financial statements; typically provide an opinion letter with representations and assurances by the reviewing accountant that are less than those in audited financial statements.

Rho The sensitivity of the option price to the risk-free rate.

Risk reversal An option position that consists of the purchase of an out-of-the-money call and the simultaneous sale of an out-of-the-money put with the same "delta," on the same underlying currency or security, and with the same expiration date.

Risk-neutral probabilities Weights that are used to compute a binomial option price. They are the probabilities that would apply if a risk-neutral investor valued an option.

Risk-neutral valuation The process by which options and other derivatives are priced by treating investors as though they were risk neutral.

Robust standard errors Standard errors of the estimated parameters of a regression that correct for the presence of heteroskedasticity in the regression's error term.

Roll When an investor moves from one series to a new one.

Root mean squared error (RMSE) The square root of the average squared forecast error; used to compare the out-of-sample forecasting performance of forecasting models.

Sales comparison approach In the context of real estate, this approach estimates value based on what similar or comparable properties (comparables) transacted for in the current market.

Sales-type leases A type of finance lease, from a lessor perspective, where the present value of the lease payments (lease receivable) exceeds the carrying value of the leased asset. The revenues earned by the lessor are operating (the profit on the sale) and financing (interest) in nature.

Sampling distribution The distribution of all distinct possible values that a statistic can assume when computed from samples of the same size randomly drawn from the same population.

Scaled earnings surprise Unexpected earnings divided by the standard deviation of analysts' earnings forecasts.

Scalper A trader who offers to buy or sell futures contracts, holding the position for only a brief period of time. Scalpers attempt to profit by buying at the bid price and selling at the higher ask price.

Scatter plot A two-dimensional plot of pairs of observations on two data series.

Scenario analysis Analysis that involves changing multiple assumptions at the same time.

Screening The application of a set of criteria to reduce a set of potential investments to a smaller set having certain desired characteristics.

Seats Memberships in a derivatives exchange.

Sector neutralizing Measure of financial reporting quality by subtracting the mean or median ratio for a given sector group from a given company's ratio.

Securities offering A merger or acquisition in which target shareholders are to receive shares of the acquirer's common stock as compensation.

Security market line (SML) The graph of the capital asset pricing model.

Self-regulating organizations Private, non-governmental organizations that both represent and regulate their members. Some self-regulating organizations are also independent regulators.

Sell-side analysts Analysts who work at brokerages.

Sensitivity analysis Analysis that shows the range of possible outcomes as specific assumptions are changed; involves changing one assumption at a time.

Serially correlated With reference to regression errors, errors that are correlated across observations.

Settlement In the case of a credit event, the process by which the two parties to a CDS contract satisfy their respective obligations.

Settlement date The date on which the parties to a swap make payments. Also called *payment date*.

Settlement period The time between settlement dates.

Settlement price The official price, designated by the clearinghouse, from which daily gains and losses will be determined and marked to market.

Shareholders' equity Total assets minus total liabilities.

Shark repellents   A pre-offer takeover defense mechanism involving the corporate charter (e.g., staggered boards of directors and supermajority provisions).

Shopping center   REITs that invest in such retail properties as regional shopping malls or community/neighborhood shopping centers.

Short   The seller of a derivative contract. Also refers to the position of being short a derivative.

Single-name CDS   Credit default swap on one specific borrower.

Sole proprietorship   A business owned and operated by a single person.

Special purpose vehicle   A non-operating entity created to carry out a specified purpose, such as leasing assets or securitizing receivables; can be a corporation, partnership, trust, limited liability, or partnership formed to facilitate a specific type of business activity. Also called *special purpose entity* or *variable interest entity*.

Speculative value   The difference between the market price of the option and its intrinsic value, determined by the uncertainty of the underlying over the remaining life of the option. Also called *time value*.

Spin-off   A form of restructuring in which shareholders of a parent company receive a proportional number of shares in a new, separate entity; shareholders end up owning stock in two different companies where there used to be one.

Split-off   A form of restructuring in which shareholders of the parent company are given shares in a newly created entity in exchange for their shares of the parent company.

Split-rate tax system   In reference to corporate taxes, a split-rate system taxes earnings to be distributed as dividends at a different rate than earnings to be retained. Corporate profits distributed as dividends are taxed at a lower rate than those retained in the business.

Spurious correlation   A correlation that misleadingly points toward associations between variables.

Stabilized NOI   In the context of real estate, the expected NOI when a renovation is complete.

Stable dividend policy   A policy in which regular dividends are paid that reflect long-run expected earnings. In contrast to a constant dividend payout ratio policy, a stable dividend policy does not reflect short-term volatility in earnings.

Standard deviation   The positive square root of the variance; a measure of dispersion in the same units as the original data.

Standard of value   A specification of how "value" is to be understood in the context of a specific valuation.

Standardized beta   With reference to fundamental factor models, the value of the attribute for an asset minus the average value of the attribute across all stocks, divided by the standard deviation of the attribute across all stocks.

Standardized unexpected earnings   (SUE) Unexpected earnings per share divided by the standard deviation of unexpected earnings per share over a specified prior time period.

Static trade-off theory of capital structure   A theory pertaining to a company's optimal capital structure; the optimal level of debt is found at the point where additional debt would cause the costs of financial distress to increase by a greater amount than the benefit of the additional tax shield.

Statistical factor models   A multifactor model in which statistical methods are applied to a set of historical returns to determine portfolios that best explain either historical return covariances or variances.

Statistical inference   Making forecasts, estimates, or judgments about a larger group from a smaller group actually observed; using a sample statistic to infer the value of an unknown population parameter.

Statistically significant   A result indicating that the null hypothesis can be rejected; with reference to an estimated regression coefficient, frequently understood to mean a result indicating that the corresponding population regression coefficient is different from 0.

Statutes   Laws enacted by legislative bodies.

Statutory merger   A merger in which one company ceases to exist as an identifiable entity and all its assets and liabilities become part of a purchasing company.

Steady state rate of growth   The constant growth rate of output (or output per capita) which can or will be sustained indefinitely once it is reached. Key ratios, such as the capital–output ratio, are constant on the steady-state growth path.

Sterilized intervention   A policy measure in which a monetary authority buys or sells its own currency to mitigate undesired exchange rate movements and simultaneously offsets the impact on the money supply with transactions in other financial instruments (usually money market instruments).

Stock purchase   An acquisition in which the acquirer gives the target company's shareholders some combination of cash and securities in exchange for shares of the target company's stock.

Storage REITs   REITs that own and operate self-storage properties, sometimes referred to as mini-warehouse facilities.

Storage costs   The costs of holding an asset, generally a function of the physical characteristics of the underlying asset.

Straight-line rent   The average annual rent under a multi-year lease agreement that contains contractual increases in rent during the life of the lease. For example if the rent is $100,000 in Year 1, $105,000 in Year 2, and $110,000 in Year 3, the average rent to be recognized each year as revenue under straight-line rent accounting is ($100,000 + $105,000 + $110,000)/3 = $105,000.

Straight-line rent adjustment   See *non-cash rent*.

Strategic transaction   A purchase involving a buyer that would benefit from certain synergies associated with owning the target firm.

Strike   See *exercise price*.

Strike price   See *exercise price*.

Strike rate   The fixed rate at which the holder of an interest rate option can buy or sell the underlying. Also called *exercise rate*.

Striking price   See *exercise price*.

Structural models   Structural models of credit analysis build on the insights of option pricing theory. They are based on the structure of a company's balance sheet.

Subsidiary merger   A merger in which the company being purchased becomes a subsidiary of the purchaser.

Substantive law   The body of law that focuses on the rights and responsibilities of entities and relationships among entities.

Succession event   A change of corporate structure of the reference entity, such as through a merger, divestiture, spinoff, or any similar action, in which ultimate responsibility for the debt in question is unclear.

Sum-of-the-parts valuation   A valuation that sums the estimated values of each of a company's businesses as if each business were an independent going concern.

Sunk cost   A cost that has already been incurred.

Supernormal growth Above average or abnormally high growth rate in earnings per share.

Surprise The actual value of a variable minus its predicted (or expected) value.

Survivorship bias Bias that may result when failed or defunct companies are excluded from membership in a group.

Sustainable growth rate The rate of dividend (and earnings) growth that can be sustained over time for a given level of return on equity, keeping the capital structure constant and without issuing additional common stock.

Swap spread The difference between the fixed rate on an interest rate swap and the rate on a Treasury note with equivalent maturity; it reflects the general level of credit risk in the market.

Swaption An option to enter into a swap.

Synthetic CDO Created by combining a portfolio of default-free securities with a combination of credit default swaps undertaken as protection sellers.

Synthetic call The combination of puts, the underlying, and risk-free bonds that replicates a call option.

Synthetic forward contract The combination of the underlying, puts, calls, and risk-free bonds that replicates a forward contract.

Synthetic lease A lease that is structured to provide a company with the tax benefits of ownership while not requiring the asset to be reflected on the company's financial statements.

Synthetic put The combination of calls, the underlying, and risk-free bonds that replicates a put option.

Systematic factors Factors that affect the average returns of a large number of different assets.

Systemic risk The risk of failure of the financial system.

Takeover A merger; the term may be applied to any transaction, but is often used in reference to hostile transactions.

Takeover premium The amount by which the takeover price for each share of stock must exceed the current stock price in order to entice shareholders to relinquish control of the company to an acquirer.

Tangible book value per share Common shareholders' equity minus intangible assets from the balance sheet, divided by the number of shares outstanding.

Target The company in a merger or acquisition that is being acquired.

Target capital structure A company's chosen proportions of debt and equity.

Target company The company in a merger or acquisition that is being acquired.

Target payout ratio A strategic corporate goal representing the long-term proportion of earnings that the company intends to distribute to shareholders as dividends.

Technical indicators Momentum indicators based on price.

Temporal method A variation of the monetary/non-monetary translation method that requires not only monetary assets and liabilities, but also non-monetary assets and liabilities that are measured at their current value on the balance sheet date to be translated at the current exchange rate. Assets and liabilities are translated at rates consistent with the timing of their measurement value. This method is typically used when the functional currency is other than the local currency.

Tender offer A public offer whereby the acquirer invites target shareholders to submit ("tender") their shares in return for the proposed payment.

Terminal price multiples The price multiple for a stock assumed to hold at a stated future time.

Terminal share price The share price at a particular point in the future.

Terminal value of the stock The analyst's estimate of a stock's value at a particular point in the future. Also called *continuing value of the stock.*

Termination date The date of the final payment on a swap; also, the swap's expiration date.

Theta The rate at which an option's time value decays.

Time series A set of observations on a variable's outcomes in different time periods.

Time to expiration The time remaining in the life of a derivative, typically expressed in years.

Time value The difference between the market price of the option and its intrinsic value, determined by the uncertainty of the underlying over the remaining life of the option. Also called *speculative value.*

Time value decay The loss in the value of an option resulting from movement of the option price towards its payoff value as the expiration day approaches.

Tobin's *q* The ratio of the market value of debt and equity to the replacement cost of total assets.

Top-down approach With respect to forecasting, an approach that usually begins at the level of the overall economy. Forecasts are then made at more narrowly defined levels, such as sector, industry, and market for a specific product.

Top-down investing An approach to investing that typically begins with macroeconomic forecasts.

Total factor productivity (TFP) A multiplicative scale factor that reflects the general level of productivity or technology in the economy. Changes in total factor productivity generate proportional changes in output for any input combination.

Total invested capital The sum of market value of common equity, book value of preferred equity, and face value of debt.

Total return swap A swap in which one party agrees to pay the total return on a security. Often used as a credit derivative, in which the underlying is a bond.

Tracking error The standard deviation of the differences between a portfolio's returns and its benchmark's returns; a synonym of active risk. Also called *tracking risk.*

Tracking portfolio A portfolio having factor sensitivities that are matched to those of a benchmark or other portfolio.

Tracking risk The standard deviation of the differences between a portfolio's returns and its benchmark's returns; a synonym of active risk. Also called *tracking error.*

Trailing P/E A stock's current market price divided by the most recent four quarters of earnings per share. Also called *current P/E.*

Trailing dividend yield Current market price divided by the most recent quarterly per-share dividend multiplied by four.

Tranche CDS A type of credit default swap that covers a combination of borrowers but only up to pre-specified levels of losses.

Transaction exposure The risk of a change in value between the transaction date and the settlement date of an asset of liability denominated in a foreign currency.

Trend A long-term pattern of movement in a particular direction.

Triangular arbitrage An arbitrage transaction involving three currencies which attempts to exploit inconsistencies among pair wise exchange rates.

UPREITs An umbrella partnership REIT under which the REIT owns an operating partnership and serves as the general partner of the operating partnership. All or most of the properties are held in the operating partnership.

Unconditional heteroskedasticity Heteroskedasticity of the error term that is not correlated with the values of the independent variable(s) in the regression.

Uncovered interest rate parity The proposition that the expected return on an uncovered (i.e., unhedged) foreign currency (risk-free) investment should equal the return on a comparable domestic currency investment.

Underlying An asset that trades in a market in which buyers and sellers meet, decide on a price, and the seller then delivers the asset to the buyer and receives payment. The underlying is the asset or other derivative on which a particular derivative is based. The market for the underlying is also referred to as the spot market.

Underlying earnings Earnings excluding nonrecurring components.

Unearned revenue A liability account for money that has been collected for goods or services that have not yet been delivered; payment received in advance of providing a good or service.

Unexpected earnings The difference between reported earnings per share and expected earnings per share.

Unit root A time series that is not covariance stationary is said to have a unit root.

Uniting of interests method A method of accounting in which combined companies were portrayed as if they had always operated as a single economic entity. Called pooling of interests under U.S. GAAP and uniting of interests under IFRS. (No longer allowed under U.S. GAAP or IFRS).

Unlimited funds An unlimited funds environment assumes that the company can raise the funds it wants for all profitable projects simply by paying the required rate of return.

Unsterilized intervention A policy measure in which a monetary authority buys or sells its own currency to mitigate undesired exchange rate movements and does not offset the impact on the money supply with transactions in other financial instruments.

Upfront payment The difference between the credit spread and the standard rate paid by the protection if the standard rate is insufficient to compensate the protection seller. Also called *upfront premium*.

Upfront premium See *upfront payment*.

Upstream A transaction between two related companies, an investor company (or a parent company) and an associate company (or a subsidiary company) such that the associate company records a profit on its income statement. An example is a sale of inventory by the associate to the investor company or by a subsidiary to a parent company.

Valuation The process of determining the value of an asset or service on the basis of variables perceived to be related to future investment returns, or on the basis of comparisons with closely similar assets.

Value at risk (VAR) A money measure of the minimum value of losses expected during a specified time period at a given level of probability.

Value of growth The difference between the actual value per share and the nogrowth value per share.

Variance The expected value (the probability-weighted average) of squared deviations from a random variable's expected value.

Variation margin Additional margin that must be deposited in an amount sufficient to bring the balance up to the initial margin requirement.

Vega The relationship between option price and volatility.

Venture capital investors Private equity investors in development-stage companies.

Vertical merger A merger involving companies at different positions of the same production chain; for example, a supplier or a distributor.

Visibility The extent to which a company's operations are predictable with substantial confidence.

Weighted average cost An inventory accounting method that averages the total cost of available inventory items over the total units available for sale.

Weighted average cost of capital (WACC) A weighted average of the after-tax required rates of return on a company's common stock, preferred stock, and long-term debt, where the weights are the fraction of each source of financing in the company's target capital structure.

Weighted harmonic mean See *harmonic mean*.

White knight A third party that is sought out by the target company's board to purchase the target in lieu of a hostile bidder.

White squire A third party that is sought out by the target company's board to purchase a substantial minority stake in the target—enough to block a hostile takeover without selling the entire company.

White-corrected standard errors A synonym for robust standard errors.

Winner's curse The tendency for the winner in certain competitive bidding situations to overpay, whether because of overestimation of intrinsic value, emotion, or information asymmetries.

Write-down A reduction in the value of an asset as stated in the balance sheet.

Zero-cost collar A transaction in which a position in the underlying is protected by buying a put and selling a call with the premium from the sale of the call offsetting the premium from the purchase of the put. It can also be used to protect a floating-rate borrower against interest rate increases with the premium on a long cap offsetting the premium on a short floor.

Index